THE POLITICS OF ANTIPOLITICS

THE POLITICS OF ANTIPOLITICS

The Military in Latin America

Revised and Updated

Edited by

BRIAN LOVEMAN
THOMAS M. DAVIES, Jr.

A Scholarly Resources Inc. Imprint
Wilmington, Delaware

Scholarly Resources Inc.
104 Greenhill Avenue
Wilmington, DE 19805-1897

Acknowledgments for permission to reprint copyrighted material appear on pages 425–26.

Library of Congress Cataloging-in-Publication Data

The Politics of antipolitics : the military in Latin America /
    edited by Brian Loveman and Thomas M. Davies, Jr. —
    Rev. and updated.
        p.   cm. — (Latin American silhouettes : studies in history
    and culture)
    ISBN 0-8420-2609-6 (alk. paper). — ISBN 0-8420-2611-8
    (pbk. : alk. paper)
    1. Civil-military relations—Latin America. 2. Latin America—
Armed Forces—Political activity. 3. Latin America—Armed
Forces. 4. Latin America—Politics and government. I. Loveman,
Brian. II. Davies, Thomas M. III. Series: Latin American
silhouettes.
JL956.C58P65   1997
322'.5'098—dc20   96-9466
                                                                    CIP

⊛The paper used in this publication meets the minimum requirements of the American National Standard for permanence of paper for printed library materials, Z39.48, 1984.

To Bernard J. Loveman

and

Thomas M. and Faith Arnold Davies

About the Editors

BRIAN LOVEMAN is professor of political science at San Diego State University. He has written numerous articles and books on Latin American history and politics including *Chile: The Legacy of Hispanic Capitalism* (1979). His most recent book, *The Constitution of Tyranny: Regimes of Exception in Spanish America* (1993), received the Hubert Herring Prize in 1995 for the best work on Latin America.

THOMAS M. DAVIES, JR., received his doctorate from the University of New Mexico. Professor of Latin American and U.S. history at San Diego State University, as well as director of its Center for Latin American Studies, he has written numerous journal articles and is the author of *Indian Integration in Peru: A Half-Century of Experience, 1900–1948* (1974) and coauthor (with Brian Loveman) of *Che Guevara on Guerrilla Warfare* (1985).

Contents

Preface to the Revised and Updated Edition

From 1978 to 1994 civilian governments succeeded military regimes throughout Latin America. Yet, seventeen years after the first edition of this book, the essential elements of antipolitics persisted in most of the region. Indeed, the military regimes from 1964 to the early 1990s battered, distorted, and discredited liberalism, populism, and social democracy so severely that the restoration of civilian government from 1978 in Ecuador to 1993 in Paraguay in many ways represented a victory for the forces of antipolitics in the Western Hemisphere.

The newer versions of antipolitics accompanied the apparent global victory of neoliberalism and "market democracy," the demise of socialism, and the era of the shrinking state. Democracy premised on the need to restrict popular movements and populist policies, and the efficacy (if not moral priority) of the market, dressed authoritarian institutions in the trappings of *protected democracy*. Military tutelage, veto power, and implicit threats to correct civilian "excesses" were (re)incorporated into the new constitutions and statutes of the Latin American polities in the 1980s and 1990s. With Marxism, communism, and "subversion" no longer tied to international (Soviet) conspiracies, military leaders and institutions were seeking to redefine and relegitimate their internal and external missions and expand their participation in economic, social, and foreign policy. They also reminded the peoples of the hemisphere that only the armed forces' patriotism and sacrifice prevented the victory of Marxism and saved their nations from the populist *political* scourge.

In the 1990s national security concerns now included the environment, drug wars, technology transfer, international trade, and even AIDS. These new security issues were added to the traditional internal order and external defense missions assigned to the armed forces. Security for fragile democracies required permanent military vigilance against the resurgence of *politiquería* and subversion. It also required military deployment to combat narcoterrorism. In addition, old and new threats to national sovereignty, recurrent border disputes, and the challenges of globalization also implied central roles for the armed forces.

The transition from military to civilian governments thus marked the victory of the forces of "Western Christian civilization" over the Communist barbarians, and also the victory of neoliberal "market democracy" over the *politiquería* of irresponsible politicians. It did not end the need for military preparedness against internal and external threats—political, economic, or even environmental.

The military had made democracy possible, albeit a particular democracy. The "cure" for the "cancer of subversion" forced "strong medicine" on the diseased body politic. After the cure came democracy, vaccinated against socialism, populism, and policy excesses. The armed forces and their civilian allies instituted democracy protected against itself, with civilian political leaders repenting their "immaturity" in the 1960s and 1970s—and under the permanent vigilance of military guardians. This was the victory of the antipoliticians, military and civilian, with the assistance and approval of the United States.

Antipolitics survived under elected governments. Democratization remained partial, fragile, and suspect. In this third edition we remind readers of the origins of antipolitics, trace its nineteenth- and early twentieth-century history, and focus on the years from 1965 to 1995 to emphasize the sometimes illusory "transitions" to democracy. We also consider why and how the military rulers acceded to the return of civilian elected governments, and the military's defense against accusations of human rights abuses—in most cases achieving for themselves impunity or pardons.

In preparing this third edition, we have revised the introductions to several sections, shortened discussion of the nineteenth century and the pre-1945 period by deleting some articles that appeared in the first two editions. As in the first two, we have eliminated most of the footnotes from the reprinted articles; readers may, of course, consult the original source for the note material. We also have omitted some speeches in Part V, "The Military Speaks for Itself," in order to permit additions on the transition to civilian rule and the human rights issue. We hope that these revisions will make this volume as useful to students of Latin American politics and military institutions in the 1990s as the earlier editions were after 1978. One thing is certain: with or without direct military rule, antipolitics persists as a foundation of Latin American politics.

B.L.
T.M.D., Jr.

I

Military Antipolitics and the Latin American Tradition

Brian Loveman and
Thomas M. Davies, Jr.

CHAPTER 1

The Politics of Antipolitics

Military leaders successful in anticolonial wars founded the Spanish American republics in the early nineteenth century. Military elites were also responsible for the creation of the Brazilian Republic in the late nineteenth century. In the 1960s and 1970s professional military officers in Latin America scanned the panorama of the hemisphere's history and blamed the ineptitude and corruption of civilian politicians as well as the imported institutions of liberal democracy for the wretched conditions in their region. In much of Latin America, professional military officers concluded that only an end to "politics" and the establishment of long-term military rule could provide the basis for modernization, economic development, and political stability. This determination, strengthened by events in Brazil after 1964, led to explicitly antipolitical military regimes in most of Latin America.

Military antipolitics originated both in military understanding of the region's history and military assessment of the Latin American dilemma in the midtwentieth century. Throughout most of the nineteenth century, "politics," that is, conflict among personalist factions and, later, political parties over ideological formulas and the spoils of rule, submerged most of the Latin American nations in bloody civil strife. In the late nineteenth and early twentieth centuries, however, military leaders sought to end the chaos and impose stability and order amid the social conflict and dislocation caused by the process of modernization. "Politics," including the demagogic appeals by civilian politicians to the emerging proletariat, promoted class conflict and instability which "forced" sectors of the military to intervene to restore order and cleanse the body politic of political corruption.

The years following World War I witnessed not only the failure of civilian experiments with political democracy but also the collapse of the Latin American export economies, a collapse which demonstrated to many military officers the folly of total dependence on foreign capitalists. When the military leaders again intervened in the 1920s and 1930s to restore order and deal with the problems that civilians refused or were unable to resolve, they pointed to civilian bungling, ineptitude, and corruption as the primary motivating factors in their decision.

In Chile in 1924 one civilian minister was told:

> Even though you now represent to us the most disgusting element in our country—politicians—all that is corrupt, the dismal factional disputes, depravity and immoralities, in other words, the causes of our national degeneration, we recognize that you, despite the fact that you must defend sinecures, hand out public jobs, support avaricious ambitions, are one of the few honest politicians.[1]

Three years earlier, a statement signed by seventeen Peruvian army officers contained the following words:

> Comrades:

> For some time now, since politics infiltrated the army, we military officers have been serving as stepping-stones for unscrupulous politicians. They use our services, and then they promote us. This must stop. Promotions must be based upon professional competence and not on political activity. . . . *We [must] assume the reins of government of the country in order to root out political influence, the worst of all plagues, and we shall shape Peru's destiny with our own hands and our own initiative.* . . . Our fatherland suffers daily from the partisan struggles of politicians who care nothing for the development and progress of the nation. It is our task to normalize the institutional life of the country. . . . *The army, drawn from all social classes of the nation, must intervene directly in the management of the affairs of state.*[2]

As the twentieth century wore on, the hopes of career military officers for modernization and industrialization were increasingly frustrated. The attitudes and aspirations imparted by the European training missions that professionalized many Latin American military establishments in the late nineteenth century conflicted with the obvious inability of civilians to create viable institutions for directing national development. Thus, while many young military officers retained kinship and class ties to the traditional elites, they harbored an ever growing disdain for civilian politicians and for politics in general.

One widely held assumption of Latin American military officers, and one also shared by many conservative civilian groups, was that "politics" was largely responsible for the poverty, instability, and economic backwardness of their nations. This assumption was not new, nor did it originate in all cases within military circles, but the depoliticization of "politics" and the establishment of an administrative regime to forge an organic, hierarchically structured polity provided a crucial ideological link between civilian propertied interests and military modernizers.

Acceptance of this ideology of antipolitics also entailed the denial of the legitimacy of labor protest, strikes, political party claims of representing diverse interests, and, more generally, of opposition to government authority, policies, and programs. Order, obedience, authority, and stability—cherished values of the Hispanic socioeconomic elites—not only dovetailed neatly with the spirit of military training, but also provided easy rationalizations for military rule. With slight alteration, these values and assumptions formed the ideological core of military antipolitics and military rule in the 1970s.

Latin American Antecedents of Antipolitics

Widespread instability and economic deterioration in early nineteenth-century Latin America contrasted markedly with the special case of Chile, where, after 1833, an institutional predecessor of military antipolitics provided the basis for economic expansion, territorial aggrandizement, and regime stability. Thus, the legal and political practices introduced in Chile during those years are useful benchmarks for the organizational assumptions of antipolitics, the political practices of antipolitics, and, from the perspective of conservative civilians and military leaders intent on "modernization," the economic successes of antipolitics.

The Chilean Constitution of 1833 concentrated authority in an all-powerful executive, the president, who was permitted to serve two five-year terms. The legislative branch was subordinate to the executive. For example, when the legislature was in recess (most of the time), the president could declare a state of siege in any part of the country, thereby suspending constitutional government in that region. The administrative officers in each province and department (*intendentes* and *gobernadores*) were named directly by the president as his "natural and immediate agents." Thus, the constitution made operative the organizational premises of antipolitics: (1) centralization of authority; (2) hierarchical rule through administrative (nonparliamentary) agencies at the provincial and local levels; (3) a "flexible" constitution, that is, a constitution that offered little effective constraint on the exercise of governmental authority; and (4) official recognition of governance through a state of siege or other regimes of exception.

These assumptions about the structure and scope of governmental authority were combined with political practices that epitomized the ideological commitment to antipolitics: (1) systematic persecution of opposition elements, including the press; (2) pragmatic repression of the regime's opponents expressing overt resistance to official policy or programs; and (3) nonrecognition of the legitimacy of active opposition or of political bargaining, negotiation, or compromise.

Repudiating the liberal principles used to justify the Latin American independence movements, the leaders of Chile's autocratic republic made no pretense of accepting a noninterventionist state mediating among conflicting pluralist interests. The Chilean state, following the classic Hispanic tradition, sought to impose order, direct and regulate economic enterprise, and maintain the "proper" relationships among the elements of an organically conceived society. These basic tenets concerning the role of governmental authority and the state apparatus were perhaps best summed up by Diego Portales, founder of the Chilean autocratic regime: "One can never understand lawyers: and, *¡Carajo!* what use are constitutions and bits of paper unless to remedy an evil that one knows to exist or is about to exist. . . ? An accursed law, then, [if it] prevents the government from going ahead freely at the opportune moment."[3]

The principles and practices of Chile's autocratic republic—an interventionist, centralized state; a flexible, "suspendable" constitution allowing for government through a state of siege at executive discretion; intolerance of opposition; repression of opponents of the regime; and maintenance of order, which is understood to include hierarchical social and class relationships—provided the ideological underpinnings for Latin America's first successful experiment with a deliberate policy of economic expansion founded upon international commerce, foreign capital, and stimulation of the nation's primary sectors, mining and agriculture.

From 1830 to 1860, in sharp contrast to the economies of most of Latin America, Chile's economy grew and prospered. Agricultural output increased, new roads were constructed, and foreign trade mushroomed. American and European entrepreneurs brought modern transport and navigation systems to the country, which contributed to the notable expansion in the mining sector. Precepts of liberal economic doctrine, particularly free trade, dominated economic policy, thereby encouraging imports at the same time that Chilean wheat found its way to California markets. Antipolitics produced both stability and economic growth.

The Spread of Antipolitics

In the late nineteenth century the social and economic implications of positivism offered a philosophical rationale for authoritarian governments' efforts to stimulate economic modernization. The main features of the Chilean autocratic republic were increasingly evident in Mexico, Guatemala, and across much of South America. As with Chile in the years 1830–60, the combination of authoritarian rule, pragmatic (nonideological) repression, and Hispanic capitalism[4] in an international economy demanding Latin America's primary products resulted in stability and economic growth. Antipolitics worked— for those who ruled. It produced stability, concentrated the benefits of economic growth in the hands of a small elite, and forced the emerging urban and industrial working classes and the rural poor to bear the costs of "development."

The United States and Antipolitics in Latin America

Then came the Mexican Revolution, the Russian Revolution, and World War I, all of which contributed to a general questioning of traditional values and governmental systems and to the emergence of new concepts about societal relationships. Civilization came to mean democracy, and Latin American elites wanted to be included in the civilized world. Unfortunately, democracy did not work very well, certainly not as well as antipolitics. Democracy, after all, required the tolerance of opposition, placed constraints on executive authority, meant mobilization of the rural and urban poor, and entailed demands for income redistribution. The potential threats to the existing order contained in liberal democracy and, after World War I, Marxism concerned U.S. policymakers as much as Latin American elites. Foreshadowing the military assistance programs of the Alliance for Progress years, the United States began to create military constabularies whose leaders (for example, Rafael Trujillo in the Dominican Republic and Anastasio Somoza in Nicaragua) recognized the viability of a new version of antipolitics founded on the coercive force of professional military establishments.

On the other hand, the professional military created by U.S. intervention or earlier German and French military missions posed a contradiction as nationalist sentiments and the desire for economic development aroused both admiration and hostility toward Western European and American ideology and society. Eventually, however, these military officers devised a developmental orientation highly consistent with the Latin American tradition, with the added touch of assigning the predominant governmental role to the military itself. Patriotism, nationalism, self-sacrifice, and absolute commitment to the national welfare and security distinguished military officers, in their own opinion, from the self-seeking, venal civilian politicians, who served special interests rather than those of the nation. The perfection of antipolitics required nonpolitical leadership and the negation of partisan strife. It required, in fact, the military.

Economic Development as a Military Mission

Speaking to the Argentine Círculo Militar in 1926, Colonel Luis Vicat told his colleagues:

> The real meaning of national defense is vast and complex; it can be defined by saying that it includes all those activities and security measures necessary to assure the tranquillity, prosperity, and independence of a nation, as well as rapid victory in case of conflict.[5]

Fifty years later, the notion that economic development was an integral part of national defense and national security, that is, a military mission, was widely held by Latin American military officers. One of the theoreticians of the Brazilian Revolution of 1964 contends:

> At the beginning of the century it was enough to maintain armed forces capable of ensuring the integrity of national boundaries and overcoming the military might of possible enemies. But this idea has [now] been replaced by another, which recognizes that national security includes everything that in one way or another affects the life of the nation.[6]

That this concept was hardly novel in Brazil can be seen in a statement made in 1952 by one of the founders of its Superior War School (ESG): "National security lies in the battle for production, in the tranquillity of the population, and in the provision of stability and a reasonable standard of living."[7]

Increasingly, there seemed to be a common assumption among military officers that only through an end to "politics" and the imposition of military rule could any developmental mission be accomplished. Officers no longer intervened merely to restore order or to act as caretakers; in the 1960s and 1970s they adopted a revised version of antipolitics to justify military rule.

Counterrevolution and Antipolitics

The internal rationale for military antipolitics was also heavily influenced by the United States' response to revolutionary change in Cuba. Convinced that communism flourished where people lived in poverty, the United States committed itself to an Alliance for Progress for Latin America. This so-called alliance featured economic and military assistance programs designed both to induce economic growth and to support, finance, and "advise" civic action and counterinsurgency programs designed to combat those forces which opposed incumbent regimes.

Summing up the objectives of American assistance programs to Latin America, former Secretary of Defense Robert McNamara declared in 1967:

> The specific objectives of military assistance are the development of Latin American forces capable of maintaining internal security against threats of violence and subversion, whether Communist-inspired and supported or "home grown"; encouraging the armed forces to support and strengthen democratic institutions and to undertake civic action projects which both contribute to the social and economic development of the country and bring the armed forces and civilian populace closer together.[8]

Despite McNamara's reassertion of the Kennedy administration's thesis that Latin American armed forces would support and strengthen democratic institutions, by 1967 it had already become evident that the Alliance for Progress's counterrevolutionary inspiration intensified the contempt of the military's "new professionals" for civilian politicians. Furthermore, the failure of the United States to distinguish clearly between "Communist" and "homegrown" insurgents fit neatly with the Hispanic tradition of antipolitics in dealing with opponents of the regime.

U.S. Military Assistance Funds for Civic Action Programs, Fiscal Year 1962 through Fiscal Year 1966 (in Thousands of Dollars)

	Fiscal Year 1962	Fiscal Year 1963	Fiscal Year 1964	Fiscal Year 1965	Fiscal Year 1966
Argentina	—	—	298	1,253	539
Bolivia	—	1,817	397	239	114

Brazil	2,200	2,156	2,097	2,386	1,961
Chile	860	2,019	1,279	391	634
Colombia	—	1,488	1,655	550	696
Costa Rica	—	—	222	13	*
Dominican Republic	—	596	59	64	122
Ecuador	1,500	323	709	476	104
El Salvador	—	534	145	99	65
Guatemala	—	863	567	133	343
Honduras	—	84	20	240	71
Mexico	—	—	—	8	20
Nicaragua	—	59	—	3	—
Panama	—	—	2	44	22
Paraguay	—	840	1,111	596	576
Peru	1,135	2,794	1,271	2,411	2,871
Uruguay	—	546	431	286	103
Venezuela	—	—	23	47	59
Region†	—	—	—	—	72
Area Total	5,695	14,119	10,286	9,239	8,372

Note: Fiscal year 1962 was the first year that civic action assistance was so identified in military assistance programs. Fiscal year 1967 is estimated to have a worldwide total of $11,810.
*Less than $500.
†Probably refers to funds not dedicated to a particular country but to region "overhead."

Still, some military officers were uneasy about the "new professionalism" that cast military officers in the role of the only force capable of resolving national problems in a disinterested and patriotic fashion. This uneasiness resulted from the lack of a systematic ideological and doctrinal rationale for prolonged military rule. Gradually this void was filled by the emergence of specialized military academic and research centers that not only developed an appropriate rationale for military rule, but also took it upon themselves to train civilians as administrators in the antipolitical military state.

Prototypical Institutions of the New Professionalism of Military Antipolitics: CAEM (Peru) and ESG (Brazil)

In the 1970s military antipolitics became a predominant political form in Latin America. No longer did military officers feel obliged to insist that intervention in politics was temporary or even undesirable. To a great extent, the openly political ambitions and activities of military elites stemmed from a new emphasis on professional training that provided a rationale for and a stimulus to the creation of military governments as instruments of development.

Prototypical in this respect were the Center for Advanced Military Studies (Centro de Altos Estudios Militares—CAEM) in Peru and the Superior War School (Escola Superior de Guerra—ESG) in Brazil. Interestingly, the military governments in Peru and Brazil, led chiefly by graduates or instructors from these institutions (and also assisted by civilian graduates), have been seen as both "rightist" (Brazil) and "leftist" (Peru) because of the policies and programs adopted in their countries. In fact, however, the basic paradigm of both regimes, "military antipolitics," is consistent either with mobilizational inclusionary programs of economic modernization (Peru, 1968–75) or with politics that demobilize social and political groups and limit political participation to encourage modernization through regressive income distribution and capital accumulation (Brazil, 1964–73, Argentina, 1976–83, Chile, 1973–1990).

Historical and environmental factors greatly influenced the particulars of public policy under the new military regimes. Where quasi-feudal land tenure systems, ethnic and cultural diversity, and relatively weak industrial economies existed, efforts to modernize through antipolitics appeared to be reformist, populist, or even "leftist." In nations with more developed capitalist economies, or more militant and well-organized labor movements, military antipolitics seemed more reactionary. In either case, law and order, restraints on autonomous popular mobilization, press censorship, restrictions on civil liberties, and intolerance of opposition underlie policy differences among the military regimes.

Although some have labeled the orientation of these institutions the "new professionalism,"[9] neither their orientations nor their attitudes were, in fact, new. Rather, the explicit concern with internal security, economic development, and social services; the ineptitude of civilian politicians; and the inadequacy of politics was the result of an amalgamation of traditional Hispanic antipolitics with the influences of military professionalization from 1880 to 1930, the Cold War ambiance, the United States-influenced counterinsurgency and Alliance for Progress programs, and, importantly, the doctrinal justification for military rule contained in the CAEM, ESG-type military educational experience. But even this doctrinal justification, including the expansion of the concept of national security to encompass all those political, economic, and social conditions that affect the power of a nation, was merely an elaboration upon the sentiments of Latin American military officers in the early twentieth century (see the remarks of Colonel Luis Vicat, cited above).

The educational experience at CAEM, for example, reinforced the long-held disdain and contempt that officers felt for civilian politicians and for "politics." Since the civilian governments had failed to stimulate development, it followed therefore that they were responsible for all of Peru's social and economic ills. Moreover, since the civilians who had governed the country belonged to the traditional elites representing agro-commercial interests, the military's anticivilian orientation coincided nicely with leftist critiques of the landed oligarchy. The military saw itself as being patriotic, self-sacrificing, and dedicated to national—not class—interests, unlike the self-interested civilians.

Thus, the Peruvian military was "leftist." Yet the basic assumptions about the role of the state, the nature of authority, and the uses of constitutions bore a much greater resemblance to Diego Portales than to Karl Marx. The military's mission, to provide internal security, required that the state have "freedom of action and the necessary resources to achieve social well-being. . . . [The state must have] the authority to adopt measures considered necessary for achieving its objectives. . . . The state is supreme within its territory."[10] If the Peruvian officers disliked their dependence upon the United States and seemed to attack certain sectors of the private economy, the philosophical basis of these measures reached back to colonial Hispanic capitalism and military nationalism, not to Marxism. CAEM provided a modern rationale for antipolitics under military direction.

In Brazil, a larger and much more industrialized society than Peru, the socioeconomic dilemmas of political leadership by the military were even more complex. Political experience under civilian regimes had been more varied and the failure of liberalism and populism more recent and more directly menacing to the military. Thus, the Brazilian variant of antipolitics included rabid anti-Marxism. Yet, allowing for Brazil's somewhat unique history in Latin America, the basic assumptions of rule held by the ESG graduates were quite familiar: the need to centralize authority, the intolerance of opposition, the contempt for civilian politics and politicians, the refusal to be constrained by constitutional limits, the propensity to govern by decree, and the censorship or closure of opposition mass media.[11]

Brazilian practice added a relatively new element to antipolitics (an element anticipated by George Orwell): government use of torture and terror as a routine instrument of rule. Variants on the Brazilian version of antipolitics, notably after 1973 in both Chile and Uruguay and after 1976 in Argentina, incorporated state terrorism into the arsenal of the public policy instruments of Latin American antipolitics.

In Argentina, after 1976, the military declared and waged a war against the internal enemy—politicians and "subversives"—which left thousands dead or "disappeared" in the late 1970s and early 1980s. Meanwhile, in Guatemala and El Salvador, thousands more died in civil wars and counterinsurgency operations as death squads, secret police, and counterintelligence units detained, arrested, and attacked labor leaders, peasants, journalists, politicians, students, clerics, and other regime opponents in efforts to extirpate the "cancer of politics" from national life.

Policy Consequences of Military Antipolitics

The assumptions of antipolitics allow for a great diversity of policy initiatives by military rulers. Antipolitics is committed neither to capitalism nor to socialism. It is antiliberal and anti-Marxist. It assumes repression of opposition, silencing or censoring of the media, and subordinating the labor movement to the objectives of the regime. It does not willingly tolerate strikes by workers or the pretensions to aristocratic privilege by traditional elites. It seeks order and progress, the latter assumed contingent upon the former. It places high priority on economic growth and is usually little concerned with income distribution except insofar as worker or white-collar discontent leads to protest and disorder. It can pragmatically emphasize either concessions or repression in obtaining its objectives. It can even use "elections," pseudopolitical parties, and plebiscites in order to give a veneer of "democratic" legitimacy to authoritarian direction of the state and society.

Military antipolitics adds several elements to those general characteristics: military leadership, a more evident linkage between the state and coercion, a more insistent demand for order and respect for hierarchy, a less tolerant attitude toward opposition, and an outright rejection of "politics," which is perceived as being the source of underdevelopment, corruption, and evil.[12]

Thus, whether military antipolitics includes programs for land reform or industrialization, expanded public health services, urban housing, or new educational facilities, the other policies of antipolitics tend to be shared. And, above all, military antipolitics produces a regime of masters and "proles," of rulers and the ruled. Sometimes the masters use torture and other forms of repression to enforce their will and maintain their power; sometimes prosperity permits the use of more pleasant instruments of persuasion. Nevertheless, the military version of antipolitics remains tied to the Portalian notion: "The stick and the cake, justly and opportunely administered, are the specifics with which any nation can be cured, however inveterate its bad habits may be."[13]

Notes

1. Raúl Aldunate Phillips, *Ruido de sables* (Santiago de Chile: Escuela Lito-Tipográfica, "La Gratitud Nacional," n.d.), p. 87.
2. Quoted in Víctor Villanueva, *Ejército peruano: del caudillaje anárquico al militarismo reformista* (Lima: Librería-Editorial Juan Mejía Baca, 1973), p. 177. The emphasis is in the original.
3. Simon Collier, *Ideas and Politics of Chilean Independence, 1808–1833* (Cambridge: Cambridge University Press, 1967), p. 345.
4. In contrast to the European liberal tradition of laissez-faire capitalism, Hispanic capitalism views private enterprise as a concession of the state. Thus, in the Hispanic system, monopoly is not the end product of capitalist development, but rather the starting point of private enterprise. The old slave monopoly, or *asiento*, of colonial days and the various concessionary monopolies, or *estancos*, of the republican period are merely two examples of this system.
5. Luis Vicat, "El desarrollo industrial como empresa militar," in Jorge Alvarez, ed., *Ejército y revolución industrial* (Buenos Aires: Talleres Gráficos Verdad, 1964), p. 25.
6. Quoted in Víctor Villanueva, *El CAEM y la revolución de la fuerza armada* (Lima: Instituto de Estudios Peruanos, 1972), p. 233.
7. Quoted in ibid.
8. U.S. Congress, House, *Foreign Assistance and Related Agencies Appropriations for 1967, Hearing before a Subcommittee of the Committee on Appropriations*, 89th Cong., 1st sess., 1967, pp. 605–6.
9. For a discussion of "new professionalism," see Alfred Stepan, "The New Professionalism of Internal Warfare and Military Role Expansion," in Alfred Stepan, ed., *Authoritarian Brazil: Origins, Policies, and Failures* (New Haven: Yale University Press, 1973), pp. 47–65.
10. Villanueva, *CAEM*, p. 156.
11. Stepan, "New Professionalism," p. 55.
12. It must be noted that there remain military officers who wish to return to a narrower professional role. Important divisions within the Latin American officer corps developed (in each of the countries upon which we focus in this book) precisely over the desirability of prolonged military rule or even military intervention. Yet in the 1970s the officers who desired an end to military rule or a return to anything approximating liberal domestic politics were clearly out of step with the dominant doctrines in the military academies and the reality of the Latin American scene. In the 1980s this trend was, at least temporarily, reversed.
13. Collier, *Ideas and Politics of Chilean Independence*, p. 359.

*Brian Loveman and
Thomas M. Davies, Jr.*

CHAPTER 2

Instability, Violence, and the Age of the Caudillos

The roots of the antipolitical military regimes of the 1960s, 1970s, and 1980s stretch far back into Iberian and colonial Latin American history. There exists a plethora of theories about and explanations for the form of Spanish colonial government and for the rise of the caudillos in the nineteenth century. One of the most popular, particularly as developed by Américo Castro, holds that the Spanish, and consequently the republican, mentality was decisively shaped by the *Reconquista* experience: El Cid and the warrior priest. Others have pointed to the institutional contributions of the highly developed Amerindian civilizations and particularly to the submissiveness of the lower orders in Aztec, Maya, and Inca cultures. Still others explain the rise of the caudillos and the political chaos of the nineteenth century in terms of the heritage from the Spanish conquistadores.[1]

More important for the study of antipolitics, however, is the approach adopted by Professor Richard M. Morse in his classic essay "Toward a Theory of Spanish American Government."[2] Morse points to the dualism and philosophical polarization present in Spanish thought. On the one hand, there was the medieval Thomistic philosophy embodied in the *Siete Partidas* (the basic source of Spanish law during this period) and practiced by Queen Isabella. The *Siete Partidas*, according to Morse,

> assumed the nuclear element of society to be, not Lockean atomistic man, but religious societal man: man with a salvable soul (that is, in relationship with God) and man in a station of life (that is, having mutual obligations with fellow humans, determinable by principles of Christian justice). The ruler, though not procedurally responsible to the people or the estates, was bound through his conscience to be the instrument of God's immutable, publicly ascertainable law.[3]

Isabella's husband, Ferdinand, on the other hand, by virtue of the nature of the Aragon Empire, with such diverse components as the Balearic Islands, Sardinia, Sicily, and Naples, was forced to adopt a strikingly different political philosophy for his regime. As Morse notes:

> Ferdinand was committed to the shifting, amoral statecraft of competing Christian princes in maintenance and expansion of a domain which, within its Christian context, was diversely composed. Ferdinand ruled under transitional conditions which precluded resorting for authority to Isabella's Thomistic sanction or to statist apologetics. Managing with sheer personal verve and cunning, he was, in the fullest sense, Machiavellian.[4]

Thus, Spanish colonial government had from the outset a "dual heritage: medieval and Renaissance, Thomistic and Machiavellian." The role of the king in this colonial system was crucial, for he was the ultimate unifying symbol. As Morse states:

> The king, even though he might be an inarticulate near-imbecile like Charles II, was symbolic throughout his realm as the guarantor of status. In Thomistic idiom, all parts of the society were ordered to the whole as the imperfect to the perfect. This ordering, inherently the responsibility of the whole multitude, devolved upon the king as a public person acting in their behalf, for the task of ordering to a given end fell to the agent best placed and fitted for the specific function.[5]

The stated objectives of this system—order, obedience (both to God and king), authority, and stability—are in many respects identical to those of the caudillos and of the later military regimes. However, the system was fragile, relying almost entirely for its continuance on subject loyalty to the crown.

Napoleon's invasion of Spain in 1808, the placing of his brother Joseph on the throne, and the subsequent criollo revolts in the colonies all had the effect of destroying the delicate political equilibrium. Gone was the supreme moral force provided by the crown, and the subsequent power struggles that emerged represented efforts to find a new basis for political order. For a time, the great liberators, such as Simón Bolívar and José de San Martín, served as surrogate kings; but with the end of the wars, the liberators either retired from the political arena or were forcibly ejected.

In the early nineteenth century, criollo leaders attempted to rule by applying the new, alien concepts of constitutionalism and liberalism, but they failed to stem the tide of personalism and localism which swept the land. "With the breakdown of the moral authority of the crown, lawlessness became widespread and was overcome not necessarily by a substitute moral authority, but rather by the personal magnetism of a given charismatic leader. Personalism rather than principle tended to prevail."[6]

Argentina's first president, Bernardino Rivadavia, summed this up best when he wrote in 1830:

> In my opinion what retards regular and stable advance in those republics stems from the vacillations and doubts that deprive all institutions of that moral force which is indispensable to them and can be given only by conviction and decision. It is evident to me, and would be easy to demonstrate, that the upheavals of our country spring much more immediately from lack of public spirit and of cooperation among responsible men in sustaining order and laws than from attacks of ungovernable, ambitious persons without merit or fitness and of indolent coveters.[7]

This leadership crisis was further compounded when most upper-class criollos also withdrew from the active direction of their newly created nations and returned to their great landed estates. The absence of these men created a tremendous vacuum, not only political but also military and moral. The old Thomistic order was truncated and replaced by a new order ruled not by statesmen or professional soldiers, but by prototypical Machiavellian leaders—the caudillos. For fifty years, the caudillos, with varying degrees of success, attempted to fill the vacuum caused by the lack of effective, legitimate political institutions—an attempt which invites comparison with the military antipoliticians after 1964.

The nineteenth-century caudillo, whether Juan Manuel de Rosas in Argentina, Ramón Castilla in Peru, or Rafael Carrera in Guatemala, had much in common with twentieth-century military elites, despite a lack of professional credentials. Neither the caudillo nor today's professional soldier is committed to political movements or interests based on traditional ideological questions of liberal or conservative, left or right. Both caudillos and professional soldiers usually justify their rule in nationalist terms of saving and maintaining the fatherland, although this appears more frequently among the latter than the former. Neither the caudillo nor today's professional soldier tolerates dissent, much less formal opposition, and both react quickly to stifle it. Finally, both the caudillo and the professional soldier employ force as the basis for their political rule.

But there are important differences as well. The professional soldier stresses military education, strict obedience to a hierarchical authority, and submission of personal desires to the well-being of the military institution and the nation. The caudillo, on the other hand, was highly individualistic and hated all laws and authority except his own. The professional soldier, then, adopts many of the precepts of the Thomistic tradition, while the caudillo opts instead for an extreme form of atomism.

The adjectives employed to describe the caudillo are as varied as they are colorful: crude, vulgar, barbaric, cruel, daring, sadistic, strong, fearless, and illiterate. As Domingo Sarmiento noted about the Argentine caudillo Juan Facundo Quiroga, his was the type of "primitive barbarism" which knew no bounds or restraints. The caudillo relied not only upon force to maintain his power, but also, more importantly, on his charisma and his unfailing ability to dominate those around him.

In contrast to the nationalistic professional soldier, most caudillos were committed only to a locality or a region. They possessed a limited sense of nationalism; and when a caudillo did become president of his nation, he still thought in regional terms, often seeking to dominate only the capital city. He ruled the remainder of his country through a rather loose alliance with other regional caudillos or *caciques*. As Hugh Hamill puts it: "Given geographic isolation and the vastness of the region, the scattered power nuclei, controlled by *caciques*, were fundamental to the emergence of a national caudillo. Whereas a *cacique* is a ruler among men, a caudillo is a ruler among *caciques*."[8] The success of his rule depended upon personalism and charisma, not on institutions. Thus, there was little institutional development in the period, be it in the civilian political arena or in the military sector.

During the Wars of Independence, the officer corps were drawn principally from the upper class. After the wars they withdrew and were replaced by men of much lower social status for whom, in the words of Edwin Lieuwen, "an army career provided the opportunity to break through the arbitrary restrictions of the old social order, to shoot one's way into a share of the power, wealth, and social prestige enjoyed by the landed oligarchy and the church hierarchy."[9] Thus the upper classes lost effective control over the military establishments which, in conjunction with regional civilian caudillos, became the arbiters in what amounted to a political system of chaos.

These so-called national armies had almost nothing in common with today's Latin American military establishments. The officers and men alike were ill trained and poorly equipped. As John Johnson has noted, the service academies which did exist were poorly organized, and attendance was not a prerequisite for professional advancement. Moreover, neither the cadets in the academies nor the enlisted men in the ranks were taught any skill that might be of use in national development, despite the fact that the various militaries consumed over half of their nations' yearly budgets.[10] In addition to being poorly trained and equipped, the enlisted men never felt part of a nation or a national institution. What loyalty they did feel was to their commander, who in turn was loyal only to himself or to another caudillo.

Although the creation of the Latin American nations was to a large extent a military achievement, in many cases it was only through the ventures of nationalistic caudillos that the territorial units were forged and maintained against European as well as Latin American enemies. As the age of caudillos gave way to that of civilian politics, the successors of the caudillos—the professional military—often saw in the venality and incapacity of civilian elites a betrayal of nations which the military had founded.

In contrast, these modern-day military officers view with respect the regimes of the great caudillos in their nations' past. Not only did the caudillos shape and defend the fatherland, but they also did it with firmness (even violence) and with dedication. They alone prevented the national disintegration which would have resulted from "politics." In short, they successfully applied the politics of antipolitics and in so doing served as vital links between traditional Hispanic politics and the antipolitical military regimes of today.

One of the best known and most successful of all Latin American caudillos was the Argentine strongman Juan Manuel de Rosas. Breaking with his family at an early age, Rosas went to the interior, where he soon gained fame for his daring and skill as a gaucho. He became wealthy in cattle ranching and later expanded into the complementary businesses of salt and slaughterhouses. In 1829 he was appointed governor of Buenos Aires province and charged with ending the chaos created by the politicians of the legislature. His solution was as efficient as it was prototypical of *caudillismo*—the carrot or the stick. Rosas totally dominated Buenos Aires province but allowed the regional caudillos to retain control of their respective provinces in return for their absolute loyalty to him. Recalcitrant caudillos were dealt with quickly and severely.

In the early years of his rule, Rosas was enormously popular with all strata of the population. The upper-class ranchers supported him because he had restored internal order and because he emphasized the cattle industry in his economic policies. The lower classes admired his prowess as a gaucho and responded to his tremendous charisma. In 1832, Rosas stepped down as governor and went south with his army to fight the Indians. He succeeded in pushing them almost to Patagonia, thereby adding to his reputation as a fierce warrior. He increased his support among the great ranchers (*estancieros*) by distributing to them the newly opened Indian lands.

The period 1832–35 saw Argentina slip back into the chaos that had been characteristic of "politics" before. Finally, in 1835, after much pleading and a rigged plebiscite, Rosas agreed to accept the governorship again. He quickly reestablished internal order, whipped the regional caudillos back into line, and repressed all opposition. Rosas tolerated no dissent, and those who dared to challenge him were either jailed, exiled, or killed, while thousands more fled into voluntary exile. Even the Catholic Church was brought into line and forced to hang Rosas's portrait next to the altars in the churches. His was a regime of terror and personalist rule. Argentina was not a true nation, rather a series of provinces held together by the power and charisma of the dictator. Still, it did survive as an entity as it might not have under the rule of "politics."

Rosas sought to rule his neighbors as he did his gauchos. He refused to accept the independence of Uruguay or even of Paraguay and was constantly meddling in the internal affairs of the former. He declared war on his Bolivian counterpart Andrés de Santa Cruz in 1837 in an effort to prevent Santa Cruz from uniting Bolivia and Peru into a strong confederation. He also successfully defended his regime and Argentina from attack by Europeans. In 1838 the French captured Martín García Island and instituted a blockade which lasted until 1840. In 1845 the French returned, this time with the British, and blockaded the entire Río de la Plata estuary. Although the blockades caused severe economic dislocations in Argentina, Rosas held out and forced the two powers to withdraw by 1848.

In 1851, Rosas sought to renew his pact with the regional caudillos, but this time his long-time supporter Justo José Urquiza, the strongman of Entre Ríos province, declared against him. Urquiza succeeded in winning over the other caudillos, in addition to getting support from both Uruguay and Brazil, and defeated Rosas's army in 1852.

Rosas had ruled for almost a quarter of a century, but his sudden defeat is indicative of the fragility of the caudillo system. Nevertheless, Rosas did establish internal order (despite the high social and political costs), and he did defend the nation against both South American and European challengers. In contrast to the weak, corrupt, and inept civilian regimes which followed, the nationalism of the Rosas regime was viewed favorably by subsequent military officers.

In Peru, one finds much the same political situation in the years following independence as that which existed in Argentina. In 1826, Simón Bolívar departed Peru, leaving behind a constitution and a caretaker government headed by Andrés de Santa Cruz. Both were overthrown in 1827, and for the next seventeen years the country was in almost constant chaos. The principals were military caudillos, veterans of the independence wars, who traded the presidency back and forth by means of *golpes* and counter *golpes*.

Finally, in 1845, Ramón Castilla assumed the presidency for the first time (he served two terms, 1845–51 and 1855–60) and initiated an era of economic prosperity, military preparedness, and political order. He was so successful that he ranks first in the pantheon of Peruvian heroes and is revered by the military today for his honesty, patriotism, and firm commitment to national defense.

Castilla was a mestizo with relatively unsophisticated manners, and this contributed to his popularity with the lower classes. Like most caudillos, he had led an active and eventful life, serving on both sides in the Wars of Independence, being captured and taken to Buenos Aires, escaping and walking back to Peru across South America. He was daring, resourceful, and charismatic.

Upon taking office, he faced the monumental task of restoring internal order, both politically and militarily. He quickly suppressed the bandit bands which had flourished between Lima and Callao and on the coastal highway to the north. He ended the political strife between Liberals and Conservatives by using both but joining neither. He used the revenues from guano exploitation to promote business and regularize the economy and the civil service, thereby inaugurating an era of unprecedented prosperity. He supported construction of the first railroad in South America, wrote the Constitution of 1860, which lasted for sixty years (longer than any other before or since), and sought to instill a new patriotism in the young nation. Like Rosas, Castilla used the carrot-and-stick technique with opponents, but he did so in a much less violent fashion. He neither executed nor jailed his enemies; rather, he sent them into exile with the understanding that they could return under very favorable circumstances anytime they decided to cooperate. In this way he avoided making any really dangerous enemies. Finally, he subdued the various regional military leaders and centralized the military command structure.

More than anyone else in the nineteenth century, Castilla was responsible for the creation of a national military force, stating that:

"Our military forces are not the instrument of tyranny or the enemies of society. . . . Imbued with a sense of the importance of their noble destiny, they are the conservers of the public tranquillity, the custodians of external and internal peace, and the loyal defenders of the constitution and the laws."[11]

Castilla greatly increased the size of the army, reopened the military academy, and purchased modern armaments. He also concentrated on improving and expanding the navy and built it into the most powerful naval force on the west coast of South America. His long-remembered thesis was that if Chile bought one ship, Peru should buy two. The fact that a civilian president, Manuel Pardo, canceled an order for two warships, which were subsequently purchased and used by Chile in the War of the Pacific (1879–83), provided added weight to Castilla's judgment, a judgment which has become an almost religious principle among today's professional soldiers in Peru.

Castilla is also remembered for his success in foreign affairs and in defense of the national boundaries. He was among the leaders of the opposition to the abortive attempt by Spain to retake Ecuador in 1845. He was also an outspoken critic of the United States' aggression against Mexico, and he sought to create a united Latin American front against the Colossus of the North. In 1859, Castilla attacked Guayaquil, Ecuador, in retaliation for the Ecuadorian government's attempt to placate European creditors by ceding them land claimed by Peru.

Finally, in 1865, Castilla, though no longer president, was the first to denounce the Vivanco-Pareja Treaty between Spain and Peru as being insulting to the national honor. The treaty was aimed at ending Spanish occupation of Peru's principal guano deposits on the Chincha Islands, which had been seized by the Spanish fleet some months earlier. What incensed Castilla was that Peru agreed to pay not only Spanish claims dating back to the War for Independence, but also the cost of the Spanish occupation of the Chinchas.

Thus, from a military point of view, Castilla stands as one of the greatest leaders in Peruvian history. He established internal order, brought about economic prosperity, enlarged and improved the armed forces, assumed a leadership role for his country in foreign affairs (including challenging the United States), and vigorously defended the national boundaries against both South American and European opponents. If one compares Castilla with subsequent civilian presidents, both in the nineteenth and twentieth centuries, one might conclude, as have thousands of Peruvian military officers, that what Peru needs is not civilian "politics," but the antipolitics of Ramón Castilla.

To the north, in Central America, a remarkably similar scene was being played out. By 1835 the United Provinces of Central America, launched in 1823 with dreams of achieving Central American unity, was in ruins. As with the confederations of Gran Colombia and Peru-Bolivia, the seeds of disunity and destruction had been sown centuries earlier by the structure of Spanish colonialism, seeds which sprouted anew in the Liberal-Conservative conflicts of the late colonial and early independence periods.

Ideological divisions between Liberals and Conservatives in Guatemala and the rest of Central America differed little from those prevalent in the rest of Latin America. Conservatives, for the most part, wanted a strong centralized government with traditional ties to the Catholic Church, that is, a continuation of the Hispanic tradition. Liberals, on the other hand, intermittently held sway in some of the provinces and looked favorably upon a United States-type model of federation. Most Liberals also sought to curb the influence of the Church and move toward the establishment of a more secular state.[12]

Although the Liberals and their leader, Manuel José Arce, had controlled the federation since its inception, Conservatives never accepted the legitimacy of their rule. Constant infighting and skirmishing finally erupted in a bloody civil war in 1826. By 1829 the Liberals and their new leader, Francisco Morazán, had overcome the Conservative forces and immediately embarked upon a program of far-reaching change. These reforms all but guaranteed the outbreak of a new civil war. As Ralph Lee Woodward has written, "The grassroots reaction against the Liberals was especially violent against foreign elements and against efforts to change traditional lifestyles and patterns of rural life."[13]

Convinced that the economic and political backwardness of their region was the direct result of Hispanic culture, institutions, economic models, land tenure patterns, and legislation, Morazán and the Guatemalan governor, Mariano Gálvez, along with their Liberal allies, sought to emulate the Lockean tradition of England and the United States, a tradition which proved totally antagonistic to the communal tradition of the region's Indian peoples and to the power of the Church and of many colonial elites.

Like their Andean counterparts José de San Martín and Simón Bolívar, the Liberals of Central America held a rather simplistic view of the "Indian problem" and rural land tenure structures. Imbued with the ideals of the French Revolution and of Thomas Jefferson, they not only misunderstood Indian culture, but also mistakenly assumed that communal landholdings necessarily inhibited economic development and limited agricultural production.[14] Their solution was the parcelization of communal lands and the granting of individual land titles to Indians. Almost everywhere these types of proposals led to massive appropriation of communal lands by nearby haciendas and other favored beneficiaries at the expense of Indian peasants.

Peasant anger over this Liberal land "redistribution" was exacerbated by government policies which encouraged and supported foreign colonization projects in sparsely populated regions. The Liberals, on the other hand, felt that lumber and agricultural concessions to foreigners, primarily British, would provide a much-needed impetus to modernization and economic progress.

Liberal attitudes toward the Catholic Church and education further inflamed the antagonism of many Indian and rural groups. Not only were most peasants deeply religious, but they also had tremendous respect, even adoration, for many local priests who were thus able to rally them against the government, particularly after a cholera epidemic swept the region in 1837. In time-honored fashion, the Church preached that the cholera was God's retribution for Liberal anticlericalism. Likewise, Liberal attempts to destroy Indian culture through mass-education programs, including the removal of children from their parents, provoked additional anger.

Added to this were Liberal policies which established a head tax (reminiscent of the old Spanish Indian tribute) and a labor draft for the construction of roads (reminiscent of the variety of Spanish forced-labor systems during the colonial period). Both fell heaviest on the rural masses.

Out of this milieu emerged José Rafael Carrera, the greatest of the midnineteenth-century Central American caudillos. Born in 1814 to a family of very modest means, Carrera has been variously characterized as "an illiterate Guatemalan Indian," a "primitive," and a "religious fanatic of strong will and messianic aspirations."[15] In fact, Carrera was a *ladino* who received no formal education, served briefly in the army as a youth, and then moved to the countryside where he married and settled down to raise pigs. In 1837 he joined the rebellion against the Liberals and organized a peasant guerrilla army, quickly gaining fame for "fearlessly leading his forces in fanatical charges against troops with better arms and training."[16] After heavy fighting, Carrera's peasant forces entered Guatemala City in January 1838 and overthrew Gálvez. Throughout 1838, chaos reigned in Guatemala as Conservatives and Liberals continued to fight and the United Provinces of Central America collapsed. Finally, in early 1840, Carrera routed the Liberal forces and took control of the nation. For the first four years, 1840–44, Carrera controlled the government through the army; in 1844 he assumed the presidency, which he held, with a brief interlude (1849–51), until his death in 1865.

Like Rosas in Argentina, Carrera possessed an enormous ego and often compared himself to Napoleon. He was also an astute politician who skillfully played Liberals and Conservatives against each other. His lower-class origins, mixed ancestry, and fame as a warrior made him immensely popular with the masses. Although rejected initially by the elites, Carrera's increasing commitment to Conservative ideals and his ability to maintain internal order ultimately won him much upper-class support as well.

Under his long regime, most of the Liberal policies were reversed or abandoned. He centralized all government operations in his hands, restored to the Church its confiscated lands, the tithe, and control of education, abolished the head tax, reinstated the colonial land tenure system, and abandoned the Liberals' attempts to Westernize the Indians and integrate them into "national" life. Moreover, Carrera sought to create a national, professional military and to foster economic growth through subsidies, tariffs, and the reactivation of the old colonial Economic Society.

Carrera also took steps to monitor and control foreigners in the country and in general adopted a highly nationalistic stance. This nationalism was most evident in his active participation to oust the filibustering William Walker from Nicaragua, an act similar to the role of Rosas against European invaders in Argentina and the role of Castilla in Peru. He also actively intervened in the affairs of his neighbors, as exemplified by the installation of one of his lieutenants, Francisco Malespín, as dictator of El Salvador.

In sum, Carrera consolidated national government in Guatemala, imposed order from the chaos of the early independence period, resisted the incursion of foreign ideas and influence, and made efforts to create a more modern military. He reestablished a centralized political system based on the traditional values of Hispanic society and the blessing of the Catholic Church—a nationalistic government which prided itself on law and order, the carrot and the stick, which would serve as a model for future military leaders of Guatemala.

Unlike Guatemala, El Salvador did not produce one outstanding nineteenth-century caudillo. In the half century from 1821 to 1872 the Liberals held power for twenty-nine years and the Conservatives for twenty-one. The reasons for this were many, but one of the most important was the omnipresence of Carrera in Guatemala. On three separate occasions (1840, 1851, 1863), Carrera intervened openly in El Salvador to dislodge Liberal governments. Nevertheless, partially as a response to Carrera's intervention in El Salvador and the rest of Central America, Liberal caudillos in El Salvador gave rise to a heroic military tradition in the first part of the nineteenth century. Among the most colorful of these, General Gerardo Barrios began his career as a youthful follower of Morazán. During the 1840s and 1850s, after a brief exile in Peru, Barrios fought against the armies of Carrera in Costa Rica, Nicaragua, and El Salvador. In 1858, as interim president, Barrios had the remains of Morazán returned from Costa Rica to El Salvador and during the next seven years challenged Carrera's forces in Central America.

In one of the many losing efforts, Barrios won the everlasting adulation of Salvadoran nationalists with his oft-quoted response to demands for his surrender: "Tell them I will not surrender. I will be buried with my soldiers." Barrios brought Colombian General José María Melo to El Salvador in 1859 to reorganize the army. For the first time, discipline and drill, along with standard uniforms, were introduced. In 1862 a French mission of four officers replaced the Colombians, and the beginnings of a proud military tradition in El Salvador were forged amongst the struggles of the Central American caudillos.[17]

Seven years later, Barrios was captured in Nicaragua, taken to El Salvador, "tried" by his opponents, and then executed. Carrera himself died only months later, ending the era of early nineteenth-century caudillos in the region. In El Salvador, however, the memory of Barrios lives among the nation's twentieth-century military leaders, including those like Oscar Osorio, who initiated the era of modernizing military regimes in the late 1940s. In 1949 the military government commemorated the anniversary of Captain General Gerardo Barrios's death with a homage and erection of a statue which would be "a model for all Salvadorans who aspire to ennoble the fatherland, with sword, struggle, and deeds."[18]

Both Carrera and Barrios must be viewed in national as well as regional terms. For the embattled military officers in Central America of the 1980s and 1990s, José Rafael Carrera and Gerardo Barrios embody the virtues of patriotism, honor, courage, military discipline, and economic development which they seek to impose upon their societies today—conflicting in their view, with the malevolent forces of "politics," venality, and subversion which threaten the fatherland. In these circumstances, as the military leaders make clear, it is their sacred duty to save the *patria* from disorder and destruction.

The nineteenth-century political experiences of both Brazil and Chile stand in sharp contrast to those of Argentina, Peru, Bolivia, and Central America. Unlike the Spanish American republics, Brazil was largely spared the violence, bloodshed, political chaos, and economic dislocation of a struggle for independence. Instead, Emperor Pedro I abdicated in favor of his son, and the transition was a smooth one. From 1831 to 1889, Pedro II ruled Brazil peacefully, and therefore the military establishment developed out of a totally different milieu.

As outlined in the introductory essay, the age of the caudillo was extremely short-lived in Chile, being replaced after 1830 with a highly centralized, autocratic republic which maintained internal order and greatly expanded the economy of the nation, but which tolerated no opposition or dissent. Thus, Chile also avoided the economic and political chaos associated with the age of the caudillos.

In most of Latin America, the age of *caudillismo* gradually came to an end after 1870. National economies demanded national policy-making. National policy-making implied effective national leadership, which in many cases meant the dominance of a truly national caudillo like Porfirio Díaz in Mexico. In other cases, such as Chile and Argentina, national political institutions developed which allowed legal transfers of power and implementation of public policy through administrative agencies.

A key to the formation of real nation-states was the emergence of national military institutions. Control of national politics required the reorganization, modernization, and professionalization of the national military establishments, which in turn meant the destruction of the old regional and personalist armies. This professionalization process did not mark an end to the military as political elites, but rather to the formation of a new national military-political elite to replace the regionalistic caudillo commanders. Latin America and Latin American military officers in particular had begun the slow road back to what Morse has called the Thomistic tradition, a road which was to culminate in the military antipolitics of the 1960s, 1970s, and 1980s.

Notes

1. For a succinct discussion of these and other causal factors, see the Introduction by Hugh M. Hamill, Jr., in his *Dictatorship in Spanish America* (New York: Alfred A. Knopf, 1965), pp. 3–25.

2. Originally published in the *Journal of the History of Ideas* 15 (1954), pp, 71–93, the essay was reprinted in abridged form in Hamill, *Dictatorship*, pp. 52–68. All citations are from the latter.

3. Morse, "Toward a Theory," pp. 53–54.

4. Ibid., pp. 54–55.

5. Ibid., p. 56.

6. Hamill, *Dictatorship*, p. 21.

7. Quoted in Morse, "Toward a Theory," p. 60.

8. Hamill, *Dictatorship*, p. 11.

9. Edwin Lieuwen, *Arms and Politics in Latin America*, rev. ed. (New York: Frederick A. Praeger, 1961), pp. 19–20.

10. John J. Johnson, *The Military and Society in Latin America* (Stanford, Calif.: Stanford University Press, 1964), pp. 50, 53.

11. Quoted in Fredrick B. Pike, *The Modern History of Peru* (New York: Frederick A. Praeger, 1967), p. 92.

12. For a cogent description and analysis of Liberal-Conservative conflict in Central America in the early nineteenth century, see Ralph Lee Woodward, Jr., *Central America: A Nation Divided*, 2d ed. (New York: Oxford University Press, 1985), pp. 92–119.

13. Ibid., p. 99.

14. See Thomas M. Davies, Jr., *Indian Integration in Peru: A Half Century of Experience, 1900–1948* (Lincoln: University of Nebraska Press, 1974), pp. 19–23; and ibid., pp. 100–101.

15. Howard I. Blutstein et al., *El Salvador: A Country Study* (Washington, D.C.: American University, 1979), p. 12; John Edwin Fagg, *Latin America: A General History*, 3d ed. (New York: Macmillan Publishing Co., 1977), p. 411; and Richard F. Nyrop, ed., *Guatemala: A Country Study* (Washington, D.C.: U.S. Government Printing Office, 1983), p. 16.

16. Woodward, *Central America*, p. 105.

17. See Pedro Zamora Castellanos, *Vida militar de Centro América*, 2d ed., 2 vols. (Guatemala: Editorial del Ejército, 1967), 2:193–205.

18. *Diario Oficial*, San Salvador, 29 August 1949, 147, no. 188, p. 3011.

II

The Latin American Nation-State and the Creation of Professional Military Establishments

One of the great illusions in post-World War II thought on Latin American development was the hope that the military establishments would be professionalized, thereby ending their periodic intervention into national politics. North American observers in particular equated military professionalism and professionalization with apolitical military establishments. In practice, however, military professionalization in the Latin American milieu actually accelerated institutional and officer involvement in the political arena.

This result surprised many North American and European specialists on Latin America. To a great extent, their surprise stemmed from a misreading of the history of the region's military professionalization during the latter part of the nineteenth and early part of the twentieth centuries, as well as of the quality and direction of this professionalization after World War II. In contrast to what North Americans expected, the introduction of professional training, organization, and staffing of Latin American military establishments by European training missions led to the creation of political as well as military elites. Indeed, key political actors in the first three decades of the twentieth century were graduates of the German or French military professionalization programs or later of the programs run by German-trained Chilean personnel. Examples are Carlos Ibáñez in Chile, José F. Uriburu in Argentina, Luis M. Sánchez Cerro in Peru, and Leitão de Carvalho in Brazil.

In part, the impact of professionalization on Latin American military institutions followed the previous European pattern, particularly that of France and Prussia, but also that experienced in Spain, Portugal, and elsewhere. Latin American officers shared with their

European counterparts increasingly antipolitical, antidemocratic, and pro-"developmental" views when confronted with the challenges of industrialization, social change, labor strife, and the rise of more inclusive political regimes. The intellectual antecedents of Latin American antipolitics, such as Colmar von der Goltz's *Das Volk in Waffen* (1883) and Louis Hubert Gonzalve Lyautey's *Le rôle social de l'officier* (1891) and *Lettres du Tonkin et de Madagascar* (1897), detested politicians, socioeconomic instability, and the rise of the democratic state. They were convinced that the military had a special responsibility for achieving national objectives and protecting their nations' "permanent interests." Thus, Lyautey's disdain for "incompetent, unstable and irresponsible parliamentarism," and Goltz's quest for a "fusion of the military and the social and industrial life of the people," would be echoed in the Latin American national security doctrines after World War II.[*]

Frederick Nunn's article presents an overview of the effects of these European military training missions around the turn of the century. Nunn concludes that "the overriding impact of fifty years of European military training or orientation on Latin American armies was to stimulate rather than lessen political interest and to motivate elitist, professional army officers to assume responsibility for the conduct of national affairs."

In Brazil, the influence of European military training missions before World War I was slight. Nevertheless, the move toward professionalization of the military played a significant political role in the late nineteenth and early twentieth centuries. As in Argentina, Chile, Peru, and Bolivia, professionalization in Brazil meant the development of a politicized, anticivilian military elite anxious to "cleanse" the Brazilian polity and lead the nation to continental hegemony. Frank McCann traces the evolution of the professionalization and concomitant politicization of the Brazilian military in the late nineteenth and early twentieth centuries.

In Central America, European military missions and the process of military professionalization occurred somewhat later, as liberal and conservative caudillos led conflicting armies throughout the region during most of the nineteenth century. In Guatemala, where no systematic study of the European military missions has yet been completed, Spanish officers helped to create the Escuela Politécnica in

[*]Frederick Nunn's *Yesterday's Soldiers: European Military Professionalism in South America, 1890–1940* (Lincoln: University of Nebraska Press, 1983) is the most important study on the influence of European military doctrine and missions in Latin America.

the early 1870s and continued to provide staff for the military school into the 1880s. Later, French officers served as advisers to the army and, after World War I, the air corps. Although the small French mission remained the dominant influence in the military school, Guatemalan officers also attended Spanish military institutions during the 1920s, and a small number were sent to the United States. In the 1930s, American officers replaced the French and Spanish influence and were also designated to head the country's military academy.

Development of foreign and European influence in the military institutions of El Salvador began even earlier than in Guatemala. As Robert Elam indicates, Colombian, Spanish, French, and Chilean officers (the latter trained by Germans) all contributed to El Salvador's military tradition—and to the central role the military officers and institutions have played in Salvadoran politics. Generals ruled the country from 1887 to 1903; professionalization in the first decades of the twentieth century set the stage for development of one of the most politicized military institutions in Latin America from the 1930s until the present.

Taken together, these descriptions and analyses of military professionalization in Latin America in the late nineteenth and early twentieth centuries suggest that, instead of creating an apolitical military, professionalization actually produced a politicized officer corps, with its own ideology of modernization, industrialization, corporate elitism, nationalism, and antipolitics.

Frederick M. Nunn

CHAPTER 3

An Overview of
the European Military
Missions in Latin America

The presence of military organizations in Latin American politics is a reality of the twentieth century just as it was of the past. Scholars are in unison on this point but disagree on the reasons for the behavior and political outlook of twentieth-century political officers. Obviously, "changing times," nationalism, and middle-class origins of officers are insufficient causes for the nationalist, reformist-authoritarian strain of contemporary military attitudes in Latin America.

One of the most important causes for the development of contemporary Latin American military attitudes toward state, nation, and society is the creation of a professional army officer corps undertaken late in the last century and early in this century by the more advanced countries and by some of the lesser republics as well. Military professionalization was undertaken in Latin America for a variety of reasons, depending on time and place. In those countries where pre-World War II professionalization was guided by Europeans—French and Germans, chiefly—it resulted in the creation of a powerful political interest group. That group, the officer corps, completed the laying of the foundations for professional militarism. And professional militarism in Latin American countries where French and German officers served bears the indelible stamp of their presence. It is the purpose of this essay to point out the significance of that presence.

For some time now we have assumed that military professionalization did not achieve the desired results—that is, depoliticization—in Latin America because of such endemic factors as fiscal problems, weak economies, political conflict, and social change. But endemic factors may be the least important reason for the failure of professionalization to preclude political activities by the military in

Latin America. The overriding impact of fifty years of European military training or orientation on Latin American armies was to stimulate rather than lessen political interest and to motivate elitist, professional army officers to assume responsibility for the conduct of national affairs. This is by no means a monocausal interpretation; it is, rather, an additional explanation for military interest in Latin American politics.

Abstention from politics, then, did not result from professional training. What did develop first was a state that can be called military professionalism, and more. For the end of military professionalism—expertise, corporateness or sense of career, and responsibility—in Latin America during the age of modernization was professional militarism: a set of attitudes that may result in the resort to political action in an attempt to find solutions for social and economic distresses by methods based on a military ethos.

A careful historical examination of the professional armies selected by Latin American military leaders and statesmen to be models for their own armies indicates that they in fact were highly political. The French and German armies were highly political, not in the sense that they intervened in the affairs of the state time and time again, but in the sense that they were professions, corporate entities, immune in theory but not in practice from civilian meddling. And they were loyal to the state and the nation more than to a specific government or administration. They were vital and potent ingredients of the political process in France and Germany at the same time they were involved in the training of Latin America's armies.

Although the histories of the German and French armies from 1871 to 1914, and then from 1918 to about 1940, are those of a high degree of professionalism, they are also histories in which partisan political issues were of vital importance to the military profession per se. To review the Dreyfus affair, the Catholic-Radical-Masonic conflict, and the catastrophe of 1914–15 in France, or the German army and the empire, . . . and the rise of Nazism would be redundant here. History has yet to record more politicized armies than those of pre-World War II France and Germany.

It can be tentatively posited that Latin Americans who learned their military science in the classroom, in war games, and on maneuvers learned other things from their mentors. If the French and Germans were exemplary in a professional way, they cannot have been less exemplary in an extraprofessional way.

European military influences—professional and extraprofessional—were most keenly felt in South America, where the military buildup was a facet of traditional international rivalries on the one hand and a component of the overall modernization process on the other between 1890 and 1940. By 1914, German missions and individual instructors were training the armies of Argentina, Bolivia, and Chile. Chileans, who had studied under the retired German Captain Emil Körner (who rose to the rank of general in Chile) and his cohorts, in turn laid the foundations for the modern armies of Colombia, Ecuador, and El Salvador. Cadets and young officers from Central America, Venezuela, and Paraguay studied in Santiago. German-trained Argentines were prominent in that country's army by 1914, and students from Bolivia, Paraguay, and Peru came to study in Buenos Aires. Colonel Hans Kundt, probably the best known of all German officers in Latin America, put in several fruitful years prior to 1914 at the military school in La Paz, Bolivia. He would later prepare and lead that country's army to disaster in the Chaco War.

The Peruvian army was under French influence through a series of missions from 1896 until 1940, except for the 1914–18 interim. And, in 1919, a French mission led by General Maurice Gamelin, later chief of the French general staff, was contracted by Brazil. With the exception of those of the countries in the Caribbean area under heavy United States influence, no Latin American army was without an attachment to French or German (and in certain specialized fields, Spanish, Swiss, or Italian) influence during the half century before World War II.

In those countries most heavily influenced by French or German military training the armies were intensely political, in a professional sense and for professional reasons, as early as 1920 and by no later than 1930. Added to the incredible difficulties of shattered economies, disrupted commercial patterns, political disharmony, and social ferment in the interwar years was the rise of the professional military as a political interest group. By the end of 1930, Argentina, Brazil, and Peru were under army-led or -created regimes. Chile was entering its sixth year of military-influenced rule. Bolivia was girding for war; so was the French-trained Paraguayan army.

The integrity of the profession and professional expertise were supposed to have been guaranteed through professionalization by consent of civilian authority, but they were not. Thus, members of the professional officer corps in Argentina, Bolivia, Brazil, Chile, Paraguay, and Peru blamed social disorder, economic collapse, and professional shortcomings on civilians and their politics long before the Cold War, Castro, and Che Guevara. And in doing so, they often displayed attitudes assimilated from France and Germany.

Having been Europeanized, they aped their mentors by holding themselves above the rest of society and by considering themselves superior to their non-Europeanized commanders. They were, they believed, models of modernity and members of a truly national institution. We know this is true in Argentina, Brazil, Chile, and Peru. As junior officers in these countries rose to positions of influence, they naturally favored alternate political systems or organizations that might guarantee them the prerequisites for professional progress.

In Chile and Brazil, European orientation had both similar and diverse results. First, French or German training tended to solidify the profession but did not make it monolithic by any means. Second, political motivation and action were tempered to the point where the status of the profession became both causal and inhibitive to the flagrant overthrow of a fragile civilian regime or system. Third, both armies were led by elitist officers who believed they represented the only true national institutions—impartial, apolitical (nonpartisan), pure, and morally superior to civilian interest groups. Fourth, virtually all professional shortcomings were blamed on civilians: the "impotent" Old Republic in Brazil and the "irresponsible" Parliamentary Republic in Chile. Fifth, Franco-German professional "differences of opinion" kept political action from taking on a personalist tone: in Chile the appeal of *Ibañismo* was more pronounced among civilians than among military men; in Brazil the officer class spawned no *manda chuva* (military caudillo) after the demise of Marshal Hermes in 1923. There are civilian "corollaries" to each of these assumptions, which should not be overlooked in an overall assessment of civil-military relations.

Among the major Latin American nations (excluding Mexico), Brazil and Chile are among the few held up as exemplary in the field of civil-military relations. Not until 1964 did the Brazilian armed forces, led by the army, actually overthrow a government with the idea of holding onto power. Even then the maintenance of power was debated fiercely within the services for some months. Since 1932 the Chilean army had refrained from such conduct until 1973, and except for isolated movements in 1935, 1938, 1939, 1945–46, 1953–55, and 1969, it had stayed "in the barracks." Here one might tentatively posit that professionalization achieved its objective purposes at least until 1964 in Brazil and until 1973 in Chile. Obviously, the existence or lack of strong national civilian political or socioeconomic groups is significant. But the fact remains that owing heavily to European training and orientation, the armies of these two nations became more capable of being intensely political for professional reasons. The nature of their political action was molded by environment as well, but their propensity for it was, and is, an inheritance based on their early twentieth-century experiences.

This is also the case in Argentina and Peru; but inherited and environmental factors vary, despite apparent similarities. German military training in Argentina, like Chile, was a pre-1914 phenomenon, but there the army was successful in eventually casting off the stigma of Germany's defeat by virtue of having asserted earlier that it was quite capable of continuing the professionalization process on its own. Also, the favored position of the army under Gen. Julio A. Roca (president, 1880–86, 1898–1904), then its politicization at the hands of Hipólito Irigoyen (president, 1916–22, 1928–30), was unequaled at the time in South America.

Argentines perpetuated the outlook of the pre-World War I German officer class themselves, and in a roughly similar milieu. Like their counterparts in Brazil, Chile, and Peru, Argentine military elitists were highly critical of civilian politics, particularly during the Radical Era (1916–30). Unlike their counterparts, the Argentine army officers functioned within a cult of personalism, exaggerated by then extant Latin American professional military standards and akin to personalism à la Seeckt and Hindenburg. Generals Agustín P. Justo and José F. Uriburu represented the politics of military factionalism in the interwar years. Uriburu represented the continuation of German military orientation fused with chauvinistic Argentine and Fascist-elitist ideas. Justo associated himself with the antipersonalist Radical faction. Despite factionalism, though, the military attitude toward civilian politics retained an authoritarian, elitist character in Argentina from World War I through and beyond the Perón years (1943–55).

As early as 1900 war minister Gen. Pablo Riccheri established limitations on foreign (German) penetration of the Argentine army by stating that the army would not copy any European military organization but would instead adapt what best suited its needs. Argentina, he reasoned, was not European, but American. Nevertheless, until 1914, German officers were in charge of the Escuela Superior de Guerra and trained all Argentine staff officers. Instruction, education, tactics, and strategy were German oriented, whereas for fortification techniques, the artillery and engineers depended more heavily on post-1871 French concepts. By 1914, Argentina's staff school instructors and administrators were strident Germanophiles. During this period, the German theory of all-out offense became the principal doctrine of the Argentine army. This, when coupled with professional attitudes toward military needs, soon took the form of army demands made in public for a national program to support mass mobilization (with two fronts always in mind!). When war appeared improbable from 1904 on, this philosophy became a demand for industrialization and economic development, not for the sake of making war but as a prerequisite to overall national greatness.

At the beginning of the twentieth century, Peru, like Argentina and Brazil, was an unintegrated nation. Geographically and socially, Peru was divided; and from the earliest stages of French military indoctrination, the army officer corps looked upon itself as the agency most capable of bringing the country together.

After the War of the Pacific (1879–84), Peru was not only lacking integration and unity, but it was in political and economic collapse. Chile had eclipsed Peru as the leading Pacific power of the continent and had begun the military reform program under German leadership in order to maintain that position "by reason or force"—the motto on the Chilean escutcheon.

Peru's contracting of a mission in 1896, like Argentina's resort to German training, was primarily in response to the Chilean military buildup. The Peruvian government, however, did not look to Germany for assistance, but to France. France had suffered defeat at the hands of the Germans, to be sure, but the reorganization of the French army in the 1880s impressed the decision makers in Lima. Furthermore, the French army, owing to a large number of Catholic and Monarchist officers, was removed (or so it appeared) from politics. French expertise in fortification, frontier defense, and military engineering appealed to Lima. Forswearing any military designs on lost territory, Peru sought to apply French defensive doctrines to her own situation. In 1896, Capt. Paul Clément was appointed a colonel in the Peruvian army and took up his duties as instructor, inspector, and reorganizer. Some seventy-five French officers served in Peru between Clément's arrival and 1940. Until the 1920s the French had great freedom in reorganizing the Peruvian army, but, as with the Germans in Argentina, held no command positions.

One of the first things Clément called for was a rigid promotion system that would allow only academy graduates to rise above the rank of *subteniente* (second lieutenant). This became law in 1899, but, unfortunately for discipline, was not rigidly applied. Other French-inspired proposals, dating in many cases from 1899, presaged by a half century proposals emanating from the now twenty-three-year-old, elite Centro de Altos Estudios Militares (CAEM). In his report of 1899, for example, Clément noted that frontiers must be accessible from the capital in time of peace as well as war, that internal lines of communication would aid the development of national unity as well as defense. He further stated that regionalism necessitated a flexibility in training, armament, tactics, and strategy, and that the officer class should seek close association with civilians. These are themes reiterated time and again in this century.

Clément also suggested that staff officers serving in the provinces should study the history, economy, politics, and society of their region in order to know all possible in case an emergency arose. "Peru has not one topographic map," he wrote, "not even of the area surrounding Lima. . . . It will be the army's job to supply one." Just above his signature to the seventy-five-page 1899 report are the words, "Throughout the country, one can sense the desire to see the army move ahead along the road to progress and obtain the prestige that corresponds to the military profession." For nearly forty years, Peruvian cadets, staff aspirants, and colonels who attended special advanced courses (which ultimately evolved into CAEM) had a steady dose of such heady stuff.

Neither Clément nor those who came after him were able to make the army immune to political issues and pressures. But because of their pervasive influence there existed no apparent divisions within the officer corps on professional issues, save those emanating from the old versus the young rivalry.

Unlike their Brazilian counterparts, however, Peruvian political officers (Col. Luis Sánchez Cerro, for example) appealed in a personalistic way to civilians as well as army officers. This lasted well into the second half of the twentieth century. Nevertheless, French emphasis on territorial unification and the awareness of having to deal with a large aboriginal population, based on French experiences in Africa and Indochina . . . laid the groundwork for the emergence of the technocratic nation builders of the 1960s. In an article published in 1933, Lt. Col. Manuel Moria wrote of the *misión civilizadora* of the army in Peru, where nationhood had yet to flourish. Transportation, communications, education and health programs for Indian conscripts, patriotism, discipline, and national economic development could all be provided by army service and supervised by the officer corps, he concluded.

Early in this century, therefore, Peruvian army officers saw themselves as nation builders in a backward and divided land. Based on published materials in military journals and given the emphasis on French training, it is possible to trace the origins of the present Peruvian *mentalidad militar* ascribed by Víctor Villanueva to French influences. Army officers today readily cite the French emphasis on communications in remote areas, frontier defense, and flexible organization in the provinces as contributory to the assumption of political responsibility. CAEM, which since 1950 has turned out a number of "intellectual officers," is a direct result of French emphasis on continued education for high-ranking officers.

Examined together, Argentina and Peru appear superficially dissimilar rather than similar. But in more detail, the similarities are evident. First, personalism continued in both armies despite professionalization and because of early politicization. In both countries the "military modernization" issue was hotly debated in civilian circles, and much published material exists that is highly critical of the alleged need for a modern military: defense of the profession by civilians did not go unrewarded in times of national crisis.

Second, both Peru and Argentina originally sought European missions out of fear—Chile being the immediate danger, so they thought, from about 1885 until 1905. Once the heavy emphasis on war subsided, though, the profession did not wither. Instead, in both countries the professional army became a political pressure group with its own mission: national integration, education, nationalization of indigenous and immigrant conscripts, and overseer of internal economic development.

Third, the army became hostile to the civilian center-left. In Argentina, some professional officers blamed the Radicals for the lack of military progress towards professionalism, but others were co-opted by that party. The end result was the smashing of traditional civilian institutions, perhaps beyond repair. The disenchantment with *Peronismo*-labor politics is a continuance of this attitude in Argentina. In Peru, the army became anti-Aprista, primarily as Luigi Einaudi says, "based on the perception of APRA as 'another unreliable civilian political entity,' " and because of Aprista attempts to subvert military discipline. Finally, the status of the profession tempered political activities less in Argentina and Peru than in Brazil and Chile, as long as European influences were prevalent. As with Brazil and Chile, these conclusions do not stand alone and cannot be separated entirely from civilian influences.

Because of the nature of civilian politics, and owing to the socioeconomic dilemma, European-trained Argentines and Peruvians did become political, but apparently less for professional reasons than in Brazil and Chile, until World War II. This may be because of politicization and the fact that civilians sought out military allies and promised them much more in Argentina and Peru than they did in

Brazil and Chile. Professional training by Europeans plus the environmental factors helped to make involvement of the profession more a constant in Argentina and Peru than in Brazil and Chile.

The Argentine, Brazilian, Chilean, and Peruvian officers who spent time in France or Germany, and Spain and Italy also, after academy and staff training at home, rose to elite status rapidly upon their return. Uriburu, Klinger, Leitão de Carvalho, the Chileans Bartolomé Blanche and Marmaduke Grove, and Luis Sánchez Cerro owed much to their French and German training.

Marshal José Felix Estigarribia of Paraguay, who directed the Chaco campaign for his country, had studied in Chile and in France at the Ecole Supérieure. Without a doubt his French staff training made him a national figure in remote, backward Paraguay.

In summary, nearly all armies in Latin America were influenced in some ways by European training in the first half of this century. Six of South America's ten countries (Bolivia and Paraguay in addition to those treated herein) had significant military missions or instructors. In Argentina, Brazil, Chile, and Peru the contracting of French or German missions was part of the overall modernization process, continental power politics, and military rivalry. War-making potential was minimal, nevertheless, with the exception of the Bolivia-Paraguay conflict. But the European impact on military activities in other spheres was great. Military professionalism in a developing Latin America was also affected by civilian meddling, financial limitations, human resources, and political instability; but the concept of professional integrity and status was very real. The concept stimulated, rather than precluded, political action in the manner called professional militarism.

Frank D. McCann, Jr.

CHAPTER 4

Origins of the "New Professionalism" of the Brazilian Military

In the course of Brazilian military history, since at least the beginning of the century, there have been debates and even violence revolving ultimately around questions of self-definition. Why have an army? What was it for? The answers as to what the army's missions were and hence what it meant to be an officer and a soldier varied across time; the variance produced conflict within the institution. This resulted from the deliberate ambiguity of the military's constitutional status. The constitutions of the Empire (1824) and the Republic (1891, 1934, 1937, 1946) specified that the military were to defend the country against foreign attack and, as the constitution of 1891 phrased it, to "maintain the laws in the interior." The political leaders wanted the military squarely between the two poles of external and internal security, so not surprisingly some officers defined their profession in terms of an exclusive external or internal orientation, while others mixed the two. Clearly such men as the Duke of Caxias in the Empire, Marshals Deodoro da Fonseca, Floriano Peixoto, Hermes da Fonseca, Pedro A. de Góes Monteiro, and Eurico Dutra fall into the latter category because they exercised both external defense and internal political roles. There appear to have been relatively fewer officers who were totally external defense oriented and therefore apolitical. A few who do come to mind are José Caetano de Faria, Estevão Leitão de Carvalho, and João B. Mascarenhas de Morais because these adhered to the legalist position that the army must obey the lawful orders of the government and because they were concerned with shaping the army into a fighting force of European quality. Yet, though their orientation was basically professional, they were drawn into internal affairs because of their desire for a modern, European-style, external defense army.

41

Perhaps it is best not to seek hard and fast definitions of professionalism but to examine currents of thought that mix and blend over time. José Murilo de Carvalho discerned three currents: that of the citizen-soldier, the professional soldier, and the corporative soldier. The first made its appearance in the 1880s serving as a means of unifying the officer corps for reformist intervention to replace the tottering monarchy with a renovating republic.

The Citizen-Soldier

The officer corps had been split since the Paraguayan war into two antagonistic groups, the *tarimbeiros* and the *doutores*, who nevertheless shared a common disdain for the political elite. The tarimbeiros were those who had come up from the ranks without attending the military school. The term referred to the *tarimba*, the hard wooden soldier's bunk that was common in old forts and barracks. They favored intervention only to strengthen the military institution, that is to say their own positions vis-à-vis the civilian elite. Their desires revolved almost exclusively around power and prestige. The doutores were the graduates of the military school, who glowed with the light of Colonel Benjamin Constant's positivist teachings. In their view, soldiers should be regarded as armed civilians, rather than as a separate caste, because industrial progress would retire armies and their weapons of destruction to the museums and pages of history. The distinction between the concepts of citizen and soldier should be extinguished in favor of a broadened view of citizenship. But they acknowledged that a weakened army could not bring about political reform and so before it could disappear, the army had to be strengthened. Given the generational fissures of the era and the differences between tarimbeiros and doutores, simultaneous reformist intervention and institutional strengthening were incompatible. The first decade of the republic did little to improve the army's martial abilities until the rude awakening of the Canudos campaign of 1897, and efforts to secure the Amazon during the Acré affair (1903–4) forced a reassessment of values.

The interventionist sentiment that flowed from, or perhaps even created, the concept of the citizen-soldier was based on resentment against an elite that ignored the officer corps, keeping salaries low, promotions slow, and arms scarce, while seeking to minimize the army's political power via increases in police and National Guard forces in and around Rio de Janeiro. Lieutenant Sebastião Bandeira, Captain Antônio Adolfo de Mena Barreto, and General Tibúrcio de

Sousa were typical of officers convinced that not only was the imperial government hostile to the army, but, in a broader sense, all civilian politicians were the enemy.

Psychologically, the officers compensated for their inferior status by counterposing it with a belief in their spiritual superiority. "There was a generalized conviction that the men in uniform were *pure*, were *vigorous*, were *patriots*; whereas the civilians were *corrupt*, were *vice-ridden*, without any public sentiment." The officers saw themselves as "saviors of the *patria*," with the obligation not only to defend their own rights and interests, but to rescue the fatherland from the civilian politicians who corrupted it. Floriano Peixoto wrote that a military dictatorship was necessary because only a "government of the sword" could "purify the blood of the social body." The vision of the officer corps as a priesthood of national purification blended with republican terminology to give form and substance to the citizen-soldier and his role in Brazilian society. But after overthrowing the imperial government, the officers discovered that running a country was not as easy as it looked from the barracks window. The civil war, the continued disagreements between tarimbeiros and doutores, resurgent regionalism, and the Canudos affair shook the officers' self-assurance, and they stepped aside for civilians.

The Professional Soldier

In the first two decades of the new century, the professional soldier embraced the citizen-soldier idea as a vehicle to reform the army. This reform in turn would lead to a widening of the army's influence, power, and roles. The professionals, whose family backgrounds and premilitary education were apparently similar to the more politically involved citizen-soldier and corporative soldier types, desired a European-style army. Nineteenth-century Brazilian history demonstrated little need for such an army. The major experiences had been internal affairs in which officers either fought against government forces as rebels or battled to suppress rebellion. The list is impressive: uprisings in Rio de Janeiro in 1831 and 1832; the *Cabanagem* in Pará from 1835 to 1840; the Sabinada in Bahia in 1837–38; the Balaiada in Maranhão in 1831–41; the Alagôas revolt of 1844; the Praieira revolt of 1848–50 in Pernambuco; and, of course, the Farroupilha in Rio Grande do Sul from 1835 to 1845. By comparison, the foreign combat had been against the United Provinces of the Rio de la Plata, 1825 to 1828; Buenos Aires' Rosas in 1852; and Paraguay's Solano López from 1865 to 1870.

   This last was "The War" for the senior officers who commanded the army at the turn of the century. The experience left its mark in a distrust of politicians who would declare war without providing adequate means or forces to fight with, and who would ignore and deprecate the victors, the wounded, the widowed, and the orphaned. Officers came to believe that only they were concerned about Brazil's defense. Another legacy of the war was a lingering bitterness between the former Argentine and Brazilian allies regarding the treaty arrangements. In the years before World War I, as Buenos Aires modernized its forces with German equipment and instructors, the Brazilian army held up their southern neighbor's energetic activities as a warning against complacency. To make matters more nerve-wracking, the undefended Amazon, with all its supposed riches, seemed a likely target for a repetition of what the powers had done to Africa and Asia. Even the great republic of the north had recently acquired an overseas empire, and the nightmare of the powers sitting around a table in some faraway chancellery dividing the Amazon and the underpopulated interior seemed possible if the nation did not create a sufficiently martial facade.

   In 1904, Minister of War Marshal Francisco de Paula Argollo complained that Brazilians placed too much faith in "the principles of international jurisprudence and the efficacy of diplomatic notes" to protect their territory. But without military force—the *ultima ratio*—the diplomats would not be able, he argued, to make their logic prevail. "The weak countries lived condemned to the degrading tutelage of the strong, who feel that they possess the right to counsel them, direct them, and even to admonish them, transforming, de facto, their independence and autonomy into a true fiction." Japan was treated with respect, he observed, because it had demonstrated military prowess. Brazil must do likewise. But how? Civilian and military enthusiasm for army reform rose and fell with equal speed. "The army is in the condition it finds itself," he lamented, "not because we ignore its necessities . . . but only because of the lack of firmness, resolution and courage on our part to realize that which we recommend and avow to be indispensable."

   So the military problem of the new century was twofold: a European-style army would have to be created because the likely enemy would employ such a force; and basic attitudes inside and outside the army would have to change. The professionals knew that Brazil was too poor to maintain a large standing army, and so they placed their hopes in developing a cadre army with large trained reserves. The easily expandable force was convincing on paper, suited the economic realities, and did not appear to threaten the political power of the regional elites.

Because the past did not provide the models that they needed for the future, the professionals did tours of duty as junior officers in the imperial Prussian army (1910–12) and later accepted a French military mission (1919–39) to organize and teach their advanced officer and general staff courses. Since their geopolitical views were shared by Foreign Minister Rio Branco and his diplomats, they had support for obtaining new foreign-made armament. But how to alter the attitudes of civilian society?

Here the professionals found ready allies in the growing urban middle class. These people were appalled at the stunning ignorance, poverty, and filthiness of the masses, and burned with resentment at the rural landowners, or *coronels*, whose armed hangers-on and elaborate alliance system kept the masses and the central government subservient. If the middle class could control an invigorated army, they might be able to impose their vision of Brazil. But they lacked the will for conflict and knew from experience in the civil war of 1893–95 that they would suffer from such internal warfare. And because they had little ability, or perhaps taste, for unified political action, they sought to reform the prevailing system from within: in historian Edgard Carone's phrase, "instead of struggle, collaboration: in place of its own ideology, the vague glorification of citizenship (*civismo*)."

Through spokespersons such as the patriotic poet Olavo Bilac, the middle class supported the establishment of a national draft lottery in 1916 to provide annual levies of recruits to be given a year of training and then returned home as reservists to spread the good work of citizenship. Bilac saw the lottery as "a promise of salvation" for Brazil. Reflecting the prevalent middle-class view that Brazil was not a cohesive, unified nation, he saw the privileged classes wanting only self-pleasure and prosperity, the lower classes living in "inertia, apathy, and superstition," and the foreign immigrants isolated from others by language and custom. The "militarization of all civilians" was the way to impart middle-class virtues to society and thereby give it the cohesion necessary to preserve itself. Military service was to be the means of massive social uplift; however, from the middle-class point of view, it was also important that it act as a leveling force bringing the upper classes down to a more reasonable level. For Bilac, "generalized military service" was:

> the complete triumph of democracy; the leveling of the classes; the school of order, discipline, cohesion; the laboratory of individual

dignity and patriotism. It is obligatory primary instruction; it is
obligatory civic education; it is obligatory cleanliness, obligatory
hygiene, obligatory muscular and psychic regeneration. The cities
are full of lazy, barefoot, ragged enemies of the "ABC's" and of
bathing—brute animals, who have only the appearance and wick-
edness of men. For these dregs of society the barracks will be
salvation.

Military service would purify them and return them to society as
"conscientious, worthy Brazilians." The military would provide the
discipline and order to reconstruct Brazil by lifting up the downcast
millions. And because he held the rural oligarchies to be primarily
responsible for the people's distressing state, he argued that only the
middle class possessed "complete intellectual and moral culture,"
"high-mindedness," and capacity to place themselves above self, class,
or partisan interests, and so they were destined "to the sacred mission of governing and directing the multitude." The military, already
possessing these high qualities, would help the middle class take
power peacefully. The nation, that is, the remade people under middle-
class leadership, would be the army; and the army, reformed, restructured, redirected, would be the nation. The officer corps in Bilac's
view was the army, its soul—"all the sensibility, all the intelligence,
all the will of the corporation of soldiers." The officer was the priest
of the cult of the nation, and as such should flee from political ambition and involvement. The officer would be the regenerator and disciplinarian, the middle class would govern and direct. The draft lottery
may have meant to the reformist professional a modern army, with a
growing reserve that would be mobilized to support Brazilian dreams
of greatness and desire for security, but to the middle class it had a
key role in developing their social vision of Brazil. For such a division of roles to work, they would have to be clearly defined and accepted. Such was not the case. The "militarization of all civilians,"
which Bilac called for, was not possible, and the effort to achieve it
via the draft lottery served to intensify the army's inward orientation. So in the 1920s, while the army was acquiring all the trappings
of a professional force, it was becoming steadily more involved internally via the very means it sought to use to professionalize itself.
   The draft lottery provided the mechanism and justification for
the army's physical expansion and contributed to its increasing involvement in society and politics. Instead of opting for one or two
national training camps, with subsequent distribution to posts throughout Brazil, the army wished to keep the soldiers in their own regions.

This would avoid the cost and administrative burden of transporting large contingents hither and yon, and would give the army a local image. But to effect this required at least one army unit in each state to receive and train the draftees and volunteers, and to do that would necessitate the increase of effectives from an authorized 18,000 men to 25,000, which was the smallest figure which would allow the army to deal with "questions of internal order" and also serve as a "nucleus of instruction." The expansion in turn also involved a higher level of military spending. After Brazil entered World War I in October 1917, the pace of expansion increased to the point where by mid-1918 every state had at least one federal army unit to serve as a reception and training center for draftees. Commanding an army that now embraced 52,000 effectives, War Minister José Caetano de Faria expressed the belief that the war demonstrated the dangers of returning "our army to the insignificant effectives that we had." Once the expansion had occurred, it would not be possible to deter the pace of growth. According to General Eurico Dutra, the number of effectives rose from 30,000 in 1920 to 50,000 in 1930, and had reached 93,000 in the midst of the Estado Nôvo in 1940. Though the proportion of soldiers to population would remain low in comparison to other countries, that is, about 1.1 soldiers per thousand, the army's size increased at a faster rate than did the population. José Murilo de Carvalho has shown that while the population increased 162 percent between 1890 and 1930, the army grew 220 percent. And while Alfred Stepan may well be correct in asserting that "political variables are frequently far more important for determining the role of the military in society than the absolute size of the armed forces," still we are confronted with the parallel developments of the army's numerical growth and its greater political involvement. Surely, by itself, the former was not the cause of the latter, but it is hard to imagine the army of 1905 providing the muscle for the Estado Nôvo or the 1964 to 1979 governments.

While the lottery and the war provided the justification for expansion in size and pace, the army used the necessity for reserves to extend its influence over state police forces and the National Guard. Under a January 1917 law, it made agreements with the state governments whereby state police and firemen would be considered auxiliary army forces. Complete control would not be secured until the Estado Nôvo in 1937–45, but this was the first step. The National Guard was denominated the army's second line and by a 1918 decree was to be remodeled. Considered a rival force by many officers, it would be abolished before the next decade was out. As a result, for the "first time among us," as Caetano de Faria happily pointed out, the army came to control "all the forces which ought to constitute the military power of the nation."

It fell to the republic's only civilian minister of war, João Pandiá Calógeras, to consolidate the numerical and spacial expansion by an ambitious building program in 1920–21—the largest before the Estado Nôvo. Taking over the ministry, he traveled throughout the country to see firsthand the army's condition. He was dismayed. "Brazil owes it to itself," he declared, "not to consent to its sons . . . being quartered in filthy *senzalas* (slave quarters)." From North to South, telegrams rained on the ministry describing the army's precarious situation—troops were without blankets, ponchos, uniforms, barracks, wagons, and, worse still, their pay was behind schedule. The expansion had taken place too precipitously, units were dangerously under strength, and as for training, Calógeras summed it up—"Instruction nil. Training areas nonexistent. . . . No training at all." With that, he inaugurated the construction of 56 new barracks in 49 locations throughout Brazil and the repair and enlargement of some 45 others in 41 places at a cost of approximately 1920 U.S. $20 million. In addition, regional headquarters, powderhouses, depots, hospitals, and infirmaries were remodeled and expanded at a total cost of approximately 1920 U.S. $2.5 million. Considering that the army's regular 1919 budget had been roughly the equivalent of U.S. $20 million and that of 1920, U.S. $27 million, these expenditures were truly extraordinary.

Not only was the army larger and present in some form in every state, but its pattern of distribution changed. Under the empire, the largest garrisons were in the frontier provinces of Rio Grande do Sul and Mato Grosso and in the capital. In 1889 the large provinces/states of Minas Gerais, São Paulo, Bahia, and Pernambuco had few national troops. The Caetano de Faria-Calógeras expansion radically altered the pattern. There was a clear tendency to place military forces "where political power was concentrated." The change was especially noticeable in Minas Gerais, São Paulo, Paraná, and Bahia. Federal troops in the first two rose from 113 and 386 in 1889 to 3,787 and 3,675 in the 1920s. Significantly, by 1933, army effectives outnumbered state police forces in Rio Grande do Sul, State of Rio de Janeiro, Paraná, Pará, and Mato Grosso. At the same time, the large states that were still attempting to cling to their old autonomy—Bahia, Minas Gerais, Pernambuco, and São Paulo—had felt compelled to increase their police forces relative to federal garrisons. Given the army's local recruitment of common soldiers, it may be, as Stepan suggests, that "the loyalty of local units is often open to question during times of great national political conflict." Even so, it is certain that the army's expansion set the stage for increasing federal involvement in the states in the 1930s.

Along with the physical expansion, the officer corps improved its technical ability to plan, coordinate, and carry out assigned missions, thanks to the improved French-advised general staff course and the reformed general staff itself. The *tenente* uprisings of the 1920s were devisive, but they provided combat experience, exposed weaknesses in military institutions, and helped draw ideological lines. The result was a growing determination to avoid future divisions within the institution and a heightened sense of membership in a separate corporate entity. The citizen-soldier and professional soldier had given the army a new self-image and the ability to carry out its tasks. But what tasks, what mission? The answer was being developed gradually since the turn of the century, and would be given expression and put into practice by the corporative soldier.

The Corporative Soldier

In his 1905 report to the president, War Minister Marshal Francisco de Paula Argollo had worried that if the army did not avoid partisan struggles, ignoring the "lying and ephemeral applause of exploitative politicians," it would lose the confidence of, and become an object of fear for, "the conservative classes of society, of whose interest it ought to be the best solid guarantee." In the first issue of the reformist Young Turk journal *A Defesa Nacional* in 1913, Bertholdo Klinger, who certainly had the proper professional credentials, wrote that the army needed to be equipped for its "conservative and stabilizing function" and "prepared to correct the internal troubles [*perturbacões*] so common in the tumultuous life of societies in formation."

If Argollo, who won his commission on the battlefield in Paraguay, represented the old army, and Klinger the new, then it appears that there were no substantial differences between them concerning the army's ultimate role; both saw it as maintaining social stability. Both could accept the legitimacy of military intervention providing it was an armywide effort and not just lieutenants and captains inciting units to mutiny and rebellion. The corporative soldier disagreed with the early version of citizen-soldier only over the form and substance of intervention. His basic requirement was that it be armywide under the direction of the general staff. In 1930, for example, Klinger was chief of staff of the so-called Movimento Pacificador that

deposed President Washington Luís. The initial intention was to promote new elections to resolve the impasse between the government
and the revolting Vargas forces, and Klinger saw the army's role as
that of arbitrator. In a message to the president, Klinger noted that
the government's use of the armed forces to solve political conflicts
had only produced ruin and that "public salvation" and "the integrity
of the nation" required delivery of "the destinies of Brazil in the
present moment to its general officers of the land and sea." His attitude was further defined in a *Defesa Nacional* article, published after
the military junta had turned the government over to Getúlio Vargas,
which argued the right of the military to intervene in the political
system, declaring that the presidency was a "general staff problem."

Perhaps the most skillful practitioner among the corporative soldiers was Pedro A. de Góes Monteiro. A highly regarded general staff
officer, who as a student in the staff school had won great praise
from the French instructors, Góes acted as Vargas's chief of staff in
1930. He embodied many of the ideas and attitudes of the citizen-
soldier and the professional soldier. But he saw the army's role in a
wider context. The armed forces [a curt nod to the navy!] were the
only national organizations and so ought to develop their own policies, their own politics. For him the army was an "essentially political instrument" whose "collective conscience" should produce a
"politics *of* the army" to avoid "politics *in* the army." Its sole objective was "the greatness of the common *patria*." He saw the army, the
people, and, in the 1930s, the Vargas regime as being in "a crusade of
national regeneration" that included "developing the physical and
spiritual health of our people," improving education, both technical
and moral, building highways and railroads for strategic and economic purposes, and encouraging the collaboration of private industry "in the work of our defense." The army's efficiency was intimately
linked to the harmonious development of all the vital forces of the
nation. And just as the army should be concerned with "National Security" [*Segurança Nacional*] (always capitalized in army literature)
in its widest sense to ensure a solid base for Brazil's greatness, so too
should one of the first concerns of good Brazilians be the army.

But while Góes's writings show a deep involvement in internal
affairs, they also demonstrate a preoccupation with discipline, with
anything that would prevent presenting a united front to society. Because the order of the day was the development and presentation of
an army policy, a "politics *of* the army," then the army had to be
"immunized against partisan seductions." Officers must not be tainted
with the slightest suspicion of being involved in factious movements

or having partisan concerns "alien to the policy (*política*) of the Army." Further, they must develop a "conscience capable of rejecting everything that would be against and accepting everything that would be useful to the principles and purposes of the Army." The individual officer was to function politically only in concert with his fellow officers and only at the direction of the general staff. This attitude would be turned into policy by 1939, when Minister Eurico Dutra reported that "the law of social conformity and the elimination of non-conformists forms the moral base of the Army's disciplinary structure and justifies the severe repression of dissident elements or rebels."

The citizen-soldiers' reformist intervention (including *tenentismo*) merged with and utilized the work of the professional soldiers to produce "the interventionism of the generals, or of the general staff, the intervention of the organization as a whole." From the 1930s onward, intervention would be controlled from above so that the army could fulfill its "immense historical responsibility of maintainer (*mantenedor*)" and "guardian of federative unity, of order and of internal progress and of national sovereignty." This self-definition supported the Estado Nôvo, then rejected the dictator when he attempted to change his political base, and underlay the various postwar administrations and the direct military rule of the past fifteen years. It may well be a new professionalism, but its roots are deep in the Brazilian past.

Robert V. Elam

CHAPTER 5

The Army and Politics in El Salvador, 1840–1927

From the dissolution of the Central American Union in 1839 to the presidential victory of Pío Romero Bosque in 1927, El Salvador experienced more than its share of militarism. Frequent armed uprisings at home, together with a dozen invasions from across its frontiers, kept the tiny republic in a state of constant turmoil and rendered the development of stable political institutions all but impossible. However, El Salvador's failure to provide stable central government did not produce regional divisions, as was the case in many of its sister republics. San Salvador remained throughout the period the undisputed capital and the center of all national activities. The diminutiveness of the country constrained the local caudillos, and the constant fear of invasion enhanced the need for political unity. Furthermore, racial, linguistic, or economic regionalisms never developed.

El Salvador sustained no particular ideological character during the last century. It vacillated between liberal and conservative leadership, accepted and rejected the idea of union, in much the same fashion as its neighbors. What remained constant in politics was the reliance upon military force. No sooner did the Constituent Assembly meet in January 1841 than it was threatened with military domination. Each subsequent political conflict, regardless of the nature of the issue, gave rise to armed hordes—hardly could they be called armies—and the brief periods of peace were used for the preparation of new rebel forces.

Because of the violent nature of Salvadoran politics, no enduring military institution developed and the division of civil and military authority remained obscure and confusing. The constitution of 1841, in effect until 1864, provided the president with the authority to use troops, and the congress with the power to raise them, for the defense of the nation. The armed forces were declared apolitical. Active officers were prohibited from serving in the congress, though no such

52

prohibition was applied to the presidency. A more serious omission was the failure to provide the chief executive with the powers of commander in chief. As a consequence, civilian presidents often found themselves wholly dependent upon the country's senior officer. The fact that generals held the presidency for a combined period of little more than two years between 1841 and 1859 is evidence that military leaders normally contented themselves with retaining real power rather than titular power.

After General Gerardo Barrios took control of the government in 1858, new emphasis was given to the task of building a formal military organization. On his request, Colombian General José María Melo arrived in 1859. As inspector general of the newly emerging army, Melo emphasized discipline and drill, issued the first standard uniforms, and organized and equipped a special squadron for the president. A French mission of four officers, which replaced Melo in 1862, introduced cavalry and artillery instruction and provided new codes and military ordinances. Prior to this, all codes and ordinances approximated those in use before independence. Not until 1864 and the promulgation of a new constitution were the presidential office and the position of commander in chief combined. Three years later, the first officer school opened in San Salvador under the direction of Spanish General Luis Pérez Gómez. However, mismanagement and limited funds prevented it from having much effect for nearly a decade.

Further reorganization was accomplished in 1879. For the first time, a fixed numerical strength was established for the army. The forces were divided into four divisions, each containing five thousand men.

Increased interest in the development of a stable military institution and greater concern with the promotion of harmonious civil-military relations were less the result of professionalization than of a changing social and economic environment. El Salvador's volcanic soil was found to be highly suitable for growing coffee, and its production was greatly encouraged by General Gerardo Barrios. His successors not only continued the policy of favoring coffee growing but also provided the newly emerging elite with further opportunity for economic and political power. Expropriation of communal lands and the development of large estates characterized the period after 1859, and the process of land concentration was nearly complete by 1912. Moreover, after 1860 the government gave up ownership of rural real estate not used for public facilities with the express condition that the land be planted in coffee.

Other measures were taken to promote economic development and political stability. General Santiago González (1871–76) initiated the building of a modern communications network with army garrisons established at key points. Port facilities were vastly improved, and commodities necessary for coffee production and industrial development were exempted from import taxes.

Little recognition was given to the inherent dangers of a one-crop economy or to the ill effects of encouraging the development of a socioeconomic system dominated by a handful of wealthy families. Those making policy saw themselves as having overcome the burdens of the nation's colonial past by developing a truly modern economy. Plantations resembled factories more than farms, and the new elite was more interested in capital investment and improved agriculture than in family traditions and local politics. Vital to the continuation of these trends was the maintenance of political harmony.

A balance between the needs of the new commercial aristocrats and those of the old conservative generals, long schooled in political intervention, was difficult to achieve, since the desire for wealth and power on the part of ambitious officers often proved insatiable. Generals held the presidency from 1887 to 1903, and not until 1911 was an understanding between civilian and military factions established. That the conflict could take on the characteristics of a barroom brawl is revealed in a dispatch to Washington, D.C., written by a U.S. representative in Central America:

> July 10, 1906. On the 5th, General Regalado, Commander of the Salvadoran army, commenced one of his drunken orgies, ordered out a Hotchkiss gun, and fired two shells into the Presidential Palace, loudly proclaiming his Government a den of thieves whom he desired to wipe out. . . . The morning of the 6th he left for the Guatemalan border where he previously had stationed 1,400 troops, and attacked a Guatemalan outpost. [President] Escalon did all in his power to get him to return to the capital.

So long as wars with neighbors threatened, the new elite resigned itself to the idea that strutting generals and strong-arm tactics were the price for national protection. But after the 1907 Washington treaty of peace and amnesty, this view began to change. Deprived of the opportunity for foreign campaigns and confronted by a powerful oligarchy determined to achieve order, the military constrained its more disreputable officers and accepted civilian political leadership. The resulting stability, which would continue until 1931, proved even more profitable for the armed forces than had the predatory struggle of the past. Defense expenditures normally absorbed over 20 percent of the total government budgets. Modern garrisons were constructed throughout the republic and the latest European arms were imported.

Indicative of the military's new role was the change in military missions and the creation of the National Guard in 1912. Beginning in 1905, a Chilean mission of five officers spent six years organizing and instructing El Salvador's army. Emphasis was given to tactics and discipline befitting a force designed for external warfare. Then, in 1912, a Spanish mission arrived to establish the National Guard and to organize the armed forces into an internal peace-keeping institution. Under the dual control of the ministries of war and government, this new corps operated as an adjunct to the army, drawing its officers from the Escuela Politécnica and its armaments and ordinance from the Ministry of War. Assignments for the National Guard were determined by the Ministry of Government, and its duties included the patrolling of agricultural estates, the surveillance of roads and ports, and the policing of remote villages and towns. By 1924 the National Guard numbered one thousand guardsmen and ninety-six officers, divided into three infantry regiments and one cavalry regiment stationed throughout the republic.

The National Police, created during the presidency of Rafael Zaldivar (1880–84), was subjected to a thorough reorganization after 1919. Like those of the new National Guard, officers of the National Police were trained in the Escuela Politécnica. Under the jurisdiction of the Ministry of War, the police served to ensure order within the urban areas of the republic.

The results, at least on the surface, were impressive. American expert Dana Munro thought that El Salvador's army was the best trained in Central America, though considerably larger than was necessary. The new National Guard, smartly dressed in pith helmets and Sam Browne belts and sporting a battery of motorcycles, added to the overall impression that the nation's armed forces had at last achieved a degree of professionalism. "Really an admirable organization," reported United States military attaché Garrard Harris to the United States Department of Commerce in 1916.

Conservative in matters of social reform, suspicious of mass political participation, and always wary of civilian authority, El Salvador's military cooperated with the government so long as its own sentiments were given ample consideration. The Meléndez-Quiñónez family, which provided the presidents from 1913 until 1927, satisfied the military. By sharing the presidency, the oligarchy avoided the danger of open political campaigns while providing the nation with order and stability. Occasional public protests were met with swift military repression, and the armed forces continued to be well paid for their efforts.

III

The Military and Latin American Politics, 1919–1945

From the end of World War I to the end of World War II, much of Latin America experienced a period of intensified urbanization and industrialization. These socioeconomic developments were accompanied by hopeful turns toward formal democracy, which were occasionally interrupted by civilian or military dictatorships.

With the onset of the economic depression of the 1930s, even the seemingly most "democratic" Latin American governments saw military elites, by themselves or in alliance with civilians, put an end to the post-World War I experiments with liberal democracy. In these years, military elites were still not willing to become permanently involved in "politics," and caretaker regimes or temporary restorationist movements followed coups. Still, divisions were developing within the military establishments themselves over the viability and utility of democratic institutions in Latin America.

Not until two decades after World War II, however, did the factions committed to long-term military rule emerge triumphant. Nevertheless, in the period 1920–45, military officers attracted to corporate, fascist, or military populist political models temporarily dominated governmental institutions in all six of the countries upon which we focus in this book: Argentina (1930, 1943, 1946); Brazil (1937–45); Chile (1927–31); Peru (1930–39); El Salvador (1931–44); and Guatemala (1931–44). Whether their programs were rightist or leftist, the military elites usually made antipolitics a basic foundation of their programs. They broke with or subordinated traditional political parties and repressed leftist parties or movements. They sought to administer national policies without the distraction of "politics" or the inconvenience of a tolerated opposition. Ironically, these antipolitical officers often belonged to secret societies or lodges— for example, the Logia General San Martín and the GOU (Grupo de

Oficiales Unidos) in Argentina—which engaged in intrainstitutional politics.

In Argentina, Brazil, Chile, and Peru, the appeals of European corporatism or fascism allowed the nationalist, hierarchical, and antipolitical inclinations of the military elites to combine with conservative or reactionary civilian sectors in new political experiments. Frequently the patronage and partisan politics characteristic of formal democracy were used as a pretext for military intervention. Leading officers blamed civilian politics for the consequences of the economic collapse of the 1930s, as well as for the intromission of party politics into the supposedly sacrosanct realms of military promotions, budget decisions, and military education.

The article by Robert Potash in this section describes an archetypal case of this phenomenon in Argentina, where after more than a half century of legal transfers of government, a military coup in 1930 set the stage for restoration of oligarchic rule and then for the reign of Juan Domingo Perón. Of particular interest are the types of justifications provided by the officers for their action against President Hipólito Yrigoyen, as well as the prominent role of the most highly professionalized military elites in Argentina (including Generals Uriburu and Justo) in the reaction against the results of fourteen years of government by the middle-class Radical party.

Also to be noted are the divisions within the military professional elites over the proper role of the military in politics and the substantive character of public policy once the military found itself in control. Clearly, civilian political cleavages had affected the Argentine military establishment, as officers, like civilians, were divided over the policies of the Radical politicians, economic nationalism, populism or oligarchic restoration, and the Argentine constitution itself. Professionalization had done much to improve the Argentine military, but it also made politics and public policy an intimate concern of the professional officer corps. The eventual emergence of Juan Perón as a military populist with a highly political antipolitical appeal was a product of the events of the 1930s in Argentina.

In Brazil, the 1930s saw the end to an era of liberal democratic experiments. Getúlio Vargas, in alliance with modernizing elements of the armed forces (including the *tenentes*) and civilian industrial interests, took power with a military movement and sought to forge a truly national political regime in a Brazil still dominated by local and regional notables with private armed retainers or state militia. The article by Ronald Schneider describes the coming to power of Vargas. Despite the fact that Vargas himself was a civilian leader, it is clear that military political thinking and support formed the foundation for the Vargas experiment in Brazil.

Military antipolitics dominated the years 1924–32 in Chile. From 1932 until 1973 no successful military coup interrupted the evolution of formal democracy. Frederick Nunn analyzes the background and consequences of the "honorable mission" of the armed forces in the period 1924–32. The lack of successful military movements in Chile from 1932 until the coup which overthrew President Salvador Allende in 1973, however, does not mean that the military was completely devoid of antipolitical officers, as periodic military protests or "strikes" from the late 1930s onward made clear.

In Peru, a civilian dictator, Augusto B. Leguía, ruled from 1919 to 1930 with the support of the armed forces. The role of the military in the Leguía administration and in the numerous coups and countercoups until 1945 is dealt with by Víctor Villanueva. Officers of the French military mission in Peru played a significant role in post-World War I politics.

In 1930 one of the officers trained by the French, Lt. Col. Luis M. Sánchez Cerro, led a successful revolt against Leguía. Owing to divisions within the military establishment, Sánchez Cerro was first elected head of the military junta and later, by popular vote, president of the republic. He allied himself with the traditional landed oligarchy against the center-left reformist elements in the Alianza Popular Revolucionaria Americana (APRA) party led by Víctor Raúl Haya de la Torre. Sánchez Cerro's regime was characterized by extreme violence, including the bloody Trujillo massacre of July 1932 and two assassination attempts against his person (the one of April 1933 being successful).

General Oscar R. Benavides, who had led a coup in 1914 and served briefly as president, assumed power and sought to end the bloodshed and establish internal order. He first tried to achieve this through a policy of liberalization and traditional politics (that is, maintaining the Constituent Congress and calling for presidential elections in 1936). When this policy failed, he resorted to antipolitics, which in the Peruvian case meant annulling the elections of 1936, dissolving the Congress, and repressing political parties, both rightist and leftist.

It is also during this period (1936–39) that the influence of fascism began to spread among the Peruvian officer corps and among certain civilian elites who were closely allied with the military. The new ideology seemingly offered a panacea for ending the chaos and bloodshed which many officers blamed on civilian politics.

In both Guatemala and El Salvador, personalist military dictator-ships dominated politics from 1931 to 1944. In the cases of both General Maximiliano Hernández Martínez in El Salvador and General Jorge Ubico in Guatemala, the economic and political crisis of the 1930s provided justification for an increased militarization of politics and a rejection of democracy. The articles by Robert Elam and Kenneth Grieb describe the growing role of the military in national politics in El Salvador and Guatemala during this period.

Robert A. Potash

CHAPTER 6

The Military and Argentine Politics

Increasing professionalism, even when accompanied by physical growth and expanded budgetary allocations, did not necessarily make for greater unity, contentment, and morale within the Argentine officer corps. Quite the contrary, a series of strains developed in the 1920s between rival groups of officers and between parts of the corps and the governing authorities. These strains were all related in one way or another to the rise of Hipólito Yrigoyen and the Unión Cívica Radical (Radical party) to political power. The process of professionalization had coincided with, and to some extent was a response to, the efforts of the Radical party to gain access to power for its growing number of middle-class adherents. From its founding in 1891, the party had been frustrated by electoral fraud from legally achieving its goals; and under Yrigoyen's leadership it had demanded electoral reform, while engaging in a series of conspiracies and revolts. These culminated in the unsuccessful revolution of February 1905, in which numerous officers took part even at risk to their professional careers. Partly in reaction to their involvement, the revised military statute enacted later that year restated the standing regulations prohibiting officers who held troop commands or any assignment under War Ministry control from participating directly or indirectly in politics, even by exercise of the franchise, and warned that "military men who do not comply with [these] proscriptions . . . will be punished for disobedience."

Such regulations did not prevent individual officers from joining the Radical cause, and even General Ricchieri, who as war minister in 1901 had authored the original prohibition on political activity by troop commanders, is said to have offered support in 1909, when serving as a field commander, in Yrigoyen's struggle for electoral reform. Conspiratorial activity involving civilians and military men continued, but no new uprising took place. The guarantees of electoral reform offered to the Radicals in 1910 by the newly elected

Conservative president, Roque Sáenz Peña, initiated instead a peaceful process of change that culminated in the election of Yrigoyen to the presidency in 1916.

The calm with which the military accepted the peaceful revolution inherent in the Radicals' rise to national power was subsequently disturbed by the policies of the new administration. The military apparently had little criticism of the international policies of Yrigoyen, especially of his determination not to break relations with Germany in World War I. On the domestic scene, however, the numerous provincial interventions had definite repercussions. Yrigoyen justified the interventions as a means of extending the honesty of the ballot to provincial government and of ending political corruption, a policy of atonement for past wrongs that he liked to call *reparación política*. But these interventions made extensive use of the army to maintain order, and critics noted that the diversion of army units to police duties seriously interfered with the training of conscripts. Moreover, the use of military forces to enable Radical party provincial politicians to take over the offices of rival political groups must have been disturbing to those officers who thought of their mission in professional military terms.

In applying the concept of *reparación* to the army itself, Yrigoyen also aroused resentment in the professional-minded officers who regarded military regulations as sacrosanct, or at least not to be disregarded at the whim of the civil authority. The president, for his part, quite naturally wanted to reward those men whose military careers had suffered because of involvement in the "cause." Acting through a civilian minister of war—in itself a break with the usual practice of appointing a high-ranking officer—Yrigoyen passed over officers eligible for promotion in favor of ex-revolutionaries and issued decrees altering the rank lists, promoting retired officers, and granting pensions regardless of the stipulations of existing laws and regulations. The alienation of many officers was increased by a 1921 legislative proposal, whose enactment President Yrigoyen urged, declaring that participation in the Radical revolts of 1890, 1893, and 1905 constituted service to the nation. This bill proposed the reincorporation into the retired list and the granting of retirement benefits for those ex-officers who had been dropped from military service, and one-grade promotions for all those now on the retired list who had been passed over because of their involvement in the revolts. Although the beneficiaries of the bill, after its enactment in modified form in 1923, proved to be relatively few, this attempt to reward personnel who, to paraphrase the words of the bill's author, placed civic obligations above military duty, was an assault on the consciences of those who had remained loyal to that duty. In arguing that there were "primordial obligations to country and constitution far superior to all military regulations," Yrigoyen's supporters unwittingly offered a rationalization for future military uprisings, of which they were to be the first victims. The tragedy was that in looking backward and trying to redress past inequities, Yrigoyen was helping to undermine the none-too-strong tradition of military aloofness from politics and to weaken the sense of unity in the officer corps.

Indeed, that unity all but disappeared in the 1920s as differences between officers hardened and factionalism grew. Evidence of this was the organization in 1921 of a secret society of officers alienated by the administration's handling of military matters. This society originated in a merging of two groups of officers: one a group of captains largely from the cavalry; the other, field grade officers of various services. The society took the name Logia General San Martín and eventually comprised some 300 officers, or about one-fifth of the total line officer strength.

A recent study of the Logia ascribes its formation to five basic factors: the toleration shown by the War Ministry to politically minded officers who used their positions to campaign for public office or to generate support for Yrigoyen; favoritism and arbitrariness in the handling of promotions; the development of deficiencies in the training of conscripts; the failure of the administration to act on army requests for adequate arms and equipment; and a general deterioration of discipline within the army that was reflected in enlisted and noncommissioned ranks as well as among the officers.

To these essentially professional concerns leading to the creation of the Logia must be added the apprehension with which certain officers viewed the spread of left-wing activities in Argentina. Still fresh in mind was the week-long breakdown of order in Buenos Aires in January 1919, the so-called *Semana Trágica*, when a minor labor dispute gave rise to bloody clashes with the authorities, mob violence, and what some regarded as an abortive attempt at social revolution. The subsequent discovery that soldiers and noncommissioned officers in at least two garrisons had been forming "soviets" exerted a direct influence on several of the officers, who two years later took the initiative in forming the Logia General San Martín. The Logia's members looked on the organization, therefore, not only as an instrument for correcting professional ills but also as a means of pressuring the government to be less tolerant of the political left. . . .

   The appointment of Agustín Justo as Alvear's minister of war in 1922 was a victory for the Logia but no less so for the persistence of factionalism. The gulf between officers who had been critical of Yrigoyen's military measures and those who had profited from them grew wider than ever, the major difference being that it was the former critics who were now the ones to enjoy positions of power. Logia members received many key assignments, including chief of the War Ministry secretariat, chief of the president's military household (Casa Militar), and director of the military and war academies. Moreover, the promotion list for superior officers, which the outgoing administration in its final weeks had submitted to the Senate, was recalled before it could be approved, and a new one was prepared.

   The Logia members waged relentless war against those officers who in their view were engaged in political activity. Not only did they secure an official decree calling for enforcement of the statutory prohibition on such activity, but they resorted to ostracism of officers who continued to violate it. The leaders of the Logia devised what they termed a blacklist of such officers and called on their members to refrain from any personal contact with those blacklisted except as required by acts of the service. The Logia's existence as a formal organization ended early in 1926. A majority of its governing committee had reached the conclusion that its mission was accomplished; and to prevent its being used for personal ambitions, they moved to dissolve it, a step that was supported by the bulk of the membership. Nevertheless, the procedures used by the Logia in its five years of existence had not eliminated factions in the officer corps. Among some of the former *logistas* there was built up a special bond that was to manifest itself in the politics of the future, while on the part of those who had suffered from the Logia, a determination developed to seek revenge against Logia members.

   . . . The inauguration in October 1928 of Hipólito Yrigoyen marked the return to the presidency of a charismatic leader, the most popular figure in Argentine history before Perón. Neither the limited achievements of Yrigoyen's first administration (1916–22) nor his six years out of office had dislodged him from the special place he enjoyed in the hearts of average Argentines. Unlike other leaders with mass followings, Yrigoyen was neither a spellbinder nor a crowd-pleaser. Indeed, he had rarely appeared in public and had carefully avoided making speeches, even during the recent electoral campaign. His strength lay rather in his personal persuasiveness, in his ability to convince those who came into direct contact with him to accept his leadership. Strong-willed, tenacious, a firm believer in his own historic mission to redeem the downtrodden, Yrigoyen projected at once a sincerity of purpose and a weight of authority that was difficult to resist. Reinforcing his appeal was the air of mystery he maintained about himself and the austerity of his private life. Even while serving in high office, he avoided ceremony as much as possible and continued the ascetic life that had been his norm for the past half century. In his predilection for conversing in low tones in shaded rooms, his preference for wearing dark, nondescript suits, and his reluctance to pose for photographs, he revealed the continuing effects of his early career as a political conspirator. . . .

The Yrigoyen administration's handling of the military construction and armaments program in its first eight months in office was the source of considerable dissatisfaction within military circles. At the close of July 1929 the U.S. ambassador, in a message devoted to analyzing the general situation, observed: "The officers of the Army and the Navy are said to be generally disgruntled with the Government because work has stopped, through failure to make payments, on barracks and many other improvements undertaken by sanction of the previous Government."

The military malaise that developed under the Yrigoyen administration had other roots than its mishandling of the capital outlay program. Much more serious from the viewpoint of the ordinary officer was the display of political favoritism in the treatment of military personnel. This favoritism took various forms: the reincorporation into the officer corps of personnel long since discharged with full credit for serving the intervening years; retroactive promotion of retired officers, contrary to explicit provisions of the military laws, with the right to collect the differential in retirement pay; and alteration in the date-of-rank of favored active-duty officers, giving them greater seniority than their contemporaries and consequently an advantage for promotion. . . .

President Yrigoyen's role in the promotion process and in other personnel decisions was not a passive one. He felt free to request changes in the lists submitted by army promotion boards, and he ordered additional promotions in response to personal appeals by individual officers. Indeed, his propensity to respond generously to individuals seeking changes in status introduced a chaotic note in personnel administration. As *La Prensa* observed in July 1930: "It is well known today in the entire national administration, even in the navy and especially in the army, that the military man or his relatives who can secure access to the president of the nation gets everything he wants, even if it is unjust or illegal.". . .

Early in the new administration, officers who were identified with the Logia or with the outgoing war minister, General Justo, were relieved of their posts and placed in an unassigned status (*disponibilidad*). This status, which some officers endured for more than a year, resulted in enforced idleness, as well as loss of the supplementary pay that went with specific assignments. Eventually many of these officers were given assignments, but others preferred to ask for retirement. Among the latter was Colonel Luis García, onetime head of the Logia and former director of the Colegio Militar, who used his retired status to fire salvo after salvo at the War Ministry from the editorial columns of the conservative Buenos Aires daily, *La Nación*. His 137 articles, published from mid-July 1929 to September 5, 1930, spelled out in convincing detail the administration's military mismanagement, seeking thereby to undermine officer corps loyalty.

Working toward the same end was General José F. Uriburu, whose retirement from active duty in May 1929 freed him of inhibitions against participating in a conspiracy. In December 1927, when approached by young nationalists to consider a military movement that would prevent the return of Yrigoyen, his reply is said to have been, "Aren't you forgetting that I am an officer on active duty?" Now, on the occasion of his retirement, he made plain his hostility to the Yrigoyen government in a speech that denounced its influence on the army. After noting that an armed force is a reflection of the nation, having the same virtues and defects, he observed:

> The weaknesses of command, which in themselves are usually an expression of the decadence of character, take on a catastrophic aspect the moment that the political power undermines its innards, by destroying through favor or threat what is most respectable in the soul of the officer: his disinterestedness. And it can be asserted without fear of error that from the very moment this sentiment begins to weaken, intrigue and base servility substitute for the common ideal of serving the country with disinterest.

. . . As the Argentine winter of 1930 set in, the administration of the aging president was being buffeted from all sides. Within his own party, disillusioned elements questioned his leadership and that of the men who surrounded him, but Yrigoyen made no move to change either his style or his advisers. Instead, he contented himself with criticism of the critics, including intemperate remarks about the role of foreigners and young people in the party. Outside the party, the barrage of criticism reached unprecedented heights. In the latter part of August, with reports that Yrigoyen was planning to intervene in Entre Ríos province, the atmosphere became explosive. Leaders of all opposition parties called on the president to change his course. A series of mass meetings sought to mobilize public opinion against the administration, while certain political figures on the right began conspiring with army officers. The stage was being set for the military intervention of September 6. . . .

General Uriburu's assumption of power in September 1930 as president of the provisional government marked the beginning of a seventeen-month period of de facto rule. In its own day and ever since, the Uriburu government has been described variously as a military regime, a civil-military government, and a personalist dictatorship. The confusion in terminology derives from the contradictory makeup of the regime. To understand its true character and the place of the military in it, it is necessary to examine the persons who made up the administration, the procedures by which it governed, the groups that supported it, and finally the policies it pursued. . . .

The Uriburu regime rested primarily on the support of the armed forces, which, as we shall see, was not unqalified; on the support of vociferous nationalist groups, including the paramilitary Legíon Cívica Argentina (Argentine Civic Legion); and on certain provincial political organizations, of which the Conservative Party of Buenos Aires was the most important. At the very beginning of his administration, however, as a result of the euphoria produced by the very success of revolution and by the pledges given to respect the constitution and work for national harmony, General Uriburu enjoyed the support, or at least the goodwill, of much broader sectors of Argentine opinion. Not only were the political parties that had worked to bring on the revolution, notably the Independent Socialists of the Federal Capital, the Democrats of Córdoba (a conservative group), and the Anti-Personalista Radicals, prepared to cooperate with the government, but parties that had opposed military intervention, the old-line Socialists and Progressive Democrats, showed a willingness to go along with the regime. Even an important sector of the divided labor movement made a public declaration of support.

Had the revolutionary government been content to serve simply in a caretaker capacity while preparing the country for early general elections, these various groups would have supported it in this task. But Uriburu's determination, publicly acknowledged early in October, to promote a series of constitutional reforms that would, among other things, alter the existing electoral and representation system, precipitated a process of political alienation. To the natural and open opposition of the Radicals was added the tacit opposition of several of the parties that had opposed the Radicals. In the absence of any public enthusiasm for his reforms, Uriburu's support was eventually narrowed to the military, the nationalists, and small conservative groups.

Military support for the Uriburu government, while sufficient to enable Uriburu to stay in power for a year and a half, was not unconditional. He had to contend not only with the threat of officers still loyal to Yrigoyen, but also with the influence and ambitions of General Justo and his supporters, who disagreed with Uriburu on the goals of the revolution. . . .

Although the Uriburu administration was able to conduct its economic policies with relatively little concern for military reactions, its political policies involved it in a dialogue with armed forces officers. The war and navy ministers were the normal channels of communication, but President Uriburu frequently spoke before military audiences to build support for his policies. Paradoxically, some of his most important political announcements were made in speeches at military installations, where politics was supposed to be regarded as a threat to morale and unity.

General Uriburu's political objective, as has already been noted, was the adoption of constitutional changes that would, in his view, prevent a repetition of an Yrigoyen-type government. While some of these changes embodied long-standing proposals to strengthen the legislative and judicial branches in relation to the executive and to shore up provincial autonomy against domination from the center, the heart of the proposed reform was alteration of the existing system of universal manhood suffrage and geographical representation. Never spelled out in detail, the proposals aimed at some sort of restricted vote and direct representation of functional groups. . . .

The Uriburu government did use its decree powers, however, to make one far-reaching innovation, the creation of the Escuela Superior Técnica, the technological counterpart of the War Academy. This institution, replacing the advanced course given at the Colegio Militar, trained military engineers and was the logical corollary of the efforts already under way to develop an armaments industry, including the production of aircraft. Under its first director, Lieutenant Colonel Manuel Savio, the Escuela Superior Técnica was to become the center for studying technical problems related to heavy industry development and the promoter of economic nationalist doctrines within the army.

The impact of the Uriburu era on the Argentine army, of course, transcended questions of size, promotions, training, and regulations to affect the very morale and outlook of the officer corps. Professional values tended to be subordinated to political issues, and what had once been regarded as beyond their competence became matters of daily discussion. The harmful effects on professional standards were evident even to officers who had supported the revolution. Writing in April 1931, Captain Perón observed to Lieutenant Colonel Sarobe, then far removed from the Argentine scene:

> I think this revolution has done great harm to the officer cadre. It will be necessary for the men who govern in the future to return things to their place. There is no other solution than to multiply the tasks. The year 1932 at the least ought to be for officers in general a year of extraordinary work of every sort; only in this way can we avoid the harm produced in the army by idleness, backbiting, and politics. Every officer will have to be kept busy in professional tasks from reveille to retreat. Otherwise this will go from bad to worse.

. . . Deterioration of discipline and intensification of rivalries within the officer corps were the inevitable consequences of the September revolution. Another result was an increased disdain for civilians and civilian politicians. Uriburu's speeches to his comrades-in-arms repeatedly denigrated politicians and inculcated the view that patriotism was somehow the monopoly of the armed forces or of special groups like the Legión Cívica. How many officers were persuaded of this view cannot be determined, but it seems likely that a good many junior officers accepted as their own the scornful attitudes of their commander in chief.

The damage inflicted on Argentine society by the revolution worked two ways. On the one hand, it made many officers unwilling to accept completely the idea that political party activity is normal and essential in a democratic society. On the other hand, it lowered civilian confidence in the armed forces as a national institution above politics and spread skepticism about its aims. As Alfredo Colmo put it, "The army will have difficulty, henceforth, in convincing anyone that it is the patrimony of the entire country, that alien passions are not playing in it nor self-centered or irresponsible elements meddling in it. It will have to work to recover its prestige and good name."

An enormous burden was thus thrust upon the Justo administration when it took control in 1932, a burden that its very pursuit of power had helped to create. Not only did it have to cope with the alienation of the Radicals and face the economic and social problems of the deepening depression, but it had to work out, in an atmosphere of considerable distrust, a viable relationship between the army and a goodly part of Argentine society. . . .

From the very beginning of his administration President Justo was extremely sensitive to the problem of military support. The bulk of the officer corps, he was well aware, was politically neutral. However, there were two potential sources of danger: on the one hand, those officers who belonged to, or sympathized with, the Radical party and who subscribed to its view that the Justo government was illegitimate in its origin; and at the other extreme, and bitterly hostile to the Radicals, the authoritarian-minded officers who had been close to Uriburu and who after the latter's death developed the myth that Justo had betrayed the ideals of the September revolution.

Justo's response to the problem was a mixture of measures designed to reduce the likelihood of further alienation of officers while safeguarding him against the subversive activities of unreconstructed elements. Perhaps his shrewdest move was the appointment of Manuel Rodríguez to the War Ministry. Rodríguez was a prestigious officer known for his deep commitment to professional standards. As minister of war, Rodríguez undertook to isolate the military from politics and to restore the discipline that had been shattered by the events of 1930–31. For one thing, he deliberately intensified the daily training schedules so as to leave little time for other activities. For another, he constantly emphasized the concept of professionalism and the primacy of military duty over other considerations. The sincerity with which General Rodríguez was able to proclaim these values undoubtedly helped maintain the loyalty of the bulk of the officer corps.

To protect his government against the politically minded officers, however, President Justo employed other means. A surveillance system was developed that included monitoring long-distance telephone calls placed through Buenos Aires and maintaining a close watch on contacts between officers and politicians. With information supplied by military intelligence personnel and by the Federal Capital Police, Justo was in a position to deal quietly with would-be conspirators, in some cases transferring them to innocuous positions, in other cases using the promise of promotion to wean them away from their allies. Arrest and retirement, however, were the usual penalties for those active-duty military personnel who carried their opposition into the open.

Justo much preferred to use indirect methods for thwarting military opposition. This is seen in the promotion of superior officers. In the list he submitted to the Senate in July 1932, the first to be approved since 1928, the grade of colonel was requested for forty-three officers, including Uriburistas and Radicals as well as members of the "Justo group." There is some reason for believing, moreover, that the president tried to exploit the mutual hostility of Radical and Uriburista officers as a means of keeping both in check. His overtures to the former through a proposed amnesty for pro-Radical officers penalized by the Uriburu regime and his concession to the former Uriburistas in not shutting down the paramilitary Legión Cívica support such an interpretation. The discontent of both groups persisted, but neither was able by itself to upset Justo's position.

The most determined efforts to overthrow him in the first two years of the administration came from the Radical side. A small group of officers and noncommissioned officers, of whom Lieutenant Colonel Atilio Cattáneo was the driving spirit, tried to organize a civil-military revolution in conjunction with leaders of the Radical party. Opposition from the Alvear wing of the party and rivalries among the military and civilian elements pledged to take part plagued the effort, as Cattáneo's memoirs attest. The first attempt, which was to consist of coordinated uprisings in the capital and several provinces, never came off because an accidental explosion a week before the planned day in December 1932 alerted the authorities and resulted in Cattáneo's arrest.

A few weeks later two Radical officers tried, unsuccessfully, to raise a regiment in Concordia, Entre Ríos, but the next major effort was scheduled to coincide with the holding of the Radical party's national convention in Santa Fe, in December 1933. This time the authorities knew the timing of the uprisings in advance, although not exactly where they would take place. Waiters on the river vessel that carried Radical party members to Santa Fe had been replaced by police agents; and on the basis of their reports, the president and his advisers waited up on the night of December 28–29 for the blows to strike. The main fighting took place in Santa Fe and Corrientes, with other disturbances in Buenos Aires province, but federal forces were easily able to restore order. A nationwide state of siege was proclaimed, and President Justo now took advantage of the situation to crack down on the entire Radical party, arresting Alvear and other moderate leaders who wanted a return to electoral politics, as well as those who frankly favored revolutionary methods.

With the failure of the 1933 movement, conspiratorial activity among the pro-Radical officers was confined to a few diehards. The party itself, recognizing the impossibility of regaining power by force, decided, despite vigorous internal dissent, to resume contesting elections in 1935. Thereafter, its contacts with the military were designed primarily to persuade the officer corps that a Radical victory at the polls would not threaten their careers. . . .

By 1937, President Justo had gained sufficient control of the political process to rig the election for his successor without fear of military intervention. Radical appeals for the army to supervise the balloting received no visible response from the officer corps, which obeyed Justo's injunction, repeated at the annual armed forces dinner on July 6, to stay clear of politics. The politically minded nationalist officers, who had as little use for the official candidate as they did for his Radical opponent, were in no position to act. Instead, they decided to await Justo's exit from office before making a new attempt to take power.

The willingness of the officer corps as a whole to leave politics to the president was undoubtedly influenced by their approval of Justo's handling of military affairs. Under his administration the modernization of the armed forces, which had been interrupted after 1928, was renewed and outlays of funds for military purposes reached unprecedented heights. . . .

The support given the Justo administration by the armed forces obscured but did not prevent the intensification of nationalistic sentiment in the officer corps and of the accompanying belief that the military should play a larger role in shaping public policy. Evidence of this trend may be seen in articles published in semiofficial and official military organs during and after the Justo era. Although the views expressed were those of individual authors, it is evident that the military men who edited the *Revista Militar* and the *Revista de Informaciones* were not opposed to having such views associated with the military establishment. A favorite theme of these articles was the great destiny that awaited Argentina and the need for the nation to prepare for an important future international role. Typical of this view was the flat assertion of a military engineer, Major Ricardo Maraimbo, that "the Argentine Republic ought to be and must be a great world power." The preparation that he and like-minded fellow officers proposed included nationalization of foreign investment, promotion of industrial self-sufficiency, intensification of patriotic sentiment through the repudiation of "utopian, internationalist, pacifist, and exotic ideas," and a substantial strengthening of the peacetime army. . . .

Not content with setting forth general goals, some officers insisted on the army's right to a major voice in foreign policy decisions. Colonel Carlos Gómez repeatedly advocated that the general staff chiefs participate in a national defense council concerned not just with defense plans but with the entire process of international relations. With reference to bordering countries, he specifically claimed the right for the military to say, "With this neighbor we ought to be friends or allies; with this other it does not matter whether we are." Strategic considerations alone, he felt, should determine the nature of Argentina's relations with her South American neighbors.

From the belief that the military had a natural right to determine foreign [policy] decisions, it was no great jump to the conclusion that this competence extended also to the domestic field. Civilian nationalists like the poet Leopoldo Lugones had long been advocating military influence in domestic matters, of course, and had seen their ideas translated into approximate reality during the Uriburu interlude.

As the Justo administration came to an end, the gap was widening between the official view of the army's role and that held by an indeterminate but increasing number of individual officers. Officially, the army was depicted as an institution without interests apart from those of the nation, one that accepted subordination to the constituted authorities, one that contributed to the general progress of the republic. Justo's first war minister had once summed this up by stating to the Congress that he was "a representative of the interests of the nation in the War Department, and not the representative of the interests of the army." But even though General Rodríguez had spoken of the army as "a weapon to be used by the civilians who have responsibility for the governments of the nation," military skepticism about the ability of such civilians to conduct its affairs was very much alive at the time the fraudulently elected Ortiz-Castillo government took power. The six years of the Justo administration had postponed, not resolved, the delicate question of the place of the military in the political process. . . .

The substitution of military for civilian government [again] in June 1943 took place under conditions quite distinct from those prevailing at the time of the first takeover thirteen years before. Missing was the atmosphere of public excitement that had preceded the Uriburu-led coup, an atmosphere deliberately fomented by Yrigoyen's opponents. The June uprisings, in contrast, came as a surprise to the general public and even to those politicians who were aware of the widespread discontent within the officer corps. The politicians were anticipating a move in September, not in June.

Still, it would be erroneous to claim that the military acted without regard for the civilian sector, or indeed without encouragement from it. The officers shared the universal concern over President Castillo's electoral plans even while they disagreed among themselves on the wisdom of his foreign policies. Moreover, the belief that it was their responsibility to take action was strengthened by their increasing contacts with political leaders, especially those of the Radical party. Without this stimulus, it is questionable whether the liberal, pro-Allied sector of the army would have risen, and without their participation the movement could not have succeeded. The inability of the nationalist sector to mount a successful coup by itself had been demonstrated time and time again in previous years.

In acting to oust the Castillo government, the military was responding to a harsh axiom of Argentine politics: that no constitutional authority is strong enough to prevent a determined president from imposing his will, even if this involves violation of the laws and the constitution itself; and that only the withdrawal of military support can call a halt to such an administration. With his control over the Senate, Dr. Castillo could be unconcerned about impeachment proceedings, and he had shown by his continued extension of the state of siege his determination to ignore hostile opinion. The belief that it was up to the military to intervene was by no means limited to military circles; many civilians would have agreed with General Rawson when he told his comrades-in-arms: "When the nation, as a result of bad rulers, is put into a situation where there are no constitutional solutions, [the military] has a duty to fulfill: to put the nation in order." But here was the rub. Could an officer corps as deeply divided as that which existed in 1943 "put the nation in order"?

Ronald M. Schneider

CHAPTER 7

The Military and Brazilian Politics to World War II

Since the establishment of the republic, there have been very few periods in Brazilian history that have not been marked either by military revolts or by heavy armed forces tutelage of the government. In the recurrent struggle between legalism and political activism within the Brazilian military, the latter has long been substantially stronger than depicted by most historians and many contemporary observers. Neglect of this fundamental fact and the corresponding overemphasis of the role of civilian politicians and political movements have distorted interpretations of Brazilian political development. While a series of civilians from São Paulo did govern the country with reasonable security after the initial years of military domination under Marshals Deodoro and Floriano, two of these three presidents faced military crises that in the context of the times posed threats to their continuance in office. Prudente de Morais (1894–98) was plagued by dissatisfaction over his handling of the Canudos "insurgency" problem and in November 1897 was saved from assassination by a veteran of that campaign only because War Minister Machado Bittencourt sacrificed his own life to save the president. Following Campos Salles's quite peaceful term (1898–1902), Rodrigues Alves survived the November 1904 revolt of the Military School at the midpoint of his administration. The first *mineiro* president, Afonso Pena (1906–09), died in office of a "moral traumatism" soon after being thwarted in his preference for a civilian as his successor and being forced to accept the candidacy of War Minister Hermes da Fonseca. Nilo Peçanha's year in office was little more than an opportunity to preside over the marshal's election, and Hermes himself was barely settled in the presidency when the naval revolt of 1910 broke out. His regime was also plagued by protracted insurgency in the northeast and south by dissident politicians. The latter problem extended into the term of Wenceslau Braz (1914–18), who otherwise enjoyed stability, although the nation's political kingmaker, Senator Pinheiro

75

Machado, was murdered (to the ill-concealed satisfaction of some officers). The military's involvement in World War I temporarily reduced its political interference and left Braz a good bit freer than he might otherwise have been.

Military involvement in politics resurged during the interwar period. Epitácio Pessoa (1919–22) was involved in rather constant friction with the armed forces because of his insistence on appointing civilians to head the war and navy ministries. By the last year of his term a grave military question had arisen as the army, behind Marshal Hermes da Fonseca, adamantly opposed the choice of Arthur Bernardes as president for the 1922–26 term. Indeed, the entire decade of the 1920s was one of repeated military uprisings, culminating in the successful 1930 Revolution. [Getúlio] Vargas himself, although heavily backed by, and to a considerable degree dependent upon, the armed forces, faced civil war in 1932 and a Communist revolt in 1935, in both of which movements regular army elements were involved, before staging his own dictatorial coup in 1937. Like Wenceslau Braz a quarter of a century earlier, Vargas also benefited from the military's concern with its wartime obligations. But with the end of World War II, Vargas was unceremoniously removed from office by the armed forces.

The transition from dictatorship to a constitutional, competitive regime after 1945 did not place undue strains upon the political process shaped by Vargas, at least so long as it received predominantly support rather than demands from the armed forces. Subsequently, however, the problems of aftermath politics in a period of emerging populism and resurgent traditional clientelism, aggravated by dislocations caused by the external influence of postwar international adjustments, gave rise to increasing tensions and a "revolution of rising frustrations." Under these conditions, Vargas's return to power through popular elections took place in 1950, only to encounter the full brunt of the participation crisis. Governing within the constraints of a constitutional system that had been consciously devised to thwart a president who might try to operate in his old style, Vargas found his tried-and-true techniques of manipulation and conciliation inadequate. His response involved a shriller demagoguery and intensified exploitation of nationalism rather than evolving a more serviceable substitute political style. In this situation, the majority of the officer corps withdrew their support from his regime.

Thus, the military's repeated intervention in the political arena in the postwar era had behind it a substantial tradition. Indeed, the relative political peace under Juscelino Kubitschek (January 1956–

January 1961) was as long a recess from major political-military crisis as the republic had yet witnessed. When Kubitschek turned over the presidential office at the end of his full term to an elected successor in a climate of normalcy, he was accomplishing something achieved only by three previous civilian presidents (Campos Salles, Rodrigues Alves, and Wenceslau Braz). Moreover, three governments fell by force in the single constitutional term between [Eurico Gaspar] Dutra and Kubitschek, while the five-year presidential period after Kubitschek saw the emergence and decline of three distinct regimes in a process of nearly continual crises that interred the old pattern of civil-military relations and brought the armed forces back to the direct exercise of power they had experienced in the infant years of the republic.

In a very similar sense to the continuity of *tenentismo* (the political militance of the junior officers entering the service after World War I) and even of the *tenentes* themselves from the 1920s through the 1960s, *Florianismo* in the form of advocacy of military rule as practiced by Marshal Floriano [Peixoto], spanned the 1890s to the early 1920s. First with the "Consolidator of the Republic" himself, then through the political career and presidency of his aide and favorite nephew, Marshal Hermes da Fonseca (1910–14), and finally with the bridge between *Florianismo* and *tenentismo* in the form of the 1921–22 campaign of the Military Club against the government under Hermes's leadership, this interventionist current left its impact on the military generation born after the establishment of the republic. Thus, if events before 1910 were just faint memories to the senior officers of the early 1960s, the same was not true of the Hermes da Fonseca administration and the period of World War I. For with few exceptions, the generals of the post-Vargas era were already cadets at this time, enrolled in military preparatory school (Colegio Militar) if not already in the academy (Escola Militar). Hence, for example, the naval revolt that broke out after Hermes's inauguration appears to have left an imprint that disposed them to react strongly to the navy insubordination in March 1964.

While the earlier military interventions and revolts were part of the armed forces' historical memory, the developments of the 1920s were directly related—through the Revolution of 1930, the 1937 coup, and the ouster of Vargas in 1945—to the developments of the 1954–64 decade.

Throughout this period, military figures were actively involved in the political life of the states, albeit more often behind the scenes than in the spotlight. In point of fact, between 1900 and 1930 the

Brazilian armed forces were an even more active factor in the politics of the nation than were their Argentine counterparts—conventional wisdom to the contrary. The Brazilian armed forces differed from the Latin American norm during the first three decades of the twentieth century more as a result of the nature of the Brazilian political system as a whole than in terms of their own particular characteristics as an institution. As the system underwent a process of change, so did the military subsystem, in response to many of the same dynamic factors.

With the beginning of the political decay and institutional deterioration of the Old Republic at the end of World War I, the military was at the center of every crisis. The increasing division within the armed forces along generational lines, which placed them on both sides of the conflict between the established order and the forces of change, nourished a continued belief, strongest within the military but accepted by much of the public, that it was national rather than institutional interests or personal ambitions that motivated their political actions, and to a considerable degree this was true. As their predecessors were the midwives of the republic in 1889, the younger officers—those emerging from the Military School toward the end of the war and after—were its gravediggers.

By 1928 the republican regime in its nearly four decades of existence had reached the same point of deterioration, and the oligarchic system a parallel degree of political decay, as had been the case with the empire in the mid-1880s. Institutions and processes that might have been suitable for the first years of republican self-government had failed to evolve beyond an amalgam with traditional practices carried over from the monarchy. Indeed, they became entrenched through the federal government's willingness to let state power structures alone as long as they cooperated in Congress and created no undue difficulty over presidential succession. The electoral process was highly fraudulent; national parties were nonexistent; and protests against the inequities of the established order were increasingly met with repression rather than compromise and evolutionary reform. The federal executive, while frequently arbitrary, often lacked the compensatory merit of strength and effectiveness. The political representatives of the patriarchal and "oligarchic" regime could not point with pride to outstanding accomplishments to justify their continued stewardship of the nation. Or rather, when they sought to do so, they were convincing only to themselves, while appearing hypocritical and self-seeking to an increasing proportion of the politically conscious public.

As long as elections might lead to change, there was no strong popular base for revolution. But the people were aware that never in the history of the republic had the government's candidate lost. Moreover, only on two widely separated occasions had the electorate been given even the shadow of a real choice rather than just an opportunity to ratify the decision of the powerful state machines (and this only when the bargaining process among the president and the governors of São Paulo, Minas Gerais, and Rio Grande do Sul had broken down). Indeed, to all intents and purposes, the selection of São Paulo's governor for the 1926–30 presidential term had taken place in 1919, when the election of Epitácio Pessoa to the presidency was understood within the political class as a temporary "emergency" interruption of the pattern of São Paulo-Minas Gerais alternation, which would give the young state executive four more years to mature. In this context, the presidential succession of 1930 turned out to be the last chance for the old republican system to demonstrate significant flexibility or adaptability. But the course of events from late 1928 on demonstrated that Brazil's political crisis was one both of men and of institutions.

The core of the revolutionary movement that eventually triumphed in October 1930 was composed of the *tenentes*, who had gained conspiratorial experience as well as a degree of popular renown during the four years of their armed struggle against the government of Arthur da Silva Bernardes (1922–26). During 1928–29 they were able to win additional adherents to their cause within the officer corps, exploiting the growing dissatisfaction with the regime's policies. The successful revolution became possible only after they formed an alliance with a broad coalition of political forces possessing a significant power base in the key states, but their proselytizing and infiltration of military units throughout the country were essential to the achievement of this purpose. Indeed, without the assurance of widespread military adhesions, the generally cautious political leaders would not have risked a revolutionary venture, particularly the coldly calculating Getúlio Vargas, in whose name the 1930 revolt was ultimately launched and who had delayed his commitment until the movement was far advanced.

Tenentismo paralleled in many respects the positivistic republicanism of the young officers in the last decade of the empire. On the intellectual side, its origins can be found in the Military Academy, reopened in 1911–12 at Realengo after being closed in the wake of the 1904 cadet revolt. There during World War I such future leaders as Eduardo Gomes, Luís Carlos Prestes, Siqueira Campos, Oswaldo

Cordeiro de Farias, Stenio Caio de Albuquerque Lima, and Ciro do Espirito Santo Cardoso (to name but one group among several who maintained a significant exchange of ideas) studied and lamented a "Brazil laden with problems, beneath the weight of the crisis and in the hands of politicians [who are] inept as well as unscrupulous and [the] instruments of oligarchies." The leaders of the academy made a conscious effort to keep the education essentially technical rather than highly theoretical, with a taste of the humanities, or at least of positivist philosophy, as had been the case at the old academy at Praia Vermelha during the years when its instructors were still the disciples of Benjamin Constant. The goal was to develop competent professional soldiers, well disciplined and obedient to constituted authority. This orientation was successful with many. But in light of the lower-middle-class origin of a large proportion of the young officers, the example of their superiors' often mixing in politics, the siren call of renewed *Florianismo* through the person of Hermes da Fonseca, and the magnitude of national problems (contrasted with the "selfish" interests of the "boss"-dominated political system), it is not surprising that a significant minority questioned the military's institutional role as a support of the established order.

The militants of both the legalist and reformist theses were greatly outnumbered at the time (as they would be three decades later) by the vast majority of officers for whom the two sides of the nation's motto, "Order and Progress," had equal importance. Since the 1891 Constitution enjoined the armed forces on the one hand to be "essentially obedient, within the limits of the law" to the president, but on the other hand declared them "obligated to support the constitutional institutions," it virtually consecrated ambivalence in ambiguous situations when the threat to the constitution's integrity appeared to come from the executive. Moreover, the increased emphasis upon study and training advocated so vigorously by the champions of professionalism and embodied in the 1920 military regulations, along with the arrival in the same year of a French training mission, which was destined to have a heavy impact upon the army's mentality, appears to have made young officers more aware of national problems than before. Growing numbers came to believe: "On the national scale, the army, and only the army, was the organized force which could be placed at the service of democratic ideals and popular demands, against the interests of the bosses and oligarchies which increasingly aggravated the burdensome conditions of survival for the unprivileged."

The spread of this reformist-activist sentiment among the military coincided with the increasing alienation of urban progressive groups who found the establishment unresponsive to their demand for a significant voice in policy-making and not at all disposed to yield to demands for any type of reform, including that of the electoral system. As had been the case forty years earlier, nearly all of the preconditions for revolution existed. Dissension within the political elite over presidential succession combined with the impact of the world economic crisis made the regime vulnerable and provided additional impetus to the formation of a revolutionary coalition capable of overthrowing the established order.

The successful revolutionary movement of 1930 was a heterogeneous amalgam of groups desiring sweeping political changes if not a new social order, with elements which, although violently opposed to the incumbent administration and the president's hand-picked successor, were devoid of any wish for more than modest political and administrative reforms. In both its civilian and military components —each crucial to its success—the revolutionary coalition was essentially, indeed almost exclusively, bourgeois in nature. The Communists, considering the October 1930 revolt to be narrowly concerned with regional rivalries within the existing system, refused to participate or support it—a fact that was to have significant implications for the postrevolution political struggles.

Presidential succession was the issue that coalesced the fragmented opposition forces into a single movement cohesive insofar as its immediate objective—attainment of power—was concerned. In 1929 the world market crisis combined with a record coffee harvest to thwart government price-support policies and trigger an economic recession. Elements linked to industry, finance, commerce, and services began to react strongly against economic policies favoring export-oriented agricultural producers. Against this background, an unusually strong opposition coalition was forged to contest the 1930 presidential election. When outgoing President Washington Luís, of São Paulo, broke with tradition and sought to impose another *Paulista* as the official candidate, Minas Gerais political leaders threw their support to the "Liberal Alliance" slate headed by Getúlio Vargas, the governor of Rio Grande do Sul. Júlio Prestes was announced the winner, but the Liberal Alliance refused to accept the allegedly fraudulent results and launched a revolt in October 1930. Alarmed at the prospect of civil war and impressed with the visible decay of the old regime in the face of this challenge, the high command of the armed forces, after a good deal of maneuvering by generals with key commands, stepped in and forced the president to resign in favor of a junta, which, it was hoped by some participants, might prove a viable alternative to the revolutionary forces.

Vargas became provisional chief executive at the head of a very heterogeneous movement. Although the *tenentes* and some "Young Turk" politicians desired a real social revolution, they lacked any coherent plan; other groups wished only to correct the evident deficiencies of the old political system. They agreed only upon a new electoral code incorporating the secret ballot, proportional representation, a system of electoral courts, and extension of the franchise to include women. Following an unsuccessful "Constitutionalist" revolt centered in São Paulo in July 1932, a constituent assembly was elected and in 1934 conferred a four-year presidential term upon Vargas. During this time both the Communists and the local fascists (known as Integralists), thriving in a situation where less ideological parties failed to take root, sought Vargas's overthrow by violent means. In November 1937, Vargas staged a coup with the acquiescence of the armed forces' leaders, assuming dictatorial powers and decreeing a semicorporate "New State" (*Estado Nôvo*). By absorbing into his regime important elements of the dominant state machines, he was able to bend the existing political system to his wishes and adapt it to his needs. Thus, he was able to govern without a formal party structure while maneuvering to neutralize critical military elements.

Vargas's fifteen-year stay in power, although interrupting Brazil's tradition of constitutional government, helped to break the hold of the traditional elite groups and brought new elements into the political arena. Moreover, Vargas gave impetus to social and economic developments that subsequently tended to give a broader base to Brazilian experiments with representative regimes in the 1946–64 period. Yet more than anything else the *Estado Nôvo* reinforced authoritarian tendencies and corporatist structures which proved barriers to the development of a pluralist system.

CHAPTER 8

The Military in
Chilean Politics, 1924–32

Prior to 1973, political orientation and motivation of Chilean army officers in the twentieth century were generally confined to the 1924–32 period. During those eight years the military functioned as a politically deliberative body in four distinct ways. First, in September 1924 the actions of junior and middle-grade officers caused President Arturo Alessandri Palma to resign his office, whereupon a junta composed of two generals and an admiral assumed executive functions. Four months later, in January 1925, a coup led by the progenitors of the 1924 movement deposed the junta and recalled Alessandri, allowing him to serve out the remaining few months of his five-year term.

Second, during the two tense years that followed, the army, under the control of a clique of colonels, steadily increased its influence in national politics while observing constitutional procedure. From the pose of an obedient, objectively controlled military organization the Chilean army moved to a position of dominance. It was the army which provided impetus for civilians to write a new constitution in 1925. In September 1925 the recalled Alessandri resigned his office a second time because of military pressure. His elected successor fared no better and by early 1927 was a pawn in the struggle between reform-minded military men and recalcitrant and antimilitarist political leaders. The army's insistence on full exercise of constitutionally provided executive powers forced him to resign. When he did so, it was only a matter of weeks before the military reform leader Colonel Carlos Ibáñez del Campo became president, the first military man to occupy the presidential chair in three-quarters of a century.

Third, Ibáñez and his civilian and military supporters governed Chile for four years, until July 1931. Applying the socioeconomic reforms called for in the new constitution, Ibáñez paid only lip service to civil liberties and democratic procedures of governance embodied in the same document. He was not a true dictator, but a rigid authoritarian, elevated to power constitutionally, who had grave doubts about traditional liberal democracy and constitutionalism.

Fourth, after the fall of Ibáñez in 1931, army officers continued to engage in intrigue and plotting for nearly fifteen months. In this last period the prestige of the armed forces suffered greatly. Plotting and effecting the overthrow of three administrations within three months in 1932 assumed an almost Parnassian quality and showed little orientation toward national issues at stake during the previous three epochs.

It is in the second of these clearly delineated periods that an aberrant civil-military relationship came to fruition. In the 1925–27 period the leaders of the Chilean state within the state were not concerned with the classic freedom from budgetary powers of parliament or with the refusal to accept democratic controls. Their concept hinged upon a refusal to accept what they considered to be an outmoded form of democracy per se. They adopted such a stance in order to see to it that a new form of democracy be realized in state and society. More than a mere withdrawal of "the most vital military matters" from all civilian controls, Chilean political officers desired to alter the very basis of those controls by changing the form of civilian administration. They partially achieved this in September 1924 when Alessandri agreed (temporarily) to designate only military men as war and navy ministers.

These politicomilitary aspirants adhered to no ideology; as politicomilitary participants they had no programmatic approach to reform. They paid prime allegiance to Chile, not to the parliamentary system of government or its adherents; not to Alessandri, its leading foe, or his civilian colleagues; not to any political party or coalition, social sector or economic group. In word and action they paid allegiance to the nation.

Only twenty-five years earlier the Republic of Chile was the supreme military and naval power on the Pacific coast of South America. Economically, the country was in the midst of a nitrate boom brought about by the successful termination of the War of the Pacific against Peru and Bolivia (1879–83). Socially and politically, Chile was stable, its homogeneous society being remarkably free from immobility (by Latin American standards) and its politics modeled after those of Great Britain in a pseudoparliamentary regime.

Within a quarter of a century, however, Chile fell under the influence of army leaders who looked with distaste on politics, believed that serious social problems were going unattended, and realized that the effects of the post-World War I recession had ruined their country's economy. Chilean politics encased in parliamentarism did not prove representative of society in a changing Chile. The country was on the threshold of social change being brought about by urbanization and increasing personnel changes at all levels of government. "Middle-class" and provincial elements were important in politics, but their voices were those of the minority until 1924. The army identified more with new social and political elements than it did with those of the past, but this did not necessarily mean that it would serve their interests.

Chile's crisis of the 1920s was essentially one of leadership. The Chilean advocates of change—who held that government action and/or constitutional reform were necessary for social and economic modernization—were a divided lot. The "social reform" parties, the Radicals and Democrats, were not at all committed to sweeping constitutional reforms proposed by the man they helped elect president in 1920. That man, Alessandri, fervently worked for a return to the presidential system (or at least an executive-legislative equilibrium) through constitutional reform as the way to provide necessary leadership and solutions for national problems. For the first four years of his presidency he failed.

Finally a ray of hope met Alessandri's gaze. In March 1924 he arranged for army officers to oversee congressional elections in certain key districts. It was this maneuver which enabled him to establish a shaky coalition majority in both houses of Congress. The 1924 elections so compromised the army that it was unable to dissociate itself from politics for over eight years. Nevertheless, it was not until early 1925 that the army became a disciplined and united political force.

Involvement of the army in the crucial March elections brought cries of intervention from all quarters. The conservative opposition to Alessandri (composed of Conservatives and many Liberals) accused the army of intervention. Even Alessandri's cohorts were uneasy about military collaboration. When Congress failed to act on Alessandri's legislative proposals, the army, already torn between old and new leaders, reacted. In September 1924, Alessandri left office because of the pressure exerted on him by both elements, and military rule was imposed on Chile. But the high command's answer to Chile's crisis (the provisional junta) was unsatisfactory to those junior- and middle-grade officers who had initiated the pressure tactics on Alessandri and Congress in September.

By January 1925, Chile's new army leaders took the initiative themselves. Led by the Comité Revolucionario (headed by Lieutenant Colonel Carlos Ibáñez del Campo and Lieutenant Colonel Marmaduke Grove Vallejo), they overthrew the interim government headed by General Luis Altamirano. Ibáñez, a cavalry officer, and Grove, an artillery officer, were long-time friends and former colleagues in the Academia de Guerra, Chile's army staff school. The clique of elite officers responsible for important political decisions in the 1925–27 period and during the subsequent presidency of Ibáñez (1927–31) were all products of the "Generation of 1912–14," the last class to enter and leave the Academia prior to the outbreak of World War I. While bent on recalling Alessandri, they let it be known that the army would, by no means, allow a restoration of traditional parliamentary politics. Ibáñez became war minister on January 23 and did not relinquish the post until 1927, when he rose to the Interior Ministry.

The coup met with little opposition except for objections from the conservative anti-Alessandri Consejo Naval, Chile's admiralty, based in Valparaíso. Once this opposition was overcome, however, nothing stood in the way of the president's return.

The next step in ensuring that the army would have its way was the creation of a transition government to administer Chile until Alessandri returned. The transition government was a junta handpicked by Ibáñez and his collaborators. From his desk in the War Ministry, Ibáñez began acting a kingmaker's role even before Alessandri arrived home. He was aided by Grove and another longtime friend and Academia cavalry colleague, Colonel Bartolomé Blanche Espejo, the subsecretary of war. In the hiatus between January 23 and March 20, when Alessandri arrived in Santiago, Ibáñez made several moves designed to strengthen his grip on the army; hence the army's position as a political force.

To preclude intra-army rivalries he transferred loyal cavalry elements from the provinces into Santiago and gave Blanche a free hand to deal with recalcitrant infantry officers who, particularly, objected to the new influence of the cavalry. He transferred the rural carabineros from the Interior Ministry and brought them under control of the War Ministry to eliminate the possibility of any armed conflict between them and the army. Included in all transfers and shifts were key promotions or assignments for Ibáñista officers.

Army influence in restored politics was evident from the outset. Fearing a civilian reaction to military intervention, Ibáñez bluntly let Alessandri know that he owed his reinstatement to the army Comité as much, or more, than to civilian resistance to the Altamirano government. In short, the army still eschewed actual political control, but demanded its just due for allowing Alessandri to finish his term in office.

Alessandri had struggled with Congress since 1920 for constitutional reform to provide a balance between the executive and legislative branches, to reform the Chilean fiscal system, separate church and state, and establish a governmental role in the labor and welfare fields. He realized these goals with the promulgation of a new constitution on September 18, 1925, but not without considerable help from the army. Though written by civilians, it is doubtful that the Constitution of 1925 would have become a reality without military pressure. It is doubtful if that military pressure could have been applied had Ibáñez and the new leaders not taken an adamant stand on the need for reform.

Doubtless, Chile would have been provided with a new constitution at this time in its history. The precise time, manner, and form of this provision, however, was dependent on the politics of the army, specifically the politics of the war minister, Ibáñez.

Ibáñez and Alessandri clashed numerous times during the winter of 1925, during and after the constitution-making process. In May and June the nitrate port of Iquique was convulsed by continuous labor agitation. Ibáñez ordered carabineros to forcibly break up demonstrations in which the Red flag was shown and refused to rescind the order when ordered to do so by Alessandri. Ibáñez received numerous telegrams congratulating him for maintaining order and discipline, but Alessandri accused him of aiding the forces of reaction and violating civil liberties. When demonstrations turned to violence, Alessandri ordered General Florentino de la Guarda, commandant of the First Division, to crush resistance to the government and placed the provinces of Antofagasta and Tarapacá under a state of siege and martial law. Guarda carried out his order to the letter and tried all agitators as "Communist revolutionaries." Concomitantly, rumors circulated in Santiago that Ibáñez had political ambitions. These rumors were summarized ably in official dispatches written by U.S. Ambassador William Miller Collier. Alessandri's enforced reliance on the army as an internal police force and rumors of a political future for the army's chieftain led to an Alessandri-Ibáñez estrangement and made the army even more a political force.

On September 29 a group of party and independent leaders presented Ibáñez with a petition requesting his declaration of intent. Ibáñez accepted the petition and declared his candidacy. The next day the cabinet resigned en masse, a customary act when a minister of state became a candidate. But the war minister's name was missing from the list of resignations. When Alessandri demanded his resignation, Ibáñez refused in an open letter to the president published October 1. Referring to himself as "chief of the revolution," he stated that his tenure in the cabinet was vital to the maintenance of public order. He then informed Alessandri that as the only cabinet member in service, his signature had to appear on any executive decree. Alessandri's response to this was his own resignation and transfer of the government to Luis Barros Borgoño.

The obdurate stand of Ibáñez in the face of Alessandri's demand for his resignation has been interpreted as evidence of his own presidential ambitions. Whatever his personal ambitions may have been at this point, they were frustrated.

Reaction to the Ibáñez-Alessandri showdown came from both the military and the civilian realm. An ill-conceived putsch attempt of October 3 failed to restore Alessandri, but some of the political leaders who petitioned Ibáñez on September 29 now expressed doubts about his motives. Further, there was military pressure exerted on him to bow out of the incipient presidential contest in favor of a civilian unity candidate. Admiral Juan Schroeders, director general of the navy, and Inspector General Navarrete both urged him to do so. Just four days after Alessandri resigned, party leaders agreed to support a colorless aristocrat, Emiliano Figueroa Larraín of the Democratic Liberal party. Ibáñez promptly withdrew his candidacy; so did the Radical Quezada.

Clearly, the impact of the military on Chilean internal affairs depended on the actions of Ibáñez. Equally clearly, the political effectiveness of Ibáñez and his cohorts depended on their control (or lack of control) of the army. Ibáñez's ambivalence during October reflected the delicate politicomilitary position into which the perhaps overhasty "acquiescence to a presidential draft" had temporarily lodged him. He stated that Figueroa was a reactionary. When José Santos Salas announced as a candidate of the Republican Social Union of Chilean Wage-Earners (Unión Sociale Republicana de Asalariados de Chile, or USRACH), Ibáñez supported him. Then he changed his mind on Figueroa; finally, he called for postponement—but not cancellation—of the elections. The elections were held as scheduled, with Figueroa the victor.

Congressional elections, held a month later, resulted in gains for the reform parties, the Radicals and Democrats; but the new leaders of Congress showed no immediate willingness to yield to presidential prerogatives established in the new constitution, and President Figueroa showed a similar lack of will to exercise them. This dual unwillingness to adjust lasted throughout 1926 and served to renew military doubts about the viability of Chilean liberal democracy.

That this attitude became dominant in the army, and then the navy, can be seen in the gradual reestablishment of Ibáñez's strong position during 1926. From the nadir of October 1925, Chile's war minister rose to a new zenith by February 1927. Figueroa retained him in the cabinet, for it was apparent that he was less a threat if kept inside the government. The state and the state within remained in conjunction once normal constitutional processes were restored and extraordinary conditions ceased to be. Because of this, military influence continued to grow.

Politics drifted to the right during 1926, but it was not until April that Ibáñez showed his obdurate side again. On April 16 he addressed the Chamber of Deputies, whose presiding officer, Conservative Rafael Luis Gumucio, the editor of *El Diario Ilustrado*, was an outspoken critic of the army since the overthrow of 1925 and opposed the new constitution. Ibáñez debunked charges that there was new plotting in the army and defended the army's (and his) actions since 1924. He said that military men were concerned about the nation's postwar difficulties and characterized the army's role since September 1924 as one of a national institution which acted for the good of the country, not for any single political faction. He reminded the deputies of the army's role in securing legislation long stalled in Congress and in the constitution-making process. The war minister concluded by stating that if Congress could not carry on the work begun by the military, the military might be forced to assume the burden.

The April 16 confrontation did nothing to bring about executive-legislative harmony; if anything, it exacerbated an already existing conflict. During the Chilean winter of 1926, the Alessandri-Congress impasse of 1920–24 was replayed with new personnel. Administration spokesmen were heckled in the Senate and Chamber, and Radicals and Conservatives refused to compromise with the executive branch on any major items of legislation. Meanwhile, Chile's economic situation continued to deteriorate. By the time Congress adjourned for the September 18 independence festivities, the Radicals led by Senate president Enrique Oyarzún and party president Pedro Aguirre Cerda had broken all relations with the administration. The Radical party, receptive to social and economic reform, would not

support measures introduced by an administration it considered reactionary and would not cooperate with it even in the face of growing pressure from Ibáñez.

Ibáñez accused the Chamber and the Senate of irresponsibility
and lack of concern for national needs. These, he claimed, made the
people susceptible to extreme leftist propaganda. He closed by challenging the right of senators and deputies to criticize the army, in or
out of congressional session. In late October 1926, Chilean politics
entered a new crisis stage.

For six weeks Chilean politics remained static, and relations between Ibáñez and the parliament continued strained. On November 13, Chile's emerging strongman tried a new tactic; he demanded
that the cabinet be reconstituted because it had proved powerless to
cope with Congress, unable to realize its reform programs, and incompetent in dealing with the Communist menace. Ibáñez turned his
attention temporarily from the legislative to the executive branch.
The cabinet resigned en masse on November 14; Ibáñez resigned in a
separate document, but in his quest for a successor, Figueroa met
with no success. So solid was Ibáñez's position by this time that no
officer would accept the War portfolio. A new cabinet (with Ibáñez
retaining his post) was sworn in on November 18. At this point, the
traditional Chilean civil-military relationship inverted.

Carlos Ibáñez del Campo attained an "unassailable position" in
November 1926, a position which allowed him a free hand to represent the interests of the state within the state and of the tight clique of
staff officers who had aligned themselves with him in January 1925
before the civil authorities of Chile. This "unassailable position" was
enhanced in January 1927 when leaders of a new naval reform movement appealed to him for support. When Ibáñez feigned ignorance of
the navy affair, the new interior minister, Manuel Rivas Vicuña, resigned in disgust. On February 9, 1927, President Figueroa appointed
Ibáñez interior minister and allowed him to form a new cabinet.

In February 1927 the Chilean state within the state ceased to be,
for its leader had become a political figure with civil authority. Within
two months of his appointment to the Interior Ministry, Ibáñez became vice president when Figueroa took a leave of absence for "personal reasons." On May 5, Figueroa officially resigned; and on
May 22, Ibáñez was elected to the presidency. The Chilean army elite,
whose advocacy of social, political, and economic reform and whose
hostility toward traditional liberal democracy were first made obvious in the crisis of 1924 and the overthrow of 1925, had succeeded in
imposing its version of reform and democracy on the state. Once this

was done military influence continued, to be sure, but in a slightly less obvious manner until the desperate days of 1931–32.

No valid appraisal of modern Chilean democracy can be made without bearing in mind the impact of the military on the internal affairs of Chile from 1924 to 1932. No valid appraisal of that octennium can be made unless the 1925–27 period is understood, for it was in that period that the Chilean army figuratively marched the nation toward reform and provided the necessary national leadership to do so.

CHAPTER 9

The Military in
Peruvian Politics, 1919–45

In 1919, Augusto B. Leguía launched his campaign for the presidency against Antero Aspíllaga, a large landholder from the north who was backed by outgoing president José Pardo and the Civilista party. The Pardo administration, however, had lost a great deal of prestige due to its bloody repression of the general strike, which had been called to demand an eight-hour day. Moreover, the traditional oligarchy was in decline, with the general populace completely opposed to it, and Leguía easily won the army-supervised elections. It was rumored that the government would refuse to accept the election results, so Leguía immediately began to conspire.

He searched for a "man on horseback," making offers to various officers with all the savoir faire he had learned from his years of business experience. Finally, he obtained the support of an officer of the Palace Guard who promised to open the doors of the National Palace at an opportune moment.

The army had seen Leguía win at the ballot box, but more importantly they had seen Pardo cut the military's share of the national budget from 25.21 percent in 1915 to 17.87 percent in 1919. Thus, they quickly decided to support Leguía, who wielded a chauvinistic slogan: "Recover the Bluff of Arica," which Peru was forced to surrender to Chile in the War of the Pacific.

In the early morning hours of July 4, 1919, the Lima garrison revolted, arrested President Pardo, and put Leguía into power. Leguía entered the palace accompanied by the legendary Andrés Cáceres, symbol of the resistance against the Chilean invasion and principal guarantor of Leguía's future military policy—the recovery of Tacna and Arica.

Despite the fact that he was a civilian, Leguía quite frankly initiated a new militarist and dictatorial period in Peru, a period that had its antecedents in the insurrection of February 4, 1914. Now the term *militarism* referred not only to specific military governments but also to military influence in a nation's politics and to the use of the military as a tool for capturing and maintaining power.

Leguía gained the presidency by means of a military coup. He had himself reelected twice without any popular backing, relying instead on the exclusive support of the armed forces, and succeeded in remaining in power against the popular will for eleven years (the *Oncenio*). The Leguía government paid very little attention to the army as an institution, but it did obtain the individual support of many officers, due principally to the concessions and gifts provided them. Military discipline kept the remainder in line. By carefully selecting loyal officers and giving them key posts, Leguía was able to elude all kinds of dangers and even to control the discontent within the army's own ranks. . . .

As a means of rewarding the sergeants who took part in the July 4 coup, Leguía promoted them to officers, thereby violating the Promotions Law. He did the same for all the officers who had participated in the barracks revolt. The process of demoralization of the army, begun by Benavides in 1914, was accelerated by Leguía's 1919 action. The illegal promotions caused a profound disquiet among military officers. Those who had been so promoted were nicknamed "horse thieves" and were looked down upon, but since they enjoyed official approval, those officers continued their careers undaunted. Not a few achieved high rank in the officer corps, and a few even succeeded in donning the embroidered uniform of a general.

Leguía then was responsible for reimplementing the system of paying for political favors with military promotions, a throwback to the previous century. A popular joke held that military officers were like gasoline—sold by the gallon. [*Galón* in Spanish means both gallon and galloon braid.] The loss of prestige engendered by this caustic joke lasted for a very long time. The army, made up of true professionals, was contaminated by the "horse thieves," who, since they were regime men, were given the highest positions. The other officers, either through discipline or prudence, obeyed these new officers, thereby giving the impression that the entire army supported the Leguía regime, which quickly changed into a dictatorship. Many officers, who had never had much moral stature, accommodated themselves easily to the system of offering their political allegiance to the dictator in return for being favored in the promotion lists. The sops to the "cooperative" officers also took other forms such as "educational trips to Europe" for undeserving men and salary increases and corresponding perquisites in a period characterized by fiscal penury. Moreover, in addition to military backing, Leguía enjoyed the decided approval of U.S. imperialism, which provided him with numerous loans.

In spite of the unconditional allegiance which the army gave to the dictator, it received very little in return, except for the gratuities offered to selected military personnel. Indeed, Leguía even tried to diminish the importance of the army. In order to create a military equilibrium and counterbalance the army, Leguía organized the Guardia Civil (Civil Guard), granting to the officers of the new institution the same prerogatives, remuneration, and even the same uniforms as army officers. The Guardia Civil even succeeded for a time in having more regular troops than the standing army.

It seems that the military officers of that period were not concerned with the state of the army. They received promotions and stipends, and they did not ask for more. Leguía neither acquired new armaments nor increased the size of the army nor tried to reorganize and modernize it. When Leguía came to power he found a military budget which absorbed 17.87 percent of the national budget. In the first year, he abruptly increased it to 22.1 percent but then steadily decreased it to 17.59 percent by 1930, the year he was overthrown. The budget of the Ministry of Government and Police, on the other hand, rose from 807,234 Peruvian pounds in 1919 to 2,090,896 pounds in 1930, a threefold increase.

Leguía did more for the navy than he did for the army, acquiring four submarines. He also supported the air force, purchasing a number of planes and founding the Palmas Aviation School. Leguía named his son Juan Leguía to be commander of the air force, with the rank of colonel even though his only qualifications were his relationship to the president and the possession of a private pilot's license from England.

Though Leguía was not a military caudillo, militarism dominated the period. The army principally, but also the other military services, acquired great political importance, with the opinions of high-ranking officers carrying more weight than those of a senator or minister. Nevertheless, that was the period in which they invented or reactivated the slogan: "The military should not intervene in politics." The intention was not to remove officers from politics, but rather, since it was now "illegal" to play politics inside the army, to give those officers loyal to the regime a better opportunity to impose their will.

It was said, as it always has been, that an officer was playing politics when he uttered one critical word against the government. On the other hand, he was applauded for attending "official receptions" in order to praise whatever action the government had taken.

Thus, eulogizing what the government had done was not "playing politics," according to that curious regime logic.

To maintain his regime, Leguía depended on the continued support of the military and the availability of foreign loans, the combination of which created a false impression of internal tranquillity and economic prosperity. The economic crisis of 1929, however, decisively brought to a close the "Leguía Century," which had lasted eleven years. The leader of the revolt was Lieutenant Colonel Luis M. Sánchez Cerro, a man with a reputation for both bravery and conspiracies and a captive of the intellectual bourgeoisie of the provinces. He was the commander of a sapper battalion in Arequipa, and that became the core of the military uprising.

Once the Arequipa revolt was known, the government adopted the necessary measures to put it down; but the economic crisis had undermined the regime, and the army found itself morally defenseless, with its high command in crisis because of the prolonged support it had lent to the dictatorship. In addition, popular pressure against the regime was mounting, and antiregime propaganda by the oligarchy became insistent.

At the beginning, Sánchez Cerro enjoyed authentic popular support and the unanimous backing of the citizenry. Of a decidedly mestizo background, in fact, a *cholo*, the insurrectionist of Arequipa could have become a true caudillo by virtue of his great charisma, his personal valor, and the fervor he was able to awaken in the masses; but he lacked political experience, he lacked a coherent ideology, and he fell victim to vanity.

An analogous thing happened to Luís Carlos Prestes in Brazil. The "Knight of Hope" roamed all over Brazil fighting against the regular army and defeating it in more than one hundred battles over a two-year period, but never found the road to attainment of his ideals. But then it is necessary to put that into proper perspective. Prestes, an army captain, was a legitimate *tenente*, a member of the *tenentismo* movement, an expression of Brazilian militarism, yes, but a progressive militarism which arose in defense of the people's rights. Prestes was the heir of Marshal Hermes da Fonseca, who had tried to stop the army from shooting at the population of Pernambuco (see Chapter 7).

Sánchez Cerro, on the other hand, lacked the democratic "pedigree" of which one could be proud. His predecessors had only fought for their own interests at the beginning and for the interests of the oligarchy afterwards; his successors did not do anything except shoot at the populace until a new type of militarism arose in Peru in 1962.

During the Sánchez Cerro period, militaristic attitudes prolifer-
ated to the extent that they assumed the characteristics of an epidemic. In the lapse of one month, six military uprisings broke out. At
one point there was a government in Lima and another in Arequipa,
and five different juntas followed in quick succession. The period
compared favorably with the most tumultuous times of the past
century.

Sánchez Cerro was elected president and took office on December 8, 1931. Though he failed to remain in power (he was assassinated in 1933), he did succeed in consolidating a third period of
militarism in Peru. Except for a brief period ruled by a civilian-led
junta, military regimes controlled the destiny of the nation throughout the 1930s. From 1948 to 1956 there was another military dictatorship, and two administrations of Manuel Prado (1939–45, 1956–62)
were contrary to the popular will, being maintained only by the armed
forces. In 1962 a new military junta ruled for one year, and in 1968
the armed forces returned to power and have ruled to the present
[1968–1980].

With the death of Sánchez Cerro, the oligarchy, terrified of the
social struggle which threatened their interests and powerless to take
power on their own, prudently pulled back and gave power to another general [who] hopefully would know how to defend their interests and continue the struggle against APRA, the political party most
hated and feared by the oligarchy, which was not aware of, or perhaps did not believe in, the venality of its leaders.

The oligarchy did not realize that, through the use of bribes, it
could have converted the APRA movement into the best tool for defending the bourgeoisie, as Manuel Prado succeeded in doing some
years later.

With the body of the tyrant still warm, the Constituent Assembly
elected General Oscar R. Benavides, then inspector general of national defense, as president of the republic to finish Sánchez Cerro's
term. The election violated the newly promulgated Constitution of
1933, which prohibited, in Article 137, the election as president of "a
member of the armed forces on active duty." But the infringement of
the constitution mattered little to them. Stopping the enemy was the
primary concern; putting a halt to the social revolution they saw coming was basic. And Benavides was chosen for the task because of the
qualities he had already demonstrated in the pro-oligarchy coup of
1914. Moreover, his background was completely acceptable.

In 1936, Sánchez Cerro's term ran out, and Benavides was supposed to step down. He called for elections and proposed the candi-

dacy of Jorge Prado for president—as he had done years before with Javier Prado and would do later with Manuel Prado, whom he finally succeeded in putting in power. The Aprista party, incapable of launching a revolution and legally prevented from running its own candidate, threw its support to Dr. Luis Antonio Eguiguren, an honest and upright, but very conservative, lawyer.

As the election returns came in, the bourgeoisie viewed with dread the victory of the Aprista candidate. Benavides, in a totally dictatorial decision, ordered the Congress to annul the elections inasmuch as Eguiguren's victory was due to Aprista votes, that is to say, votes of an "international party" which was prohibited by the constitution from taking part in politics. Benavides also ordered the Congress, whose legal term had likewise ended, to recess and delegate all legislative powers to the president.

Benavides first used these new powers to name three vice presidents: General Ernesto Montagne as first vice president, General Antonio Rodríguez as second vice president, and General Federico Hurtado as third vice president. Benavides had become an all-powerful dictator, and the most curious thing is that his dictatorship was "constitutional" and "legal" in that it had been approved by the Congress which, at least in theory, represented the will of the people. The armed forces not only accepted passively the trampling of democracy and the violation of the constitution, they went even further and congratulated the dictator on his actions and promised him their complete support.

The military dictatorship continued along the road of oppression and bloodshed. To the end of improving on the means of repression, Benavides contracted a fascist Italian police mission which brought and implemented the most modern systems of repression and torture. He created the Assault Battalion, a motorized unit which specialized in breaking up demonstrations, equipped it specially for its mission, and assigned its command to several civilian politicians.

The campaign of Nazification of the army was effectively carried out. Magazines in Spanish, seemingly technical in nature but full of political propaganda, circulated freely. The military services adopted German techniques, and Hitler's rantings were well received within the army, which had always been inclined to applaud certain types of attitudes, particularly when they were backed up with brilliant and spectacular military deeds.

Benavides approved of this campaign of penetration and pushed it throughout the country. The principal newspapers of the capital, although they were enemies of the regime, played the same game.

Carleton Beals lists the headlines of one Lima daily to show how it exalted the totalitarian powers and eulogized their activities. Beals also details the diverse activities of Nazi-fascist penetration in the Benavides dictatorship.

At the same time, APRA, realizing that it could not come to power by means of a popular uprising, turned to the army as a possible vehicle for achieving power. The first officer they approached was General Antonio Rodríguez, second vice president and minister of government in the Benavides administration. Convinced he was the "chosen man" to lead the country out of oppression, Rodríguez and a few friends revolted in the early hours of February 19, 1939, taking advantage of the absence of the president, who was on board a navy ship taking a pleasure cruise off the coast. The conspirators captured the National Palace, something which was relatively easy because of Rodríguez's high position. They then obtained the support of the Guardia Republicana (Republican Guard), which in turn captured the Lima penitentiary and freed all the political prisoners. But then all action ceased.

The movement, well planned from a political point of view, was not equally well planned militarily. The conspirators remained in the palace without taking any further action until the Assault Battalion arrived and killed Rodríguez with a burst of machine-gun fire. The other officers did not know what to do; they were incapable of taking any action at all. The Aprista party, which according to the agreed-upon plan should have taken to the streets as soon as the palace was captured, likewise did nothing. The "popular support" offered by APRA never materialized.

From that moment, when they persuaded General Rodríguez to revolt, the Apristas have continued to interact with military officers. The antimilitarist party that APRA originally was henceforth had to praise the generals, apparently submit itself to their will, and approve of army intervention in politics. APRA has openly urged the armed forces to leave their barracks and take power, many times begging that they do so "in defense of the constitution." Aprista newspapers, pamphlets, and speeches are full of such calls.

Thus, the militarism that had long counted on the complacency and tolerance of the oligarchy, then on the consent of the rich bourgeoisie, henceforth could count on the support and cooperation of a party which called itself "antimilitarist" and "of Marxist extraction," and which was popularly based even though it was directed by a sector of the petit bourgeoisie.

Benavides was president on three occasions: in 1914, when he took power by force; in 1933, when the Congress gave it to him; and in 1936, when that same Congress extended his term. In none of these cases was he elected by the people, nor did he ever enjoy any popular support. Benavides never counted on any party to back him nor did he try to organize one. It was enough that the armed forces supported him, together with his own background and experience as a dictator.

These were the times in which Hitler and Mussolini shone like stars of the first magnitude in the world arena. These were the times in which a Peruvian author wrote: "We are walking triumphantly on top of the decaying body of the god of liberty." These were the times in which dictatorship was considered to be the best system of government ever invented by man and democracy only an obstacle to the progress of civilization. To imitate those men of the Old World was the dream of all the apprentice dictators of Latin America.

But Benavides demonstrated that he was not an apprentice; his period of apprenticeship had already passed. He was a man of his time, a dictator in every sense of the word. He was also the last great man of Peruvian militarism.

Despite the fact that he was a military man and had governed with the exclusive support of the armed forces, Benavides reduced military expenditures during his administration from 24.11 percent of the national budget to 21 percent, increasing instead expenditures on public works and social programs.

However, there were several reasons why the military dictator did not give much importance to the armed forces. Not one of the Aprista conspiracies against his government ever crystallized; all were smothered at the outset, so he never had to call upon the armed forces. In order to sustain his slogan of "Order, Peace, and Work," in order to put down uprisings, and in order to uncover conspiracies, Benavides never had to go beyond the police, particularly the investigative police and his own well-paid secret police. The armed forces served only as guarantors of the stability of the dictatorship, not as an active instrument of repression.

The recurrence of militarism in Peru with the coup of Sánchez Cerro and its consolidation under Benavides were not isolated incidents in Latin America. On the contrary, they constituted what we might say was characteristic of the period. During these years, there were only four countries ruled by popularly elected civilians: Colombia, Uruguay, Chile, and Costa Rica.

Europe was dominated by Hitler, Mussolini, Franco, and Salazar—four dictators backed by their respective armed forces. The dictatorship of Stalin in the Soviet Union completes the picture of an epoch that was characterized by the crisis of bourgeois democracy on a worldwide scale.

In 1939, Manuel Prado became president of the republic. APRA came out of hiding, the Aprista prisoners were set free, and there was a type of undeclared amnesty. It was not what APRA wanted, however, for semilegality hardly suited them. Prado did not fulfill his part of the political bargain, and APRA moved into open opposition and subsequently back into hiding.

The Prado government was constitutional in origin, but it lost its claim to constitutionality by violating statutory guarantees. The armed forces, in obedience to that same constitution, had to defend the government. It is said that the Prado government was oligarchical and consequently the military supported the oligarchy. This is true, but it is also true that the army, according to the constitution, does not question; it only obeys. It could also be said that if the oligarchy is in power, the armed forces are not responsible, but rather the people who elected it. Nevertheless, the army did uphold that tyrannical regime.

On the one hand, the armed forces were accused of collaboration with tyranny, and, on the other, they were urged to revolt. APRA did both at once. In some clandestine publications, APRA invoked the constitution and reminded the armed forces, with frequent insistency, of their duty to respect the constitution. In other fliers and broadsides, APRA blamed the armed forces for the state of the country. At the same time, Apristas sought contacts with high military officers and tried to conspire for the overthrow of the Prado regime. Those same officers, however, were satisfied with the government and invoked the classic slogan used when they want to remain passive: "We do not get involved in politics."

The Aprista party held a leadership convention in 1942 and among other things issued a "Political Declaration," which held that the Prado regime was carrying out "an antidemocratic policy of persecution of APRA and a policy of denying citizen rights." The party also issued a call to the armed forces to come out in defense of the constitution, an action which "would not constitute subversion of the public order, but rather would mean the preservation of constitutional order and of the democratic norms of the nation which every Peruvian has the civic duty to respect and defend."

But the ranking officers of the armed forces remained deaf to Aprista demands. Only when the party shared power in 1945 did those same officers declare their long-standing sympathy for *Aprismo*. It should be noted, and many observers have already written on the subject, that this phenomenon is common in Latin America. The high command of the armed forces always identifies with the oligarchy that governs their respective nations, while the younger officers, on the other hand, try to get closer to the people and support them in their struggle for social change.

At any rate, the armed forces are constantly pressured by the bourgeoisie to leave their barracks and intervene in the political process of the country. The Aprista party, representing the petit bourgeoisie, acted the same way with the two military strata: officers and enlisted men, and within the first, senior and junior officers. To the first they talked about the necessity of respecting the constitution, of returning to the democratic course, and of fighting against communism, which is to say they emphasized conservative positions.

To the younger officers and to the enlisted men, the Apristas spoke of establishing social justice, of the great changes needed by the country, and of the destruction of the oligarchy. The Aprista preachings had a greater impact among the junior officers than on the senior ones. In addition, the Apristas knew of the honesty of the younger officers, so they talked to them of the fatherland, not of the party, of the people and not of *Aprismo*. What APRA wanted was to take power, but they wanted someone else to do it for them. Therefore, they encouraged the militaristic attitudes of the army. . . .

At the beginning of 1945, the end of the Axis powers was in sight, the fall of German Nazism and of Mussolini's fascism was imminent. The fervent admirers of those ideas in Peru were crestfallen. The generals who before had had no objections to heaping praise on the totalitarian dictators now preferred to turn their attention to the Allied officers and speak of the advantages of democracy, including in that term the Red Army, which had succeeded in resisting Hitler's army.

CHAPTER 10

The Military and Politics in El Salvador, 1927–45

The elections of 1927 deviated from the traditional political pattern. The elite erred in transferring its power to Dr. Pio Romero Bosque, an outsider, for this marked the end of its political control. Faithful to his inaugural pledge, the new president unmuzzled the press, raised the general state of siege, restored constitutional rights, and granted the university autonomy. He declared amnesty, and most political exiles of the previous six administrations returned. Though he had served as war minister (1923–25), Romero Bosque did not hesitate to indict the former president for financial malfeasance. In particular, Romero Bosque accused him of entering into an unwritten agreement with senior officers which transferred funds to the Ministry of War that were officially assigned to other ministries. A three-month investigation failed to uncover proof but did create fear and suspicion in the armed services.

In addition, Romero Bosque initiated a reform of the officer training system and of the laws regulating officer promotion. The efforts of Chilean and Spanish missions had been only partially successful in modernizing the military. Overlapping laws, vaguely written regulations, and inadequate systems of advancement and retirement still prevailed. Part of the problem stemmed from the overabundance of senior officers who had gained their rank and office through service in the campaigns of 1906 and 1907. The lack of a reserve corps before 1921, the absence of a regularized system of promotion before 1913, and the inadequate retirement law of 1916 allowed older, ill-trained officers to establish themselves so firmly in control of the armed services that they remained long after structural reforms had taken place. It was not uncommon as late as 1920 to find regimental commanders sufficiently influential to dictate the selection of their staffs or to move their officer corps with them when they were transferred to another regiment. Graduates of the Escuela Politécnica either attached themselves to one of the provincial military chiefs or found their professional opportunities sharply curtailed. When an insurrection of cadets resulted in the closing of the Escuela Politécnica in February 1922, the integration of new and old officers ceased to be a problem. During the next five years, as civilian influence increased and as old-time officers were retired, El Salvador found itself in the unusual position of having too few officers to direct its military. As a consequence, a new school, the Escuela Militar, was founded in January 1927. Between August 8, 1927, and December 30, 1930, 125 second lieutenants were graduated, and the process of integrating the new with the old began once again.

Much had taken place between the closing of the Escuela Politécnica in 1922 and the founding of the Escuela Militar in 1927 to alter the process of integration. The experiences of World War I resulted in new methods of military organization and a changed view of the role of the officer. The new school, free from the accumulated traditions so burdensome to the old Escuela Politécnica, reflected these experiences. Instruction now emphasized the importance of small-group action directed by individual officers to implement the strategy of high command.

Texts and manuals stressed the need for qualified personnel in the lower echelons of the officer corps and detailed the duties and responsibilities of each rank. Specialization further minimized tradition by establishing for each grade a prescribed program of study. The objects were to ensure recognition and respect from superior officers as well as those of inferior rank and to destroy the tendency to equate senior rank with superior knowledge in all fields of military activity.

Opposition to Romero Bosque's military reorganization was inevitable. On December 6, 1927, Colonel Juan Aberle and Major Alfaro Noguera took possession of the capital's central police barracks in an attempt to force the president's resignation. Poorly planned and executed, the uprising was quickly repressed. The following April, a group of senior officers protested the new promotion laws and threatened to withdraw their support of the government. Romero Bosque responded by transferring all the conspiring officers to regiments of unquestionable loyalty. However, the maneuver did not hush rumors that the protest was aimed at the president's overall civil-military policy rather than at the specific issue of promotion. Another source of irritation was the resignation of the highly respected minister of war, Dr. Alberto Gómez Zárate, and the appointment of Romero Bosque's son to that high post.

A further cause of dissatisfaction with the new administration was Romero Bosque's lack of concern over the growth of left-wing extremist groups. By mid-1930 terrorism in the rural areas had reached alarming proportions, and confiscated propaganda indicated that it was being initiated and directed by a hard core of foreign Communists. Ranking officers claimed that it was impossible to maintain order in an atmosphere of governmental indifference and requested that Romero Bosque take a strong stand against all subversive activities. He replied in August by ordering the expulsion of all foreigners found "employing Communist subversion." A request to use army troops was denied, and the National Guard continued to carry the responsibility for rural order.

Clearly, the relationship between the military and the government, essentially static for thirteen years, showed signs of fundamental change during the presidency of Pio Romero Bosque. Wisely avoiding a direct challenge to the older officers whenever possible, the president undermined their power by establishing the Escuela Militar and rewriting the promotion laws. Also, he assured the advancement of junior officers by insisting upon the strict application of the new law of officer retirement. That he was successful in maintaining junior officer support is evident in their attitude toward the presidential campaign of late 1930 and the election of early 1931.

To crown his achievements in the area of civil liberties, Romero Bosque guaranteed that his successor would be the choice of the people. The three days of balloting in January 1931 represented the first free presidential elections in the nation's history. In response to the presidential orders, officers took up positions in each population center to act as observers and coordinators of the balloting. Other military personnel formed an election center in the presidential palace to register calculations as the votes were telegraphed from outlying polls. Everything seemed to suggest that Romero Bosque had succeeded in his policy of military reorganization.

On March 1, 1931, labor candidate Arturo Araujo was sworn into office on the basis of a clear victory at the polls. Proposing broad social and economic reforms, the wealthy engineer and his supporters had barnstormed the country in an unprecedented fashion, promising land to the peasants and the elimination of taxes. The day after Arturo Araujo moved to the presidential palace, his supporters began forming queues outside in the hope of collecting their share of the promised land. Each day the crowds came and were turned away, and each day the newly elected president lost support.

To be sure, the troubles that marred Araujo's nine-month administration were not all his own doing. The Great Depression affected the entire nation as the bottom fell out of the coffee market. Conditions of the workers, instead of improving as Araujo and his party workers had promised, became worse. Incidents of violence broke out everywhere.

The new president's handling of the military was uncommonly harsh. In February a group of officers gathered in the Círculo Militar to draft and sign a memorandum asking Araujo to abolish certain injustices which existed in the armed forces. Their demands were simple and direct: first, that pay be equalized among both officers and enlisted men of all fourteen departments; second, that the military be paid on a monthly instead of a daily basis; and third, that pay be received during the first days of each month. When the memorandum was placed in front of Araujo, he praised it but failed to put its suggestions into practice.

In the month of July, another incident increased tensions between the army and the government. Araujo ordered the eleven officers enrolled in the medical, engineering, and law schools of the National University to resign their commissions and remain as students or leave the school for posts in active service. As officers, stated Araujo, they were part of the military profession and had no place in a civilian program of studies.

Although the above-described incidents are admittedly isolated, they do point out some of the reasons for the growing resentment felt by many army officers toward the Araujo administration. They also reveal the new president's incapacity to understand the military's political role during the preceding eighteen years. Consequently, when the government sharply reduced the military budget in August and called for the elimination of the positions of a number of officers who were on the payroll but who had not actively served for years, it did so in a climate of suspicion. Though eventually rescinded, the order irreparably damaged civil-military relations, and plans for a revolt were soon under way.

Worst of all, Araujo neglected the first requisite for a Latin American president, which is to assure prompt payment of the military. From September through November 1931 officers in every department went without their salaries. Then, on November 30, after a series of appeals, Araujo promised that the government would pay all salaries. The promise, however, was broken, and a revolt began two days later.

Araujo was a political newcomer without firsthand knowledge of the power relationships developed since 1913. Incapable of exerting informal influence like his predecessor, Araujo relied upon formal patterns of authority that had remained largely unchanged and ignored since the nineteenth century. As a result, officers in revolt in December 1931 justified their actions not only on grounds of public discontent with Araujo's administration but also on grounds of preservation of their institution.

In addition, because of grave economic hardships, the frequency of peasant uprisings increased. The military's inability to quell rural violence placed the army in a poor light. Newspaper articles questioning the capabilities of the army began to appear in early 1931, and civilian criticism mounted. In defense, the officers claimed that the administration's failure to curb Communist infiltration and the imposition of restrictions upon the military made it impossible for them to act decisively. Given the freedom to consider the situation strictly in military terms, they argued, the army could quickly restore peace and order.

On the second day of the revolt, the Military Directorate transferred full executive powers to the vice president, General Maximiliano Hernández Martínez, who had been released the previous day, December 3, after having been held prisoner in Fort El Zapote since the early hours of the revolt. Contrary to popular opinion, the vice president had not taken part in the planning of the revolt. The directorate made the decision only after careful deliberation with prominent lawyers. As is commonly the case following the establishment of a government by force, those in command saw the need to legitimatize their powers. Legitimacy, they reasoned, would ensure recognition as well as cause dissident elements to hesitate before acting against the new regime, hence the appointment of Hernández Martínez to administer a caretaker government. The directorate, however, retained the power to make military appointments until its disbandment on December 12.

A worrisome issue for the new government was the question of diplomatic recognition. The United States, initiator and major supporter of the Treaty of Washington of 1923, viewed the new government with suspicion. Specific criteria as to the manner in which a revolutionary government must proceed when organizing itself had been agreed upon. The U.S. State Department immediately requested its minister to Colombia, Jefferson Caffery, to go to El Salvador to study the situation. Since Hernández Martínez had been a part of the overthrown government, Caffery concluded that the government would require a new president if it expected to comply with the treaty of 1923 and thus gain recognition. Generally, civilians found this position unacceptable. Some Salvadorans argued that the treaty was not applicable, since their National Assembly had withheld ratification of various clauses of the 1923 treaty, particularly those clauses relating to the functions of the vice president of the republic. *El Espectador* viewed the problem in another way:

> The movement of the second should neither be classified as a revolution nor a *Golpe de Estado*, because in reality it was neither one nor the other. Juridically speaking, its true name or denomination in Spanish political terminology, already generally accepted, is that of *pronunciamiento militar*. This differs from the above types in that it does not include the breaking of Article II of the General Treaty of Peace and Amnesty . . . which is *now being used* to negate the possibility of recognition for the government of Martínez.

Finally, the suspension of diplomatic relations was viewed as a kind of subtle imperialism such as the United States had employed in Nicaragua, and the new president used growing anti-U.S. feeling to enhance his own position. Whereas Hernández Martínez viewed nonrecognition as a source of strength, political opponents saw it as a basic weakness. Liberals hoped that the desire for recognition would compel the new regime to initiate sweeping political reforms and to usher in a period of genuinely democratic government. Revolutionists believed that nonrecognition would sufficiently weaken the government to allow them to establish a socialist government in its place. Consequently, the suspension of diplomatic relations helped to turn sporadic outbreaks of rural violence into a general peasant uprising in the early months of 1932.

The causes of the massive 1932 revolt are not difficult to find. Like most Latin American countries before World War II, El Salvador had for years suffered from a bottom-heavy social structure based upon subsistence and export agriculture. Burdened by economic problems generated beyond the frontiers, the family dynasty sought ways to protect the nation's elite, often at the expense of the lower classes. No pressure groups existed that were willing or able to represent the masses, whose living conditions grew steadily worse.

In 1925, with the assistance of Mexican and Guatemalan agents, the first organized Communist group was established in San Salvador. The following year, under the direction of this group, the Regional Federation of Salvadoran Workers was founded. Not until 1929, however, did labor leaders consider their movement anything but urban, and Communist labor propaganda was confined to San Salvador and other population centers. But after a congress held in the capital in mid-July of that year, labor's platform was redirected to include rural workers. Increasingly, the Federation's publications encouraged the class struggle and emphasized the important role of the peasant.

In late December 1929 leaders of the Federation established the first national Communist Party. Though the labor and Communist organizations appeared to act independently after 1929, their leadership was in fact provided by the same men. The Regional Federation now urged the establishment of worker cells in all factories and places of business, and both organizations broadcast an intense stream of propaganda directed toward the overthrow of the government.

President Bosque's efforts to curb the movement's growth, and the weak opposition afforded by his successor, seemed only to strengthen the labor-Communist alliance and to increase foreign assistance to the movement. Even before the 1931 presidential elections, the movement had won substantial support from intellectuals and workers. However, it was not until the last weeks of Araujo's presidency that a conscious effort was made to infiltrate the military. Two objectives characterized this phase of the movement: first, a broad campaign to subvert the rank and file; and second, an effort to cultivate a hard core of Communists and Communist sympathizers among the officer class. Manifestos now began by addressing the "workers, peasants, and soldiers of the nation" and called for an all-out struggle against the existing government. One circular dated January 14, 1932, reminded soldiers:

> Above all, the soldier is a worker or a peasant whom the rich exploit in factories, shops, and fields. When he is still a youth, he is taken to the barracks where he is forced to bear arms in defense of the wealth which he has produced for the rich as a worker or peasant.
>
> The discontent which the soldier feels in the barracks from the oppression by which he lives is the result of the fact that a soldier, enduring the lies of chiefs and officers, feels that they are his enemies, because the same chiefs and officers belong to the same class which exploited him in the factories, shops, and fields.

Then, on the twenty-first, a sequel was published: ". . . COMRADE SOLDIERS: Don't fire a single shot at the revolutionary workers and peasants. Kill the chiefs and officers. Place yourselves under the orders of the Comrade Soldiers who have been named Red Comrades by this Central Committee." Loyal officers soon grew aware of the deep inroads being made in the ranks of the military. In some instances, soldiers went to their superiors with reports of Communist activity. In one case, a report by an enlisted man led to the discovery and elimination of a plot to assassinate all the commissioned officers of a barracks and to use the military arms to equip a civil-military "Red Army."

Despite precautions, barracks revolts did break out and had to be quelled by force. After one such outbreak, in the First Regiment of Cavalry, the government declared a state of siege in six of the fourteen departments, restricted the press, and ordered the arrest of the directors of the Communist mouthpiece, *Red Star*. The hardest blow to the movement, however, came with the execution of Agustín Farabundo Martí on February 1, shortly after his arrest for the third time. Without his leadership, and with the capture of a number of his lieutenants, the rebel organization broke into discordant factions. Without leadership, peasant bands struck out in a wanton and blind destruction of anything resembling the traditional order.

Under the guise of meeting a national emergency, President Hernández Martínez replaced civilian bureaucrats with military officers at both the national and provincial levels. Little objection was heard. In an article entitled "Para que el pueblo sepa y no se confié," a student publication boldly noted that the majority of public administrative offices had been filled with military officers: "assaulted," in a word, "by a pack of robbers." But such sentiments never reached the regular press.

In addition, the conflict demanded the utilization of a large share of the nation's armed services and provided a long-needed outlet for the officers' military desires. The majority of officers had seen no previous field service, and they eagerly looked forward to the opportunity to direct military action. Furthermore, those who served best proved by their actions a willingness to support the new regime. Officers who opposed the December coup and who failed to make their peace with the new government were eliminated as burdensome baggage in the drive for order.

Hernández Martínez's government, as a consequence, emerged from the revolutionary experience of 1932 supported by a more devoted and united armed force than had existed in the nation for many years. In addition, the government could boast having gained the following of most of the urban populations, as well as the wholehearted support of the landowners, some of whom owed their lives to government protection. In late January the government recommended that the

> honorable laboring men of every population center of El Salvador organize themselves . . . into militias patterned after the Italian *Fascio*, the Spanish armed corps (*somatenes*) or the patriotic youth groups of *Acción France*, for the defense at any time of our

families and homes against the deadly and ferocious attacks of the gangs of villains that fill the ranks of the Red Army that hopes to drown in blood the free and generous nation left to us by our ancestors.

Though militias were never established, groups of upper-class citizens of the capital were armed by the military to patrol the streets. On the suggestion of a prominent banker, these citizens were given carte blanche to shoot any "Communist" on sight.

Both in material and in psychological terms, the Communist-inspired revolution of 1932 proved costly. Six population centers, together with the capital, had been affected. So great was the death toll in rural areas, and through mass executions staged in the capital, that the chief of the Department of Sanitation feared a major epidemic would result from the slowly decomposing bodies. By the end of January, the number of deaths had risen to the point where burial became impractical, and the chief of operations ordered the incineration of bodies. Night after night San Salvador was disturbed by the rumble of military trucks carrying the captured into the city and by bursts of machine-gun fire as "justice" was hurriedly rendered. It remains impossible to render an accurate count of the number killed during January and February of 1932. Estimates as high as twenty-five thousand are not uncommon.

By mid-February, the country was beginning to return to normal. Clearly, the new regime was in firm command and further displayed its strength and character by naming three army officers as president designates. To remain in opposition to or moderate toward government policy was impossible. All adversaries were labeled Communist or Communist sympathizers. Opportunity for the development of loyal opposition did not exist.

Despite the passing of more than five decades, horrifying details of terrorism still remain clear in the minds of many El Salvadorans, and fear of a similar occurrence has in part shaped the legislation and policies of governments ever since 1932.

By dealing successfully, if brutally, with the question of disorder, Hernández Martínez acquired the right to advance the process of militarization. The waning of antimilitary sentiment, which had been growing under Romero Bosque and Araujo, provided the new president with a free hand to build a loyal military establishment. By spring 1934 little doubt existed as to the character of the regime. Civilians had been gradually replaced by army officers. Three generals added glitter to the cabinet, the treasury minister was a captain, and the director of the government printing house was a colonel. All but one of the governors of the fourteen departments were military men. The subordinate offices of all government branches were filled with loyal officers. The armed forces became the "dictator's praetorian guard."

By fall 1934 the dictator was ready to exhibit his military's strength, and a crowd of some ten thousand witnessed the first modern war maneuvers in the nation's history. A total of two thousand men participated, including cavalry, artillery, and air force. Demonstrations in aerial bombardment, artillery and machine-gun fire, and mass troop movements were conducted. Hernández Martínez proudly unveiled the first domestic-made tank, equipped with six heavy machine guns.

Related to the establishment of military dictatorship was the increasing identity of El Salvador with the Axis powers. The brief experiment in party politics and representative democracy had failed. It was now the military's mission to redeem the country. The economic crisis during Araujo's administration only deepened the military's distaste for political liberalism and heightened its desire for a more elitist form of government. Communist subversion in 1932 strengthened this view. As early as 1936, Salvadoran officers began training in Italy and Germany. Pro-Axis officers held key military and government posts until late in 1941. In March 1938 a contract was signed whereby Italy agreed to supply El Salvador with four Caproni fighters and spare parts in exchange for $200,000 worth of coffee. The following October, six Caproni bombers arrived, as well as three Fiat tanks and three heavy tractors capable of being quickly converted into armored cars. To assist in the training of drivers and mechanics, a group of Italian technicians accompanied the equipment.

Significant too was the appointment of General Eberhardt Bohnstedt as director of the Escuela Militar in 1938. With the rank of colonel in the German army, Bohnstedt replaced Colonel Ernesto Bará, of French descent and a veteran of French campaigns in World War I.

Little doubt remained as to Hernández Martínez's policy when, in June 1940, it was decreed a national crime to express sympathy for the Allied cause. When Italy declared war the same month, three hundred Blackshirts paraded through downtown San Salvador. The unfavorable reaction on the part of spectators was quickly suppressed by the police.

By fall 1940 the nation was clearly suffering from the high price of Axis sympathy. Unreliable trade with Italy and Germany produced severe shortages. Sharply declining exports to the Axis nations and a corresponding decrease in production caused the unemployment of 20 percent of the work force. In the face of growing hostility at home and pressure from abroad, Hernández Martínez reversed his policy by publicly denouncing European totalitarianism and praising the Allied cause in October 1940.

One cause of the change in foreign policy was the sharp increase in military opposition to the Axis powers. Even though officers remained divided on ideological grounds, armament shortages and the unavailability of European matériel made the abandonment of the pro-Axis stance appear to be the most profitable course of action. Furthermore, the United States had clearly shown itself willing to replace Europe as El Salvador's major arms supplier. When Defense Minister General Salvador Castañeda Castro requested thirty-five thousand rifles from the U.S. military attaché in June of 1940, Colonel J. B. Pate informed him that he was confident that a way would be found "to help our exceptionally loyal friends in this matter." Castañeda boasted that his country could raise an army of forty thousand men and added that the armed forces were overwhelmingly in favor of the Allies. It was only a matter of time, he continued, before his government would denounce German and Italian aggression.

Despite a willingness to change his international views, Hernández Martínez remained uniform in his approach to domestic politics. Throughout his rule, the overriding principle was the retention of power. In August 1934 the presidency was transferred to General Andrés Ignacio Menéndez, minister of war, to enable Hernández Martínez to campaign for the March 1935 elections. According to the arrangement, Menéndez's first act was to appoint Hernández Martínez as his minister of war to ensure his own resumption of that office after the election. To mark the occasion, amnesty was decreed for all minor crimes against the state, and sentences were reduced for serious crimes committed by military personnel.

Preparations for Hernández Martínez's campaign began in late 1933, though newspapers were prohibited from carrying political news until December 1934, when the National Assembly belatedly announced the election. Opposition candidates had little time to campaign, and Hernández Martínez was inaugurated the following March.

The 1939 election presented a more difficult problem. Reelection was prohibited by the constitution, and civilian opposition to *continuismo* was widespread. Citizens prided themselves on the fact that no president had held consecutive terms since the nineteenth century. Nonetheless, Hernández Martínez clearly had no intention of relinquishing control, and campaigning for a "reform" of the electoral laws was well advanced by the middle of 1937. Every conceivable device was used to convince the country of the wisdom of constitutional change and the need for Hernández Martínez's reelection. Well-planned campaigns were conducted by the government-controlled radio stations, as well as by the press. Motion pictures of organized demonstrations were employed, and thirty thousand Hernández Martínez supporters were reported to have welcomed convention participants when they convened in November 1938 to write a new constitution. The new constitution, effected January 20, 1939, extended future presidential terms from four to six years, and the convention itself elected Hernández Martínez to a second term. Further, to ensure political order, military courts were granted the right to try all intended or committed crimes against the peace, and additional measures were taken by the Defense Ministry to tighten public surveillance.

No amount of military might or constitutional maneuvering could stay the tide of growing national discontent. The state of siege remained in effect until Hernández Martínez's fall in 1944. Periodic uprisings reflected the profound social and economic changes which had taken place since World War I. Following the trend of the whole of Latin America, El Salvador had become a partially urbanized nation, and by 1936 over a third of the population were city dwellers. This group, cognizant of national events, demanded better living standards and formed a hard core of discontent not easily controlled by oppressive measures. Increasingly, the population realized the need for basic political and economic reform, and few people were willing to accept the world depression as the sole reason for their ills.

Occasional efforts to dislodge the military dictatorship were met with swift military repression. A strong army, a National Guard to control the rural sectors, and a secret police force that was reported to be the best in Central America ensured that revolts rarely went beyond the planning stage. Malcontents had a way of simply disappearing, and every available jail in San Salvador was kept full.

Ostensibly, the Constitutional Assembly which convened in January 1944 assembled for the purpose of amending the constitution to permit the expropriation of German property, but its main business was to alter the election laws to allow Hernández Martínez a fourth term. March 1 marked his inauguration, and the dictator celebrated the event in a gala evening of toasts and well-wishing. Opposition groups, however, concluded that the time to act had arrived.

Leading civilian opponents knew that the foundation of military support constructed by the dictator was showing serious signs of wear. In late 1943, members of the clandestine Acción Democrática Salvadoreña had met with seven junior and senior officers of the army and air force to choose a director for the anti-Martínez movement. Civilians consciously fanned unrest within the army's officer corps by pointing to the inequity of division of spoils and the arbitrary system of promotion. Their hope, of course, was that the overthrow of Hernández Martínez would end personal aggrandizement on the part of all officers. Even the dictator had lost faith in the army's willingness to support him. Despite his efforts to transform the army into a personal guard, every unsuccessful revolt during his administration had included army officers. As a consequence, the dictator increasingly devoted more attention to the other services. After 1937 the air force and National Police received larger percentages of the defense budgets, and the National Guard was given the largest share of the new equipment.

Much of the advantage Hernández Martínez gained by building the National Guard, the National Police, and the air force to offset the army was lost in September 1941, when the government called for the creation of a civilian militia. Fashioned from the membership of Hernández Martínez's Pro-Patria party, this group came to be recognized as a counterbalance to the armed forces. The fact that the civilian militia remained small and poorly armed did not keep it from being a source of concern for all the military services.

Under these circumstances, it was no surprise that when a revolt was staged on April 2, 1944, many of those involved were members of the armed forces. By April 3 all resistance in the capital had been crushed. On the following day, troops under the command of Subsecretary of Defense General Fidel Cristino Garay reestablished government control in Santa Ana, the only place outside the capital to enter into open rebellion.

Though short in duration, the revolt had been costly in lives and property lost. Although sources vary as to the number of fatalities, a cautious estimate would place the total in excess of two hundred. At least half this number were civilians. The worst tragedy occurred when twenty-two truckloads of civilians, heeding the rebel call to arms, were ambushed by troops under the command of General Garay about midway between Santa Ana and San Salvador. Earlier in the day, fire caused by rebel bombs aimed at the police barracks had spread in the downtown area, and two square blocks were completely destroyed. Six planes that had fallen into the hands of rebel pilots were also destroyed. These six, together with three planes that escaped, constituted 75 percent of the planes registered in the country.

Hernández Martínez had been successful in riding out the first stage of revolt, but it appeared that the dictator had lost faith in his capacity to control the nation. Repeatedly in the days that followed, statements from the presidential palace emphasized the return to tranquillity, the insignificant number of "traitors" who had taken part in the abortive revolt, and the fact that the armed forces of the nation steadfastly supported the government. The reign of terror now imposed had all the earmarks of a government uncertain of its ability to remain intact. If there were those who stood in horror of the events of April 2, it was the entire nation that was repulsed by the inhumanity that followed. No sooner had a semblance of order returned than the dictator named a Council of War to judge and prosecute those who had led the rebellion. By its orders, ten officers were executed on the morning of the tenth, whereas nine others were sentenced to death in absentia. Of this number, only two held the rank of colonel and one the rank of general. The following day the executions included the first civilian. To make it clear that continued subversion was futile, the executions were held on a downtown street in full view of the public, and martial law was proclaimed throughout the republic. All newspapers were suspended with the exception of the government-owned *Diario Nuevo* and *El Gran Diario*.

By the last week of April, eighteen more officers and civilians had been condemned or executed, bringing the total to forty-three. Civilian opposition to the regime's heavy-handedness continued to mount. Initially, university students declared themselves on strike in protest to the continued bloodshed. They were followed by secondary students and employees of the banks and commercial houses of the city. By the end of the month, most of the professionals in San Salvador, and many subordinate personnel in several ministries, were staying at home, and the city's activities were slowing to a halt. On the evening of May 5, President Hernández Martínez spoke over the two government-owned radio stations. He lamented the poor coverage by foreign newspapers of the events of April 2 and then announced that the nation was at peace and working, with the exception of the capital, where "seditious elements were carrying on a war of nerves." Even to those in opposition, it was a pathetic speech. It revealed the dictator's resolute belief that the people, in truth, still supported him.

Hernández Martínez had reason to plead. Nothing he had done had persuaded the capital to return to work. That morning, banks had closed their doors. For the fifth consecutive day, jeering, taunting crowds filled the streets, obviously hoping to incite police action. In a last effort to maintain his power, Hernández Martínez gave up hope of regaining the allegiance of the professional and business community and directed his appeal to the workers and peasants. With the assistance of loyal landowners, eight hundred peasants armed with machetes had been transported to the capital on April 6 and quartered in various military barracks. The combination of radio and printed appeals to the lower classes, and the appearance of armed peasants in the streets, aroused memories of the 1932 revolution. These memories were sufficient to inspire grave fears and to prompt some government employees and businessmen to return to work.

Still, the strike continued, and rumors of impending uprisings spread freely through the city. On April 7, Hernández Martínez had called a meeting of his cabinet in the salon of the Ministry of Foreign Relations. The dictator requested a continuation of power until the end of the month. He was certain that order could be restored, and though he admitted opposition by the armed forces, he spoke of the small number involved and the divisions that separated them. Despite his assurances, only the minister of the treasury, Escobar Serrano, agreed. The rest of the cabinet remained silent. That same afternoon, having already resigned himself to abdication, Hernández Martínez called a second meeting which included cabinet members and also a handful of loyal followers. Five designees to the presidency were chosen and their names left with the dictator.

On May 8, Hernández Martínez spoke over the government's radio stations and announced that he was resigning. The following day, as the strike brought the capital to a complete standstill, it was announced that the Legislative Assembly had chosen General Andrés Ignacio Menéndez to succeed to the presidency.

Just prior to this announcement, but anticipating the selection of Menéndez, a group of junior officers had approached General Luis Andreu and proposed that he assume control of a military directorate and thus guarantee continued military control. Andreu, a recognized wheelhorse of the Hernández Martínez regime and probably better informed about the circumstances of the coming selection, refused. It was common knowledge that many junior officers had for years found Menéndez to be too absolutely honest, too much of a disciplinarian, a soldier who would do nothing that did not conform to the strict letter of the military law.

Menéndez, above intrigue and without political aspirations, had probably been selected by Hernández Martínez as a safe compromise. The old dictator favored Menéndez, since he could be trusted to hand over the presidency if Hernández Martínez managed to return. Military equipment had been dispatched to strategic areas throughout the republic. The assignment of devoted followers to the governorships of those areas during the first week of May suggested the use of such equipment to regain the country for Hernández Martínez.

Whether or not Hernández Martínez could regain political control was of little consequence to most senior officers. They had enjoyed extramilitary power and ample budgets too long to take their chances under a civilian regime. The failure of the April 2 rebellion had the effect of cleansing from the military all officers who might have shown a willingness to accept civilian government. The few that escaped execution either remained outside the country or returned in support of Menéndez. As a consequence, liberal civilians urged that the strike continue until fundamental rights were restored and the nation freed of military control.

No one could doubt that the country remained in the hands of the military. Trucks loaded with troops patrolled the capital, and manifestos from the Defense Ministry circulated daily. The only remaining question was whether Menéndez or a military directorate was in charge of the country.

On May 10 the provisional president named his cabinet, which included representatives from the various political factions operating in the nation. At the same time, the National Congress, still dominated by friends of Hernández Martínez, extended amnesty to all political refugees and prisoners. Liberty of the press was reestablished. A manifesto was circulated to the effect that the new chief executive offered his word of honor as a soldier that all "noble aspirations would be sympathetically received" by him and his government.

At the very least, liberal civilians had successfully challenged Hernández Martínez and had introduced a period of expectation and adjustment. However, at best, the nation still remained under military control and still lacked a truly constitutional framework.

Kenneth J. Grieb

CHAPTER 11

The Guatemalan Military and the Revolution of 1944

Under the watchwords honesty, efficiency, and progress, General Jorge Ubico held Guatemala in the firm grip of a highly *personalista* progressive-military dictatorship for thirteen years. The platform of his Liberal Progressive Party emphasized development, and the stern caudillo devoted much of his attention to public works projects, particularly a vast expansion of the transportation and communications facilities. A highly successful road construction program gradually helped create an essential element of the economic infrastructure, opening new areas to settlement and cultivation, while encompassing a greater portion of the population in the money economy. These efforts resulted in a considerable expansion and transformation of the economy during Ubico's thirteen-year rule, with the effects increasing during the later portion of his tenure. This upsurge of commerce naturally brought attendant opportunities for small industry and the service professions, and resulted in the expansion of the government bureaucracy. These factors led to the establishment of a considerable number of middle-level managerial, sales, clerical, and other white-collar positions, which vastly expanded the middle class. The impact of this phenomenon was greatest in the capital, where industry, commerce, and governmental offices were concentrated. Economic development thus greatly enlarged the middle class in the capital, creating a potentially new political force. Since Guatemala was run by and for a tiny oligarchy composed of the military officer caste and the owners of the estates that produced the country's export crops, the regime ignored the newly emergent middle class. Although the economic expansion brought undeniable benefits, the expanding middle class became increasingly frustrated with its systematic exclusion from positions of political power.

Since the army has traditionally constituted one of the principal elements of the power structure throughout Guatemalan history, it is scarcely surprising that General Ubico's regime was military in character. The economic progress he fostered had its price in an immense security apparatus which maintained careful surveillance over all activities. Press censorship stifled criticism, while political opponents were exiled or harassed, and election control assured a subservient Congress. Perceiving that support of the officer caste was essential to maintaining himself in power and as a product of this caste himself a partisan of its predominance, Ubico judiciously cultivated this group to such an extent that his government became increasingly militarized during its protracted tenure. Gradually, officers replaced civilian governors in the provinces, and eventually the posts of *jefe político* and governor became synonymous. This process became more evident during the latter portion of his rule, since the effect was cumulative, as supporters rose to higher rank. By 1944 the Guatemalan army boasted 80 generals to command its 15,000 men. Inevitably these promotions fell to old line, politically appointed officers, but like other benefits of the Ubico regime, these rewards had their price. Since generals considerably outnumbered commands, it became customary for the "surplus" generals who did not occupy active command positions to assemble daily at the National Palace, in the President's outer office, where they awaited the Chief Executive's pleasure. Many of the generals thus became virtual "errand boys" whom Ubico employed to handle any situations that arose during the course of the day. Ubico required complete subservience from his officials, and placed the entire security apparatus under his personal control. The police reported directly to the Chief Executive rather than to the Minister of Gobernación, and the President conferred daily with his Minister of War, an aged officer selected primarily for his loyalty. While promotions and decorations were frequent, Ubico applied his austerity program to the army, with the result that the average conscript was paid a mere $3 per month, and even the generals had to settle for a modest salary of $125, far below the standards of other Latin American armies.

Just as with the economy, part of Ubico's program to strengthen the military sowed the seeds of dissent. In the case of the army, this stemmed from the President's efforts to increase professionalism among the officers through upgrading the Escuela Politécnica, the Guatemalan military academy. At Ubico's personal request, a U.S. Army officer assumed command of the school, and in accordance with Ubico's directive to "make the Escuela Politécnica as near like West Point as was possible under conditions here," stiffened requirements and discipline, introducing a system based on merit. The academy was thus drastically reformed during Ubico's tenure, with a modernized curriculum, a merit system, and a considerable expansion in size. These reforms gradually produced an expanding corps of well-trained, professionalized junior officers. Since they owed their graduation solely to merit, they included some individuals of middle-class origin, thus introducing a new element into the officer corps.

The events of 1944 become understandable only when viewed in this perspective. In both the civilian and the military spheres, the government failed to recognize the situation created by its own programs, and attempted to continue administering the nation as if no changes had occurred. The result was the disaffection of the young professionals in civilian and military life, which increased as the regime clung to office, gradually producing an explosive situation.

A revolt in Salvador, which unseated another long-standing dictatorship during May 1944, increased the tension in Guatemala. The winds of change had swept into a neighboring country, and the parallel between the regime of General Maximiliano Hernández Martínez in Salvador and that of Ubico was obvious. U.S. Ambassador Boaz Long reported that Ubico was disturbed by the Salvadoran turn of events. Significantly, the Guatemalan President was extremely critical of Martínez's attempts to suppress the rebellion, condemning the resulting bloodbath. Ubico stated that such a situation "would not happen" in Guatemala. The success of the Salvadoran uprising emboldened the Guatemalan opposition, and provided exiles with a base of operations on the border. Student leaders promptly announced plans to boycott the June 30 celebration commemorating the founding of the official Liberal Party. In an effort to counteract the discontent, Ubico decreed a 15 percent increase in all salaries to alleviate the pressures caused by wartime inflation, but this token came far too late.

Protests by university students regarding internal campus grievances provided the spark that ignited the volatile situation. A small coterie of law school students had begun meeting several years earlier, and in 1942 had revived the defunct Law Students Association. The Medical Students Association was resurrected at the same time, and other campus elements followed suit. By late 1943 the groups had coalesced to form the University Students Association to coordinate their activities. In June 1944 medical and law students petitioned for the removal of their Deans. To the surprise of all, the government yielded. This unusual gesture was interpreted as a sign of weakness, and campus leaders immediately determined to press for further concessions to gain political leverage. As one of the few organized sectors of the populace, the students constituted almost the only group capable of initiating a challenge to the administration. The fact that a considerable number of the students came from middle-class families denied political power increased their frustration with the regime's rigid control of intellectual activity. With the normal rashness of youth, they were more willing to risk political activity to redress the grievances their parents were content to decry in private. Upon receiving word of the government concession, the University Students Association endorsed sweeping demands for educational reforms and dismissals throughout the entire university and called for a general university strike. Attempting to placate the dissidents, the President's private secretary, Lic. Ernesto Rivas, summoned protest leaders to the palace and offered concessions in return for a pledge to terminate the demonstrations. Sensing their new-found political power, the students refused. Their ultimatum caused Ubico to convene the first cabinet meeting of his thirteen-year regime. The ministers concluded that further concessions would encourage demands by other sectors, and decided to suppress the student factions.

A presidential decree suspending constitutional guarantees, issued in accordance with the cabinet decision, converted the internal campus problem into a national political issue. Despite the government's announcement that the measures were directed exclusively at campus dissidents and its pledge to rescind the decree as rapidly as possible, lawyers and other professional men interpreted the suspension of constitutional guarantees as a general threat. Although student demonstrators surging through the capital were quickly dispersed by troops and police, driving the leaders to asylum in the Mexican Embassy, several small, clandestine associations of lawyers emerged, and promptly marshalled widespread support. By June 24 a student-sponsored general strike, endorsed by some labor groups and a substantial portion of the middle class, brought the capital to a standstill. A group of 311 professional men petitioned the government for restoration of constitutional rights and a general liberalization of restrictions. The demonstrations and the broad support they elicited caught the administration completely by surprise. Responding instinctively with harsh measures, the government decreed martial law, sealed the nation's borders, and rushed reinforcements to the capital, stationing troops at strategic points throughout the city. The regime also adopted the novel expedient of announcing immediate payment of the entire foreign debt, totaling $8 million, to empty the treasury and remove what officials considered a "temptation to the opposition." Even these desperate measures failed to alleviate the situation. While the security forces effectively dispersed large demonstrations, they proved unable to cope with the new tactics that moved small groups of people to the Central Plaza, where they suddenly combined. Army units ringing the palace eventually fired on these mobs, furnishing the movement with martyrs. Passive resistance became the order of the day, in view of the government's preponderance of force, and demonstrations were abandoned in preference for a general strike supported by the capital's businessmen, which paralyzed the city. Militarization of the railroad and transportation workers failed to break the strike. . . . Perceiving that his own continuance in office was impossible, Ubico opted for preserving military control by stepping aside. . . . If the President was to relinquish his post, however, his successor must be someone whose selection would placate public opinion. . . . Consequently, Ubico decided to form a military junta. . . .

Hasty selection of the junta indicated that all concerned considered military control the only important aspect. None of the three [Federico Ponce Vaides, Eduardo Villagrán Ariza, and Buenaventura Pindea] were confidants of Ubico, or had played a pivotal role in his regime. . . . The three were simply available—and that was all that was considered necessary. The generals, collectively, constituted the real repository of the presidency, with the junta officers as figureheads.

Ubico's resignation produced widespread jubilation, but the resulting turmoil, coupled with the relaxation of government controls, merely exacerbated the political crisis. While waiting for Congress to assemble, the junta acted to remove the principal legal irritants by terminating the stringent measures imposed during the outbreak. The decree suspending constitutional guarantees was immediately revoked, along with various other measures generally blamed for the burgeoning inflation, such as restrictions on the sale of agricultural products and the slaughter of cattle. To complete the evidence of change, the military commanders withdrew the troops to fixed positions around the palace and other governmental installations, terminating patrols within the city and abandoning efforts to prevent street demonstrations. These policies were designed to emphasize the end of the Ubico era and create an appearance of revolutionary victory, while masking the army's continued dominance. . . .

Installation of General Ponce as provisional president confirmed the military control, and indicated that the change in government was more apparent than real. . . .

It quickly became apparent that the military was still in control, and governmental transfer resembled a changing of the guard rather than a significant alteration of the power structure. Although a new general occupied the presidential chair, it was still firmly in the hands of a military "strongman." Despite several new cabinet appointments, a substantial portion of the Ubiquista officials continued in office on a "temporary" basis, including such key individuals as Minister of Foreign Relations Carlos Salazar, Military Commander of the Plaza General Rodrico Anzueta, and Private Secretary to the Presidency Ernesto Rivas. Although Ubico had refused to participate in the selection of the junta or the provisional president, once Ponce assumed office, Ubico received a constant stream of visitors at his home, including several members of the government, causing speculation that the ex-president was still in control. While Ubico and Ponce were not on close personal terms, holdover administrators might well have turned to their old mentor for "advice." The former chief executive and his generals had shrewdly created the appearance of yielding to popular pressure, while effectively maintaining power in the hope that this maneuver would placate the discontented masses.

Agitation continued, and although the opposition leaders initially refrained from condemning Ponce, they launched a major effort to organize the masses in preparation for the forthcoming elections. *El Imparcial* bristled with articles relating experiences of individuals imprisoned by Ubico and of students injured in clashes with police during the recent demonstrations, in an attempt to elicit support and sympathy from the populace by emphasizing the harshest aspects of the old regime. Direct criticism of the provisional president was initially limited to editorials urging him to renounce any intention of becoming a candidate in the forthcoming elections, as rumors to this effect were already circulating. Ponce immediately obliged, declaring that he would not enter the elections under any circumstances. The dissidents formed several peasant and labor unions, attempting to channel the widespread popular support into disciplined groups. A plethora of minuscule political movements emerged, with new parties surfacing weekly. American embassy officials prefaced their reports with the comment that the rapid proliferation of parties rendered all analyses transmitted by mail obsolete by the time they reached Washington. . . .

It became obvious to the generals that a mere change of presidents would not be sufficient to enable "business as usual," and that the free rein granted to popular feeling was increasing discontent. The military leaders and the oligarchy had hoped that merely substituting another general for Ubico, and then installing a civilian oligarch as a facade, would calm public sentiment and stifle the surge for social reform. They apparently calculated that removing restrictions would permit a brief orgy of popular enthusiasm which would exhaust itself and dissipate the energies of the opposition leaders. Instead of fading, however, the dissidents continued to gain strength.

With the emergence of an opposition that posed an effective electoral threat, the generals edged toward the familiar tactics of repression. The decision was apparently reached late in August, when American officials learned that a representative of the regime visited Salvador, to confer with military leaders who had regained control of that country after suppressing a similar outbreak. Rumors that Ponce would enter the list as a presidential aspirant increased, and by mid-September many Guatemalans were convinced that the General intended to retain power. Ponce began to sound out the Assembly regarding passage of a constitutional amendment permitting the provisional executive to become a candidate without resigning. Manuel Melgar, the new secretary to the President, summoned the Deputies in small groups, asking them to inscribe their names on lists supporting the constitutional amendment, but encountered considerable resistance. The regime also prepared to employ the rural Indian masses to counter the agitation in the capital. This strategy became apparent when several hundred Indians, armed with machetes and clubs, were transported into the city in government trucks to participate in a national holiday on September 15. They paraded through the streets with photos of Ponce pinned to their clothes, and then were quartered at the government-owned finca "La Aurora" on the edge of the capital for several days. The presence of this group terrorized the entire city. It was evident that the government intended the measure as a warning.

Following these preparations, the Ponce regime began to suppress its opposition ruthlessly. During the latter part of September, a radio station and several newspapers were ordered closed, and attempts were made to persuade others to temporarily suspend operations "voluntarily." On October 1, Alejandro Cordova, the owner-editor of *El Imparcial*, the leading anti-administration periodical, was assassinated by "unknown individuals." The crime occurred a few days after the minister of war summoned him and warned him to cease his attacks on the regime, while offering him a substantial sum of money to close his paper and "take a vacation" until after the election. A few days later, Cordova's successor was compelled to jump out his office window to escape pursuing police, fleeing to the protection of the Mexican Embassy. . . . Some thirty-six hours after the publisher's assassination, ex-president Ubico called at the U.S. Embassy to provide his personal analysis of the political situation. The former executive . . . stated that the situation rendered it essential that Ponce continue in office. The following day, Ponce visited the ambassador, who noted that the provisional president's analysis of the situation was identical with Ubico's. Results of the October 13 elections to fill vacancies in Congress confirmed Ponce's determination to retain power. In the words of the American chargé, the official returns indicated that the government-supported slate "won by a handsome, not to say fantastic, margin, garnering 48,530 votes out of a total of 44,571" ballots cast. Invigorated by its "success," the regime ordered the arrest and deportation of Juan José Arévalo [who had returned from exile in Argentina to become the leading civilian candidate for the presidency with the support of the various revolutionary groups].

The generals were not the only component of the military, however, and the revolutionaries found a fertile field for their propaganda among the disgruntled, professionalized junior officers. The student and middle-class leaders had learned from painful experience that although passive tactics could compel the resignation of the executive, their effects were purely negative. Working outside the power structure, they could exert no influence over the choice of a successor. It was evident to the dissident leaders that the revolution had been aborted by the generals, and that only possession of sufficient force to counteract the army could bring a change in the power structure. Given the realities of Guatemala, this force could come from only one source—inside the very military the revolutionaries sought to overthrow. Consequently, during the weeks following Ponce's installation, the revolutionaries launched a new strategy—seeking to subvert the army from within. They quickly discovered that ample opportunity to split the military existed. Expansion of the Polytechnic School had produced a substantial corps of well-trained, professionalized junior officers, who considered themselves better prepared than their commanders, many of whom had begun their careers prior to the establishment of the military academy, and owed their rank to political maneuvering. The rigidity of the regime and the social system denied the younger officers opportunities they felt they deserved. Since Ubico stressed austerity, military wages were extremely modest. If a general's salary of $125 a month looked meager to the senior commanders when compared to those in other countries, it appeared absolutely princely to the subalterns. The newly commissioned lieutenant found upon completing the arduous course at the academy that his stipend was a mere $24 a month. Naturally the junior officers chafed at such scales. In addition, Ubico was extremely reluctant to send officers abroad for advanced training, thus barring a potential "fringe benefit." Approaching the junior officers coincided with the civilian emphasis on a youth movement. Revolutionary propaganda also stressed the superior training of the junior officers, and the political origins of the generals. Junior officers were informed that Ubico, Ponce, and their cohorts had besmirched the name of the army by corrupt practices, thus reducing its standing within the nation. Finally, the revolutionaries found it necessary to produce a counterargument to military loyalty, which had been instilled in the young officers. In doing so, the rebel leaders ironically were compelled to espouse the theory that the army had a duty not merely to defend the government, but also to uphold the constitution. The concept of the army as the custodian of the constitution was the only possible rationale to counter the military loyalty, as it appealed to the officers' sense of duty. To overthrow a military regime, it proved necessary to propagate the notion that the military was above the government, and had a duty to oust corrupt, unrepresentative, and unconstitutional regimes.

The resulting split in the military ranks proved to be the key to the overthrow of the Ponce regime, which became possible only after the revolutionaries had secured the support of a substantial portion of the army. By October 1944 the American chargé reported that only six of the officers who had graduated from the military academy during recent years were on duty in the capital, and those six included the President's sons. Even with such stringent dispersal of recent academy graduates, the chargé noted "decided mistrust" between those junior officers stationed in the capital, and the senior commanders.

On October 20, a few days after Arévalo and several of his key supporters had issued a manifesto calling for revolt, the Ponce regime fell abruptly when the presidential guard rebelled under the leadership of junior officers. While all other garrisons in the capital initially remained loyal, the government's previous decision to concentrate heavy armaments in the hands of the *guardia de honor* proved decisive, for, in addition to being well supplied with artillery and machine guns, the guard had control of the country's twelve tanks. The revolt was essentially military in character, led by Major Francisco Javier Arana, commander of the tank battalion, and Captain Jacobo Arbenz, who had recently been dismissed from the service. Both Arbenz and Arana had long been considered leaders of the junior officers, and Arbenz had been particularly popular with the cadets while serving as a professor at the military academy. A fierce battle ensued, but government forces were hopelessly outgunned, and the tank battalion enabled the rebel troops to seize most of the capital. Ponce's efforts to borrow weapons and ammunition from neighboring countries proved futile, and a lucky hit by an artillery shell on the magazine of one of the loyal forts completed the debacle. Negotiations were initiated shortly after the fighting began, culminating in the surrender of the government forces. The departure of numerous leaders of the oligarchy for exile, including cabinet members and senior army officers, indicated the scope of the turnover. Unlike the resignation of Ubico, this transition produced a sharp break.

The successful revolt ousted the old military elite, and placed the younger officers in control. The new junta consisted of Major Arana, Captain Arbenz, and a civilian, Jorge Toriello Garrido. Despite the civilian representative, Arana and Arbenz held the effective power. The military regime had been ousted only by a military revolt, and it was replaced by a predominantly military junta, although the latter was pledged to install a civilian, Arévalo, as eventual president. The new junta promptly purged the bureaucracy and the senior army commands to remove adherents of the old regime, thus completing the transfer of power. Of course, the purges also opened places for the young rebel leaders. Military pay was immediately increased substantially. Although the new regime enjoyed considerable popularity, it found it necessary to proceed cautiously, and the junta ruled "with an iron hand in a silk glove." Supporters of Arévalo swept the November Assembly elections, and a presidential ballot was immediately scheduled for December. As expected, Arévalo scored an overwhelming triumph. His installation in office completed the transition begun by the junta.

There was, of course, a price for the support of the young officers, which had enabled Arévalo to take office. Despite the idealistic rhetoric, the leaders of the revolt received the traditional rewards. Arana rose from Major to full Colonel, and Arbenz from Captain to Lieutenant Colonel. Arana also became Minister of Defense, and hence effective commander of the armed forces. The officers and men who had supported the uprising had already received their share—higher salaries, an opportunity to study abroad, and promotions resulting from vacancies created by the purge of supporters of the old regime. More importantly, the new Constitution made the armed forces virtually independent of the government. This autonomy measure appeared on the agenda which the junta prepared for the Assembly in what the American ambassador described as "a Constitutional curiosity" attempting to "dictate by executive action the provisions of a new Constitution." The Assembly accepted the proposal, which was strongly endorsed by Arévalo. Its avowed purpose was to divorce the army from politics by terminating political promotions based on loyalty and preventing manipulation of the army for political purposes. Hopefully, it would cause the army to devote its concern to professional matters and remove itself from politics. But autonomy could also have the reverse effect, particularly when combined with the idea that the military was the guardian of the Constitution. Throughout his term of office, Arévalo was careful to praise the army effusively, and champion its autonomy. This was the cost of military support, and granting favors and praise to the army differed little from the policy of previous regimes. There was little friction because of the alliance between young officers and young intellectuals who shared ideals about improving the country. But the implications for the future remained, and reform was dependent upon the commitment of the professionalized officer corps.

IV

The United States and
the Latin American Military

After World War II the United States sought to incorporate Latin American military establishments into the Western defense alliances against the expansion of international socialism. The Río Pact of 1947 bound Latin American nations, at least formally, to a collective security arrangement explicitly oriented against "Communist" intervention. But just as only Brazil had actually sent armed forces to fight against the Axis powers in World War II, only Colombia participated in the war to "contain communism" in Korea. Thus, the military establishments remained largely without a serious professional mission to perform in regard to defending their nations against external threats. Then came the Cuban Revolution. On January 27, 1959, shortly after the victory of Fidel Castro over Fulgencio Batista's dictatorship, Ernesto "Che" Guevara outlined the implications of the Cuban Revolution for the rest of Latin America:

> The example of our revolution for Latin America and the lessons it implies have destroyed all the café theories; we have shown that a small group of resolute men supported by the people and not afraid to die if necessary can take on a disciplined regular army and completely defeat it. This is the basic lesson. There is another, which our brothers in Latin America in economically the same position agriculturally as ourselves should take up, and that is there must be an agrarian revolution and fighting in the countryside and the mountains. The revolution must be taken from there to the cities. . . .

It did not matter that Batista's army was hardly disciplined or that Fidel's *guerrilleros* never "completely defeated" a regular army in pitched battle. The Cuban experience was to provide an inspiration to Latin American revolutionaries such as Chilean presidential candidate Salvador Allende, who proclaimed in 1960:

Cuba's fate resembles that of all Latin American countries. They are all underdeveloped—producers of raw materials and importers of industrial products. In all these countries, imperialism has deformed the economy, made big profits, and established its political influence. The Cuban Revolution is a national revolution, but it is also a revolution of the whole of Latin America. It has shown the way for the liberation of all our peoples.

If many on the political left saw Cuba as a hope for the future, policymakers in the United States and traditional power holders in Latin America came more and more to fear the spread of the Cuban Revolution or its principles to the rest of the region. Furthermore, the fate of the Cuban officer corps was not lost on the military establishments in the rest of the hemisphere.

From 1961 onward, the United States, in cooperation with Latin American governments and military elites, organized a counterthrust to the Cuban Revolution: the Alliance for Progress. The Alliance, however, came more and more to be an alliance between Washington policymakers and Latin American counterrevolutionaries and military elites.

Theorists and policymakers drew attention to the threat of Communist subversion and the need for U.S. counterinsurgency programs to prevent the spread of revolution throughout the hemisphere. The article reprinted here by Walt Rostow, one of the best-known intellectuals and policymakers advocating these programs in the 1960s, illustrates clearly the underpinnings of U.S. policy during this period. Entitled "Guerrilla Warfare in Underdeveloped Areas," this article notes emphatically the view that guerrilla warfare in the Third World represents "a systematic attempt by the Communists to impose a serious disease on those societies attempting the transition to modernization."

During 1962 and 1963 the United States expanded its counterinsurgency programs and training capabilities. These included the army's Special Forces, the Southern Command in the Panama Canal Zone, and the center at Fort Bragg, North Carolina. The Agency for International Development (AID) established the Inter-American Police Academy in the Canal Zone in 1962. From 1962 to 1968 military missions provided training, support, and personnel to assist Latin American regimes in the destruction of guerrilla movements and other opposition (at times even banditry) to incumbent governments. These combined U.S.-local military efforts were overwhelmingly successful, culminating in 1967 with the death of Che Guevara and the defeat of his guerrilla band in Bolivia.

The training received by Latin American military officers and police officials as part of the counterinsurgency programs had more than simple technical substance and implications. This training not only prepared officers to lead troops against insurgents, but also led them to ask questions about why such operations were necessary in their countries. The answers to these questions involved complex relationships among (1) international communism, (2) Cuba, (3) the lack of economic development in their countries, and (4) the ineptitude and corruption of civilian politicians.

In the United States, there were some policymakers who resisted its role in fomenting counterrevolution and military rule in Latin America. Despite such objections, however, the U.S. role in assisting, training, and buttressing military expansion and rule in the region continued.

As guerrilla forces and revolutionary political movements became more sophisticated, especially after the death of Che Guevara in 1967, there was growing concern about urban- as well as rural-based guerrilla movements. By 1975 over seventy thousand Latin Americans had been trained in the United States, in the Canal Zone, or in various Latin American countries by U.S. military instructors.

Most of the Latin American guerrilla movements failed or were defeated. But in Nicaragua in 1979 the Sandinista revolutionaries spearheaded a popular insurrection which toppled the Somoza dictatorship. Meanwhile, government forces, supported by U.S. military assistance, were stalemated in El Salvador. Renewed concern for Communist subversion brought a new focus on what came to be called "low-intensity warfare." In 1985, Colonel John D. Waghelstein, an officer recently responsible for direction of U.S. military programs in El Salvador, published an appeal in *Military Review* for the U.S. military establishment to develop further its low-intensity warfare capabilities to deal with the existing threats. Thus, his "Post-Vietnam Counterinsurgency Doctrine" offers insight into the definition of the politico-military mission in Latin America in the 1980s.

With *perestroika* and the declared end to the Cold War, the U.S. military and the Latin American armed forces were obliged to reconsider the meaning of national security and defense missions. As the U.S. Southern Command sought to reorient its programs for the region, it developed new roles for itself and made efforts to incorporate Latin Americans into the "new security agenda." In particular, this included concern for democratization, human rights, the "war on drugs," environmental protection, and undocumented immigration in the hemisphere. Latin American military establishments were not altogether convinced that traditional security issues such as boundary disputes and territorial conflicts, regional arms races, internal order, and military modernization had disappeared. They were also concerned that Washington slighted the sovereignty of particular Latin American countries in its war on drugs or the focus on environmental protection. Nevertheless, the new SOUTHCOM agenda reflected the post-*perestroika* hemispheric policies of the United States. The Latin American militaries were challenged to respond, if not to agree with them. In "The U.S. Southern Command: A Strategy for the Future," three American officers spell out the essential elements of this new hemispheric policy for the 1990s.

W. W. Rostow

CHAPTER 12

Guerrilla Warfare in Underdeveloped Areas

It does not require much imagination to understand why President Kennedy took the problem of guerrilla warfare seriously. When this administration came to responsibility, it faced four major crises: Cuba, the Congo, Laos, and Vietnam. Each represented a successful Communist breaching—over the previous two years—of the Cold War truce lines which had emerged from World War II and its aftermath. In different ways, each had arisen from the efforts of the international Communist movement to exploit the inherent instabilities of the underdeveloped areas of the non-Communist world, and each had a guerrilla-warfare component.

Cuba, of course, differed from the other cases. The Cuban revolution against Batista was a broad-based national insurrection. But that revolution was tragically captured from within by the Communist apparatus, and now Latin America faces the danger of Cuba's being used as the base for training, supply, and direction of guerrilla warfare in the hemisphere.

More than that, Mr. Khrushchev, in his report to the Moscow conference of Communist Parties (published January 6, 1961), had explained at great length that the Communists fully support what he called wars of national liberation and would march in the front rank with the peoples waging such struggles. The military arm of Mr. Khrushchev's January 1961 doctrine is, clearly, guerrilla warfare.

Faced with these four crises pressing in on the president from day to day, and faced with the candidly stated position of Mr. Khrushchev, we have, indeed, begun to take the problem of guerrilla warfare seriously.

To understand this problem, however, one must begin with the great revolutionary process that is going forward in the southern half of the world, for the guerrilla-warfare problem in these regions is a product of that revolutionary process and the Communist effort and intent to exploit it.

What is happening throughout Latin America, Africa, the Middle East, and Asia is this: Old societies are changing their ways in order to create and maintain a national personality on the world scene and to bring to their peoples the benefits modern technology can offer. This process is truly revolutionary. It touches every aspect of the traditional life—economic, social, and political. The introduction of modern technology brings about not merely new methods of production, but a new style of family life, new links between the villages and the cities, the beginnings of national politics, and a new relationship to the world outside.

Like all revolutions, the revolution of modernization is disturbing. Individual men are torn between the commitment to the old, familiar way of life and the attractions of a modern way of life. The power of old social groups—notably the landlord, who usually dominates the traditional society—is reduced. Power moves toward those who command the tools of modern technology, including modern weapons. Men and women in the villages and the cities, feeling that the old ways of life are shaken and that new possibilities are open to them, express old resentments and new hopes.

This is the grand arena of revolutionary change, which the Communists are exploiting with great energy. They believe that their techniques of organization—based on small disciplined cadres of conspirators—are ideally suited to grasp and to hold power in these turbulent settings. They believe that the weak transitional governments that one is likely to find during this modernization process are highly vulnerable to subversion and to guerrilla warfare. And whatever Communist doctrines of historical inevitability may be, Communists know that their time to seize power in the underdeveloped areas is limited. They know that as momentum takes hold in an underdeveloped area—and the fundamental social problems inherited from the traditional society are solved—their chances to seize power decline.

It is on the weakest nations, facing their most difficult transitional moments, that the Communists concentrate their attention. They are the scavengers of the modernization process. They believe that the techniques of political centralization under dictatorial control—and the projected image of Soviet and Chinese Communist economic progress—will persuade hesitant men, faced with great transitional problems, that the Communist model should be adopted for modernization, even at the cost of surrendering human liberty. They believe that they can exploit effectively the resentments built up in many of these areas against colonial rule and that they can associate themselves effectively with the desire of the emerging nations for independence, for status on the world scene, and for material progress.

This is a formidable program, for the history of this century teaches us that Communism is not the long-run wave of the future toward which societies are naturally drawn. But, on the contrary, it is one particular form of modern society to which a nation may fall prey during the transitional process. Communism is best understood as a disease of the transition to modernization.

What is our reply to this historical conception and strategy? What is the American purpose and the American strategy? We, too, recognize that a revolutionary process is under way. We are dedicated to the proposition that this revolutionary process of modernization shall be permitted to go forward in independence, with increasing degrees of human freedom. We seek two results: first, that truly independent nations shall emerge on the world scene; and, second, that each nation will be permitted to fashion out of its own culture and its own ambitions the kind of modern society it wants. The same religious and philosophical beliefs which decree that we respect the uniqueness of each individual make it natural that we respect the uniqueness of each national society. Moreover, we Americans are confident that if the independence of this process can be maintained over the coming years and decades, these societies will choose their own version of what we would recognize as a democratic, open society.

These are our commitments of policy and of faith. The United States has no interest in political satellites. Where we have military pacts, we have them because governments feel directly endangered by outside military action and we are prepared to help protect their independence against such military action. But, to use Mao Tse-tung's famous phrase, we do not seek nations which "lean to one side." We seek nations which will stand up straight. And we do so for a reason: because we are deeply confident that nations which stand up straight will protect their independence and move in their own ways and in their own time toward human freedom and political democracy.

Thus, our central task in the underdeveloped areas, as we see it, is to protect the independence of the revolutionary process now going forward. This is our mission, and it is our ultimate strength. For this is not—and cannot be—the mission of Communism. And in time, through the fog of propaganda and the honest confusions of men caught up in the business of making new nations, this fundamental difference will become increasingly clear in the southern half of the world. The American interest will be served if our children live in an environment of strong, assertive, independent nations capable, because they are strong, of assuming collective responsibility for the peace.

The diffusion of power is the basis for freedom within our own society, and we have no reason to fear it on the world scene. But this outcome would be a defeat for Communism—not for Russia as a national state, but for Communism. Despite all the Communist talk of aiding movements of national independence, they are driven in the end, by the nature of their system, to violate the independence of nations. Despite all the Communist talk of American imperialism, we are committed, by the nature of our system, to support the cause of national independence. And the truth will out.

The victory we seek will see no ticker-tape parades down Broadway, no climactic battles, no great American celebrations of victory. It is a victory that will take many years and decades of hard work and dedication—by many people—to bring about. This will not be a victory of the United States over the Soviet Union. It will not be a victory of capitalism over socialism. It will be a victory of men and nations that aim to stand up straight, over the forces that wish to entrap and to exploit their revolutionary aspirations of modernization. What this victory involves, in the end, is the assertion by nations of their right to independence and by men and women of their right to freedom as they understand it. And we deeply believe this victory will come—on both sides of the Iron Curtain.

If Americans do not seek victory in the usual sense, what do we seek? What is the national interest of the United States? Why do we Americans expend our treasure and assume the risks of modern war in this global struggle? For Americans, the reward of victory will be, simply, this: It will permit American society to continue to develop along the old humane lines which go back to our birth as a nation, and which read deeper into history than that—back to the Mediterranean roots of Western life. We are struggling to maintain an environment on the world scene that will permit our open society to survive and to flourish.

To make this vision come true places a great burden on the United States at this phase of history. The preservation of independence has many dimensions.

The United States has the primary responsibility for deterring the Communists from using nuclear weapons in the pursuit of their ambitions. The United States has a major responsibility for deterring the kind of overt aggression with conventional forces that was launched in June 1950, in Korea.

The United States has the primary responsibility for assisting the economies of those hard-pressed states on the periphery of the Communist bloc, under acute military or quasi-military pressure, which they cannot bear from their own resources; for example, South Korea, Vietnam, Taiwan, Pakistan, Iran. The United States has a special responsibility of leadership in bringing not merely its own resources, but the resources of all the free world to bear in aiding the long-run development of those nations which are serious about modernizing their economy and their social life. And, as President Kennedy made clear, he regarded no program of his administration as more important than his program for long-term economic development, dramatized, for example, by the Alliance for Progress, in Latin America. Independence cannot be maintained by military measures alone. Modern societies must be built, and we are prepared to help build them.

Finally, the United States has a role to play in learning to deter the outbreak of guerrilla warfare, if possible, and to deal with it, if necessary.

It is, of course, obvious that the primary responsibility for dealing with guerrilla warfare in the underdeveloped areas cannot be American. There are many ways in which we can help—and we are searching our minds and our imaginations to learn better how to help; but a guerrilla war must be fought primarily by those on the spot. This is so for a quite particular reason. A guerrilla war is an intimate affair, fought not merely with weapons, but fought in the minds of the men who live in the villages and in the hills, fought by the spirit and policy of those who run the local government. An outsider cannot, by himself, win a guerrilla war. He can help create conditions in which it can be won, and he can directly assist those prepared to fight for their independence. We are determined to help destroy this international disease, that is, guerrilla war, designed, initiated, supplied, and led from outside an independent nation.

Although, as leader of the free world, the United States has special responsibilities which it accepts in this common venture of deterrence, it is important that the whole international community begin to accept its responsibility for dealing with this form of aggression. It is important that the world become clear in mind, for example, that the operation run from Hanoi against Vietnam is as certain a form of aggression as the violation of the 38th Parallel by the North Korean armies in June 1950.

In my conversations with representatives of foreign governments, I am sometimes lectured that this or that government within the free world is not popular; they tell me that guerrilla warfare cannot be won unless the peoples are dissatisfied. These are, at best, half-truths. The truth is that guerrilla warfare, mounted from external bases— with rights of sanctuary—is a terrible burden to carry for any government in a society making its way toward modernization. For instance, it requires somewhere between ten and twenty soldiers to control one guerrilla in an organized operation. Moreover, the guerrilla force has this advantage: Its task is merely to destroy, while the government must build, and protect what it is building. A guerrilla war mounted from outside a transitional nation is a crude act of international vandalism. There will be no peace in the world if the international community accepts the outcome of a guerrilla war, mounted from outside a nation, as tantamount to a free election.

The sending of men and arms across international boundaries and the direction of guerrilla war from outside a sovereign nation is aggression; and this is a fact which the whole international community must confront and whose consequent responsibilities it must accept. Without such international action, those against whom aggression is mounted will be driven inevitably to seek out and engage the ultimate source of the aggression they confront.

In facing the problem of guerrilla war, I have one observation to make as a historian. It is now fashionable to read the learned works of Mao Tse-tung and Che Guevara on guerrilla warfare. This is, indeed, proper. One should read with care and without passion into the minds of one's enemies. But it is historically inaccurate and psychologically dangerous to think that these men created the strategy and tactics of guerrilla war to which we are now responding. Guerrilla warfare is not a form of military and psychological magic created by the Communists. There is no rule or parable in the Communist texts that was not known at an earlier time in history. The operation of [Francis] Marion's men in relation to the Battle of Cowpens in the American Revolution was, for example, governed by rules that Mao merely echoed. Che Guevara knows nothing of this business that T. E. Lawrence did not know or that was not practiced, for example, in the Peninsular campaign during the Napoleonic Wars, a century earlier. The orchestration of professional troops, militia, and guerrilla fighters is an old game, whose rules can be studied and learned.

My point is that we are up against a form of warfare that is powerful and effective only when we do not put our minds clearly to work on how to deal with it. I, for one, believe that with purposeful efforts, most nations which might now be susceptible to guerrilla warfare could handle their border areas in ways which would make them very unattractive to the initiation of this ugly game. We can learn to prevent the emergence of the famous sea in which Mao Tse-tung taught his men to swim. This requires, of course, not merely a proper military program of deterrence, but programs of village development, communications, and indoctrination. The best way to fight a guerrilla war is to prevent it from happening. And this can be done.

Similarly, I am confident that we can deal with the kind of operation now under way in Vietnam. It is an extremely dangerous operation, and it could overwhelm Vietnam if the Vietnamese—aided by the free world—do not deal with it. But it is an unsubtle operation, by the book, based more on murder than on political or psychological appeal.

When Communists speak of wars of national liberation and of their support for "progressive forces," I think of the systematic program of assassination now going forward in which the principal victims are the health, agriculture, and education officers in Vietnamese villages. The Viet Cong are not trying to persuade the peasants of Vietnam that Communism is good; they are trying to persuade them that their lives are insecure unless they cooperate with them. With resolution and confidence on all sides, and with the assumption of international responsibility for the frontier problem, I believe we are going to bring this threat to the independence of Vietnam under control.

My view is, then, that we confront in guerrilla warfare in the underdeveloped areas a systematic attempt by the Communists to impose a serious disease on those societies attempting the transition to modernization. This attempt is a present danger in Southeast Asia. It could quickly become a major danger in Africa and Latin America. It is our task to prevent that disease, if possible, and to eliminate it where it is imposed.

Every American should be aware of the military and the creative dimensions of the job. Those with whom I have the privilege of working are dedicated to that mission with every resource of mind and spirit at our command.

Col. John D. Waghelstein,
U.S. Army

CHAPTER 13

Post-Vietnam
Counterinsurgency Doctrine

In the post-Vietnam era, counterinsurgency has virtually become a nonsubject in the U.S. military educational system. The term *counterinsurgency* has been replaced by the less controversial *low-intensity conflict.* A recently proposed definition of low-intensity conflict for the revised Army field manual on that subject reads:

> The limited use of power for political purposes by nations or organizations . . . to coerce, control or defend a population, to control or defend a territory or establish or defend rights. It includes military operations by or against irregular forces, peacekeeping operations, terrorism, counter-terrorism, rescue operations, *and military assistance under conditions of armed conflict.* This form of conflict does not include protracted engagements of opposing regular forces. [Emphasis added]

The problem with this is that low-intensity conflict is a description of the level of violence from a military viewpoint. This kind of conflict is more accurately described as revolutionary and counter-revolutionary warfare. It is *total war* at the grass-roots level—one that uses *all* of the weapons of total war, including political, economic, and psychological warfare with the military aspect being a distant fourth in many cases. The subordination of the military in counterinsurgency has always created problems for the U.S. military establishment. This kind of conflict is fundamentally different from the American way of war.

Low-intensity conflict and counterinsurgency involve two distinct uses of the U.S. military. The first, as demonstrated in the Grenada operation [1983], is the surgical application of force—a role for which U.S. units are trained and equipped. The second use involves assisting an ally in politico-military operations to combat armed insurgents, a role for which the U.S. military is unprepared. The state of preparedness for this second role is at its lowest point in twenty years.

Low-intensity conflict instruction at the U.S. Army Command and General Staff College [USACGSC], Fort Leavenworth, Kansas, includes an analysis of insurgency—the causes, the catalysts, and the role of the sponsor in generating insurgency, as well as ways the United States can best *assist* besieged friendly governments in countering insurgencies. Developmental or consolidative campaigns aimed at the root causes of insurgency are studied, as well as methods of mobilizing human and material resources and ways of neutralizing the armed guerrilla threat. In short, the doctrine stresses a balanced approach of development, mobilization, and neutralization.

Additionally, there is a careful analysis of various types of insurgencies and the social groups and political forces existing in each. Case studies are used (for example, Venezuela, 1959–63), as well as the macro approach. The situation-specific aspects of each insurgency are stressed to preclude another "cookie cutter" disaster—for example, trying to apply a Malayan strategic hamlet solution to Vietnam. What little doctrine there is is sound and provides some useful tools to those officers who may be called upon to operate in a counterinsurgency environment.

The real problem is not the doctrine but the amount of emphasis that the services place on the subject. For example, by 1977, a paltry forty hours of the one-year-course core curriculum were devoted to the study of low-intensity conflict at the USACGSC. Two years later, the low-intensity conflict course had been reduced to eight hours. In the branch schools, the subject was discontinued altogether. The U.S. Army still does not regard guerrilla warfare, insurgency, and counterinsurgency as being unique and is unwilling to devote substantial resources to preparing for our most likely form of involvement.

A recent study by Captain Andrew F. Krepenevitch of the Department of Social Sciences, U.S. Military Academy, West Point, New York, details the Army's failure in the early 1960s to make any serious attempt at developing counterinsurgency doctrine and training. Many of the same criticisms are being leveled today:

> *The Administration's emphasis on developing a counterinsurgency capability impacted heavily on the Army brass. They were, in effect, being told to alter radically the Army's method of operation, a method that had been eminently successful in prior conflicts. The notion that a group of novice civilians ([John F.] Kennedy, [Robert S.] McNamara, and the "Whiz Kids") should require the Army*

to deemphasize what had been its strong suit (i.e., heavy units, massed firepower, high technology) in favor of stripped-down light infantry units encountered strong organizational resistance. [Emphasis added.]

Statements from the Army's leadership bear out the organization's disinterest in the President's proposals and their conviction that the concept [the conventional approach to war] could handle any problems that might crop up at the lower end of the conflict spectrum:

General Lyman Lemnitzer, Army Chairman of the JCS (Joint Chiefs of Staff), 1960–1962: stated that the new administration was "oversold" on the importance of guerrilla warfare.

General George Decker, Army Chief of Staff, 1960–1962: countered a presidential lecture to the Chiefs on counter-insurgency with the reply "any good soldier can handle guerrillas."

General Earle Wheeler, Army Chief of Staff, 1962–1964: "The essence of the problem in Vietnam is military." [Emphasis added.]

General Maxwell Taylor, Chairman of the JCS, 1962–1964: recalling his reaction to JFK's proposals: "It (counterinsurgency) is just a form of small war, a guerrilla operation in which we have a long record against the Indians. Any well-trained organization can shift the tempo to that which might be required in this kind of situation. *All this cloud of dust that's coming out of the White House really isn't necessary.* [Emphasis added.] . . .

The Army's disinterest with regard to the development of counterinsurgency capability was demonstrated not only in that mechanistic approach in which it addressed this requirement in the 1960s, but also in the manner in which once the "aberration" of Vietnam ended, the organization discarded what had always been an unwanted appendage to its concepts. [Emphasis added.]

Given the proposition that low-intensity conflict is our most likely form of involvement in the Third World, it appears that the Army is still preparing for the wrong war by emphasizing the Soviet threat on the plains of Europe [fondly called the "Fulda Gap" mentality]. This concern should not preclude preparations to assist our allies in meeting the threat of internal subversion and guerrilla warfare.

The triumph of the Sandinistas in Nicaragua, the insurgency of El Salvador, and Cuba's renewed efforts in the Caribbean Basin have conspired to force the Army to reevaluate its priorities; and, like St. Paul on the road to Damascus, many have become converts and begun to reassess our capability. The USACGSC curriculum is now back to a modest thirty-two hours, and old counterinsurgency lesson plans are being dusted off at the service schools. And serious work, albeit modest, is beginning in the service schools, staff colleges, and senior service schools.

The Special Forces, faced with drastic personnel cuts in 1979, have been resuscitated and are expanding modestly. Somewhat surprisingly, senior naval officers were instrumental in saving the Special Forces as they questioned the diminution of their "unconventional warfare" assets in the Pacific and Caribbean regions. The 8th Special Action Force (SAF) for Latin America was deactivated in 1973, and the Latin American counterinsurgency capability was reduced to a single Special Forces battalion at Fort Gulick, Panama. The 7th Special Forces Group (Airborne) at Fort Bragg, North Carolina, is now oriented toward the region and presently provides the bulk of the training assistance for Honduras and El Salvador. Apparently, the nadir of our Special Forces capability has been reached and is being expanded slightly to meet the new challenges of the 1980s and 1990s.

What concerns many of us is that these welcome changes stop far short of a serious commitment by the services to devote the personnel and curriculum hours that are needed for adequate instruction *throughout the various educational systems*—the place where long-term changes are made. Thirty-two hours at the Army's mid-level staff college hardly constitute a renaissance for low-intensity conflict. And a few hours of counterinsurgency-related tactical training do not adequately prepare our junior officers for this most likely arena.

Nor are the other services any better prepared than the Army. The Air Force devotes twenty-six hours to low-intensity conflict and counterinsurgency at the Air Command and Staff College, Maxwell Air Force Base, Alabama, and there are no units today with the training and capabilities that would be equivalent to those of the Air Commandos of the 1960s. The Navy and the Air Force still do not have foreign area officer programs that adequately prepare officers for duty in advisory or training assistance roles. The Air Force officers sent to El Salvador during my tenure there were fine pilots and administrators. However, they were totally lacking in language qualification and regional preparation, not to mention the unique aspects of insurgency and counterinsurgency.

Fortunately, the Navy was able to find two superb sea-air-land team (SEAL) officers for duty in El Salvador, but the personnel managers constantly attempted to push "blue water" conventional sailors into what was essentially a brown water, low-intensity conflict situation. All of the services are having difficulty providing counterinsurgency-trained, area-oriented, and language-qualified senior officers for El Salvador. The psychological operations and civil affairs capabilities needed to support our advisory effort in Central

America are inadequate. It may be that the U.S. defense establishment is still wary of becoming involved in another Vietnam.

I recently heard two comments from more conventionally oriented colleagues: "Who gives a damn about a bunch of chili-dip countries?" and, "It smells like NUC-Mam to me." While these comments
may not reflect Department of Defense policy, they do portray some
traditionalists' indifferent and "gun-shy" attitudes toward small wars
which we are unprepared to fight.

Given today's realities, however, failure to adequately prepare
for low-intensity conflict is inexcusable. I remember the attitude of
the Army personnel wallahs early in the 1960s. They did everything
they could to discourage combat arms officers from serving at the
Vietnamese unit and subsector levels. "What you need is troop duty
in Europe with a 'Regular' (for example, conventional) unit." After
U.S. troop units were committed to Vietnam, duty with the Military
Assistance Command, Vietnam, was still considered to be less
"career-enhancing" than duty with a U.S. unit. Despite the lessons of
post-World War II insurgencies and the experiences of officers such
as Generals William B. Rosson, Edward Landsdale, or John K.
Singlaub, we are essentially where we were when Kennedy became
president.

Our track record in dealing with insurgencies in Latin America
may account, in part, for our present indifference. In the 1960s, with
our help, most guerrilla movements in the region were effectively
neutralized by Latin American armies. In 1964, the peak year of the
mobile training team effort, we provided 275 of these teams from the
8th SAF in Panama alone. By 1970 the number was down to 70, and
most of those were technical assistance teams of one or two specialists each. Our Latin American allies had by then established their
own training centers and cadres, and they were capable of putting
rural guerrillas and urban-based terrorists supported by Fidel Castro
out of business. In 1967, for example, a fifteen-man Special Forces
mobile training team trained the Bolivian Rangers that made short
work of Ernesto "Che" Guevara's adventure. By the late 1960s it
appeared that Castro would have to look elsewhere for excitement.

Nicaragua (1979) changed all that. The Marxist-Leninists used a
popularly based insurgency to achieve power. Castro has finally convinced Moscow that revolution in Central America is possible without waiting for *all* objective conditions to exist. The changed role of
the Latin American church since the Medellín, Colombia, Conference (1968) and the subsequent radicalization of some churchmen
and women have added a new dimension to insurgency.

Most importantly, the effective orchestration of U.S. public opinion by sympathetic interest and front groups and their impact on congressional security assistance support has given new life to Castro-supported, Marxist-Leninist insurgencies. More sophisticated planning and coordination is evident in El Salvador, in Grenada, and throughout the region. While Castro has learned from the mistakes of the 1960s, we still appear to have difficulty recovering from our Vietnam hangover.

A recent book on Central America, *Rift and Revolution: The Central American Imbroglio*, contains a superb chapter on "Revolutionary Movements in Central America" by Ernest Evans. Evans concludes:

> For both doctrinal and organizational reasons revolutionary warfare goes deeply against the grain of the U.S. military. The doctrinal problem is that in the U.S. military there has always been a widely shared belief that military issues are and should be kept separate from political issues. The organizational problem is that the U.S. military is a big-unit, high-technology military. Wars against guerrillas, however, for the most part, require small units and fairly simple technology. Although the U.S. military could, of course, modify its organizational patterns, the war in Vietnam demonstrated that the U.S. military is extremely reluctant to modify its big-unit, high-technology orientation.

The fear of becoming involved in another quagmire is evident everywhere in the Department of Defense and, as a result, we are not adequately prepared for any involvement short of commitment of U.S. combat units. Security, training, and advisory assistance are the keys to success in counterinsurgency and, if utilized early enough, will preclude the need for the deployment of U.S. troops in a role for which, given our present conventional preoccupation, we are inadequately trained and doctrinally unsuited. The U.S. counterinsurgency effort, to be effective, must have security, advisory, and training assistance experts who can assess the situation, advise the host country forces on the proper counterinsurgency techniques and training, and equip those forces to do the job. They must be supported by theater and unified command staff officers who understand that counterinsurgency is not just the application of high technology, more logistics, firepower, and mobility.

In many respects, real counterinsurgency techniques are a step toward the primitive (for example, *less* firepower that is more surgically applied). The keys to popular support, the sine qua non in counterinsurgency, include psychological operations, civic action, and grass-roots human intelligence work, all of which runs counter to the conventional U.S. concept of war. To be effective in our advice, we should be sending our best trained counterinsurgency experts to assist our allies. We should not, as has generally been the case, send conventionally oriented officers to create a miniature U.S. defense establishment.

Snarled security assistance legislation, arbitrary restrictions on numbers of trainers (for example, a fifty-five-man level in El Salvador), constraints on the trainers' in-country activities (terms of reference), as well as a lack of emphasis in the Army's educational system and a paucity of fully qualified officers in the services, indicate that we still have a long way to go to meet the challenge.

Col. Antonio J. Ramos, USAF,
Col. Ronald C. Oates, USMC, and
Lt. Col. Timothy L. McMahon, USA*

CHAPTER 14

The U.S. Southern Command: A Strategy for the Future

The U.S. Southern Command's (USSOUTHCOM) Southern Theater Strategy is a broad and comprehensive plan that focuses on the future. The theater strategy describes ends, ways and means to achieve U.S. policy objectives throughout the region. Our theater strategy is more than a response or an accommodation to the changes taking place in the world. Our strategy promotes change by describing the future and providing a road map for progress.

Recent events throughout the world have shown that change may be the only constant principle. The decline of former empires and adversaries, the commitment to democracy and progress and the spread of our ideals and values are the bright side of a changing world. The rise of new nations and regional powers, the friction of ethnic and religious differences and the proliferation of conventional and mass destruction weapons may be the dark side of that changing world. This changing world is a place where we face new risks and nontraditional threats to our national and regional security, but it is also a place where we face new challenges and extraordinary opportunities.

The keys to countering the risks and exploiting the opportunities are recognizing that change will occur; understanding the reasons for change; establishing our vision for the future beyond the bow curve of change and working to build that future.

We cannot stop the changes from occurring, but we can influence the process and focus. We can lead the world toward a community of free, stable and prosperous nations acting in concert with one an-

---

*The views expressed in this article are those of the authors and do not purport to reflect the position of the Department of the Army, the Department of Defense, or any other government office or agency.—Editor

148 The Politics of Antipolitics

other and in accordance with the values and ideals of democracy. We can promote positive, ordered change by focusing our resources toward a positive view of the future.

A key objective of the U.S. National Security Strategy is stability, both promoting and maintaining regional stability throughout the world. While promoting stability, we should not confine our strategic approach to maintaining the status quo. We need to expand the definition of stability to include promoting positive, ordered change— promoting progress toward our vision of the future.

The foundation of our theater strategy is a vision of what the region can become. Our theater strategic objectives, theater priorities and operational plans and programs derive from that end state. Our strategy is focused to the future and promotes positive, ordered change.

Risks and Opportunities

Our approach to developing a strategy for the Southern Theater began with an assessment of risks and opportunities—risks to U.S. and host nation interests throughout the theater as well as opportunities that the United States and host nations might take advantage of. Our assessment of risks and opportunities showed an operational environment different from most other unified commands.

For the most part, nontraditional threats put our interests in the theater at risk. Those threats include drug production and trafficking, depressed economies, fragile democracies, ongoing insurgencies and recalcitrant military institutions. While these threats are nontraditional, they are nonetheless dangerous and represent clear risks to host nation sovereignty, as well as U.S. interests.

Our assessment also showed the potential for stronger and more responsive democracies, economic growth, social reform and even greater cooperation among the host nations in the theater. That potential environment fits the vision for the future we describe in our theater strategy.

Simply stated, our goal is to counter or eliminate the risks while expanding on the opportunities that exist in the theater. That goal, in combination with our vision and theater strategic objectives, represents our strategic end state. Establishing a set of strategic goals and objectives, based on a risk-opportunity assessment, was a critical step in developing a strategy for the future.

Our operating environment is a mix of risks and opportunities. We developed our theater strategy as a means to prioritize and provide military resources to counter the risks and exploit the opportunities—but risks and opportunities are means to an end. The end—our basic focus, strategic rationale and strategic foundation—is to protect, defend and promote U.S. interests in the Southern Theater.

During the course of strategy development, we identified the reasons for U.S. interests in the Southern Theater and studied each host nation in terms of those interests. We concluded that each nation in the theater represents some level of strategic importance to the U.S. strategy, and that the key to achieving our objective was to provide the right type and amount of resources to the right host nation.

The reasons for U.S. interests in the theater are:

• Regional Security. Insurgency, terrorism or other activities that threaten the security of a host nation. The principal focus is on those nations where insurgencies are ongoing.

• Established Democracies. Democratic government for more than 12 years.

• Emerging Democracies. Democratic government for less than 12 years. Also includes embattled or endangered democracies.

• Drugs. Drug protection and trafficking and other drug-associated activities occurring in the host nation. The principal focus is on the drug source area (the Andean ridge nations of Colombia, Bolivia and Peru); the secondary focus is on the transit area (Central America) and the countries surrounding the drug source area; the tertiary focus is on the potential source and transit area (the remaining South American nations).

• Promote Interests. The host nation has sufficient power to influence other nations in the theater and the potential to act in accordance with U.S. interests.

• U.S. Prestige. The principal focus is toward achieving U.S. policy objectives in the host nation. The secondary focus is toward maintaining U.S. influence in other international affairs—U.S. success in one area can translate into greater influence in other areas of foreign policy.

• Resources. There is a need for natural resources available in the host nation.

• Sea Lines of Communication. Critical sea lines of communication (SLOCs) are the Panama Canal, the approaches to the canal, the southeast Pacific and the Drake Passage. The host nation has the ability to protect or assist U.S. protection of SLOCs.

• Basing/Access. The United States maintains bases or basing rights in the host nation.

• Host Nation Power. The host nation is a "leading nation" in the theater based on elements of national power.

• Arms Control. The host nation produces and exports arms.

• Nuclear Technology. The host nation possesses nuclear technology.

Our theater strategy drives our resource programs. The key to providing resources is to establish priorities among the host nations, within our operational programs and in accordance with our strategic interests. Our analysis of U.S. interests and how those interests apply to the host nations allows us to establish main, supporting and economy of force efforts within our major operational programs.

Theater Strategic Objectives. Our theater strategic objectives show much more than a focus on the future, although future focus is a key element. Our strategic objectives prescribe a broad and comprehensive strategy that is more than a military strategy. We require more than a list of military forces and description of military operations designed solely to achieve military objectives. In order to achieve our theater strategic objectives, we require the cooperation and participation of many U.S. government agencies.

In fact, in most cases, USSOUTHCOM is not the lead U.S. agency in the host nations. U.S. ambassadors and their country teams are the focal points for most of our operational plans and programs in the theater. Our theater strategic objectives show the political-military (and economic) focus. Our theater strategic objectives, in priority order, are:

• Strengthen host nation democratic institutions.

• Assist host nations in eliminating threats to regional security.

• Support continued economic and social progress.

• Assist host nations in defeating drug production and trafficking.

• With the government of Panama, ensure an open and neutral Panama Canal.

• Enhance the role of the military in democratic society.

We developed these objectives to support achieving our strategic end state. The objectives are based on our strategic assessment of the theater and an analysis of other U.S. strategic documents, including the U.S. National Security Strategy, the U.S. National Military Strategy and the Joint Strategic Capabilities Plan.

The danger of establishing priorities among our theater strategic objectives, particularly with limited resources, is that we may achieve one or two of our strategic objectives to the detriment of our other objectives. We cannot afford to focus resources only toward our first and second strategic objectives and lose the opportunity for achieving the others.

The solution is to strike a balance among our theater strategic objectives, to view our objectives as mutually supporting and to apply our resources in a way to achieve multiple objectives. In other words, success in one objective area should support success in others. In terms of our objectives and priorities, the logic is that a host nation with strong democratic institutions, a strong economy and responsive social programs, and a competent and supportive military has a better chance for success in combating the nontraditional threats it faces.

USSOUTHCOM Priorities

We reviewed the tasks assigned to the command by the president, the secretary of defense, the chairman of the Joint Chiefs of Staff and the resources available to the command. It was clear that we had to focus on specific objective areas in the near- to midterm. Our priority programs, with explanations, are:

• Support counterdrug efforts. Provide military resource support to the U.S. ambassadors, host nations and other U.S. agencies.

• Facilitate implementation of the peace accords in El Salvador. Refocus our military resources toward restructuring the armed forces of El Salvador and integrating the former FMLN into the mainstream of El Salvadoran society.

• Promote liberty in Panama and implement the Panama Canal treaties. Assist the Government of Panama in fulfilling its citizens' expectations and demonstrating the benefits of democracy to its citizens. At the same time, develop and execute command plans in support of treaty implementation.

• Enhance the role of the military in the democracies of Central and South America. Assist the host nation militaries in their efforts to restructure and redefine their roles in support of developing democracies.

• Take care of troops and their families. These priorities are linked with national strategies through our strategic end state and strategic objectives. Operational plans and resource programs are developed in accordance with these priorities to achieve our theater strategic objectives.

A Theater in Transition. The conventional wisdom is that the Southern Theater is a theater in conflict. That description of the theater derives from the risks and threats to U.S. and host nation interests and security. A better way of describing the theater, how-ever, is that it is a theater in transition—a theater moving toward a positive future.

We are optimistic about the theater. Our reasons for optimism include the choices being made for democracy, the efforts toward economic and social reform, evidence of increased cooperation and consensus and the recognition that we share common interests with the host nations. Our regional counterdrug programs, for example, demonstrate both increased cooperation as well as the recognition that the United States and the host nations share common interests.

We can promote these positive trends and achieve our theater stra-tegic objectives if our national policies, and sufficient resources to give meaning to those policies, are constant and consistent. Con-versely, if our national policies toward the region change every two to four years, and resources wax and wane, then we put our interests and our ability to achieve our strategic objectives at risk.

The opportunity equation is simple and straightforward. We want to promote strong democracies, economic and social progress in the theater; reduce threats to regional security; protect and promote our interests; create an environment that allows progress toward increased opportunities for the host nations and the United States. Building that progressive environment, in cooperation with the host nations, re-quires resources and commitment.

The phrase "The Unknown and the Uncertain" has gained some popularity recently. Our view of that notion is that the threats to U.S. interests and regional security in the Southern Theater are both known and certain. The threats are not quite the former Warsaw Pact, nor the Republican Guards, for that matter. The threats that do exist in the theater, however, put our interests and host nation security at risk.

More than anything else, the command is supporting nations at war. The host nations are waging war against drug producers and traffickers, and insurgent and terrorist groups. In some cases, those forces have joined together for mutual benefit. In all cases, these non-traditional enemies are dangerous. The danger increases when host nation democracies are fragile, their economies stagnant and their military forces are learning to support the democratic process.

U.S. Military Assistance. A key point to keep in mind is that the host nations are in the lead. The host nations conduct counterdrug, counterinsurgency and nation building operations. USSOUTHCOM assists all of these efforts.

Our forces for supporting and assisting the host nations are not airborne divisions, fighter-bomber wings or carrier battle groups. Our forces of choice are tactical analysis teams, planning assistance teams, engineer, medical, civil affairs and psychological operations units. Our ways and means are security assistance training and equipment, counterdrug intelligence and operational assistance, nation building assistance, international military training and education and humanitarian assistance.

These ways and means are significant. During this year, for example, we plan to deploy nearly 20,000 soldiers, sailors, airmen and Marines throughout the theater. They will support and assist host nation forces in training for their counterdrug, counterinsurgency, nation building and humanitarian assistance operations.

Interagency Operations. The command cannot go it alone. We cannot achieve our strategic objectives without the full play of all U.S. government agencies. Clearly, the Department of State is the lead agency in developing and executing U.S. foreign policy, and our operational programs and resources are instruments of policy. Throughout the theater, we support the State Department agenda by supporting the U.S. ambassadors.

The interagency team for the theater consists of more than 19 U.S. ambassadors and one commander in chief. The roles played by the Department of Justice, the Drug Enforcement Administration, the U.S. Coast Guard, the U.S. Customs Service, the Agency for International Development, the other unified commands and host nations, for example, are critical to the success of our Counterdrug Campaign Plan. These agencies, and others, play key roles in all of our operational plans.

While the U.S. ambassadors are the focal points in each host nation, the command occupies a unique regionwide vantage point. We have the ability to serve as a focal point for coordinating theaterwide plans and programs and provide a regional focus along with our command and control capabilities, staff planning and operations expertise and military resources.

We need more than joint and combined plans and operations to achieve our strategic objectives. We need the full dimension of U.S. and host nation capabilities. We need to build one team for the region and focus that team toward a common fight.

Peacetime Engagement and Forward Presence Operations

In August 1990, President George Bush described the strategic concept of peacetime engagement in his address to the Aspen Institute.

He restated that concept in his annual National Security Strategy. In fact, the president was describing our principal operational method. By focusing on the potential causes of conflict in a host nation, we can prevent conflict from developing and assist in legitimizing a democratic government. The National Military Strategy of the United States describes the concept of forward presence operations to achieve those ends.

The commander in chief, USSOUTHCOM Peacetime Engagement Operations Plan, prescribes our major operational plans and programs—our operations short of war—designed to achieve our strategic end state. The plans and programs included are counterdrug and counterinsurgency support efforts and plans to enhance the role of host nation military forces and nation assistance programs. Our planning efforts also include the development of supporting operational plans—a regionwide counterdrug campaign plan, for example.

The principal focus of our Peacetime Engagement Operations Plan is the host nation. We want to develop the capabilities of host nation forces to meet host nation goals and objectives, insofar as those goals and objectives are consistent with our interests.

The U.S. ambassador to the host nation is a key player in our peacetime engagement efforts. He balances U.S. interests with host nation goals and objectives and specifies the capabilities, including military capabilities, the host nation needs to meet its objectives. In the context of peacetime engagement and forward presence, we provide resources, support and assistance through the U.S. ambassador, to develop those capabilities.

To execute our Peacetime Engagement Operations Plan, we needed to develop principal and supporting objectives for each of our major operational plans and programs. The principal objectives are:

• Counterdrug support and assistance. The reduction, or possible elimination, of drug production and trafficking in the theater and the flow of illegal drugs into the United States.

• Counterinsurgency support and assistance. An environment in the host nations throughout the theater where change and development occur without violence.

• Enhancing the role of the military in democratic society. Host nation military forces that can defend their nations against internal and external security threats support the continued development of democracy and protect and promote the human rights of their citizens.

• Nation assistance. Self-sustaining institutions and capabilities for nation building and development in the host nations throughout the theater.

The success of U.S. policy toward Central and South America is evident. We can measure success in terms of elected democracies throughout the region, the resolution of long-standing conflicts and the increasing potential for economic and social development. However, the continued development of democracy, and continued economic and social economic progress in the region are far from certain. Stability in the region is not assured and the root causes of internal conflict have not been completely resolved.

While the changing world presents uncertainty in some quarters, it also provides a strategic window of opportunity for refocusing our efforts and resources toward the Western Hemisphere. While threats have diminished in some quarters, very real threats to U.S. interests and security remain in Central and South America. While the future is unknown in some quarters, we have defined the future in the Southern Theater.

The United States is approaching a decision point concerning its policies toward Central and South America. U.S. policymakers, as well as the agencies that execute U.S. policy, must respond to the changes which have occurred, and are occurring, in the region. In order to develop and implement cogent policy objectives for the region, U.S. policymakers must focus on a vision of what the region can become by the beginning of the 21st century and beyond.

The opportunities for the United States represented by that strategic vision of the future are significant. We have the opportunity to promote our interests and achieve our theater strategic objectives, build mutual interests and objectives throughout the region and shape the future.

V

The Military Speaks for Itself

In the years following the Cuban Revolution, the military antipoliticians who dominated Latin America took on distinctive policy agendas from country to country. Differing policy emphases flowed from national political legacies as varied as *Peronismo* in Argentina and the Peruvian military's seeming commitment to destroy the vestiges of neofeudalism in the Peruvian Andes. Despite national idiosyncrasies, however, the following selection of speeches and policy statements by prominent military leaders in Argentina, Brazil, Chile, Peru, El Salvador, and Guatemala make clear an underlying unity of commitment to economic developmentalism and to antipolitics. Whether we turn to Videla in Argentina or Velasco in Peru, we find civilian corruption, deceit, or even treason blamed for the ills of the Latin American nations. We also hear military officers promising to restore law, order, stability, and social discipline—and to repress opposition elements, whether rightist or leftist.

Without ignoring the diversity of viewpoints and ideological orientation within the military establishments of Latin America, we have chosen the selections herein in order to provide (1) an initial statement by military leaders of the rationale for military rule in each country; and (2) an assessment by those responsible for military rule of the evolution of the military regimes and their public policy initiatives. Our choice of speeches or policy statements was also influenced by the peculiarities of each case. In Argentina, Chile, and Peru, where military antipolitics was initially associated with the extended influence of particular officers, the choice was relatively easy. In Brazil, El Salvador, and Guatemala, where a succession of military officers exercised authority, we have included selections from at least two military political leaders. An effort has been made to illustrate the differences and similarities among the military leaders in each of these countries.

CHAPTER 15

Argentina

THE ARMED FORCES' DECISION TO ASSUME THE DIRECTION OF THE STATE, 1976

Since all constitutional mechanisms have been exhausted and since all possibility of rectifications within the institutional framework has ended and since the impossibility of recovery through normal processes has been irrefutably demonstrated, the armed forces must put an end to the situation which has burdened the nation and compromised its future.

Our people have suffered a new frustration. We have faced a tremendous political vacuum capable of sinking us into anarchy and dissolution. We have also been faced with the national government's inability to call the people together; with the repeated and successive contradictions evidenced by the adoption of all kinds of measures; with the lack of a government-directed strategy to confront subversion; with the total lack of solutions for the basic problems of the nation which have resulted in the steady increase of extremism; with the total absence of ethical and moral examples which the directors of the state should exhibit; with the manifest irresponsibility in the management of the economy which has exhausted the production apparatus; and with the speculation and the generalized corruption—all of which translates into an irreparable loss of greatness and of faith.

The armed forces have assumed the direction of the state in fulfillment of their unrenounceable obligation. They do so only after calm meditation about the irreparable consequences to the destiny of the nation that would be caused by the adoption of a different stance. This decision is aimed at ending misrule, corruption, and the scourge of subversion, but it is only directed at those who are guilty of crimes or abuse of power. It is a decision for the fatherland and does not suppose, therefore, to discriminate against any civic group or social sector whatever. It rejects, therefore, the disruptive actions of all extremists and the corrupting effect of demagoguery.

During the period which begins today, the armed forces will develop a program governed by clearly defined standards, by internal order and hard work, by the total observance of ethical and moral principles, by justice, and by the integral organization of man and by the respect of his rights and dignity. Thus, the republic will succeed in unifying all Argentines and will achieve the total recuperation of the national sovereignty. . . . To achieve these goals, we call upon all the men and women, without exception, who inhabit this land, to join together in a common effort.

Besides those shared aspirations, all the representative sectors of the country ought to feel clearly identified with and committed to the common undertaking that will contribute to the greatness of the fatherland.

This government will never be controlled by special-interest groups, nor will it favor any one group. It will be imbued with a profound national spirit and will only respond to the most sacred interests of the nation and of its inhabitants.

Upon incurring such a far-reaching obligation, the armed forces issue a firm summons to the . . . citizenry. In this new stage, there is a battle post for each citizen. The task before us is both arduous and pressing. It will not be free of sacrifices, but it is undertaken with the absolute conviction that this example will be followed from top to bottom and with faith in the future of Argentina.

This process will be conducted with absolute firmness and with a spirit of service. Beginning now, this newly assumed responsibility imposes on the authorities the rigorous task of eradicating, once and for all, the vices which afflict the nation.

To achieve that, we will continue fighting, without quarter, all forms of subversion, both open and clandestine, and will eradicate all forms of demagoguery. We will tolerate neither corruption nor venality in any form or circumstance, or any transgression against the law, or any opposition to the process of restoration which has been initiated.

The armed forces have assumed control of the republic. And we want the entire country to understand the profound and unequivocal meaning of our actions so that the responsibility and the collective efforts accompanying this undertaking, which seeks the common good, will bring about, with the help of God, complete national recovery.

Signed:

Lt. Gen. Jorge Rafael Videla, commander in chief of the army

Adm. Emilio Eduardo Massera, commander in chief of the navy

Brig. Gen. Orlando Ramón Agosti, commander in chief of the air force

---

Translated and edited from a text of the radio announcement by the three commanding generals of the armed forces (March 25, 1976), published in *La Nación* (Buenos Aires), March 29, 1976.

A TIME FOR FUNDAMENTAL REORGANIZATION OF THE NATION, 1976
SPEECH BY GENERAL JORGE RAFAEL VIDELA

To the people of the Argentine Republic:

The country is passing through one of the most difficult periods in its history. With the country on the point of national disintegration, the intervention of the armed forces was the only possible alternative in the face of the deterioration provoked by misgovernment, corruption, and complacency.

. . . The armed forces, conscious of the fact that the continuation of this process did not offer an acceptable future for the country, put forth the only possible answer to this critical situation. Such a decision, predicated on the mission and the very essence of the military institution, was planned and executed with temperateness, responsibility, firmness, and a balance that has earned the gratitude of the Argentine people.

But it should be abundantly clear that the events which took place on March 24, 1976, represent more than the mere overthrow of a government. On the contrary, they signify the final closing of a historic cycle and the opening of a new one whose fundamental characteristic will be manifested by the reorganization of the nation, a task undertaken with a true spirit of service by the armed forces.

This process of national reorganization will require time and effort; it will require a broad capacity for living together; it will exact from each one his personal quota of sacrifice; and it will necessarily count on the sincere and complete confidence of all Argentines. The attainment of this confidence is, above all else, the most difficult of the endeavors which we have undertaken.

For many years, so many promises have been unfulfilled, so many plans and projects have failed, and so deep has been the national frustration that many of our fellow citizens no longer have faith in the word of their government leaders, even to the point of believing that public employees do not serve the people but only serve themselves. Thus, they were convinced that justice had ceased to exist for the Argentine citizen.

We will begin then by establishing a just order within which it will be incumbent upon each [one] to work and [to] sacrifice; in which the fruits of this effort will be transformed into better living conditions for all; in which the honest and exemplary citizen will find support and encouragement; in which those who violate the law will be severely punished regardless of their rank, their power, or their supposed influence. In this way, the people will regain confidence and faith in those who govern them, and we will have established that point of departure indispensable for confronting the grave crisis which afflicts our country.

It is unnecessary to list the tragic conditions under which the country lives; each inhabitant of the fatherland knows and suffers intensely from them day after day. Nevertheless, it is worthwhile to point out some of the most important components of this situation.

The management of the state had never been so disorderly, directed with inefficiency [because] . . . of general administrative corruption and accompanying demagoguery. For the first time in its history, the nation came to the point of suspending all payments. A vacillating and unrealistic economic leadership carried the country toward recession and the beginnings of unemployment, with its inevitable sequel of anguish and desperation, a condition which we have inherited and which we will seek to alleviate.

The indiscriminate use of violence by all sides engulfed the inhabitants of the nation in an atmosphere of insecurity and overwhelming fear. Finally, institutional stagnation, manifested in the unsuccessful attempts to produce in time the urgent and profound evolution which the country required, led to a total paralysis of the state, with a power vacuum incapable of revitalizing it. . . .

Profoundly respectful of constitutional powers, the natural underpinning of democratic institutions, the armed forces, on repeated occasions, sent clear warnings to the government about the dangers that existed and also about the shortcomings of its senseless acts. Their voice went unheard, and as a consequence not one essential measure was adopted. Therefore, every hope of institutional change was completely dashed. In the face of this dramatic situation, the armed forces assumed control of the national government.

This conscious and responsibly taken action was not motivated by an interest in or a desire for power. It was in response to the demands of an indispensable obligation emanating from the armed forces' specific mission to safeguard the highest interests of the nation.

Faced with that imperative, the armed forces, as an institution, have filled the existing power vacuum and also as an institution, inspired by an authentic spirit of service to the nation, have provided a response to the national crisis by establishing objectives and guidelines for the government to develop. For us, respect for human rights is not only born out of the rule of law and of international declarations, but also it is the result of our profound and Christian belief in the preeminent dignity of man as a fundamental value.

And it is precisely to ensure the just protection of the natural rights of man that we assume the full exercise of authority; not to infringe upon liberty but to reaffirm it; not to twist justice but to impose it. After reestablishing an effective authority, which will be revitalized at all levels, we will turn to the organization of the state, whose performance will be based on the permanence and stability of juridical norms which will guarantee the primacy of law and the observance of it by the governors and governed alike.

. . . Even though the armed forces have suspended all political party activity in order to achieve internal peace, they reiterate their decision to guarantee freedom of opinion in the future to those movements authentically national in expression and [having] a proven spirit of service.

A similar attitude determines our policy in the area of labor relations, directed as much at management as at labor. Both labor and management should confine their activities to defending the legitimate aspirations of their members and avoid intruding into areas foreign to their competence.

Likewise, we trust that both workers and businessmen will be conscious of the sacrifices required in these early days and also of the unavoidable necessity of postponing requests that are just in periods of prosperity but which are unattainable in times of emergency. . . .

This immense task which we have undertaken has only one beneficiary: the Argentine people. All the government measures are aimed both at achieving general well-being through productive labor and at developing a genuine spirit of social justice in order to form a vigorous, organized, and unified society that is spiritually and culturally prepared to forge a better future.

No one should expect immediate solutions or spectacular changes in the present situation. The armed forces are cognizant of the magnitude of the task to be performed: they are aware of the profound problems to be resolved; and they know of the special interests that will oppose them on this road that everyone should travel together. But we have to travel this road with firmness, a firmness that is expressed in our decision to complete the process with a profound love of nation and without concessions to anyone. . . .

Speech by Gen. Jorge Rafael Videla. Translated and edited from *La Nación* (Buenos Aires), April 5, 1976.

FINAL DOCUMENT OF THE MILITARY JUNTA REGARDING THE WAR AGAINST SUBVERSION AND TERRORISM: THE FUNDAMENTAL CONCEPTS, 1983

Introduction

This historical synthesis of a painful, yet still near, past is intended to be a message of faith and a recognition of the struggle for liberty, justice, and the right to life.

It is addressed, first of all, to us, the people of a nation, a nation victim of an aggression it did not deserve, invaluable and dedicated participant in the final victory. Second, it is addressed to the world of free men who belong and will continue to belong to the republic, loyal to its historical destiny.

An experience which the nation must never repeat is presented for the reflection of the Argentine people and of the world with the deep desire that, by the grace of God, the brothers of our America and the peoples of other continents will pick up and understand the message, and avoid a similar experience.

The Facts

After the mid-1960s the Argentine Republic began to suffer the aggression of terrorism, which sought both to modify the concept our community holds regarding man and the state and to capture power through violence.

Thefts of arms, assaults on banks and other institutions, kidnappings, extortion, and assassinations on a growing scale made the public aware of the criminal activity of the three most powerful terrorist groups. The actions of these groups, designed to paralyze the population, were characterized by a permanent and indiscriminate violation of the most fundamental human rights: assassinations, tortures, and prolonged detentions, incontrovertible proofs of their criminal acts and intentions.

Their victims came from every social stratum: workers, priests, intellectuals, businessmen, journalists, public employees, military judges, public safety agents, political leaders, union members, and even children.

Active members and decided sympathizers of the terrorist organizations occupied eminent positions in the national cabinet, in the provincial legislatures, and in the judicial branch. Not even the religious organizations nor the police were immune to this infiltration.

Their insidious activity caused the deviation of thousands of young people, many of them still adolescents, incorporated into bands through various recruitment techniques or simply through fear. Many died facing the forces of order; others committed suicide to avoid capture; others deserted trying to hide themselves from both the authorities and their own bands.

In order to have a clear idea of the magnitude of the terrorist activity in terms of numbers, it is worth emphasizing that in the year 1974, there were 21 surprise attacks against units of the legal forces, 466 attacks with explosive devices, and 16 robberies of large sums of money; 117 persons were kidnapped and 110 were assassinated. The year 1976 marked the apex of the violence. Kidnappings reached 600 and assassinations 646, with an average of two victims daily from terrorism; 4,150 terrorist actions were registered, including attacks on localities, actions of armed propaganda, intimidations through extortion, and attacks with explosives.

An examination of newspapers for the years 1973–79 reveals that in that period there were 742 confrontations, resulting in the deaths of 2,050 persons, a figure which does not include the casualties suffered by the government forces.

Between 1969 and 1979, 21,642 terrorist acts were registered. This figure is in direct relation to the magnitude of the subversive structure, which at its height included 25,000 subversives, of which 15,000 were combatants, that is to say, individuals who were technically trained and ideologically fanaticized to kill.

The nature and characteristics of these systematic and persistent surprise attacks forced the adoption of classified procedures in the spreading war. The strictest secrecy had to be imposed on all information regarding military actions and successes, as well as on recent discoveries and planned operations. It became imperative not to alert the enemy, not to reveal our own intentions, thereby recapturing the initiative and the element of surprise which, until that moment, was in the hands of our opponents.

During all these operations, it was practically impossible to establish with precision either the total number of casualties suffered by the bands of criminal terrorists or the identities of their members, even when the cadavers remained behind after an episode. This was due to the fact that they participated using false names, or using nicknames known as "war names," and to the fact that their structure of cells, method of operation, and division of labor made it impossible to have at our disposal a more complete picture of the events.

The efforts made by the armed security and police forces to reestablish peace and order produced increasingly positive results. Terrorist aggression slackened and Argentine society began to recuperate, in terms of peace and security, the ground it had lost. Thus, a painful and cruel period was ended in which the victory finally achieved held the same meaning as that of the defeat of the subversives. This was because Argentine society remained loyal to its traditions, faithful to its conscience, and firm in its decision. For each social sector, the subversives had drawn up and set in motion distinct methodologies, all of which converged on the final goal of destroying those sectors, but this, too, failed to affect the most solid values of a peaceful and free people.

The Principles and Procedures

The exceptional conditions under which the country lived during the period of terrorist aggression meant that the essential elements of the state were affected to such a degree that their very survival was made difficult.

The exercise of human rights was left to the mercy of the selective or indiscriminate violence employed by the terrorist actions. These took the form of assassinations, kidnappings, "revolutionary trials," forced departures from the country, and compulsory contributions.

The government's ability to act was seriously compromised by subversive infiltration and by the political vacuum caused by the death of President Juan Perón. In that crucial, historic moment, the armed forces were summoned by the constitutional government to confront the subversion (Decree No. 261 of January 5, 1975, and Decree No. 272 of October 6, 1975).

In order to procure the common good, the national government, via its legal mandate and through the armed forces as intermediary, ordered the reestablishment of the rights of every inhabitant and of the essential conditions guaranteeing the inviolability of the national territory and of the social contract, thereby facilitating the government's ability to function. The armed security and police forces acted in defense of the national community whose essential rights were not secure, and contrary to subversive actions, the armed forces did not use their power directly against innocent third parties, even though these might have suffered consequences indirectly.

The actions undertaken were the result of assessments of what had to be done in an all-out war, with a measure of the passion which both combat and defense of one's own life generate, within an ambience stained daily by innocent blood, and by destruction, and before a society in which panic reigned. Within this almost apocalyptic framework, errors were committed which, as always happens in every military conflict, could have passed, at times, the limits of respect for fundamental human rights. These errors are subject to God's judgment, to each person's conscience, and to the comprehension of man.

The armed forces hope that this painful experience will enlighten our people, so that we all can find the means compatible with the ethics and the democratic spirit of our institutions.

The Results of the Conflict

It is necessary to point out clearly that there are many unhealed wounds in Argentine society: long years of profound insecurity, frequent moments of terror, loss of family members and loved ones who fell as a result of an attack as unjustified as it was cunning, mutilations, lengthy detentions, and disappearance of people. All this, individual and collective, physical and spiritual, is the result of a war which Argentines must overcome.

The armed forces, faithful to the goal of seeking to heal the wounds left by the struggle and desirous of clarifying the points of doubt which could exist, place in the Ministry of the Interior, at the disposition of everyone, the following information:

—A list of the members of terrorist organizations at present convicted and processed by the federal courts and the councils of war, as well as of those detained by orders of the national executive branch by virtue of Article 23 of the national constitution;

—Requests for the whereabouts of persons (presumably disappeared) registered by the Ministry of the Interior from 1974 to the present;

—Requests for the whereabouts of persons whose cases have been resolved either juridically or administratively;

—Casualties produced by terrorist activity.

It is the theme of disappearances which most strongly batters legitimate humanitarian sentiments, and it is that theme which is employed so insidiously to shock the good faith of those who neither knew about nor lived under the events which took us to the brink. The experience of living through it permits us to affirm that many of the disappearances were a consequence of the terrorists' methods of operation.

The terrorists changed their true names. They knew each other by what were called "war names," and they prepared abundant forged personal documents. These same people are tied to what has been called the "passage to clandestinity," where they decide to join terrorist organizations in a surreptitious manner, abandoning their families, work, and social mediums. This is the most typical case: The family members report a disappearance whose reason they cannot explain, or, if they know the reason, that they do not want to explain.

Therefore, some "disappeared ones" whose absence has been reported appear later carrying out terrorist activities. In other cases, the terrorists secretly leave the country and live in the exterior under a false identity. Others, after exiling themselves, return to the country with forged papers. And finally, there also exist fugitive terrorists, either inside or outside the republic.

There are also cases of deserters from the various organizations who live today with false identities, inside or outside the country, in order to protect their own lives.

Many of those who died in confrontations with the legal forces either carried no identification at all or had false documents and, in many cases, had their fingerprints obliterated. Faced with imminent capture, other terrorists committed suicide, normally by swallowing cyanide pills. In these cases, the bodies were not claimed, and given the impossibility of identifying them, they were buried legally as "unknowns."

Moreover, whenever possible, the terrorists carried the bodies of their dead from the site of the battle. These bodies, as well as those of the wounded who died later, were either destroyed or buried clandestinely by the terrorists themselves.

The struggle for hegemony among the terrorists led to assassinations and kidnappings among the distinct organizations. The terrorists, in compliance with a pseudorevolutionary code, made a parody of justice and assassinated those of their members who defected or failed in their assigned missions. The bodies were buried with false identities or in unknown places and circumstances.

During the struggle, the legal forces infiltrated men into the terrorist organizations. If discovered, they were killed, and their burial place was never made known.

Moreover, there have been cases of persons reported as missing who later appeared and led normal lives without this fact having been made known to the proper judicial or administrative authorities.

Finally, the list of "disappeared ones" may be artificially increased by including those cases not attributable to the terrorist phenomenon but rather to events which habitually occur in all large urban centers.

It is appropriate to emphasize that the reports of supposed kidnappings are the subject of judicial investigation and that a large number of trials for the presumed crime of illegal deprivation of liberty have been initiated officially by the appropriate judges.

The possibility that persons considered "disappeared" might be found buried as unknowns has always been one of the principal hypotheses accepted by the government. We agree with the judgment in the report drawn up by the Inter-American Commission on Human Rights, which visited the country in 1979, when it states that, in certain cemeteries, one can verify the interment of unidentified persons who died in a violent manner, most of them in confrontations with the legal forces.

It is also said of the "disappeared ones" that they will be found detained by the Argentine government in unknown sites in the country. This is nothing more than a lie for political ends. There no longer exist in the republic secret detention sites, nor are there in the prisons persons clandestinely detained.

It should be made definitively clear that those who figure in the lists of "disappeared ones," and who are not in exile or underground, are considered to be dead, in judicial and administrative terms, even when it has not been possible to determine either the cause or place of the death or the site of burial.

Final Considerations

The victory achieved at such a high price depended upon the general assent of the citizenry who understood the complex phenomenon of subversion and expressed, through its leaders, its repudiation of violence. From this attitude on the part of the population, it is clear that the desire of the entire nation is to put an end once and for all to a painful period in our history, in order to begin, in union and liberty, the definitive constitutional institutionalization of the republic.

In order to achieve success on this road, it is absolutely essential that we have the equilibrium sufficient to comprehend that which has happened, without forgetting the circumstances which carried us to the very edge of disintegration or the responsibilities which, by commission or omission, will correspond to the distinct sectors of the community, for not traveling again that painful road.

Those who gave their lives to combat the terrorist scourge merit our eternal homage of respect and appreciation. Those who knew how to sustain the principles of a style of life based on respect for the fundamental rights of people and on the values of liberty, peace, and democracy, risking their personal security and that of their families (political leaders, priests, businessmen, labor leaders, magistrates, or simple citizens), merit the recognition of the nation.

Those who placed their intelligence, goodwill, solidarity, and piety, indeed, the whole weight of their being, at the service of the reconciliation of the Argentine family are worthy of recognition and respect. . . .

Going beyond ideological differences and joining with them by virtue of being children of God, we say to those who lost their lives by enrolling in the terrorist organizations which attacked the very society that had nurtured them, you will receive your pardon.

Those who have recognized their error and have atoned for their mistakes deserve help. In its generosity, the Argentine society is willing to take them back into the fold.

Reconciliation constitutes a difficult beginning of an era of maturity and responsibility realistically assumed by everyone. The scars represent not only a painful memory, but also the foundation of a strong democracy, of a united and free people, a people which learned that subversion and terrorism constitute the inexorable death of liberty.

The armed forces are delivering this information to the citizenry so that they, in common, can judge this sad period of our history, which as such is a problem which touches all Argentines and one which all Argentines should resolve in common if we want to assure the survival of the republic.

Because of all of that expressed above, the military junta declares the following:

1. That the information and explanations furnished in this document represent the sum total of everything the armed forces have at

their disposal to inform the nation about the results and consequences of the war against subversion and terrorism;

2. That within this frame of reference, one that was not desired by the armed forces, who had it forced upon them in order to defend the system of national life, only history can judge with exactitude who bears the direct responsibility for unjust methods and innocent deaths;

3. That the activities of the members of the armed forces in operations carried out during the successful war constitute acts of military service;

4. That the armed forces acted, as they will every time that it is necessary, in obedience to an emergency order from the national government, taking advantage of all the experience gleaned from this painful circumstance in national life;

5. That the armed forces submit to the people and to the judgment of history these decisions, which translate into an attitude having as its goal the common good, identified in that instance with the survival of the community, and whose content they assume with the authentic sorrow of Christians who recognize the errors which could have been committed in the carrying out of the assigned mission.

Original Spanish version provided to editors by the Argentine embassy, Washington, DC.

CHAPTER 16

Brazil

Gentlemen Members of the National Congress:

When I addressed the nation for the first time as president of the republic, I promised all Brazilians that I would relentlessly promote the general welfare. I did not ignore, at that moment, either the responsibility attached to such a gesture, nor the magnitude of the tasks ahead. I was also convinced that the whole nation would respond to my dramatic call to collaborate, even with some sacrifice, in order to resume the development process and to achieve true social justice.

After almost three years, I bring before Your Excellencies an account of my government, as a testimony of how much has been demanded from the Brazilian people so that they could regain confidence in the ideals of their government.

There was no break in this process, and the struggle included all areas of activity. The initial steps of the program called for implanting radical structural reforms, a stoical and permanent inflationary decompression, along with the overriding objective of boosting the national economy and revitalizing the country's management.

But no social change can take place without having [an] effect on the balance of political forces. The defects of the infrastructure always incite the former privileged groups to resist the new laws promoting equality; the new institutions still arouse stubborn opposition . . . and the memory of old habits stirs up discontent and regret in a permanent struggle to retake the government.

For that very reason, the rupture of the juridical order existing until March 31, 1964, called for the adoption of certain political measures in order to provide an adequate transition according to the terms and the ideas of the revolution.

I want to emphasize, of course, the application of Articles 7 and 10 of the First Institutional Act, strengthened later by Articles 14 and 15 of Institutional Act number 2.

In the exercise of such prerogatives, some legislative measures were canceled, and the political rights of persons indicated by the members of the National Security Council were suspended. I repeat, these decrees were political measures of the revolution. They were not inspired by a simplistic whim to punish. On the contrary, a rigorous verification of responsibilities was conducted in every case. And it must be remembered that every revolutionary process presupposes, in its own context, measures of a repressive nature. Very few, however, have proceeded with as much justice and moderation as the March 1964 movement. . . .

Since 1945 the legislation and dynamics of the representative system have deeply misguided and profoundly distorted the will of the people. A multiplicity of parties and the abuse of economic power in the electoral campaigns were two of the basic causes.

. . . In turn, the effects of multipartyism on the administrative life of the country provoked a continuous instability, with the obvious consequences. As an example, let it be remembered that the average term in office for the ministers of state, from 1946 to 1964, did not reach 224 days.

. . . [In this context] it is once more fitting to review the serious weakening of democratic institutions in the phase prior to the revolution. A social and political crisis, which reached unbearable levels, became a factor in the deteriorating internal and external economic situation, then already very critical.

As an unavoidable consequence, there occurred a decline in the efficiency of all aspects of national activity. Confronted with the need to reveal the implications of such a situation in relation to national development, we shall now undertake a brief analysis of the Brazilian situation as of March 1964, focusing especially on the socioeconomic aspects.

Despite the various structural limitations that tended to conspire against self-sustained and rapid development, the Brazilian economy experienced satisfactory performance in the period from World War II to the year 1961, and especially between the years 1947–61. During that period the gross domestic product grew at an average annual rate of 5.8 percent (equivalent to 3 percent per capita). The . . . expansion of the industrial sector through the substitution of domestic products for imported goods was the most important stimulus.

However, this process of development took place against the backdrop of a social and economic structure unfavorable to lasting economic progress. Alongside the rapid growth of the manufacturing sector, the conditions of the agrarian sector—in which more than 50 percent of the national population existed at a low standard of living—remained almost unchanged, victim of the reigning technical backwardness in the rural sector and of the unsatisfactory levels of education, health, and hygiene.

Likewise, an archaic financial structure, highly sensitive to inflationary pressure, persisted along with a lack of basic services (transportation, energy, silos and warehouses, and communications), aggravated over and over by incorrect economic policies. An opportunistic and myopic view of the economic relations of the country with the rest of the world led to neglect of exports, which constituted the main determining element of the external purchasing power of the country. As a consequence, the Brazilian capacity to import stagnated.

Finally, during the entire above-mentioned period, that is, from after the war to 1961, the Brazilian economy developed within an atmosphere of continuous inflation of variable but bearable intensity, to the point of having permitted the satisfactory evolution of the gross domestic product, at least until 1961. In the meantime, the presence of those inflationary pressures, with partial control by government officials, was harmful enough to produce undesirable distortions in the system of relative prices and to give way to speculative activities, one consequence of which was the weakening of the money and capital market and the rates of savings and exports. The extraordinary growth of the Brazilian population and the resulting increase in the demand for new jobs, linked to the vulnerability of the public administration to political pressure, encouraged the transformation of employment in the public sector into "political spoils." This undermined operational efficiency and generated increasing deficits. The consolidated deficits of the government in turn were traditionally financed with currency issues, a source of new inflationary pressures. It ended in a vicious circle. . . .

Starting in 1962, several circumstances tended to increase the government expenses, independent of the comparative increase in the fiscal revenues, with a consequent progressive evolution of deficits in the case of the National Treasury and an increase of the rate of inflation. There were also serious signs of a worsening of the balance-of-payments situation and the reduction of import capacity. The deficiency of the economic infrastructure became more acute, creating a climate of uncertainty and uneasiness. As a consequence, the level of investments and the growth rate of the economy declined, and the weaknesses of the national economy became more evident.

As a result of all this, increases in the general level of prices, which had reached an average of 15 percent per year between 1941 and 1946 [and] rose to 20 percent in the period from 1951 to 1958, suffered a rapid acceleration starting in 1959. The rate of increase in the cost of living rose in that year to 52 percent in Guanabara, and, after going down in 1960, started rising progressively until reaching 55 percent in 1962 and 81 percent in 1963. In the first quarter of 1964 it reached 25 percent and, given its rate of acceleration, it could have very well reached 150 percent by the end of the year. . . . The social and political atmosphere of the previous administration could not have been more unfavorable. The following factors should be underlined: the constant political tension created by the disharmony between the federal executive on the one hand and the national Congress and the state governments on the other, distrustful of the anticonstitutionalist intentions and desires of the old regime [to maintain itself in power]; a penchant toward state property and control that created a continuous discouragement and threat to private investors; the Communist infiltration, generating apprehensions about the overthrow of the social and economic order; the successive paralysis of production by the "strike commands." Not only did urban activities suffer but also investments in farming and cattle raising were discouraged. . . . Political instability and administrative improvisation prevailed, producing a lack of national direction . . . the entrepreneurial classes suffered from a crisis of distrust; the working classes found themselves frustrated because of the impossibility of their realizing the demagogic promises; finally, certain, more restless groups, such as the students, not finding an outlet for their idealistic impulses, slipped into the error of subversive solutions. . . .

To summarize, when this government took power, the financial and economic situation was truly gloomy. To the structural deficiencies of the national economy had been added temporary troubles which underscored these [deficiencies], disrupted internal markets, pushed the increase in prices to the verge of extreme inflation, generated a crisis of confidence [and] a slowdown in the flow of investments and in the rate of economic development. [These troubles also] increased the level of unemployment, and, finally, they damaged the country's credit abroad. The most urgent task, therefore, was to contain the extraordinary rise of the general level of prices, to recover the minimum necessary order for the functioning of the national economy, to overcome the crisis of confidence, and to return to the entrepreneurs and to the workers the tranquillity necessary for productive activities. . . .

Reprinted and edited from Mensagem ao Congresso Nacional Remedita pelo Presidente de la República na Abertura da Sessão Legislativa de 1967 (Message to the National Congress by the president of the Republic at the opening of the legislative session of 1967). Translated by Cecilia Ubilla.

SPEECH BY PRESIDENT ERNESTO GEISEL
BEFORE THE BRAZILIAN CABINET, 1974

. . . In a previous public statement I have already pointed out that the modernizing Revolution of 1964 bases all of its strategic doctrine on the two pillars of development and security, recognizing, of course, that in essence the first of the two is the dominant one. In more precise terms, one can say that the strategic action of the revolution has been and will continue to be exercised in such a way as to promote for the Brazilian people at all levels, at every stage, the maximum possible development with a minimum of indispensable security.

Likewise, in the area of national security the process is also essentially integrated, since this process is the same as national development, though applied to a more specialized and more restricted area. The minimum of indispensable security results, therefore, from an interaction duly balanced . . . in each of its integrated components.

. . . It is clear that we have received a valuable heritage from the governments of the revolution, which in these last ten years managed to raise Brazil to an outstanding position among the new world powers, with an internal market which places Brazil among the ten largest of the Western world, and a gross domestic product, this year, on the order of $66 billion. After a phase of pressing sacrifices, during which combating inflation, remodeling economic institutions, and reestablishing internal credibility became priorities, and, parallel to this, the creation of a climate of order, stability, dedication to work, and faith in the future—we begin to see indications of highly satisfactory performance: rates of growth of actual product, since 1968, between 9 percent and 11.5 percent a year; inflation on the decline and neutralized in regard to its major distortions, because of corrections in monetary policy and the system of minidevaluations; balance-of-payments surpluses, permitting the accumulation of reserves, [which amounted] in December 1973 to more than $6 billion.

Thanks to the impressive dynamism of the economy under President Médici, the country recorded the highest level of prosperity in modern history, with expectations that per capita income will exceed $600 in 1974.

The great expansion and diversification of our external sector, accomplished in those ten years, increased foreign trade to a value of

$12 billion in 1973, which will enable the country to face the most serious challenges of the future confidently.

It is not less certain, however, that the drastic changes which have taken place in the world scene—such as the serious energy crisis, the shortage of basic foods and raw materials in general and the shortage of oil and its by-products in particular; the instability of the international monetary system, already in a painful search for a new order; the inflation which has spread over the entire world at alarming rates; the political and social tensions, aggravated by the ferment of the irresponsible calls to violence, which disturb the life of many nations, in a setting of transition toward the still not well-defined new international order—all of these have serious repercussions on the national scene, especially in a year of intense political activity such as 1974. . . .

The great success achieved and the spirit of unity of the governments of the revolution . . . suggest that the major thrusts of government policy be continued.

Continuity, however, does not mean immobility. And if we intend to adapt to those new external circumstances, which represent a serious challenge, we must not only improve the institutional mechanisms for the coordination of development and security policy, but also take care of new objectives and of new priorities which derive, naturally, from the high level of progress already attained by the country.

. . . In regard to domestic politics, we shall welcome sincere movements toward gradual but sure democratic progress, expanding honest and mutually respectful dialogue and encouraging more participation from responsible elites and from the people in general . . . in order to create a climate of basic consensus and to proceed to the institutionalization of the principles of the Revolution of 1964. I am anxious to see the extraordinary instruments with which the government has armed itself to maintain an atmosphere of security and order which is fundamental for socioeconomic progress . . . used less frequently [and] . . . made unnecessary by a creative political imagination which will install, at the opportune moment, efficacious safeguards . . . within the constitutional context.

It is evident that this will not solely depend on the federal executive power, since, to a great extent, it calls for the sincere and effective collaboration of the other powers of the nation as well as that of the other government organs in the state and even municipal centers, including conscientious discipline and their own ironing out of difficulties. It will necessarily depend on the spirit of debate of the restless and disoriented minorities, disturbers of the country's life, irresponsible or demagogic, resorting even to deceit, intrigue, or violence—[and their] recognition of the general repudiation [of their doctrines] and the full recognition of today's unquestionable reality: the definitive implantation of our revolutionary doctrine.

One must not accuse this doctrine of being antidemocratic when . . . it is essentially aiming at perfecting, in realistic terms, democratic practices and adapting them in a way better suited to the characteristics of our people and to the current stage of the social and political revolution of the country, yet safe from the attacks—overt or covert—of those who in the name of liberal democracy only wish, in fact, to destroy it or to corrupt it for their own benefit. . . .

Reprinted and edited from *O Estado* (São Paulo), March 20, 1974. Translated by Cecilia Ubilla.

SPEECH BY PRESIDENT JOÃO FIGUEIREDO
TO THE BRAZILIAN NATION ON THE
SIXTEENTH ANNIVERSARY OF THE REVOLUTION (1980)

On this date sixteen years ago, the Armed Forces of the Nation were confronted with the historic mission of halting the most menacing political threat to the aspirations of our people ever experienced by us. The Brazilian family reacted with resolution and vitality against that imminent destruction of our traditional political institutions.

Under the pretext of protecting the poor and needy, democracy's enemies actually sought to exploit a peace-loving and orderly people by negating their rights as well as the social progress already achieved. Furthermore, they attempted to subjugate Brazil to interests which were ideologically, politically, and economically opposed to our own.

However, the nation was not as passive as those who wished to destroy it imagined. Throughout Brazil, a vehement outcry came forth and grew against the attempted denial of our values and the disrespect for law and order. In the barracks, on our ships, and in our air force, a unified view solidified our determination. We could not leave the nation to the mercy of subversion, demagogy, civil hatred, distrust, and class struggle.

These concerns were as profound as they were universal. We knew and felt that most Brazilians also shared these concerns. We also knew and felt how superficial was the uproar of those who said they spoke for the people but in fact were repudiated by them.

The "Nation in Arms" responded in concrete terms to all the appeals heard throughout Brazil.

Marshal Castello Branco described the revolution [the coup of 1964] as "an inevitable stage in our evolution." Brazil's commitment to democracy led the nation to "progress without damaging our people's fundamental characteristics and feelings."

Only those who oppose the revolution for the sake of opposition itself would deny our firm determination to achieve the goals we first announced some sixteen years ago. In fact, we should not worry about the opposition, because they fail to acknowledge the evidence. They are blind and mute, refusing to see or to answer. They are less perceptive than rocks.

The course that we are taking in order to create a more just, politically open, and pluralistic society is the same course chosen by the revolutionaries of 1922, 1924, 1930, and 1945. Such a society is founded upon personal and civil rights written in the constitution. Man's progress and the fulfillment of his political aspirations are the only and final objectives of every State action.

Therefore, in the lawful State, order is a necessary, a priori, and undeniable requirement. Marshal Costa e Silva affirmed that order is "a projection of the spirit upon an external reality which disciplines it, gives it meaning, and makes it possible for social groups to flourish."

Derived from liberty itself, order is thus distinct from the silence imposed by the tyrant's intransigent hands. Order does not call for a monolithic conformity with official truth. It is from within the legal order that different opinions are expressed; this attribute characterizes genuinely free societies.

For these reasons, I say that democracy, justice, equality, the rule of law, and respect for the will of the majority, are the foundations for the political and social structure. And let us not deceive ourselves. If one of these basic elements is missing, then none will exist.

At the same time, the revolution occurred in order to address the impasses that were rapidly accumulating and threatening to destroy the nation's chances for economic development. For the first time, we had experienced negative growth in our per capita national product. Our credit abroad was in shambles; almost all our exports faced a crisis. In addition, there appeared to be no future or incentives for our industry, commerce, and agriculture.

Faced with this gloomy picture, the revolutionary governments brought progress despite the economic difficulties. Today, we face the difficulties produced by economic growth, rather than those of stagnation and despair. In the words of President Emílio Médici, the revolution "will be considered by history as the period in which the nation's greatness was constructed."

The statistics confirm the development experienced by all sectors. In many respects, Brazil has grown more during these sixteen years than during the ninety-five years since the Proclamation of the Republic [1889].

Yet, if it was not possible to achieve even more, or if in certain cases the actual results did not meet our expectations, it is essential to recognize that this is due to the difficult international situation we experienced: the petroleum crisis and imported inflation. The historical circumstances, known to all Brazilians, prompted mistakes or forced us to change our plans.

All this would not matter in a totalitarian regime. These regimes would change the historical records or alter history itself. The central goals of our revolution, in contrast, are to reform (and always as quickly as possible) and to realize the ideals of supporting, defending, and sustaining democracy as the legitimate political form of government.

With this same frankness, I recognize that we were only partially successful in fighting inflation and in improving the foreign trade balance. To this end, the Brazilian people have been making great sacrifices, especially wage earners and the less fortunate classes in general. We must recognize, however, that this indispensable sacrifice should be divided equitably, with the greatest share relegated to the wealthy.

As I have already stated on other occasions, the producers, industrial and commercial, will need to accept lower profit margins in order to maintain lower prices for consumers. I hope that they do this voluntarily.

In the face of all these difficulties, we continue as resolute today as we were in the first minutes of the revolution. If the political opening consciously initiated by my honorable predecessor appears to emphasize the occasional errors rather than the great and permanent accomplishments, then I suggest that we should not forget President Ernesto Geisel's warning. He affirmed that we have the duty to remind those who had not lived through the inauspicious times of the nightmare and affliction which shrouded our well-intentioned hearts during the prolonged vigil over the nation's agony. Those times were "the abyss of incapacity, vacillation, corruption, and disorder that were subverting all of Brazil's institutions."

Brazilians: The revolutionary process has not ended; it continues with the implementation of the goals we have proposed. Naturally, the revolutionary methods will not be as evident as before, but the ideals are permanent, or we would not be "in the beginning of a new era," to use the words of President Emílio Médici.

As I have already promised to make this country a democracy, I now affirm to all Brazilians that we, the 1964 revolutionaries, shall not deviate from our course of pursuing the normalization of the political process.

Every day, one can see that democratic privileges are more evident among us. This is proof of the government's uncompromising intention to struggle for a democracy founded upon our moral and spiritual values. In accordance with the desires of Brazilians, the government rests upon Christian principles that have accompanied us since our formation as a people.

Translated, reprinted, and edited from João Figueiredo, *Discursos, 1980* (Brasília: Presidencia da República, 1981), vol. 2, pp. 39–44.

CHAPTER 17

Chile

THE REASONS OF THE JUNTA, 1973

In Order of the Day No. 5, the Junta outlines for the public benefit the reasons which moved it to assume control of the country.

The text of the order is as follows:

Order of the Day No. 5

Whereas:

1. The Allende government has exceeded the bounds of legitimacy by violating the fundamental rights of liberty, of speech, and of education; the right to congregate, to strike, and to petition; the right to own property and, in general, the right to a worthy and stable existence;

2. the government has destroyed national unity, encouraged sterile and, in many cases, cruel class wranglings, disdained the invaluable help which every Chilean could give to preserve the country's welfare, and engendered a blind fratricidal struggle based on ideas alien to our national heritage which have been proven false and ineffective;

3. the government has shown itself to be incapable of assuring a peaceful association among Chileans by nonobservance of the common law on many occasions;

4. the government has placed itself outside the law on multiple occasions, resorting to arbitrary, dubious, ill-mentioned, and even flagrantly erroneous interpretations of it, which, for various reasons, have escaped sanction;

5. by the use of subterfuge, which the government was pleased to call *resquicios legales* [legal loopholes], some laws have not been promulgated, others have been flouted, and a situation of illegitimacy engendered;

6. the government has repeatedly failed to observe the mutual respect which one power of the state owes to another, disregarding decisions approved by Congress, by the courts of

justice, and by the comptroller general of the republic, offering unacceptable excuses for so doing or none at all;

7. the supreme authority has deliberately exceeded its attributes . . . gravely compromising the rights and liberties of all;

8. the president himself has been unable to disguise the fact that the exercise of his personal authority is subject to decisions taken by committees of the political parties which support him, impairing the image of maximum authority which the constitution confers upon him;

9. the agricultural, commercial, and industrial economies of the country are in a state either of stagnation or recession and inflation is rampant, but there are no signs whatever that the government is interested in them, except as a mere spectator;

10. anarchy, stifling of liberties, moral and economic chaos, and, as far as the government is concerned, absolute irresponsibility and incapacity have led the country to ruin, preventing it from occupying its proper place among the leading nations of the continent;

11. the foregoing justify our opinion that the internal and external security of the country is in dire peril, that our very existence as an independent state is in danger, and that the continuance in power of the government is fatal to the interest of the republic and the welfare of its people;

12. that, moreover, the foregoing, viewed in the light of our national and historical idiosyncracies, is sufficient to justify our determination to oust an illegitimate, immoral government, no longer representative of national sentiment, in order to avoid the greater evils which threaten the country, there being no other reasonable method holding out promise of success, and it being our objective to reestablish normal economic and social conditions in the country, with peace, tranquillity, and security for all;

13. for the foregoing reasons the armed forces have taken upon themselves the moral duty, which the country imposes upon them, of deposing the government, which, although legitimate in the early exercise of its power, has since fallen into flagrant illegitimacy, assuming power for ourselves only for so long as circumstances so demand and counting on the support of the vast majority, all of which, before God and his-

tory, justifies our action; and hence whatever regulations, norms, and instructions we may think fit to lay down for the attainment of our objectives aimed at the common good and the maximum patriotic interest;

14. Consequently, the very legitimacy of the said norms obliges all, and especially those in authority, to abide by them.

Signed: Government Junta of the Armed Forces and Carabineros of Chile

Santiago, September 11, 1973

Reprinted and edited from *Three Years of Destruction* Asimpres (Chilean Printers Association, n.d.).

CHILE SHOULD NOT FALL INTO THE VICES OF THE PAST
SPEECH BY GENERAL AUGUSTO PINOCHET, 1983

I want to put those politicians who are anxious to recoup power on notice that we will not tolerate either limits or conditions being put upon the exercise of authority beyond those established by the legitimately approved constitutional provisions, which are an expression of an authentic consensus which no one can ignore.

On September 11, 1980, the country opted for a renovated democracy, one distinct from that defenseless system which carried us to the very edge of a confrontation between brothers and one which, also to differentiate it from that system, is fundamentally inspired by traditional national values which, throughout our history, gave our fatherland its own physiognomy.

This nationalistic democracy does not accept international ideological commitments, or economic linkages with these ideologies, which, in the end, preclude liberty and self-determination.

On numerous occasions, I have pointed out that the democracy which we approved cannot be confused with the traditional democracy which we knew until 1970; that sectors which are confused or have unstated designs are seeking to reestablish it, knowing that such conduct will cast the country headlong into *politiquería* and the chaos we have already known; and that we are repelling and will continue to repel the permanent aggression of Soviet imperialism.

Our historical experience confirms that political parties, as they were called under the old constitutional framework, tended to transform themselves into monopolistic sources for the generation of power; that they made social conflict more acute; and that in the electoral struggle in which they engaged, ethical limits disappeared, thereby allowing for any maneuver whatsoever to injure their adversaries, including the defamation and dishonoring of individuals and of families.

Moreover, that concept of political parties accepts those who obey foreign orders and who even receive economic support from the outside, constituting themselves as true advance men of international ideologies foreign to our reality.

As a result, there exists a profound difference between the constitution approved by the citizenry and the political plan elaborated by one of the opposition groups on the occasion of the 1980 plebiscite.

Through an intensive campaign, those opposition groups have insisted upon the reestablishment of the old democratic system with only minor adjustments which maintain its defects and vacuousness.

It is my duty to call to the attention of my fellow citizens that which, without doubt, would lead to a fatal confusion.

When the government and the opposition speak of "returning to full democracy," they are not referring to the same thing. Between the one philosophy and the other, there are profound differences which no one should ignore.

In the face of a totalitarian threat, and in order not to return to the vices of the past, the government over which I preside is delineating, within the framework established by the constitution, a political system which will give to the intermediate bodies of the society (those no longer contaminated by the disease of partisanship) the administration and government of the regions and municipalities, a system whose goal is the establishment of an authentic and effective democracy.

The foregoing does not mean the elimination of political parties, but rather the placing of them in their true role as currents of opinion framed within a juridical order which will save the country from excesses, as parties whose bases are those consecrated by the people of Chile in their new constitution.

Only in this way will we preserve our most sacred republican traditions, avoid the distortions which an unbridling of partisanship would bring, and give to democracy an authentically representative dimension.

In order to avoid falling anew into the vices of the past, we will continue, with a firm stance, in the work of renovating completely our institutional system to the end of banishing forever the inveterate habits which are an inevitable consequence of the excesses which Chilean partisanship brought down upon itself during various generations.

There is no doubt that we Chileans will not allow ourselves to be dragged down either by false ideals of apparent salvation or by the hallucinatory demagogy of a few politicians from the past.

Translated and reprinted from *Pinochet: Patria y democracia* (Santiago: Editorial Andrés Bello, 1983), pp. 27–29.

CHAPTER 18

Peru

MANIFESTO OF THE REVOLUTIONARY GOVERNMENT OF PERU, 1968

Upon assuming power in Peru, the armed forces want to make known to the Peruvian people the underlying causes for their far-reaching and historic decision, a decision which marks the beginning of the definitive emancipation of our fatherland.

Powerful economic forces, both national and foreign, in complicity with contemptible Peruvians motivated by [the desire for] unbridled speculation and profit, have monopolized the economic and political power of the nation. These forces have frustrated the people's desire for basic structural reforms by maintaining the existing unjust social and economic order which allows a privileged few to monopolize the national riches, thereby forcing the great majority to suffer economic deprivation inimical to human dignity.

The economic growth rate of the country has been poor, creating a crisis which not only adversely affects the financial condition of the nation, but which also weighs heavily on the great mass of our citizens. The contracts for our natural resources have been ruinous, thereby forcing us into a dependent relationship with the great economic powers, compromising our national sovereignty and dignity, and postponing indefinitely the reforms necessary to overcome our present state of underdevelopment.

Overwhelming personal ambition in the exercise of the responsibilities of the executive and legislative branches in the discharging of public and administrative duties, as well as in other fields of the nation's activities, has produced immoral acts which the public has repudiated. This selfishness has also destroyed public faith and confidence in the government, a confidence which must be restored if the people are to overcome their feeling of frustration and the false conception of government that has come about because of the lack of action and responsiveness on the part of those charged with rectifying this unfortunate situation and with improving Peru's present world image.

In 1963 the Peruvian people went to the polls with a profound democratic faith and voted for the recently ousted regime in the belief that that government's program of reform and revolutionary change would become a reality. Our history will record the overwhelming popular support enjoyed by that now defunct government, as well as the loyal and dedicated cooperation offered by the armed forces, support with which it should have been able to implement its program of action. But instead of dedicating their efforts to finding executive and legislative solutions to the nation's ills, that government's leaders, with other corrupt politicians, scorned the popular will and moved to defend those powerful interest groups which had thwarted the aspirations of the people. They subordinated the collective welfare to their . . . ambition for personal aggrandizement. Proof of this can be seen in the government's lack of direction, its compromises, its immorality, its surrender [of natural resources], its corruption, its improvisation—in the absence of any social sensitivity, characteristics of a government so bad that it should not be allowed to remain in office.

The armed forces have observed with patriotic concern the political, economic, and social crisis which has gripped the nation. The armed forces had hoped that a combination of good judgment and hard work would enable the nation to overcome the crisis and to improve the lot of the people through the democratic process, but that hope too was shattered.

The culmination of all these blunders came with the fraudulent and unbridled use of extraordinary powers which were granted unconstitutionally to the executive. One example was the pseudosolution, a national surrender, in the La Brea y Pariñas affair, a surrender which clearly demonstrated that the moral decline of the nation had reached such . . . extremes as to jeopardize Peru's very future. It was because of this that the armed forces, fulfilling their constitutional obligations, are acting to defend one of Peru's natural sources of wealth, which since it is Peruvian, should be for Peruvians.

As the people come to understand better the revolutionary stance of the armed forces, they will see it as the road to salvation for the republic and the way to move definitively toward the attainment of our national goals.

The action of the Revolutionary Government will be shaped by the necessity of transforming the structure of the state in such a manner as to permit efficient governmental operation; of transforming the social, political, and economic structures of the country; of maintaining a definitively nationalist posture, a clear, independent position internationally, and a firm defense of national sovereignty and dignity; of reestablishing fully the principles of authority, of respect for and obedience to the law, and of the predominance of justice and morality in all areas of national endeavor.

The Revolutionary Government promises that it will respect all the international agreements that Peru has ratified, that it will remain faithful to the principles of our Western, Christian tradition, and that it will encourage foreign investment that subjects itself to the interests and laws of the nation.

The Revolutionary Government, clearly identified as it is with the aspirations of the people, issues a call to work with the armed forces to achieve social justice, dynamic national development, and the reestablishment of those moral values which will assure our fatherland of its greatest destiny.

Reprinted and edited from Perú, Comando Conjunto de la Fuerza Armada, *3 de Octubre de 1968: ¿Por Qué?* (Lima: n.p., 1968).

SPEECH BY JUAN VELASCO ALVARADO, 1969*

Fellow Citizens:

Upon completing the first year of government, I am here tonight, on behalf of the armed forces, not only as the chief of state, but also principally as the chief of the revolution. But this title carries with it a meaning radically different from those of the past. . . . To be the chief of the revolution is to be the leader of a team of men who are profoundly identified with the revolutionary spirit of the armed forces, on whose behalf was initiated a year ago the process of transforming our country.

This is not a personalist government. There is no one preordained nor irreplaceable among us; nobody has a monopoly on either wisdom or power. We are a team that is carrying out the revolution that Peru needs, the revolution that others proclaimed, only to betray once they were in power. But we know that this will not be understood by those who in reality are no more than simple *caciques* of a new breed, extremists of personalism, vanity, and political fraud.

During the year that ends today, we have begun the process of national transformation that the armed forces promised the country

---

*This speech was given on the first anniversary of the military takeover in Peru.

on October 3, 1968. In this brief period, we have completed an enormous task, but it has only been the beginning of the revolutionary process. There still remains an immense job which will require long years of effort and struggle. We will finish it regardless of the obstacles because that is what the urgent needs of our people demand and because that is what the armed forces committed themselves to doing when they assumed the responsibility of governing the country.

Faced with this duty, on whose fulfillment the very destiny of Peru depends, we assign little importance to the selfish cries and false protests of those who always used power for their own profit and benefit. Today there is a chorus of voices, known to everyone, that demands the immediate return to constitutionality, that aspires to encourage a vanity which we do not possess, in order to suggest our sudden retirement and our participation in an electoral contest through which they hope to restore that formal democracy which they debased to the point of converting it into a great hypocrisy—speaking of liberty to a people victimized by exploitation, misery, hunger, corruption, surrender, and venality.

Because of that, I want to repeat that not one of us has political ambitions. We are not interested in competing in the electoral arena. We have not come to play the game of politics. We have come to make a revolution. And, if in order to make it we are required to act politically, we should not be confused with those criollo politicians who did so much damage to the country. . . .

Certainly those people do not want to understand what has happened in Peru, but we are living a *revolution*, and it is time that everyone understood it. Every genuine revolution substitutes one economic, political, and social system for another which is qualitatively different. Just as the French Revolution was not made to shore up the monarchy, ours was not launched to defend the established order in Peru, but rather to alter it fundamentally in all of its essential aspects.

Some people expected very different things and were confident, as had been the custom, that we came to power for the sole purpose of calling elections and returning to them all their privileges. The people who thought that way were and are mistaken. One cannot ask this revolution to respect the institutional norms of the system against which it revolted. This revolution has to create, and is now creating, its own institutional structure. . . . Our proposals have nothing to do with the traditional forms of criollo politics that we have banished forever from Peru.

For that reason, our legitimacy does not come from votes, from the votes of a rotten political system, because that system never acted in defense of the true interests of the Peruvian people. Our legitimacy has its origins in the incontrovertible fact that we are transforming this country, precisely to defend and interpret the interests of that people who were cheated and sold out with impunity. This is the only legitimacy of an authentic revolution like ours.

Of what value to the true man of the people was the liberty they spoke of and then traded away in the back rooms of the National Palace and the Congress? What did these defenders of formal democracy and constitutional rights ever do to resolve, once and for all, the fundamental problems that afflicted Peru and her people? . . . Where are the profound reforms that they promised so often at election time and then, once in power, whisked out of sight in order to serve the oligarchy? . . .

Nevertheless, do not think we have any interest whatsoever in refuting the charges that are hurled against the revolution. The best defense of the revolution lies in its accomplishments. . . . We do not talk of revolution; we are making one. That is our best justification before Peru and before history. All honorable Peruvians are conscious of the fact that, for the first time, we have begun to attack in toto the fundamental problems of the country.

There is plenary proof of our deeds. There is that handful of far-reaching accomplishments that greatly surpass everything that was achieved by past governments. There is the recovery of our petroleum from the hands of a foreign company which previously, because of bribery or fear, influenced the politicians that governed this country from both the [executive branch] and the Congress. There is the new Agrarian Reform Law that benefits the campesinos and breaks the back of the oligarchy, which until recently was all powerful. There is the General Water Law that at last fulfills the dreams of thousands of farmers whose rights were always trampled upon to benefit the *latifundistas*.

There is the new mining policy which ends the old practices which were prejudicial to the interests of Peru. There is the law which puts a stop to the abusive speculation in lands for urban expansion and which will contribute, in a very important way, to remedying the problem of urban housing. There is the initiation of a policy of state control over the Central Reserve Bank, which now does not represent private interests but the interests of the nation. Finally, there is the new international policy, not of submission but of dignity, whose course is limited solely to the interests of Peru.

All of this, and much more, has been achieved in scarcely one year of government action. There are those who assert that the power of propaganda is very great, and possibly this is so. But no propaganda can erase from the minds of all Peruvians the conviction that this government is doing the things that no other dared to attempt, either because of fear or selfishness. Nevertheless, it is completely understandable that incredulity and skepticism still persist in this country where so often promises were betrayed and where political chicanery was substituted for politics. . . .

We have wanted to do much more than we have done for the good of Peru, but there exist monumental obstacles that the citizenry ought to know about. We found Peru in a profound economic crisis; we did not inherit a bonanza situation. The last administration left an external debt of more than 37 billion *soles* [more than $860 million]. What great or important thing for our people was done with this immense sum of money? Which great reforms were financed by that enormous debt, which the past government borrowed from other countries? It is necessary to speak plainly: a large part of those 37 billion *soles* was squandered in the unparalleled corruption that devastated this country during the last regime. Where are those who trafficked in the misery of the poor? It is necessary to make known that some of them escaped justice by taking refuge in the international organizations which they always served with no care for the reputation or the future of their fatherland. The day will come when we will settle accounts with those who betrayed the trust of the people. We have no reason to speak in euphemisms. A revolution implies also a different language without halftones and without subterfuge.

But the limitations that the revolution has to overcome are not based solely on the heavy burden of the huge foreign debt that the last government contracted and that Peru has to repay. There is another very important limitation. The oligarchy that has seen its interests affected by the Agrarian Reform Law is not investing its money in the country. This is the great conspiracy of the economic right, its great antirevolutionary strategy, its great treason to the cause of the Peruvian people. It persists in this manner in order to create a fictitious economic crisis that will endanger the stability of the government. The excuse for not investing is that there does not exist in the country a "climate of confidence." This venal phrase is the refrain, as well as the psychological weapon, that the right uses day after day to cover with a smoke screen its true, antipatriotic intentions.

What type of "confidence" do the great proprietors of wealth demand? A "confidence" that permits them to maintain the luxury and the privileges that are not justified except by the bad habits of inveterate exploiters of the Peruvian people? . . . This type of confidence they are not going to have while we are governing because on this type of confidence are based the injustices that submerged the great majority of our people in misery and exploitation.

But there are conditions of authentic confidence for all those who understand that wealth should also fulfill a constructive social responsibility. There is confidence and government backing for investment that promotes the economic development of the country within a framework of respect for the just expectations of capital and for the legitimate rights of the workers. There is confidence because there is total political stability in the country, because social violence no longer exists, and because the people clearly support this government. . . . There is confidence because private investment enjoys all the guarantees that any modern business requires.

From the beginning, the Revolutionary Government declared its support of and encouragement to private investment, including the foreign investment that complies with the laws of the country. There exist then all the conditions of legitimate confidence that honorable investment requires. Many businessmen now understand this, and there are very clear indications of a new and positive tendency in the investment field. But the oligarchical sectors of national capitalism are plotting against the revolution through their control of the economic apparatus, assisted by an ultrareactionary press. . . . The Peruvian people ought to have a very clear idea of the oligarchy's true economic conspiracy because the Revolutionary Government will not maintain forever its serene attitude of waiting for these people to recover their sense of reality and abandon their pernicious, anti-Peruvian position.

The immense task of realizing effective changes is being carried out by this government without violence and without bloodshed. Ours is the only revolution that, having succeeded in initiating profound transformations, is executing them peaceably. In other countries, agrarian reforms less advanced than ours cost thousands of lives over years of brutal, fratricidal struggle. Until now, Peru has escaped that fate of blood and death, and we are confident that this will continue to be the case in the future. But we understand that the experience our fatherland is living through today represents a conquest without precedents. Without any doubt, this revolution is a radically new phenomenon; it cannot be understood within traditional models. For that reason, the Peruvian example excites interest, expectation, and admiration in the rest of the world and particularly in our Latin American continent.

. . . There are, to be sure, very powerful forces behind the campaign to confound the ongoing revolution. These forces dictate the course of that propaganda which, on one side, demagogically urges deceitful extremism and, on the other, insinuates that our revolution has entered a mellowing phase. Both antirevolutionary postures have the same source of inspiration—the purses of those who pay for them. These two strategies are clearly perceivable. One of them holds that the revolution has gone too far, too fast. But we will not commit that error. The other antirevolutionary strategy persists in presenting us as a movement overcome by complacency, without energy, and incapable of moving beyond that which we have done. Naturally, to halt the march of a revolution which has only recently begun would be another regrettable error, [one] which we are not going to commit. We know very well that, in order to succeed, the reforms initiated must necessarily be complemented by others that are equally indispensable. For us, the transformation of this country is a complex and integral process which will have to be attacked from distinct fronts and with different plans of action. Because of this, the revolution has a program, and that program will be carried out methodically and in its totality.

The two strategies of the oligarchy move in unison, in perfect concert, from within and from without. The conspiratorial action of the adversaries of the revolution functions at these two levels. One of their principal instruments is the synchronized propaganda and twisting of the truth that operates through certain foreign news agencies, through some internationally circulated magazines, and through the majority of the newspapers printed in Peru, newspapers that represent and defend the interests of the Peruvian oligarchy and its foreign accomplices.

The vast majority of Peruvian newspapermen have little or nothing to do with this insidious campaign of lies because they are not responsible for the editorial policies adopted by the majority of newspaper owners. In general, that immense majority of newspapermen really sympathize with the revolution. But those who control and monopolize the ownership of the press are members of the oligarchy, enemies of the transformation we are realizing.

. . . The revolution will go forward until it achieves its objectives, without haste and without hesitancy, by its own route and with its own methodology. We have learned how to resist pressures. We will not be provoked, but we will be implacable in the defense of the revolution on whose success depends the future of Peru. Do not confuse tolerance with weakness. In the Peru of today, the lines are clearly drawn. This revolution will be defended whatever the price. Its adversaries, within and without, should understand this with no room for error. The armed forces will sustain it, and the people will daily defend it more because they will feel it to be theirs.

. . . Thus, if we feel our duty and commitment is to the revolution, we have to be vigilant that it always be an example of purity, honesty, efficiency, sacrifice, and generosity. We have to create an awareness of the immense task that a revolution entails. It will be necessary to correct, from day to day, the errors that are inevitably committed in the mundane operation of the revolution. We have the honesty, the humility, the wisdom, and the valor that others have never had to recognize our errors and correct them.

Far from weakening the revolution, this will strengthen it because it will give it added moral authority. But we will be supremely demanding of ourselves; we will aspire to be a bit better each day; and we will encourage the honest criticism which is an invaluable contribution in every creative effort. Above all, we will never forget the sacred duty of always being loyal to this revolution on which depends the future of our fatherland.

. . . I want to close by directing myself first to those who are not yet involved in the revolution and, second, to the campesinos of the country. To the first group I want to say, in the name of the Revolutionary Government, that in this national mission there is a place for every Peruvian who sincerely desires a profound change in our country. Only those who identify with the oligarchy or with the hated past against which we revolted will be excluded from the revolution. This is a minority in Peru. The great majority of the blue-collar and white-collar workers, the intellectuals, the industrialists, the students, and the professionals, that is to say, the true people of Peru, have no reason to identify with the past nor to defend the interests of the enemies of the revolution. It is for them and with them that we are making this revolution.

My final words this evening will be for the campesinos because the revolution has begun the agrarian reform, the agrarian reform that many dreamed of but very few believed would some day be realized in our country, the agrarian reform that is awakening the campesino and exciting the admiration and respect of the whole world. Nevertheless, as we predicted the day it was promulgated only three months ago, it is now the target of sabotage and obstructionism.

To those campesinos for whom we effected the agrarian reform, today we say that you should not be deceived, that you should remember those who when in power dictated a reform law designed to defend the great landowners, that you should understand that the propaganda of those who seek to confound and create confusion cannot be sincere, and that you should be ready to defend with your own lives, if necessary, the lands and water that are and will be yours.

In great part, the future of the revolution depends upon the efforts and the responsibility of the campesinos to make the agrarian reform a success. There exist, and there will continue to exist, problems of implementation. But the campesinos should be alert to the enemies of this reform because they are the enemies of the revolution. The campesinos should never forget that this reform and this revolution are being carried out for all the people, for all the poor of Peru. The benefits of the agrarian reform will be felt in other sectors of our society that were equally exploited by the same oligarchy that submerged the peasantry in misery. The revolution began in the countryside, but it will not stop there. The horizon of the revolution is the same horizon of the fatherland.

If we are in power, we have to accept the responsibility for both triumphs and defeats. On us depends the future of the revolution, but it will succeed. We have on our side the might of right, but we also have the right of might.

Reprinted, translated, and edited from *Perú. Velasco: La voz de la revolución* (Lima: Ediciones Participación, 1972), 1:89–108.

SPEECH BY FRANCISCO MORALES BERMÚDEZ, 1976

My dear countrymen:

There are many ways in which the chief of state can set forth the guidelines and policies of the Revolutionary Government of the Armed Forces which he represents.

During this second phase of the revolution, we have addressed you many times through statements, speeches, press conferences, and direct dialogue with the people both at the palace and in the different regions of our country.

Today I want to avail myself of another means of communication—television and radio—in order to come into your homes for a while and deal in a most sincere manner with matters that concern our beloved country. . . .

Today's speech or talk, on this the last day of summer, has the purpose of outlining the main problem areas and situations that our country and the revolutionary process are experiencing. One hears repeatedly that the government's authority is weakened, thereby weakening authority at all levels.

This is a confused situation which should be fully clarified by calmly identifying the real causes. In the first place, we have to admit that there obviously has been a change in the methods and political management of the government, as we stated publicly on August 29. [On this day Morales Bermúdez replaced Juan Velasco Alvarado as president of Peru. Ed.]

We have opened the channels of dialogue and of freedom of expression which were very limited during the first phase of the revolution. This has enlarged the scope of political debate, a characteristic of the "Revolution with Freedom" that we practice. But we are also facing a typical situation wherein the intense propaganda of leftist and rightist opponents, who can now express their opinions, with the psychological fear of many of being considered "less than revolutionary," has led to a confusion between the need to establish authority and the need for repression and rightist fascism. The result is to endanger the revolutionary process, to which contribute, paradoxically, through their lack of lucidity and clear political vision, not only the opponents of the process but also its supporters who still do not comprehend the essence of revolutionary humanism.

. . . Another cause of this apparent weakening of governmental authority can also be identified. It has been barely seven months since we initiated the second phase of the revolution and assumed the responsibility of leading the country. We did so at the request of the armed forces in conjunction with the police forces, fully conscious of the great political and economic difficulties which this responsibility would entail. In the areas of economics and finance, my five years' experience as minister of economy and finance [1969 through 1973] and my assumption of the premiership in 1974, where I devoted most of my time to the economic affairs of the country, made it evident to me, as I announced publicly, that an economic crisis was approaching. . . .

As there was no hiatus between the first phase and the second phase of the revolution, because we followed a strict norm of revolutionary ethics, we have in fact absorbed all the virtues and defects of the revolution since its inception. The Revolutionary Government is now suffering a natural attrition after exercising power for over seven years, seven years of profound structural changes within a model that seeks to be original and unique and that has the problems of identification and attitude to which we referred above. But this phenomenon does not have its origin in the second phase, because credibility was already lost in the latter part of the first phase. We now have the obligation and the moral and patriotic duty to regain that credibility. We should acknowledge frankly and humbly the mistakes which undoubtedly have been made, for to err is human. Moreover, it would be impossible to hide them, for any period of time, just by denying them. . . .

I would now like to convey to you some reflections on the doctrinary and political-doctrinary aspects of the revolution. In order to have no possible doubt, we ought to set forth the present and immediate political objectives. In short, these are: to consolidate the revolutionary process, avoiding its degeneration into Communist statism or its return to already outdated forms of prerevolutionary capitalism, and to complete the structural reforms in order to turn Peru, in time, into a humanist, socialist, Christian, solidary, pluralist society, truly democratic and fully participatory. That is to say, to attain the final objectives of a fully participatory social democracy. This objective runs parallel to the development of the country, to make it a great, strong, and prosperous nation. Therefore, the corresponding plan for the achievement of these goals will, without any shadow of a doubt, be conceived in such a manner as to merit the enthusiastic support of the majority of the Peruvian people. . . .

And when in order to eliminate all doubts we must practice self-criticism, we shall do so; and we shall begin doing so now in this speech. Since the first phase of the revolution, we have had the tendency of not stating in a clear, simple, and unmistakable fashion what we believe, what we seek, and what we stand for. In order to avoid being accused of not being sufficiently revolutionary, or of being petit bourgeois defenders of privilege, or of not wanting to free ourselves from the past, or of thinking with certain prejudices, we frequently adopted attitudes which consisted of either dressing up or toning down our real thoughts. We then hid these thoughts behind a certain type of jargon, which interested and committed propagandists, both foreign and domestic, termed *revolutionary*. However, if we are right, and we are; if our revolutionary objective is superior, and it is; from the moment we affirm the validity of our actions and from the moment we no longer fear to state in a clear and unequivocal manner, for example, that we disagree with certain measures that are considered "revolutionary" only because Marxists preach them, we will dispel this fear that has been imbued from within and abroad, and we will affirm ourselves and reaffirm our own superior ideology. In the end what will endure is not what is thought of us today, but rather what we finally achieve, and for that reason it is essential to define everything clearly.

. . . The principles of the Peruvian Revolution are humanistic and Christian. Nothing can be clearer than this or the consequences derived therefrom. The essence of both principles is that man is the end and not the means or the instrument of others. The human condition is a constant, and therefore no one has the right to manipulate or use human beings as objects for profit or power.

If we want to achieve justice, justly, and freedom, freely, we must . . . use proper methods. For this reason, our revolution cannot be imposed by blood and fire because that would mean the manipulation of the masses and the sacrifice of many people for the sake of an uncertain future. This fact reveals that in the realm of practical politics, the most acute problem which a movement such as ours has to face is how to carry out profound structural change while still guaranteeing personal freedom. The solution we have found is gradualism. Gradualism should not be confused with reformism because reformism places a limit on the amount of change and also because reformism, in reality, only demands palliatives to prevent the traditionally privileged groups from losing power. Gradualism does not mean stopping halfway down the path, but rather means advancing by stages, with each stage being characterized by effective solutions to the problems within the limits of existing resources. . . .

We want to make this perfectly clear, because if we do not proceed in this manner the economic system will collapse and we will be left with only two alternatives: either the revolution will be truncated and [will] die, or an implacable socialist dictatorship will have to be imposed by violent means, which will preclude the people from having true participation in the collective decisions. If anyone knows of another way in which the problem of harmonizing structural transformation while maintaining people's freedom can be solved, please let us know, as we shall be very grateful indeed.

. . . My dear fellow countrymen: The armed forces, with the police forces, are and always will be bound to the revolutionary process and will defend this revolution to the end.

It should be remembered that this revolutionary process is the creation of the armed forces, who initiated the revolution on October 3, 1968, and who now direct the process in this second phase. The armed forces, guardians of the nation, are a permanent institution. The rulers are representatives of their institutions, but while men change, the institutions live on. There is no difference in either our principles or our objectives; what has changed are our methods and procedures of governing.

It was the armed forces that decided to change the political leadership last August 29. The armed forces understood long ago that the desire of our country to be free and sovereign abroad necessarily required that the people be free from all forms of domestic exploitation. The armed forces also understand that national dignity begins by acknowledging and respecting the dignity of each citizen.

Therefore, the progress of this revolutionary process is indissolubly and unshakeably linked to the armed forces. Its zealous efforts to avoid distortions and to frustrate attempts to thwart it are therefore understandable. Thus, the revolution is the very embodiment of our military conscience, and when its goals and objectives are achieved, it will make every officer, every soldier, every man in uniform feel satisfaction in having accomplished his mission and will maintain each one of them in constant vigil to prevent the original design from being distorted.

A revolution which thus exalts justice, freedom, work, participation, solidarity, creativity, honesty, and respect for human dignity is a revolution which deserves [our] living for, deserves defending and dying for. . . .

Reprinted, edited, and translated from *La revolución peruana: Consideraciones, políticas y económicas del momento actual* (Lima: Empresa Editora Perú, 1976), pp. 3–43.

CHAPTER 19

El Salvador

SPEECH BY COLONEL ARTURO ARMANDO MOLINA
ON THE OCCASION OF THE DAY OF
THE SALVADORAN SOLDIER, 1977

On this day, as I gaze out upon the representatives of the various military corps of the republic, I could do nothing less than recall the years 1945–49, when, in the lecture halls of our glorious Military Academy "Captain General Gerardo Barrios," I learned the reasons which, over the span of my life, have justified my legitimate pride in being a Salvadoran military officer.

I learned, for example, that the armed forces of El Salvador were born to be promoters of the independence and decolonization process, and, from that point forward, they were the very embodiment of the fatherland, defending its integrity against the invasion forces of Iturbide, or in the "National War" of the five Central American countries, or against the filibusters of William Walker, and maintaining until our day a gallant attitude of rejection of any attempt at foreign meddling in the internal affairs of the country.

From their birth, the armed forces, by mandate of the people, assumed the role as depository of the nation's values and of its sacred symbols. And all of its members learned to live and to die for our National Anthem, our Coat of Arms, and our Flag, which in its colors are united the desires of achieving greatness and the love of peace of all Salvadorans.

Moreover, in our primary schools and later in our Military Academy, they taught us to respect devoutly the memory of our Founding Fathers and of all our patriots who in war and peace placed their goodwill and intelligence at the service of the republic. From that is derived the intense emotion we feel for the names of General Francisco Morazán, hero of Central America; Captain General Gerardo Barrios, whose *epos* and sacrifice illuminate the efforts to achieve the economic and social development of the country; of General Francisco Menéndez, champion of national education; of General Francisco Malespín, founder of the University of El Salvador; of General

Ramón Belloso, who commanded our troops against the filibusters; and of so many others and even of those who governed in more recent times, whose figures, with all their defects and virtues, have begun to reshape history, such as General Maximiliano Hernández Martínez and Lt. Col. Oscar Osorio.

But, above all, I learned that discipline, respect for hierarchy, and honor and veneration for the fatherland were not abstract concepts, but rather norms of conduct which are indispensable to abiding by our oath as soldiers to defend the national sovereignty and to maintain internal security and public order as bases for development.

If we search for explanations for this constant line of greatness and patriotic love over more than 155 years, we would be able to find them in the origin of the armed forces, composed of men of the people with no commitments beyond those of loyalty to their superiors, to the national sentiment, and to the fatherland.

We would be able to find that line in the awareness that the aspirations of the people are converted into objectives of the State and of its institutions, beginning with ours. And it is for this reason that the men in uniform have engaged not only in bellicose battles but also in social battles to improve the conditions of life of our supreme commander, which is the Salvadoran people. Because if loving the fatherland means wanting it to be more just each day and wanting the fruits of the labor of its inhabitants to benefit everyone in proportion to their efforts, then the armed forces have always supported government measures for the socioeconomic development of the country through an orderly, pacific, and constitutional process. The armed forces have always carried on high the flag of liberation and never one of oppression or dictatorship, and even less have they been at the service of private interests who could be opposed to the national interest.

Nevertheless, in recent decades, and with greater intensity in the last few years, our armed forces have been attacked by international subversion and its terrorist groups who consider us, with just reason, to be the strongest barrier against those stateless individuals who carry out the assignments sent to them from the outside, from where they also receive orders, training, and money designed to establish a Communist dictatorship in El Salvador. The destruction of the armed forces is one of the essential goals of these ideological mercenaries who have betrayed every national sentiment. In the realization of the objective, they employ the most cowardly and unscrupulous methods: from cowardly, criminal attacks to kidnappings and extortion to the astute exploitation of ambitious politicians or of the anger of frustrated persons who, with shameful goals, dare to prefabricate violations of constitutional procedures, thereby converting themselves into conscious or unconscious allies of subversion against constitutional order.

Nevertheless, for the tranquillity of the Salvadoran people, I can state categorically that the armed forces, faithful to their tradition, will always carry out the mandate of Article 112 of the constitution: defend the sovereignty and territorial integrity of the republic, see that the law is obeyed, maintain public order, guarantee constitutional rights, and keep particular vigil to ensure that the norm of alternation of president of the republic is not violated.

And I ought to assure you, in the name of each and every member of our institution, that El Salvador has had, has now, and will have for centuries and centuries, one single army dedicated to fulfilling its duty, to continuing to be the iron barrier mentioned in our National Anthem, and to destroying those who dare to stain our sovereignty like those who take up arms against the Salvadoran people, which is the modern form of invasion attempted by the mercenaries of international subversion.

Present and Future Generations of Soldiers

A few moments ago, we celebrated the solemn ceremony of delivering the banner, which embodies the spirit of our nationality, to the various military corps of the republic, . . . who will have custody of it as a treasure of each one of them.

Since the time of ancient Greece, in a community of sentiments which combined the culture of Athens with the stoicism and bravery of Sparta, across time, the flag has been the symbol of the fatherland, and the soldiers have dedicated their lives to serving it and to defending it. I am sure that the love of God, Union, and Liberty, which constitute the emblem of our National Flag, will be the maximum inspiration to maintain it always on high, in defense against whatever aggression, internal or external, even at the cost of the maximum sacrifice, if necessary.

It is for that blue and white of our flag that I solemnly declare to all Salvadorans that democracy will live as long as the army lives, and as the founder of our institution, General Manuel José Arce, said, "The army will live as long as the Republic lives."

Comrades in Arms

I am fifty-four days away from handing over the constitutional mandate to whomever the Salvadoran people choose as their future governor. This is the last time, then, on the occasion of the Day of the Soldier, that I will speak to you as your commander in chief. And, since one does not express appreciation for the carrying out of one's duty, I only want to state before the nation that you have been loyal and that you have demonstrated a capacity for sacrifice and patriotic love by supporting all the measures taken by the Government of the Republic to benefit the great majority of the people.

What I want to tell you is not only that your commander in chief is proud of each and every one of you, but also that the exemplary behavior which you exhibited during the fifty-eight months and eight days of my government makes me personally even more satisfied for having chosen a military career and for being an officer, particularly a Salvadoran soldier.

Because it is also due to your support, comrades, that in my speeches to the Salvadoran people I have been able to speak always with my head held high with determination, decision, and strength.

First Infantry Brigade,
San Salvador, May 8, 1977

Translated and reprinted from Mensaje al Pueblo Salvadoreño, con Motivo de las Elecciones Presidenciales del 20 de Febrero de 1977, *Mensajes y discursos del señor presidente de la república, Coronel Arturo Armando Molina*, vol. 10, pp. 40–48.

PROCLAMATION OF THE ARMED FORCES OF
THE REPUBLIC OF EL SALVADOR, 1979

A. The armed forces of El Salvador, fully conscious of their sacred duties for the Salvadoran people and in full agreement with the clamor of all the nation's inhabitants against a government which
 1. has violated the human rights of the multitude,
 2. has fomented and tolerated corruption in public administration and in the justice system,
 3. has created a veritable economic and social disaster, and
 4. has profoundly impaired the reputation of the country and of the noble armed forces;

B. Convinced that the previously mentioned problems are the product of antiquated economic, social, and political structures which have traditionally prevailed in the country and which do not offer to the majority of the inhabitants the minimal conditions necessary to live like human beings (on the other hand, the corruption and lack of ability of the regime provoking distrust in the private sector because hundreds of millions of *colones* [Salvadoran monetary unit] have fled the country, thereby accentuating the economic crisis to the detriment of the popular classes);

C. Knowing with certainty that each government in turn, likewise the product of scandalous electoral frauds, has adopted inadequate programs of development in which the timid changes in the structure have been blocked by the economic and political power of the conservative sectors which, at all times, have defended their ancestral privileges as the dominant classes, even endangering the socially conscientious capital of the country which has manifested its interest in achieving a just economic development for the population;

D. Firmly convinced that the previous conditions are the fundamental cause of the economic and social chaos and of the violence the country is currently suffering, violence which can be overcome only with the arrival to power of a government that guarantees the operation of an authentically democratic regime;

Therefore, the armed forces, whose members have always been identified with the people, decided, based on the right of revolt which all peoples possess when their government fails to carry out the law, to depose the government of General Carlos Humberto Romero and to replace it with a Revolutionary Junta of Government composed primarily of civilians whose absolute honesty and competence will be beyond all doubt. Said junta will assume the powers of state with the end of creating the conditions in our country which will allow all Salvadorans to have peace and to live in accord with the dignity of a human being.

While the conditions necessary to hold truly free elections, where the people can decide their future, are being established, it is of imperative necessity, in view of the chaotic political and social state in which the country lives, to adopt a Program of Emergency which will contain urgent measures intended to create a climate of tranquility and to establish the bases upon which the profound transformations of the economic, social, and political structures of the country will be sustained.

The features of this Program of Emergency are the following:

I. *Cease the violence and the corruption*
    A. Effectively dissolving ORDEN (Organización Democrática Nacionalista)* and combatting extremist organizations which, by their actions, violate human rights
    B. Eradicating corrupt practices in public administration and in the justice system

II. *Guarantee the existence of human rights*
    A. Creating the ambience propitious for achieving truly free elections within a reasonable time frame
    B. Permitting the formation of political parties of all ideologies in such a manner as to strengthen the democratic system
    C. Granting general amnesty to all political prisoners and to those in exile
    D. Recognizing and respecting the right of all labor sectors to organize
    E. Stimulating freedom of speech in accord with ethical norms

III. *Adopt measures which will lead to an equitable distribution of the national wealth, increasing, at the same time, in an accelerated fashion, the gross national product*
    A. Creating solid bases for initiating a process of agrarian reform
    B. Providing greater economic opportunities for the population through reforms in the financial, tax, and foreign commerce sectors of the country
    C. Adopting protective measures for the consumer in order to offset the effects of inflation
    D. Implementing special development programs whose goals will be to increase national production and to create additional sources of employment
    E. Recognizing and guaranteeing the rights of housing, food, education, and health for all the inhabitants of the country
    F. Guaranteeing private property within a social function

---

*ORDEN was formed in the 1960s, with government support, to dispense patronage and provide intelligence on subversive activity to the state security apparatus. [Ed.]

IV. *Channel, in a positive fashion, the foreign relations of the country*
   A. Reestablishing relations with the sister country of Honduras in the shortest time possible
   B. Strengthening ties with the sister people of Nicaragua and its government
   C. Tightening the ties which unite us with the peoples and governments of the sister republics of Guatemala, Costa Rica, and Panama
   D. Establishing cordial relations with all the countries of the world who are willing to support the struggles of our people and respect our sovereignty
   E. Guaranteeing the fulfillment of standing international commitments

In order to obtain the accelerated accomplishment of these goals which the Salvadoran people are justly demanding, the Revolutionary Junta of Government will form a cabinet composed of honest and capable individuals, representatives of diverse sectors, who will put into play all their patriotism in the performance of such lofty functions.

In this moment of true national emergency, we are putting out a special call to the popular sectors and to socially conscious capital so that they can contribute to beginning a new era for El Salvador, an era characterized by the principles of peace and effective respect for the human rights of the entire citizenry.

Translated and reprinted from Lt. Col. Mariano Castro Morán, *Función política del ejército salvadoreño en el presente siglo*, UCA/Editores (San Salvador, 1984), appendix 14, pp. 412–15.

CHAPTER 20

Guatemala

SPEECH BY CARLOS MANUEL ARANA OSORIO, 1974

On a day like yesterday, four years ago, I received from the people of Guatemala the mandate to assume the Presidency of the Republic, and the electors, as much as I, are aware of the reasons why I was elected.

In that period, the country was dominated by political terrorism, and we were threatened with the danger that our democratic system might be destroyed by armed violence from the extreme left. Many homes still weep for their dead, and in the eastern part of the country, the tombs of sacrificed peasants still burn with pain. It would be desirable for many Guatemalans to undertake a retrospective analysis of what occurred then, in order to better appreciate the changes operating in this new Guatemala, free of fear and uncertainty.

The express mandate which the people conferred on me was to end that tragedy and that danger.

In my presidential acceptance speech, I warned that peace in our country was not then, nor is it today, a simple problem of repressing the subversive activity of the extreme left. I also stated that it is indispensable to go to the root causes. Thus it is necessary, at the same time, to know how to differentiate between the armed activity through which Communist organizations intend to achieve power and the conditions which move the poorest and most forsaken people to a desire for violent changes and to a clear attack on the institutions.

Interpreting the country's realities thusly, as president, I have fulfilled the mission with which you entrusted me, confronting the violence as much in its illicit armed forms of ideological expression as in the social and economic conditions which enable subversion to flourish.

These have been four difficult and complex years. The national problems which accumulated over such a long time became much more acute due both to the growing population and to our inadequate resources. Such resources were gravely affected by the pressures and consequences exercised over us by the international situation.

In our time, there is not one country, big or small, powerful or weak, developed or underdeveloped, that is not affected by world events. Guatemala's principal markets are the United States, Japan, Germany, and others in the European region; these transfer to our nation all the positive and negative aspects which their economies possess. It is a commonly known fact that our age, more than any other, is characterized by an economy of intense and continuous relationships, of reciprocal actions and interactions. He who tries to deny this is deliberately lying, whether he has a doctorate in economics or lacks even the ability to occupy the most modest post of constable in the smallest village.

During the last three years, three world economic events occurred which led to repercussions in every country and which produced an inflationary process affecting Guatemala. The first was the devaluation of the dollar, which declined 8 percent in 1971, and 10 percent in February 1973. Among other consequences, this forced the revaluation of the Japanese yen, which drove up the prices of those items we import from Japan.

In 1972 the United States sold practically all of its wheat reserves to Russia. Following this sale, there was a worldwide drought which produced an increase in the price of wheat and all other grains. As a result, there was an increase in the price of concentrated foods which are used to feed the livestock whose meat feeds human beings. The consequence was that Guatemala's imports of grains and concentrated foods cost much more.

The third event took place in November 1973, when the Arab-Israeli War precipitated the oil crisis, resulting in price increases which have continued until today, with derivative price increases for all other products.

Nevertheless, the effects of the international economic situation have been smaller and less grave in Guatemala than in countries of comparable development. Despite this, however, my government has been irresponsibly and demagogically criticized and selfishly attacked by politicians of the opposition, attacked demagogically, irresponsibly, and out of self-interest because to a greater or lesser degree, in one way or another, the leaders of the opposition have participated in the government of the republic and in my own government.

As is well known, the principal local leader of the Christian Democratic Party asked for, and received, the support of my government, and his political conduct was, until very recently, one of complete solidarity with the president of the republic. Numerous events and activities of said party were carried out in consultation with the president, which means that Christian Democracy lacks the moral authority to censure the government. Until very recently, I repeat, it acted in consultation with my government, which it considered to be "very good," "excellent." Thus, the change in its way of thinking is nothing more than a matter of momentary, electoral convenience.

On the other hand, the presidential candidate of the opposition served in the current government for three important years, performing delicate functions. During that entire time, he was never heard to make any observation or criticism. But now, now that he has joined the opposition, it turns out that "there are no liberties" and that all of his ex-colleagues in the government are "bad," he being a strange exception, in accord, of course, with his own opinion.

I appeal to your conscience and good judgment, my beloved compatriots, to answer and judge such serpentine conduct.

The same is true of the mayor of Guatemala City, who also spoke recently of the errors of the government. Not even two years ago, this same government provided the guarantees necessary to obtain domestic and foreign loans for the municipality. I authorized those guarantees because the funds were designated for service works for the residents and because what interests me is the well-being of all citizens regardless of their political affiliation.

Now it turns out that he thinks in a manner distinct from the government and that he speaks in a manner quite distinct from the way he spoke to me in private. But I ask: Why does the mayor see the mote in another's eye and not the beam in his own? And I also ask: Where are the projects that should have been completed with the funds which the government authorized?

This, then, is the position of my opposition.

In the face of this, I ask all of you who live in the interior of the country: Do you accept as just those attacks by the opposition?

I know that you are answering with a resounding NO, because in each village, in each town, in each city, and in the entire country, there are thousands of Guatemalans who are being helped by my government's projects; there are thousands of families who now have what they never knew existed; there are millions of inhabitants who are receiving the benefits of our works.

As all the people know, I am just a simple and sincere man. I can assure you that, with your support and with the support of the reality about which no one can lie, in the past years we have carried out physical and social works without precedent in the history of the country.

But if this is not believed, there are the works. They are in full view of everyone. They are at the service of the population of the entire country.

And if that is not sufficient, all Guatemalans know that I have been the only president who, before handing over power, has personally visited each department to verify that the works promised have been carried out; and I have verified that they have been carried out, and the inhabitants of every village know it.

Instead of closing myself up in the National Palace and only superficially seeing the problems and needs of the people, I have traveled to the most distant villages and attended to the popular needs in those places; without sparing any effort, I flew by plane and by helicopter; I rode in vehicles and on mules; I walked on foot by day and night. And I returned some time later to confirm that the projects had been carried out. Those works are there, all over the country, and only political passion or political maliciousness or political lies can deny them.

Because of this, and because I am seriously worried about what the future life of Guatemala might be, I come before you tonight to solicit your greatest serenity and your firmest maturity in electing the new government this Sunday; may your decision be the best for the national interest.

I am also worried about the threat of a socialist regime because it will destroy not only our democratic institutions, but also everything that the people, through me, have built for their well-being.

A National Plan of Development is in process; numerous public works projects and health and education programs are under way; valuable plans are being developed which will bear positive results. But the moment is approaching when we Guatemalans must elect a new government.

Elections constitute the most important characteristic of democracy. The vote is the means through which the people express their sovereign will, and through the vote, political differences are resolved; civic ideals are manifested in the vote, and only through the vote should a new government be created.

As your president, I ask each and every one of the registered voters to go to the polls and exercise the constitutional right of suffrage. I ask all of them, without any discrimination, to vote to elect the government which they believe should govern Guatemala.

I further ask that those determined, responsible citizens who are of clear conscience reject violence and the insolent demagogues of second-class politics and that they vote for the candidates who will guarantee the maintenance of our democracy.

The government will not play games or tricks of any type to pervert the suffrage, nor will it allow any candidate to claim victory until he has been so declared officially by the proper authorities, after receiving the vote totals from the entire republic.

As your president, I ask you to vote for the candidates who promise to continue the work I have carried out. It would be extremely serious for Guatemala if a government was elected which paralyzed or postponed that which we have achieved.

In my capacity as a citizen, I ask my friends, my followers, and also all those who have benefited from my government, to vote for General Kjell Eugenio Laugerud García. And I want to explain clearly and sincerely why I ask you to vote for General Laugerud.

The world in which we live is divided into two political and economic systems: that of socialism and that of democracy. In spite of its faults, the democratic system is the best system of life known today because it is based upon the principles and the objectives for which man has fought since his origin.

Those principles and objectives can be summarized as follows: that every human being has natural rights to liberty, justice, and the opportunity to progress; that he is equal before the law; that the sum of the wills expresses sovereignty; that sovereignty comes from the people; and, that the State should act with the primordial goal of guaranteeing the inhabitants of a nation the natural rights of man, as well as economic well-being, social justice, and peace.

Within the democratic system there exists private property. The family also exists, and it should be protected. Intellectual freedom prevails over the dogmas which the State seeks to impose. And, in sum, education, health, and the physical well-being of the inhabitants are not the privileges of a minority, but rights common to all. Finally, the people govern through their representatives, who are elected by the vote.

But democracy has faults, imperfections, and injustices. There is a great deal of poverty, with many illiterates and many sick bodies, and the needy and indigent do not always receive help. In this are to be found the beginnings of groups who propose changes in the institutions. And such groups are then divided among those who seek the progress of the nation through means of violent revolution and those who promote it, develop it, and carry it out through peaceful means.

Guatemala needs peaceful and progressive changes, but it must reject violent changes.

An officer of excellent orientation within the army, a man formed within rigid moral norms, a military commander of great professional virtues, General Laugerud represents the new spirit of the military, as does his clear and unequivocal conviction that our institutions must be reformed.

As a citizen, I ask that you vote for General Laugerud because he will know how to put into practice the principle that the security of the country, its physical and moral progress, as well as its development and social peace, depend upon popular satisfaction.

Popular satisfaction is the product of better justice in the distribution of the riches which the nation can produce. Popular satisfaction is the result of greater equity in the protection of the inhabitants, as much in the areas of health and education as in the opportunities to rise economically, participate in the culture, and guarantee moral values.

I know, I am sure, that General Laugerud has the intellectual capacity, the honesty, the probity, and the determination to stimulate the progress of the country.

I also know that, because of his maturity and his sensitivity, he will lead the government with firmness and with justice, moving toward the realization of the ideal which he calls: "to create well-being for those who do not have it without taking it away from those who do."

I ask, therefore, that you vote for General Laugerud. I ask this because I am sure that he will be the desirable and able governor which Guatemala needs for the upcoming years.

Good night, and may God protect Guatemala and enlighten you to vote this Sunday.

Translated and reprinted from *El Imparcial* (Guatemala City), March 2, 1974.

SPEECH BY GENERAL JOSÉ EFRAÍN RÍOS MONTT, 1982

My fellow citizens, in the name of the armed forces, I want to present to you my most cordial greetings and my gratitude for the opportunity you are giving me to enter your homes.

Today, the officer corps of the army, wishing to show its professional spirit, desiring to reintegrate itself within the dignity of a people, and attempting to revive our values, carried out a military movement over which, by chance, I preside. I preside with a government junta, a government junta which I want to introduce at this time; General Maldonado and Colonel Gordillo are here.

We three make up a junta which is drawing up a political program to present to the Guatemalan people a solution, a reality, a plan of action—a solution to this incomprehensible mode of life we have had from a political point of view and a reality, we are soldiers; in my capacity as general, I have the capability, the responsibility, to act from a political point of view, not for *politiquería* which everyone confounds with politics, but rather in my capacity as general within a strategic concept. Strategy, my fellow citizens, is the origin of every political task, and within that strategy is a policy of security, a policy of defense, an economic policy, a social policy, and a foreign policy.

Therefore, within those parameters, we are going to present to you a program of work; I only wanted to take advantage of this opportunity to tell you, my fellow citizens, that the people of Guatemala are celebrating and that we, the soldiers, full of rejoicing and enthusiasm, are pledging our word to provide political solutions to the political problems, economic solutions to the economic problems, and social solutions to the great social problems which we face.

My fellow citizens, you will understand that in a military movement, a capability is demonstrated, a dignity is demonstrated, but fundamentally, there is a maximum degree of morality. I want to tell you, fellow citizens, that, in the first place, I am trusting in God, my Lord, my King, that he may enlighten me because only He gives and only He takes away authority. I am trusting in my God so that I will not defraud the officer corps or, less yet, a people, a people which has not been respected, a people which has been insulted.

Eight years ago I was deceived; four years ago they deceived us; and now, just a few days ago, they deceived us again. Guatemalans, we are both conscious and convinced that the army is not just the soldiers who wear a uniform, but that all you citizens have the obligation and the responsibility to walk arm in arm with us toward a more tranquil future. I trust that God Our Lord will spread His mantle of mercy on Guatemala; I trust that God Our Lord will enlighten us; and I trust that God Our Lord will permit that you and we can give a new face to the political business of the nation.

There are many doubts, and in the judgment of you citizens, there are many more; among all of us there is a great deal of concern, but there is also a great deal of seriousness and responsibility.

We want to tell you, fellow citizens, that responsible to you and responsible to our God who will judge us and, above all, responsible to the younger officers who want to rid themselves of the millstone of manipulative commanders, before all of you, we promise fidelity. What we need is that you comprehend and understand that you should help us. We are not suspending any individual rights; we are guaranteeing human rights, but, please, let us make of liberty the expression of responsibility; let us make of liberty a way of life; let us make of liberty a citizen task.

At this moment, the political parties have nothing to do. We are going to present them with a declaration, and we are going to see if they are true political parties, because they have been only electoral political parties, not political parties which offer political solutions to a people needing political solutions. For that reason, fellow citizens, we want your comprehension, we want your support, because really, if we do not have your support, the armed forces will have to come out to repair Guatemala. And, hear me well, the subversion cannot continue. The political task is going to be carried out, and it will be done from a political point of view. Arms are only for the army; arms are only for the army. Please, all you civilians who are armed, take your machine guns down from your roofs and surrender them; take the pistols from your belts and replace them with machetes for work. We need work, we need responsibility, we need honorableness.

There is a challenge to Guatemala and we accept that challenge; there is no one who can touch us. We will build a country; we will build a nation; but we will build a country and a nation in which the population is integrated, a territorial reality which should demonstrate humility and identify itself with ideas and ideals, for us, God, and Guatemala, and for you, God, and Guatemala, because only thusly can we work hand in hand for Guatemala.

I want to thank you very much for the opportunity you have given me, and again be reassured, fellow citizens, that the Army of Guatemala, through me, pledges its word of honor, its word as professional soldiers, that it will make every effort possible, even dying, to benefit the political situation of the fatherland. We do not want any more *politiqueros*; we do not want the same faces; we do not want them to come and congratulate us. Do not even come near us. We are professional soldiers, and we are in a political and social position to guarantee you Guatemalans a future within the framework of peace, tranquility, and justice.

Please, you men of subversion, take note of the following: Only the Army of Guatemala should have arms; give up your arms because if you do not, then we will take them away. And, listen well, you will not be found murdered alongside the road; anyone who breaks the law will be shot, but not murdered. We want to respect human rights, because exercising those is the only means of learning to live democratically. For that reason, I would ask you, in the first place, to pray to God, Our Savior, to allow us to continue developing in peace the program we are going to present to you, and, in the second place, for your collaboration, your tranquility, and your peace. The peace of Guatemala does not depend upon armed actions; the peace of Guatemala depends upon you the men, you the women, you the children. Yes, the peace of Guatemala is in your hearts, and once there is peace in your hearts, there will be peace in your homes and peace in the society. Please, no more drinks, no more anything. Work, Guatemala needs work, because if there are no sources of labor, there is no confidence and no authority, and there was none of these before.

Today, with morality, Guatemalans, we state to you, before God, that we pledge the word of the armed forces to guarantee you peace, work, and security.

Translated and reprinted from *Mensajes del presidente de la república, General José Efraín Ríos Montt* (Tipografía Nacional de Guatemala, 1982), pp. 9–10.

SPEECH BY GENERAL OSCAR HUMBERTO MEJÍA VICTORES, 1986

To the People of Guatemala:

May the first words of the last message that I deliver to the nation in my capacity as head of state be a cordial and respectful greeting to the high dignitaries from friendly countries who, honoring us with their presence, share with us these transcendental and historic moments in the political life of Guatemala.

Two and one-half years ago, on August 8, 1983, at the decision of the Army of Guatemala, I assumed the position of chief of state, determined to rechannel and strengthen the process of political liberalization which our institution was encouraging.

I accepted the responsibility which was entrusted to me with the firm conviction that the country needed to return to institutional democracy. In name and representation of the Army of Guatemala, I committed myself to generating a process of national reconciliation which would permit Guatemalans to express themselves freely within the framework of an authentically democratic and pluralistic system.

We established as priority goals the return to constitutional government, the pacification of the country, and the elevation of Guatemala anew to the position she deserves in the international community. Concomitantly, we committed ourselves to confronting, within the limits of our possibilities, the grave economic and social crisis which profoundly affected our country. The task of realizing that was difficult and complex, but we undertook it and finalized it with the assistance of distinct social, economic, and political sectors of the country.

The people and the government responded to the challenges which the circumstances raised, and although we must recognize that, above all in the economic and social arenas, we were not able to achieve all the results desired, I can affirm today, in this solemn ceremony, that the pledge I made as a soldier, the pledge of the Army of Guatemala, has been fulfilled.

It is pertinent, on this occasion, to refer in general terms to some of the principal problems which affected Guatemala when we received the government, as well as to the way in which we resolved them. A climate of uncertainty existed at that time, and the people of Guatemala found themselves confused, disoriented, and frustrated in political matters. Above all, the timetable for a return to constitutionality was uncertain, and there also existed—and why not point it out—a profound crisis of credibility and confidence. Faced with that situation, we adopted the measures we believed most adequate to restore to Guatemalans faith in their institutions. We lifted the State of Siege which restricted both the free expression of beliefs and the political and labor rights of the citizenry.

The so-called Tribunals of Special Jurisdiction were abolished, and a broad and generous Amnesty Law was issued so that all of those compatriots who had, in one form or another, participated in or collaborated with the terrorist subversive groups could rejoin their communities of origin and dedicate themselves to their normal occupations. The Supreme Electoral Tribunal was established and given all the support it required. Apropos to this, the corresponding legal measures were issued, and, simultaneously, we initiated a process of frank and sincere consultation with the leadership of all the political parties, as well as with those committees in the process of forming parties and registering them. We listened to their proposals, we analyzed them, and, in common accord, we established the stages of the democratization process.

Elections were called to form a National Constituent Assembly, and I can affirm with deep satisfaction that the Guatemalan people responded as never before, gathering to vote in unprecedented numbers to elect their representatives who would write the new Constitution of the Republic. The results of those elections were respected, and for the first time in a long time, there was no opposition whatsoever to any of the participating political parties. After arduous labor, the National Constituent Assembly promulgated the Political Constitution of the Republic of Guatemala, which will go into complete effect after this day.

Our Magna Carta, which all Guatemalans should respect and obey, contains norms which guarantee the functioning of a modern state with emphasis on the separation of powers and the protection of human rights.

When we convoked general elections for president, vice president, deputies to the Congress of the Republic, and municipal councils, we reaffirmed the absolute neutrality of the government and we offered to guarantee free and honest elections. Last November 3, the people of Guatemala again went to the polls in an orderly and exemplary fashion. Since none of the presidential candidates obtained an absolute majority of votes, however, we resorted to a system novel in our country, a second round of elections which, fortunately, took place on December 8. These last two elections, just as with the first one, occurred with observers from various countries and international organizations present. We are extremely pleased that all of them, without exception, including the international press, recognized that the elections were impeccably honest.

On another matter, I also ought to mention that we succeeded in pacifying those areas dominated by conflict. With particular vigor, we actuated development programs for rural communities, and the system of interinstitutional coordination functioned efficiently.

I point with particular satisfaction to the foreign policy of my government. In the past, for reasons of a distinct nature, the prestige of Guatemala had been adversely affected, and she found herself virtually isolated from the international community. From the outset of our administration, we established a clear and precise policy of respect for the fundamental principles of international law. With regard to the crisis in our region, we adopted a considered, balanced, and constructive attitude, convinced that we Central Americans should find politico-diplomatic solutions to resolve our differences.

We recognize that the problems are extremely serious and complex, but we are convinced that they can be confronted if we act in good faith and demonstrate an authentic political will to find formulas of conciliation that will assure the peace.

We have firmly supported the efforts of the Contadora Group, and this is a propitious moment to thank Colombia, Mexico, Panama, and Venezuela for their tireless work over the past three years. I also want to recognize the Support Group of Contadora and the member nations of the European Economic Community for their contribution in this area.

We have acted with independence, dignity, responsibility, and realism, and we have restored to the word *sovereignty* its true meaning and dimension. With legitimate pride, I can say that now we are listened to and respected.

Guatemala, like other sister countries of Latin America, has been affected by an acute economic crisis of both internal and external origin. Within the limits of our possibilities, we tried to adopt policies which, on the one hand, contributed to alleviating the social problems and, on the other, contributed to the reactivization of our economy. We sponsored a great national dialogue with the distinct representative sectors of the country, with whom the situation was analyzed with a positive attitude and with a great deal of objectivity.

All of them cooperated and suggested distinct alternatives for overcoming the crisis. In this area, there is a long way to go, but I repeat that it is imperative that there be efforts and sacrifices from everyone; at the same time, we must ensure that the interests of a few do not prevail over those of the majority. In spite of all the obstacles, a certain economic stability has been achieved, and the outlook for the prices of our principal export products allows us to predict better times ahead. Regarding the work of my government, I have provided details in the Record of Works which has been placed in the hands of the National Congress.

Mr. President, Mr. Vice President, Members of Congress, People of Guatemala: Upon completing this message, I want to state publicly my respect for and appreciation to the Supreme Electoral Tribunal, to the National Constituent Assembly, and to the Supreme Court, who have completed, with great ability, the delicate task entrusted to them. Furthermore, I want to express my personal appreciation to my cabinet, to my collaborators, and, above all, to the Army of Guatemala for its loyalty and esprit de corps. I leave with the tranquility produced by having done my duty, and I exhort all Guatemalans to defend the peace and democracy that has cost us so much to win, and to work and act with responsibility in order to achieve those great national objectives. And, in offering my very best wishes for the success of the new government, I reaffirm that we should look to the future with faith and confidence, emphasizing the positive over the negative. May everything be well with our beloved fatherland, Guatemala.

Translated and reprinted from a government press release of the Secretaría de Relaciones Públicas, Presidencia de la República, 1986.

VI

Policies and Consequences of Military Rule

The antipolitical military governments which emerged after 1964 defined for themselves immediate *defensive* missions to rescue their nations from the threat of subversion and chaos. They also identified a range of economic and social objectives to wrest their countries from the verge of economic collapse. In the short term, the military leadership vowed to defeat subversion, prevent a collapse of the institutional order, overcome economic crisis, and prevent the political victory of Marxist groups in their respective societies. In some cases, for example, Argentina, Guatemala, and El Salvador, ongoing urban and rural guerrilla warfare confronted the armed forces with identifiable military targets as well as a political threat. In other cases, for example, Brazil in 1964 or Chile in 1973, populist policies of incumbent governments and direct threats to military discipline by reformist or socialist politicians led to military coups, though no significant internal *military* threat by opposition movements existed.

The defensive aspects of the military programs implied severe repression of political organizations and social movements, suppression of civil liberties and civil rights, and radical transformation of previous political practices. The level of repression corresponded, to some extent, to the military leaders' perceptions of the severity of the populist or revolutionary threat facing their respective nations. In countries where revolutionary guerrilla movements or political violence preceded the military interventions, for example, Guatemala (1954, 1963–1985), El Salvador (1972), Argentina (1976), and Uruguay (1971–73), extensive brutalization of opposition leadership and systematic persecution, torture, and assassination became routine instruments of military rule. This also occurred where high levels of popular mobilization or threats by populist governments to military discipline and the prevailing socioeconomic order precipitated military action, such as in Brazil (1964) and Chile (1973). Even when preintervention political mobilization was limited, as in Peru (1968), the new military regimes moved quickly to restrict the activities of labor, student, and religious organizations and to limit, suspend, or outlaw the activities of political parties. They also curtailed civil liberties and sought to control the content of the mass media through censoring or closing the opposition press.

The defensive projects of the antipolitical regimes also entailed adoption of new, but ostensibly temporary, decrees or "institutional acts" to serve as the "legal" basis for military governments. These measures, sometimes dignified as amendments to previous constitutions, varied in language but shared in practice a focus on centralizing authority in the executive branch, and limiting or eliminating the role of traditional legislative and judicial institutions. The emergency measures also provided almost unlimited legal discretion for the government to defend the nation against threats to internal security. The new military leaders based some of their actions on the authority of existing constitutional provisions for states of constitutional exception, for example, state of siege, civil war, or threats to internal security. In most cases, even where existing constitutions provided plausible legal foundations for military action, the new governments also adopted "institutional acts," "revolutionary statutes," or "constitutional acts" to provide the appearance of a legal basis for government action. Nowhere did the military regimes neglect to create *some* immediate, formal rationale for repression and for other regime initiatives. In some cases, the military utilized periodic elections (Guatemala, Brazil, El Salvador) or plebiscites (Chile, Uruguay) in efforts to "legitimize" governments, policies, or new constitutions.

With time, these temporary measures became the foundations of the new institutionality which the military elites and their civilian allies sought to impose after the initial defensive mission was achieved. In no case, however, did these efforts to establish new political institutions and practices survive intact the eventual demise of military rule. By the end of 1986 only Chile remained subject to the broad constitutional and legislative institutions imposed by the authoritarian regime—though significant remnants of the military government's innovations persisted in Argentina, Brazil, El Salvador, Guatemala, and Peru.

In the social and economic sphere, all the military leadership groups which came to power in the 1960s and 1970s promised to promote economic growth and to overcome the obstacles to economic development which had impeded progress in the region for centuries. Uniformly blaming the plight of their nations on the demagogy, corruption, venality, and incompetence of their civilian predecessors, the military antipoliticians adopted a wide range of economic projects and policies. The diversity of economic programs corresponded to the unique economic problems and resources of an emergent international economic power like Brazil, the impoverished and less developed economies of Peru, El Salvador, or Guatemala, or the more industrialized and complex societies of Chile and Argentina. These economic projects ranged from an emphasis on expansion of the role of the public sector and massive government investments in Brazil, to Chile's post-1973 experiment with the most radical neoliberal program of "privatization" of economic activity and reduction of the role of the public sector ever experienced in Latin America. Neoliberal policies emphasized economic stabilization through monetary controls to decrease growth in money supply, restrictions on credit, reduction of government expenditures and the role of the public sector, and varying degrees of privatization of provision of social services. In addition, neoliberal policies encouraged transfer of public enterprises to the private sector and attraction of foreign investment to stimulate the local economy.

The stabilization programs typically relied upon wage restraints and relaxation of price regulations, which led frequently to real income declines for workers, small farmers, and the growing numbers of unemployed and underemployed. Reductions in public services made health care, educational opportunities, social services, and housing less accessible to the majority of the population. In some cases, university enrollments declined markedly along with the decreasing opportunities in technical and vocational institutions.

Trade policies under neoliberal approaches focused on an economic opening for freer commerce through reduction or elimination of protective tariffs. These measures were adopted to encourage increased efficiency of domestic firms and to reduce the price of imported consumer goods and products used as inputs in local industry and agriculture. Some of the military governments also encouraged foreign investment to spur economic growth. Only in Chile, however, was a more or less "pure" neoliberal approach tested for a period of time; elsewhere, part or almost all of this model was rejected. For example, the Brazilian and Peruvian military regimes expanded public investments and state enterprises in key economic sectors. They also adopted protective tariffs and exchange controls to shelter domestic industries from foreign competition. Likewise in Argentina, some hesitancy by the military rulers and their civilian advisers to allow massive competition with domestic firms somewhat insulated Argentine producers in comparison with their Chilean counterparts. Despite some movement toward privatization and a rhetoric emphasizing the role of the market in economic policy, the Argentine military regime expanded the role of state enterprises in the economy.

Whatever the *specific* array of economic policies adopted, however, the new military regimes viewed economic modernization and economic growth as an extension of the military mission to provide for national security. Economic development and national security were viewed as inseparable. This was made clear in military professional journals, in public policy declarations, and in the considerable attention given to economic issues in military academies and institutions. It was also made clear in the dramatic economic innovations, of all sorts, introduced by military presidents and their civilian technocratic collaborators.

In most cases, important differences of opinion existed within the military leadership over the content of economic policy, as well as over the overall character of the new political institutionality to be created. Nevertheless, whether the new policies favored expansion of the public sector and an interventionist state role or an array of neoliberal measures to spur growth and stabilization, in part through reducing the role and size of the public sector, agreement existed that responsibility for directing the economic and social transformation of their nations had passed from the old political class to the military saviors. This occurred very early in El Salvador (perhaps as early as the government of Colonel Osorio in the early 1950s), in the 1960s in Brazil, Peru, and Guatemala, and somewhat later in Uruguay and Chile.

In addition to the short-term defensive projects and the commitment to economic modernization, the military elites gradually defined their intentions to create a new political institutionality to replace the defective democratic systems of the past. According to the military leadership, the old political institutions and practices gave rise to corruption, failed to solve pressing national problems, and allowed the advance of subversive, antinationalistic forces within these nations. The rejection of the old institutions brought forth in their place a variety of antipolitical projects, labeled everything from "reorganization of the nation" by General Videla in Argentina to "authoritarian democracy" by General Pinochet in Chile. In Brazil and Guatemala, military governments even utilized manipulated elections and the facade of parliamentary institutions to avoid a total departure from the old legitimacy—while adopting new "constitutional" or "institutional" acts that in practice made a tragic mockery of democratic institutions.

Whatever the name given to the new political projects and whatever their detail from country to country, they all proscribed political participation for "subversive" groups and outlawed political movements proclaiming "subversive" ideologies. They all gave to the State a tutorial role in defining and achieving the common interest for a society viewed as an organic community. The new institutionality proposed by the military governments typically introduced exclusionary and demobilizational measures to restrict or prohibit participation by designated political and social forces and to outlaw certain ideological visions of society—especially those of Marxism.

Universally critical of the defects of pluralist liberal democracy, the military regimes sought to eliminate mobilizational politics and autonomous groups which opposed the new economic and political order. In certain cases, for example, Peru, this even included a frontal assault on wealthy landowners, industrialists, and the conservative mass media. In most cases, the left and center of the political spectrum—party, labor, student, and mass organizations—bore the brunt of antipolitics.

A common innovation in these projects, which represented in many respects a reaffirmation of traditional Hispanic visions of politics and society updated to respond to the realities and challenges of more complex industrializing societies, was the reemphasis on the key role of the State in shaping or directing the society and economy, and the new emphasis on the central role of military institutions in controlling, staffing, and managing the State apparatus. Military leaders justified these innovations by noting the historical failure of civilian politicians and the liberal democratic State to provide political order and social harmony, and their failure to orchestrate the economic modernization requisite for development and national security. That is, previous governments had failed to utilize the State, either directly or indirectly, to advance the common welfare—the fundamental purpose of political authority in the philosophical tradition of Hispanic America.

This militarization of the State went further in some cases than in others, but it invariably placed military officers, both active duty and retired, in key policy-making positions in local government, in public enterprises, and in posts in the public administration previously occupied almost exclusively by civilians. In some countries, educational institutions from the primary level to the universities were assigned military directors and the faculties purged of "subversives." In other cases, military administrators even took over the day-to-day direction of farms and plantations, mines, and industrial enterprises. Of course, in every case, civilian advisers, technicians, and supporters collaborated with the military administration's efforts to create a new political system and to respond to the socioeconomic crises confronting these nations.

These changes in political systems and public policy offered military officers new types of economic opportunities and also new temptations. Sometimes military personnel proved susceptible to some of the opportunities for private enrichment and corruption for which they had long condemned civilian politicians. Corruption corroded professional morale and pride in the armed forces. Scandals involving a variety of improprieties tarnished the image of officers and the military institutions from Peru and Argentina to Guatemala. In Guatemala and Peru (as in Bolivia, Colombia, and Mexico), the lure of the narcotics trade further undermined the claims of morality, honesty, and selflessness which the military elites proclaimed so righteously. Military budgets increased, and acquisition of expensive weapons systems added to burgeoning national debts. Military compensation, both for military and nonmilitary government assignments, increased considerably.

Most important, military elites took on the responsibility for their countries' economic performance and the public sector's delivery of goods and services to the population. These responsibilities would prove heavy as increased energy prices, international recessions, renewed inflation, a growing debt burden, and, in the early 1980s, severe economic recession eroded support for the military governments, support previously derived from economic expansion. Resurgence of labor conflict and even political violence further challenged the military governments. These conditions all intensified internal divisions within the military institutions.

Over time, controversies within the armed forces concerning the direction and specific content of social and economic policy weakened the resolve and capabilities of military governments. At times these controversies almost amounted to the functional equivalent of conflicts between political parties and interest groups in a civilian regime. Supporters of rejected policies lost prestige or even career opportunities, whereas proponents of adopted policies furthered both their military and political careers. As these sorts of cleavages permeated the military regimes, solidarity was lost and civilian movements allied themselves with like-minded military factions.

Politics reappeared within the armed forces much to the distress of antipoliticians.

Even where impressive economic growth occurred or profound social change modified the old order (as in Brazil and Peru), the military political projects gradually collapsed in the late 1970s and early 1980s. Everywhere, the military governments failed in their self-assigned mission of creating a new political institutionality. Calls for redemocratization became the battle cry of the opposition. Resurgent political parties, student movements, labor unions, and religious organizations all pressured for political liberalization. Even business, commercial, and professional groups who had previously allied themselves with the antipolitical military regimes withdrew their support and urged a return to civilian government. The defection of these groups proved a pivotal turning point for the military regimes in Argentina, Uruguay, Brazil, and Guatemala. Only in Chile did the military-imposed constitution (1980) survive after the transition to civilian government in 1990.

Failure to consolidate the new antipolitical institutions did not mean that the antipolitical military regimes failed to alter, and in some cases radically transform, the social, economic, and political realities of their respective countries. The policies and programs of the military governments restructured national economies in a number of ways. In some cases this meant dramatic increases in industrialization, changes in land tenure and agricultural systems, and severe adjustments in occupational and social structure. To finance new economic initiatives and to pay for acquisition of new weapons and matériel, the military governments contracted large debts to foreign commercial banks and international financial institutions. These debts, like the changes in socioeconomic structure, did not disappear when the military leaders withdrew from direct policy-making responsibility.

In other cases, particularly where neoliberal policies emphasizing freer trade were adopted, industrial sectors shrank, as domestic firms could not compete with the wave of imports made possible by removal of tariff and other trade barriers. This led, in turn, to rising unemployment. Increased concentration of income and a relative shift in economic power to financial, banking, and commercial conglomerates upset the fundamental configuration of economies based upon import-substitution industrialization since the 1930s and 1940s. The consequences of all these changes, and of others discussed in the case studies which follow, provided immediate challenges for the civilian governments which replaced the military regimes.

The experience of the antipolitical regimes also deeply scarred the political and cultural life of these nations. Conscious of the brutal reality of antidemocratic practices during the decades of military rule, opposition movements which allied to oust the military governments greatly feared a reversion to the recent past. Yet this vivid memory could not produce, in itself, viable political coalitions or fundamental social consensus. A new legitimacy remained to be created even where the symbols and rhetoric of "redemocratization" served as the immediate rationale for transitions from military rule.

Extrication of the military from direct government responsibility coincided almost everywhere with new constitutions or modification of existing constitutions and with new electoral legislation. These new constitutions and electoral laws reintroduced party politics, social and civil liberties, a relatively free press and media, and a renewed struggle to redefine the long-term destinies of the nations of Latin America. New conceptions of democracy and democratization competed with older versions of liberal democracy for support by the recently elected civilian leadership. Ominously, the traditional democratic Left and the old Marxist movements once again challenged the legitimacy of the capitalist order while military leaders and advocates of exclusionary authoritarian politics warily observed the emerging political situation.

Under the extremely unfavorable circumstances of international recession, debt crises, and negative economic growth (1981–85), the new civilian governments replaced the antipolitical military regimes. Yet the transition from military to civilian regimes did not destroy the old military institutions, eliminate their coercive power or influence, or end the support by certain social sectors for authoritarian, nonparticipatory politics. Failure of the antipolitical regimes did not automatically create a new consensus on the nations' political futures. Pressures by students, workers, peasants, business associations, and government employees to meet long-postponed needs for housing, education, improved employment opportunities, and social services exceeded the capabilities and resources of many of these new governments. The threat of renewed social mobilization and political activism—strikes, farm occupations, food riots, urban land invasions, and demands for trials and punishment of the ousted military rulers and their subordinates for human rights violations—all added to the dilemmas facing the new civilian authorities. Eventually the new civilian leaders agreed, either privately or through public policy, to limit the extent of prosecutions of military and police officers for human rights violations during the period of military rule (though selected military leaders were tried and sentenced to prison—most dramatically in Argentina).

The failure of these newly elected civilian governments was possible if only because agreement on the definition of success was not easily forthcoming. The old cleavages emerged quickly: Peronism versus Radicalism in Argentina; Apristas, Communists, the new Right, and a radical Left in Peru, including the rise of Sendero Luminoso and other politico-guerrilla movements; reemergence of traditional political movements and regionalism in Brazil; a weak civilian party system in Guatemala, with an ongoing guerrilla struggle; continuing civil war in El Salvador into the 1990s and then a fragile "peace accord" (1992); and in Chile the transition to an elected government in 1990 and a second election in 1994, without overcoming the legacy of the military-imposed 1980 constitution.

If the failure of these new civilian experiments is to be avoided, a clear understanding of the common legacy and idiosyncratic impacts of the antipolitical military regimes is essential. Of course, such an understanding is no guarantee of successful democratization, but, at least, it may draw attention to the risks of reliving the politics of the recent past and of refusing to confront the challenges of the present. The country studies which follow review the effects of military antipolitics in the six countries on which this volume has focused.

Juan E. Corradi

CHAPTER 21

Military Government and State Terrorism in Argentina

The last one hundred years of Argentine history can be neatly divided in two halves. From 1880 through 1930 it was mainly a success story, a legend of rapid economic growth, of fabulous fortunes made at the top but trickling down the social ladder, of immigration, mobility, and exceptionalism. The country was in the hands of an oligarchy of landowners in dependent association with British capital. But the wealth generated by agrarian exports opened the doors to millions of Southern Europeans that flocked to rapidly growing cities, changed the cultural texture, found new occupations, and entertained new hopes. Social progress turned into political demand, and the general prosperity, coupled with the rulers' liberal bent, allowed the extension of citizenship to a rising middle class. The next fifty years were years of turbulence ending in disappointment. They were marked, overwhelmingly, by the irruption of organized labor as a political force in a context of economic uncertainty and institutional improvisation. Argentina muddled through the industrial era unable to work out satisfactory arrangements of political conviviality. This gave rise to another, darker legend of wasted opportunities, of dereliction from great promises. Nevertheless, Argentina managed to avoid the true tragedies of the century: It did not become enmeshed in serious international conflict; its crises were never catastrophic; its political errings were more colorful than dreadful. Just as it had grown in happy nonchalance, it now seemed to falter blandly. Then suddenly, in the seventies, it caught up with the horrors of our era.

Since the ouster of the first Peronist regime (1955) through 1966, military interventions periodically interrupted the constitutional process in Argentina, but allowed it to resume its course after a while. The political regime was one of exclusionary democracy, characterized by the proscription of the main political force—Peronism—from direct participation. This system was bidimensional: It consisted of an institutional political facade (parties, parliament, and the executive) and a parallel network of negotiations in camera between corporate interests (unions, business groups, landed, financial, and trade interests, and so forth), in unstable interface, which was periodically "corrected" by military interventions. The military did not stand above politics, but were part of the political process itself—one of the several actors that brought into the political arena disparate power resources. A second phase began in 1966, when the military seized power with the explicit purpose of suspending politics indefinitely and steering an ambitious program of development in dependent association with transnational capital.

The order of priorities was as follows: economic development first, social recomposition second, and political institutionalization last. However, the destruction of the existing political fabric and the social tensions brought about by the developmental process had puzzling unintended consequences that brought down the regime. The discontent of crucial social actors could not be mediated by institutional mechanisms. Instead, it generated new political alliances (notably a rapprochement between labor and middle-class sectors, between Peronists and former anti-Peronists) and a climate of generalized insurrection that threatened the state and forced the military to retreat to the barracks. A formidable amount of social power had accumulated on the margins of institutions, and the military could neither suppress nor channel it. In addition, the new mobilization carried, in its wake, the first significant anticapitalist challenge in modern Argentine history. The task of defusing the explosive mix fell on none other than Perón, who was the predictable winner of the first truly open elections since 1955. But Perón was the victim of his own success: He could not create a viable political system capable of taming the very forces that brought him back to power. After Perón's death in office (1974), his followers were even less able to control the situation. The Peronist government failed abysmally on all fronts: political stability, economic management, and the maintenance of law and order. The Peronist civilian interlude of 1973–76 was characterized by the progressive subjection of political institutions to a "siege of terror" by leftist and rightist paramilitary groups. It ended with a new seizure of power by the armed forces in 1976. The new dictatorship was the most radical of all military experiments in Argentine history. It was determined to become more impersonal, autonomous, permanent, repressive, and deeply "structural" than anything before.

The military regime installed after the March 24, 1976, coup against the government of Isabel Perón was a response to the prolonged state of war of all against all that had hitherto characterized

Argentine politics. It also embodied the "learnings" of military and corporate elites from past failures. The leaders of the armed forces and their business associates proclaimed that their objective was not merely to terminate the untenable disorder of the Peronist years, but to transform the very bases of Argentine society as well. The junta vowed to abolish terrorism, to revitalize the economy by freeing it from the trammels of state guidance, to cut the Gordian knot of stalemated conflict by reducing the number of significant social actors and disciplining the remaining ones. In short, it sought to undo what had been built haphazardly since the onset of industrialization. The vision was baptized, immodestly, a "process of national reorganization," echoing another, founding process of national organization drafted by the political generation of 1837 and carried out by that of 1880 (a process that set the ground rules for Argentine preindustrial growth and modernization until 1930).

Five years later, the first military president, General Videla, finished his mandate and conveyed power to a new president-elect, General Viola. At that point, the regime began to falter. Viola was very soon replaced by the army commander, General Galtieri. After the debacle of the South Atlantic war, the latter was replaced by General Bignone, who presided over a difficult transition to an uncertain civilian rule.

An important restructuration of power took place in Argentina after 1976. It was accompanied by significant changes in ideology. Argentina in 1976 is a particularly complex case in which internal decay produced a movement for the forced reintegration of society around new or partially new patterns of behavior.

The military and civilian elites that seized power in 1976 had a draconian definition of the situation, reeking of medical imagery: "diagnosis," "social pathology," "cancer," "surgery," "extirpation of diseased tissues," and so forth. Civil society was seriously ill. The disease that afflicted the country and which came, as it were, from below had to be met by decisive action from above. The explicit intention of the government of the armed forces was to close the historic cycle that Peronism had opened in the forties and initiate a new one. The political crisis of the seventies was perceived by both the military and some entrepreneurial elites as a basic threat to stable domination. Their critique went beyond the existing political regime that gave such a prominent place to Peronism: It focused on the social bases of the political system. Illness as political metaphor served to bridge the two major components of ideological inputs to the forced reorganization of society: to articulate the discourse of warriors and the discourse of free-enterprise conservatives.

After 1976 the main feature of the military process that took over Argentine life was the conversion of the previous populist public mores into a state-political practice and discourse in which everything was reduced to a simple dichotomy: the paradigm Friend-Foe. By reducing political rivals to ideological nonexistence, such discourse frames them for "treatment." The construction and maintenance of this order of discourse involves the deployment of particular nondiscursive sanctions which may be characterized as practices of abjection (expulsion, confinement, torture, "disappearance," and extermination).

The Terror Process

. . . To wage its war against subversion, the Argentine junta organized and armed many separate units within the armed forces and the police. These units operated with total autonomy and impunity, having a free hand in the selection of their victims. This strategy had several advantages for the government: It became a network very difficult to infiltrate, precisely because of its decentralized, protean nature; it was largely immune to the influence of even well-placed relatives of the victims; and it allowed the central government to disclaim responsibility for violations of human rights. Terror went through an intense phase in Argentina from 1976 through 1979. It then abated, although the repressive apparatus was seemingly still in place, or in a state of latency. During the terror phase, somewhere between 10,000 and 30,000 persons were liquidated. The extermination was largely secret—a fact that makes a precise estimate of the number of victims difficult. They rather belong to a category of nonpersons, between the dead and the living, for which Argentina has become sadly famous: those who have never been heard of again, the *desaparecidos*. Although repression was presented as a war against armed subversion, terror spilled over well beyond the limited zone of counterinsurgency operations. It affected nonviolent opponents of the regime, and also potential and imaginary opponents. It threatened, for a while, to become total. The main categories affected were, in addition to members of guerrilla organizations which were effectively decimated, lower and intermediate union cadres, students, civilian politicians, and professional groups (lawyers, psychiatrists, artists, social scientists, clergy, etc.), as well as relatives of initial victims.

The terror process of Argentina has served three main and two subsidiary functions. As part of a "dirty war" against armed insurgency, it eliminated those engaged in or suspected of active hostility to the power structure. It also functioned as a mechanism of deterrence, aimed at intimidating other opponents. It sought to destroy institutional alternatives and postponed the reintegration of the disorganized groups into new organizational patterns. Furthermore, it sought the prophylactic elimination of potential opponents, identified on the basis of an ideological diagnosis of the social "disease." Indirectly, the terror process helped the military to extend control across the country. This thorough penetration of the institutional fabric of society should not be confused, however, with the consolidation of an "authoritarian-bureaucratic" state. It was a narrower and more particularistic seizure of the state apparatus by corporate groups. It was also part of a strategy to transform the country's economic structure *without*, however, strengthening the levers of bureaucratic command over the economy. Rather, the economy was streamlined and forcefully reprivatized.

Like an old kingdom of West Africa, Argentina was governed by both a visible and an invisible government, by dignified military officers managing the administrative machinery of the state and by secret terroristic associations, by hidden executioners, agents from the state *absconditus* that intervened in ordinary life at certain moments, unpredictable to the victims, holding sway by virtue of the widespread fear of their powers and through the extreme violence associated with their acts. The dissociation of the invisible government from the social relations of ordinary life, the withdrawal of the state from the public sphere—a process paralleled and reinforced by the abandonment of social regulation to the "automatic" mechanisms of the market—made systematic terrorism possible. By attributing their acts to the imperatives of national security, the officials were freed from ordinary responsibility for those acts, although they were held responsible to the highest orders of military command. In essence, the state became a quasi-private and violent affair. To the privatization of civil existence under terror corresponds an increasing privatization of state power and violence.

Many allies and critics of the regime have projected an image of it as an authoritarian state representing power externally and social regulation internally—even if the latter was often reduced to mere police regulation, without an intrinsic bond of community among the governed. The acquisition and consolidation of power by the military regime issued not Leviathan but Behemoth. Something resembling a dual state existed in Argentina during these years of intense repression (i.e., a state within which two systems operated). One served as a mark for the other, under the remnants of the constitution—applied only with respect to those provisions that have not been amended by the military government—to which a new body of law has been attached, comprised of laws and decrees, institutional acts and statutes, specific provisions, resolutions, and instructions enacted since March 24, 1976. The other served under individual measures in which expediency, arbitrariness, and considerations of military security override all law. But the second system was contained in the first and acted upon it in an utterly destructive way. The seeds of that destruction are often contained in texts that have the semblance of law but none of its substance. For instance, by virtue of the Institutional Act of June 18, 1976, the military junta assumed "the power and responsibility to consider the actions of those individuals who have injured the national interest," on grounds as vague and ill-defined as "failure to observe basic moral principles in the exercise of public, political, or union offices or activities that involve the public interest." The Act led to the enactment of special laws, to the exercise of arbitrary power designed to intimidate particular groups and individuals on the basis of acts committed prior to the existence of such "laws." The generic ground on which laws rest; the discretionary nature of the powers that they grant; the creation and functioning of special bodies to which they grant jurisdictional powers; the application of their provisions on a retroactive basis; the punitive measures which they authorize; the disqualification from holding office; the restriction against practicing one's profession; the confiscation of property; the loss of citizenship, liberty, and life to which they lead, suggest, as in the case of Nazi Germany, that "we are confronted with a form of society in which the ruling groups control the rest of the population directly, without the mediation of that rational though coercive apparatus known as the state."

In 1976 the military groups that seized power benefited from the disappointment of large sectors of the population with a nominally democratic system that delivered them to chaos. Yet, after six years of rule, a majority longed again for structures of representation and binding compromise, for something as undramatic as the acknowledgment of social complexity, some measure of democratic participation, and modest economic growth. Coercion and fear appeared to them, in retrospect, as another form of disorder. As mentioned previously, on the level of official ideology, the operating metaphors of law and order were medical and, more precisely, surgical. They

corresponded to a self-presentation of the regime as punishing definite acts of subversion and breaking up seditious organizations, on
the one hand, and as establishing the bases for "sound" economic
behavior, on the other. These metaphors provided a common definition of the situation for the military-technocratic elites; they bridged
the vision of national security with free-enterprise and technocratic
utopias. Yet, behind the manifest discourse, there developed a culture of fear corresponding to the terror process.

Pseudo-Conservatism

The initial years of the Argentine military regime—the years of terror—were characterized by a sense of timelessness at the top and
anxiety at the bottom. Democracy remained suspended sine die. Perón
had been dead for four years. The guerrilla movement was defeated
in a bloody campaign. Terror reached a peak of intensity. Lawlessness became, paradoxically, an official routine. It consumed even the
suspect. Mass silence reigned, with one exception: For several months
in 1978, Argentines were allowed to pour out on the streets to attend
and celebrate the world soccer championship. The outpour of collective enthusiasm was routed to a safe channel, controlled and manipulated by the regime, and acted as a safety valve for suppressed
mobilization. The "Here I am" that was shouted in the streets was a
nativist identification with the country's glory. Politics and independent culture were frozen, but cheering in the stadiums was allowed.
While the regime acknowledged that it held nearly 3,500 political
prisoners, while countless others disappeared every day, when the
armed forces had seized command of all major institutions and many
minor ones, from the general labor confederation to charitable associations, public life returned to a primordial state. The national sport
came to mean solidarity on the cheap. It carried, no doubt, populist
undertones and reminiscences of another era, but the regime felt confident enough to feign a bond of consensus with the masses and reap
political profit from the event. Four years later it would try the experiment again on more dangerous ground, when it decided to occupy militarily the Malvinas Islands, tap nationalist feelings, and
manipulate opinion through a brief totalitarian mobilization which
backfired after the defeat, resuscitating populist mythology. These
two episodes were the closest the regime came to fascism. For most
of the time it preferred to combine nativism with an emphasis on
discipline in a more quietistic manner, avoiding organized mass mobilization. Because of its predominantly diffuse style, the regime may

be called pseudo-conservative rather than fascist. In military circles around power, the sense of a crusade against political and cultural subversion was strong.

What guided the crusaders was a notion that culture and politics should be strictly subordinated to small-town morality, religion, and national security. These are supposed to form the core of an "Argentine life-style" that is the antithesis of "communism" and a bulwark against it. The simplicities of this official view are not without paradox. The ideas of the moral crusaders are reactive and antimodern, yet Argentine culture is nothing but a by-product of modern enlightenment. In consequence, the ruling ideology produces the disconcerting spectacle of a young country defending old values, a community of recent settlers endorsing traditions they never had, conservatives with little to conserve. In fact, the conservatism of officers (many of them the children and grandchildren of immigrants) who want to stamp out sociology, psychoanalysis, and even some branches of modern mathematics is phony. It is a form of corporate paranoia, a universe plagued with demons and full of ill-digested values. This sense of cultural siege drove these officers to be critical of modern Western culture in the name of a myth of that culture which they pretended to guard against nameless "traitors."

Economics and Desocialization

The central feature of state action is neither compromise nor mobilization, but withdrawal from the pressures of organized social sectors and immunity from popular demands. Liberal economic policies and a free-enterprise ideology are pieces of that political strategy. They are designed to destroy preexisting patterns of economic behavior and political alliance.

Argentine economic liberalism rested on two ground rules: to open the internal to the international market, and to free capital markets. The ostensive purpose of policy was to reduce inflation. Several successive measures were adopted to that effect. They were not successful in terms of the stated objective, but they had several other functions that were perfectly in accordance with the global political vision of the regime. They were: a drastic rollback of real wages (1976–77), a reduction of the money supply (1977–78), and a modulated exchange rate that produced a revaluation of the currency (1978–81). Their impact on general economic activity was cyclical until 1979 and persistently recessionary since. This pattern was accompanied by a spectacular increase in the foreign debt, until Argentina became the third-ranking debtor nation in the world, and probably the first in per capita terms.

The foremost victims of these policies were workers with fixed incomes. But other groups were also affected negatively. After 1978, farmers and exporters suffered from the overvalued currency. National industry, which saw increased benefits and expansion in 1977 and 1979, was forced to contract a debt so burdensome that it collapsed in the 1980s. Only some financial sectors did spectacularly well. The period 1976–82 may well look in retrospect as one in which a dependent national economy was ravaged by international finance capital. The political effects were completely in line with the intentions of the power holders. The labor sector was fragmented and its bargaining power significantly reduced. A large number of workers literally disappeared from the social map of Argentina, first through a combination of demographic stagnation, retirement, transfer of personnel to service and self-employed categories, and migration; and then through the increase of unemployment. The national business class was severely affected by the enormous pressures on the international market on which it depended, by debt and bankruptcy. Curiously, its wail has been louder than the protest of the workers. Also disgruntled were the agarian exporters, although their position remained more solid than that of industrial entrepreneurs. The key to the whole policy was a financial manipulation that channeled resources toward a speculative economy. For some time, the bitter pill of deindustrialization was coated with what came to be known popularly as "sweet money" (*plata dulce*). The prototype of the new *homo oeconomicus* produced by the regime was the anomic speculator. If we now join the new pattern of induced economic action with the effects of political repression, we complete the picture of the social climate generated by the regime. Jointly, they further sapped the sagging public spirit.

The arbitrariness of security procedures, the tales of disappearances, the fear that anyone could be picked up, confined citizens to looking after themselves and their immediate families. Silence, denial, rationalization, mere self-regard became social norms. Everyone tended to become security conscious, metabolizing in the microcosm of the neighborhood, the job, or in the intimacy of family life the brutal thrust coming from above. Politically intimidated, Argentines were also harried by inflation and by the economic strategies to which they had to turn in order to cope. Argentina became a land of wheelers and dealers, of speculators and moonlighters, some making or losing paper fortunes overnight, others running ever faster in order to stand still. The carrot was no less demoralizing than the stick. Imagine individuals who run with their paychecks and pocket calculators to study the day's posted interest rates, then place their earnings in thirty-day, even seven-day, instruments, while inflation and interest yields race each other on a three-digit lane. A speculative economy urges the individual to secure maximum value. Everything conspires, from the police state to wild market forces, to turn a person into a maximizing consumer rather than a cooperating citizen, discouraging and eroding feelings of social obligation. The combined timelessness of terror and the high velocity of money, the disorienting abstractions of political and economic processes, explain why traditional social conventions, such as fellowship and civil conviviality, gave way to a pervasive cynicism. . . .

The consequence of institutional failure was an added flow of power to military authorities, and an attempt by the latter to extensively overhaul the status quo. At this juncture the rulers imposed a draconian model of a better system and sought frantically to prevent other groups from developing alternatives. The model was based on a charter myth combining the doctrines of national security and free enterprise. It had clear totalitarian elements, notably the recourse to terror, the attempt to pulverize old structures—albeit through market mechanisms—and the use of ideological controls to dissolve previous identities.

Yet, the project of the power holders also contained a number of contradictions and self-checks. First, there was a tension between the economic and the military "logics" of the regime. The corporate interests of the officers often clashed with the designs of free-market technocrats. Moreover, the radical and autonomous nature of policies deprived the regime of stable alliances among crucial economic sectors. Second, the combination of physical coercion and economic disarticulation managed to stifle organized social and political opposition but failed to provide substitute structures of participation and isolated the regime from society. The latter became increasingly opaque to the rulers. This situation in turn made potential opposition less predictable. The lack of early feedback signals from society compounded rather than corrected the strategic and tactical errors of the regime. When these errors were perceived, it was too late. At that point the regime changed course in a fitful manner, trying to escape from one crisis by jumping into another. Thus, when the indication of economic malfunctioning became clear, the rulers switched channels and prepared a mass mobilization for a war which, much to their dismay, actually took place and which they lost. In so acting, they opened a Pandora's box of resentment, retribution, old populist myths, and alternative ideologies.

Riordan Roett

CHAPTER 22

The Post-1964
Military Republic in Brazil

After 1964, the Brazilian political system experienced a number of institutional modifications. A series of unique, extraconstitutional decrees, known as Institutional Acts, were utilized during the early years of the Military Republic to reorganize political life.

The Institutional Acts were a significant and interesting event in Brazilian political life. These documents constituted the justification for military intervention and also provided a political framework within which major institutional and structural reforms were made. While not canceling the Constitution, whether that of 1946 or 1967, the acts superseded and restricted the purview of that document. . . . They represented a running commentary on the inadequacies of the 1946 Republic, as well as formal notification to the nation that the changes introduced in 1964 were to be considered permanent. . . .

After 1964, seventeen Institutional Acts and more than one hundred Complementary Acts were issued. The Complementary Acts spelled out the specific intent of the more general principles involved in the Institutional Acts. It is clear from the working of the acts that they were decreed by the armed forces acting in a dual role: that of the representatives of the movement of March 31, the Revolution, a role which has a life of its own apart from any institutional or constitutional restraints, and as the executive power of the Brazilian government.

The 1967 Constitution emerged, in part, from a feeling that the changes brought about by the early Institutional Acts and the Complementary Acts required incorporation into the Constitution; the 1946 document no longer served the needs of the nation. With the First Constitutional Amendment of October 1969, it became clear that the 1967 Constitution was an impermanent statement to be ignored when required by the interests of the armed forces in their efforts to restore the status quo to Brazil. Not until the mid-1970s would a slow process of juridical normalization begin with the cancellation of the

Institutional Acts. Indeed, by then they had accomplished their purpose. The regime, in the late 1970s, turned to other means to maintain its control over political life, such as the unilateral establishment of the electoral rules for 1982 and the promulgation of a new National Security Law which, the opposition argued, gave the regime power similar to that embodied in the acts.

Institutional Act No. 1, April 9, 1964

The presidency of Brazil was declared vacant on the night of April 1, 1964, by the president of the Senate. The president of the Chamber of Deputies was sworn in as acting president on April 2. The nation—and the civilian political elite—waited.

After a week of negotiation over the course of the March 31 coup, the armed forces decided to act unilaterally. The political initiative passed to the military; it remained in their hands throughout the second half of the 1960s. On April 9 the three military ministers issued an Institutional Act which would become known as Institutional Act No. 1 when others appeared. The act did not rest on any constitutional justification; its authority derived from the moral force of the Revolution itself. No further justification was deemed necessary by the armed forces.

The preamble of the act states the reason for its issuance:

> The successful Revolution invests itself with the exercise of the Constituent Power, which manifests itself by popular election or by Revolution. This is the most expressive and radical form of the Constituent Power. Thus, the successful Revolution, like the Constituent Power, is legitimized by itself. The Revolution dismisses the former government and is qualified to set up a new one. The Revolution holds in itself the normative strength inherent to the Constituent Power, and establishes judicial norms without being limited by previous norms.

The act vastly strengthened the powers of the chief executive. While the 1946 Constitution remained in force, it was subject to modification by the act. The president received the power to propose amendments to the Constitution, which the Congress had to consider within thirty days; only a majority vote, as opposed to the two-thirds vote stipulated in the 1946 Constitution, was needed for approval. Only the president could submit expenditure measures to Congress, and the Congress could not increase the amount stipulated in the bills. The power to declare a state of siege without congressional approval was given to the president, and the executive was granted the power to suppress the political rights of "political undesirables" for a period of ten years.

The act decreed that the election of the new president to replace President Goulart and of the vice president would be by an absolute majority of the Congress, to take place within two days of the promulgation of the act. On April 11, 1964, General Humberto Castello Branco, a leader of the March 31 coup, was elected president. The date for the election of Castello Branco's successor, who was to assume office in January 1966, was set for October 3, 1965.

Article X of the act, which gave the president the right to revoke legislative mandates and to suspend political rights, was to expire on June 15, 1964. The military government moved quickly to revoke the mandates of those members of Congress identified with the defeated left. By the deadline, former president Goulart, as well as six governors and more than 40 members of Congress, plus some 300 individuals active in political life, had had their rights suspended. Under Article VII, which gave the president the power to expel people from the civil service without regard for existing legislation guaranteeing employment, it is estimated that approximately 9,000 people were fired by November 9, the cutoff date stated in the act.

As the military became accustomed to its new political role, it was clear its task would not be completed by January 1966, when the presidential term of Castello Branco would terminate. In July 1964 a constitutional amendment extended the president's term of office until March 15, 1967; new presidential elections were set for November 1966.

With the decision to extend the president's term, implying a military commitment to retain power for an indefinite period, a number of events in 1965 helped to determine the political strategy of the regime. The first was the election, in the mayoral race in São Paulo in March 1965, of a candidate backed by former president Quadros. The victory of a man identified by some as a representative of the populist tradition in Brazilian politics (even though a military officer) provided the impetus required for a move away from the economic emphasis of the Revolution into the political arena.

On July 15, 1965, two laws dealing with elections and political parties were announced. These represented the first substantive revision of the pre-1964 political rules of the game. The Electoral Code reduced the number of parties by increasing the minimum requirements that parties had to meet to achieve or maintain legal status. Electoral alliances were forbidden; candidates were required to reside in the area they sought to represent; voters were required to choose legislators from the same party in order to strengthen party discipline; and the running mates of successful gubernatorial and presidential candidates were automatically elected. These reforms were an attempt to deal with one of the problems perceived by the military as most debilitating in the pre-1964 era: the weak and diffuse multiparty system. It was hoped that these reforms would introduce some coherence into the political system.

The Political Party Statute stipulated stringent procedures for the organization of new political parties. Individuals were forbidden to run for more than one office in any election. Residence and party membership requirements were specified for candidates. It was hoped that this law would help to control the problem of representation, so abused before 1964, when there were few requirements linking a candidate to his constituency.

Also promulgated on July 15 was an Ineligibilities Law. It prevented former ministers in the Goulart government (those appointed after the January 1963 plebiscite) from candidacy. Its primary purpose was to prevent the candidacy of several prominent antiregime politicians in the upcoming state elections.

Although the three proposals were submitted to Congress for consideration, two became law without final action of that body. When the time period for consideration expired, the president, using the authority granted to him by the Institutional Act, acted unilaterally. The Political Party Statute was passed by the Congress, but fourteen items introduced during floor debate were vetoed by the president. It appeared in the form in which it was originally submitted to the Congress.

The gubernatorial elections of October 1965 were a critical event in the unfolding of the military regime. Despite the warning and fears of many members of the armed forces, the Castello Branco government determined to hold open, competitive elections. Two candidates identified as opponents of the regime (Israel Pinheiro in Minas Gerais and Negrão de Lima in Guanabara), both supported by former president Kubitschek, were victorious.

Immediately the military hard-liners pressed the government to annul the elections. In order to fulfill his promise to allow the inauguration of all candidates elected, President Castello Branco promulgated Institutional Act No. 2. With the publication of the second act, the military regime made a basic decision to restructure national politics to try to ensure that the legacy of the 1946 Republic would be effectively neutralized. The elections seem to have been the determining factor in the decision of Castello Branco and the moderate wing of the military that the unity of the armed forces was more important for the future development of Brazil than was the constitutional principle of direct elections.

Institutional Acts Nos. 2, 3, and 4

Institutional Act No. 2 determined that only the president could create new positions in the civil service; further restricted the time allowed to Congress to consider legislation before it became law automatically; increased the number of members of the Supreme Court (which had been viewed as a last holdout against the more blatantly unconstitutional actions of the revolutionary government); reserved the right of nomination of all federal judges to the president of the Republic; reorganized the Supreme Military Tribunal; stipulated that civilians accused of crimes against national security were to be submitted to military justice; decreed the indirect election of the president and vice president by an absolute majority of the federal Congress; permitted the president to declare a state of siege for 180 days to prevent "the subversion of internal order"; extended the right of the Revolution to suspend individual political rights for ten years; established restrictions on the activities of those whose political rights were removed; gave the president the right to intervene in the states of the federation, for other than the reasons stipulated in the Constitution, in order to assure the execution of a federal law and in order to prevent or punish the subversion of order; abolished existing political parties and canceled their registration; excluded from judicial competence all acts of the Supreme Revolutionary Command and of the federal government in the first and second acts and in the complementary acts to follow, plus resolutions, passed since March 31, 1964, of state assemblies that cancelled the mandates of legislators; and gave the president the power to recess Congress, legislative assemblies, and chambers of municipal councilors. The second act was to remain in force until March 15, 1967, the date of the inauguration of Castello Branco's successor. . . .

The complementary acts announced through 1965 and 1966 served to implement or elaborate on the institutional acts. Perhaps the most notorious complementary act promulgated during this time was the 23rd, of October 20, 1966; it confirmed the growing centralization of power in the hands of the military and strengthened the determination of the government to allow little, if any, organized opposition to its plans. It was preceded by the removal of six federal deputies from office on October 12 and a break with the government by the ARENA congressional leadership. Complementary Act No. 23 decreed the recess of the federal Congress until November 22, 1966—after the scheduled elections. The act stated that there existed in the Congress "a group of counterrevolutionary elements whose objective was to disturb the public peace and upset the coming election of November 15, thus compromising the prestige and the authority of the legislative power. . . ." A precedent had been established, allowing the executive power to quiet the legislative branch successfully whenever it suited the government's needs.

With the indirect election by the National Congress of Marshal Costa e Silva to succeed Castello Branco, the succession issue was settled. Costa e Silva ran unopposed; attempts by the MDB to launch a rival candidacy had failed. Federal senators and deputies, state deputies, mayors, and municipal councilmen were selected in direct elections on November 15. ARENA won overwhelmingly, electing senators from fifteen states and approximately two-thirds of the new deputies.

Institutional Act No. 4 of December 7, 1966, convoked an extraordinary meeting of Congress to vote and promulgate a new constitution. The preamble of the fourth act stated that it had become necessary to give the country a new constitution that would "represent the institutionalization of the ideas and principles of the Revolution." The Constitution was promulgated on January 24, 1967. It further strengthened the executive power and weakened any hope of opposition groups to use the constitution to justify opposition to the regime.

The Costa e Silva Government

The Failure of the Opposition to Unite

With the inauguration of President Costa e Silva on March 15, 1967, the Revolution entered a new phase. The early efforts at controlling inflation seemed to be working; the needed structural reforms of the political system had been undertaken; and the crisis of confidence within the military seemed to have been overcome with the acceptance by Castello Branco of the Costa e Silva candidacy. The main political event of the first year of the second military government was the discussion about the formation of a united front of opposition forces.

The only significant attempt to organize a united political front against the military regime occurred between 1966 and 1968. Former governor Carlos Lacerda of Guanabara, who saw his presidential ambitions destroyed by the military, assumed his traditional role in Brazilian politics and took the offensive against the regime. When former presidents Kubitschek and Goulart were contacted, they evinced some interest in a united opposition movement.

In September, Lacerda met with Goulart in Montevideo and signed a pact with his former political enemy to proceed with the organization of the front. Upon his return, the executive committee of the MDB announced that it would not support the front; ex-president Jânio Quadros let it be known that he would not join the movement. The ex-president of the PTB, Lutero Vargas, attacked the idea in October. And in a speech that received widespread publicity, Interior Minister Albuquerque Lima condemned the front as an attempt to take Brazil back to the days before 1964.

By early 1968 the movement to form a united opposition front appeared badly fragmented. By the end of 1968, Lacerda had his political rights cancelled, and the moving force behind the front collapsed into silence. The movement was declared illegal; moreover, members of Congress supporting it were expelled from the Congress and banned from political activity for ten years. . . .

The Crisis of December 1968

Throughout the last half of 1968, it became apparent that the division within the regime had deepened between those who supported a moderate, semiconstitutional policy favoring limited civilian participation and the hardline nationalists who argued for military preeminence in all matters. The president seemed to favor a more moderate line; the leading proponent of a rigorous, nationalist development policy, carried out by the military, was the interior minister, General Alfonso Albuquerque Lima.

Albuquerque Lima had a large following among the younger members of the officer corps. He believed in the necessity of prolonged military rule in order to modernize Brazil, a task the civilian politicians in the 1946–64 period had failed miserably in achieving. For him, modernization meant structural reform of things such as the land-tenure system, the development and integration of the Amazon, the necessity of reducing regional imbalance, and so on. The general believed that a great nation like Brazil could no longer ignore its underdeveloped regions; such a policy of neglect threatened national security and modernization.

The two positions were brought into confrontation over the issue of a speech made on the floor of the Congress by Deputy Márcio

Moreira Alves. He urged Brazilians to boycott military parades on Independence Day and asked that parents not allow their daughters to date military personnel. The nationalists found this address disgraceful and expected that the government would take appropriate action against the deputy. President Costa e Silva attempted to utilize legal channels to convince the Congress to remove Alves's congressional immunity, but the Congress balked.

In late October, a group of captains of the First Army stationed in Rio de Janeiro issued a manifesto. The document took note of their sacrifices for the Revolution, including their state of near-poverty amidst the plenty enjoyed by some. The message was unmistakable— the government was not responding to the basic needs of the nation. The modernization of the country required firm and decisive leadership; abrasive and insolent disregard for national priorities from civilians was not to be tolerated.

On December 12, 1968, the Congress met to consider the insistent request of the government that it lift Alves's immunity. Of the members of Congress, 216 voted against the government, 141 in favor, and 15 cast blank ballots. The government's demand had been rejected. In the face of this blatant disrespect for military authority, the government moved quickly to regain control of a rapidly deteriorating situation.

Institutional Act No. 5, December 13, 1968
The fifth act stated that the "revolutionary process unfolding could not be detained." The very institutions given to the nation by the Revolution for its defense were being used to destroy it, said the preamble of the act. The fifth act empowered the president to recess the National Congress, legislative assemblies, and municipal councils by complementary acts. These bodies would convene again only when called by the president. In addition, the president could decree intervention in the states when in the national interest and without regard for the constitutional restrictions on intervention; he could suspend the political rights of any citizen for ten years and cancel election mandates without regard for constitutional limitations. The national state of siege was prolonged; the confiscation of personal goods illicitly gained was allowed; the right of habeas corpus was suspended in cases of political crimes against national security and the social and economic order; and the restrictions to be placed on those who lost their political rights were increased and more explicitly designated.

Complementary Act No. 38, of December 13, 1968, decreed the recess of Congress. With the closing of the legislature, the regime had determined the immediate future of the Revolution of March 31, 1964. It would be a period of outright military rule without the inconvenience of elected, civilian interference. The economic planning process, which represented the only significant accomplishment of the regime, would continue unfettered. The possibilities for "humanizing" the Revolution gave way to the necessity of internal security, that is, precluding overt opposition from civilian political groups, and development, to be determined by the military regime and its civilian supporters. The issuance of the act seemed to secure the leadership of the president within the regime. Albuquerque Lima's abrupt departure in January 1969 indicated that the government felt sufficiently in control to eliminate his symbolic presence in the cabinet.

The first eight months of 1969 saw a flurry of revolutionary legislation. Institutional Act No. 6 (February 1, 1969) amended the 1967 Constitution (Article 113) and stipulated that the Supreme Court would consist of eleven members nominated by the president. It also said that the Supreme Military Tribunal would be responsible for trying all those accused of national security crimes. . . .

All of the institutional acts confirmed the assumption of supreme legislative power by the military regime. . . . The acts and the promulgation of political decisions by means of the acts affirmed the willingness of the regime to pursue its twin themes of security and development.

The President Incapacitated

Two dramatic events in August and September of 1969 demonstrated both the potential vulnerability and the military's predominance in the 1964 regime: the incapacitation of President Costa e Silva and the kidnapping of U.S. Ambassador C. Burke Elbrick in Rio de Janeiro.

A massive stroke incapacitated President Costa e Silva in late August. By the 1967 Constitution, Vice President Pedro Aleixo, a civilian from Minas Gerais and old-line member of the defunct UDN, was next in succession. It was clear that the armed forces would determine if the constitutional succession would be observed. Within forty-eight hours of the president's illness, Institutional Act No. 12 (August 31, 1969) was issued. The military had decided against the Constitution. The ministers of the navy, the army, and the air force promulgated the act "in the name of the president of the Republic

. . . temporarily impeded from exercising his functions for reasons of health." The document stated:

> The situation that the country is experiencing . . . precludes the transfer of the responsibilities of supreme authority and supreme command of the Armed Forces, exercised by His Excellency, to other officials, in accordance with the constitutional provision.
>
> As an imperative of National Security, it falls to the ministers of the Navy, of the Army and of the Air Force to assume, for as long as the head of the Nation is incapacitated, the duties given to His Excellency by the constitutional documents in force.
>
> The Nation can have confidence in the patriotism of its military chiefs who, in this hour, as always, will know how to honor the historic legacy of their predecessors, loyal to the spirit of nationalism, the Christian formation of its people, contrary to extremist ideologies and violent solutions, in moments of political or institutional crisis.

The act, relatively short in length, stipulated that military ministers would act on behalf of the president, that the previously published institutional and complementary acts would remain in full force, and that all the acts and complementary acts would be beyond judicial purview.

The new act demonstrated the willingness of the armed forces to violate the Constitution they themselves had promulgated in 1967. No mention was made of the vice president; none was required, really. It was clear that the ministers represented the general will of the military in assuming supreme command of the nation.

The U.S. Ambassador Disappears

On Thursday, September 4, 1969, U.S. Ambassador Elbrick was taken at gunpoint from his limousine in Rio de Janeiro. His kidnappers left a note in which they identified themselves as members of revolutionary movements; it demanded the release of fifteen political prisoners held by the regime in exchange for the life of the ambassador. A note found in the ambassador's car, addressed "to the Brazilian people," stated:

> With the kidnapping of the Ambassador we want to demonstrate that it is possible to defeat the dictatorship and the exploitation if we arm and organize ourselves. We show up where the enemy least expects us and we disappear immediately, tearing out the dictatorship, bringing terror and fear to the exploiters, the hope and certainty of victory to the midst of the exploited.

The demands of the kidnappers were that their manifesto be published and that the fifteen prisoners be taken to Algeria, Chile, or Mexico, where they would be granted political asylum. A time limit of forty-eight hours was stated. The manifesto ended with a warning to the regime from the terrorists: "Now it is an eye for an eye, and a tooth for a tooth."

The government, in the hands of the military ministers, responded immediately. The fifteen political prisoners were rounded up from their places of detention and placed aboard a plane for Mexico; the manifesto appeared in the Brazilian newspapers. The list of prisoners included some of the leading critics and opponents of the regime. Amidst rumors that members of the officer corps were "unhappy" over the government's decision, Institutional Act No. 13 (September 5, 1969) appeared. It empowered the executive to banish from the national territory any Brazilian considered dangerous to national security.

Institutional Act No. 14, issued the same day, stated: "[It is considered] that acts of adverse psychological warfare and revolutionary or subversive war, that disturb the life of the country and maintain it in a climate of intranquility and agitation, deserve more severe repression. . . ." The act amended the Constitution (Article 150) and established the penalties of death, perpetual imprisonment, banishment, or confiscation of goods for those guilty of participating in psychological, revolutionary, or subversive war against the state.

The Urban Guerrilla Movement in Brazil

The kidnapping of the U.S. ambassador dramatically publicized the existence, previously deemphasized by the regime, of a network of guerrilla bands operating in the cities of Brazil. The movement posed a most serious threat to the stability of the regime during the 1967–69 period. By challenging the authority of the government, the terrorist groups hoped to weaken the support for the military from the middle and upper urban sectors. If the government could not secure public order, what else justified its continuation? The terrorists had begun to have a real impact on the public mind with a series of daring bank robberies—more than a hundred by the end of 1969—and public bombings.

The terrorist groups stemmed from dissident elements of the Moscow-oriented Brazilian Communist party (PCB), led for decades by Luís Carlos Prestes. The first breakoff had been with the formation of the revolutionary Communist Party of Brazil (PCdoB) with a decidedly Maoist or Fidelist orientation. Other fragments represented Trotskyite and Marxist variants.

The more prominent of the groups was the National Liberating Alliance (ALN) founded early in 1967, led by former Communist party deputy Carlos Marighella. Committed to terrorist and guerrilla warfare, Marighella became the mastermind of the movement; the ALN combined within its ranks a number of smaller terrorist bands who looked to Marighella for leadership and ideological inspiration.

A group that worked closely with the ALN but maintained its own identity was that led by ex-captain Carlos Lamarca. Called the Popular Revolutionary Vanguard (VPR), it merged with another group called the National Liberation Command (COLINA) in June-July 1969 to form the Armed Revolutionary Vanguard (VAR), referred to as VAR-Palmares. Palmares was the site of an unsuccessful slave revolt in the late nineteenth century in the Brazilian Northeast. The VPR, in turn, resulted from a fusion of other fragmented terrorist groups. Under Lamarca's daring leadership, the VAR-Palmares became a romantic symbol of protest against the regime and attracted many students to its ranks. Disillusioned by military rule, they accepted Lamarca's leadership in, and Marighella's ideological justification for, armed insurrection. A pamphlet entitled "The Mini-Manual of the Urban Guerrilla" by Carlos Marighella, which appeared in the middle of 1969, offered a sophisticated and incisive summary of the bankruptcy of the regime and the necessity of undermining it by urban revolutionary warfare.

The movement was not a monolithic entity. It was splintered and represented antagonistic views of Brazilian society, ranging from reformist to revolutionary-anarchistic. A congress of VAR-Palmares, held in September 1969 to debate the future of the organization, resulted in further fragmentation of that group. The murder of Marighella in São Paulo on November 26 weakened the revolutionary left considerably. The loss of Marighella and the continuing fragmentation of the radical left were accompanied by increasing effectiveness on the part of the regime. In the state of Guanabara, the Center of Operations of Internal Defense (CODI) brought together all the civilian police and armed forces units working on security. A similar movement in São Paulo, Operation Bandeirante (OBAN), united all federal and state police units. OBAN was successful in uncovering clandestine groups of many of the terrorist organizations and by the end of 1969 had made more than 400 arrests.

By 1972 it seemed that this challenge to the regime had been effectively counteracted. The terrorist groups had not weakened the regime in the eyes of its strongest supporters, the middle and upper sectors. On the contrary, these groups interpreted the guerrilla movement as added justification for strong and effective government. The promptness and humaneness with which the government dealt with the kidnappings of foreign diplomats (in contrast with the Guatemalan government, which had refused to negotiate with similar terrorists who then murdered the West German ambassador to Guatemala) reassured the international community that the regime was willing and able to release political prisoners without severely undermining its internal support. The death of Carlos Lamarca in a gun battle with security police in September 1971 deprived the guerrillas of their principal leader.

While the period following the 1964 Revolution had witnessed strong and often arbitrary conduct by the Military Republic, the opening of the guerrilla offensive legitimated the expansion and consolidation of a complex security and intelligence network. At both the state and federal levels, a series of coordinating institutions either emerged or were reorganized to confront and destroy the subversive offensive and its adherents. Given the diversity of Brazil, the differences in state police and federal military jurisdictions, the level of perception of threat by individual security and military commanders, and the operation of "private" groups such as the infamous "Death Squads" in São Paulo, the challenge of coordinating intelligence efforts was overwhelming. Inevitably, local and state excesses occurred that were unknown or overlooked at the national level. As the armed forces became deeply involved in cooperating with police and security units working within each of the four army regions, allegations of direct military involvement in torture and interrogation sessions grew. . . .

Constitutional Amendment No. 1, October 20, 1969

As the regime surmounted the challenge to its authority represented by the kidnapping of the U.S. ambassador, it became clear that the president's incapacitation was permanent. The country confronted the task of selecting its fifth chief executive in the 1960s.

The immediate issue concerned the constitutional succession—would Vice President Aleixo be allowed to assume the presidency? The answer of the armed forces emerged on October 14, 1969, with the announcement of Institutional Act No. 16. The high command of the armed forces—that is, the three service chiefs—promulgated the document:

> . . . considering that the superior interests of the country require the immediate and permanent filling of the office of the President of the Republic; . . . considering that Institutional Act No. 12 (of August 13 [31], 1969) . . . attributes to the military ministers the right to substitute for the President of the Republic in his temporary incapacitation. . . . Article 1. The position of the President of the Republic is declared vacant. . . . Article 2. The position of Vice President of the Republic is also declared vacant. . . .

By using an institutional act, with Congress in recess, the prerogatives of that body were exercised by the executive power. By precluding the constitutional succession of the civilian vice president, the military prepared the way for the creation of a more rigidly authoritarian government to succeed Costa e Silva.

The internal dynamics of the selection process for the new chief executive are not fully known. It is commonly accepted that the officer corps of the three services was polled. At the time there were approximately 118 army generals, 60 admirals, and 61 air force brigadiers. These, plus other command officers (an estimated total of about 13,000 men), were asked to nominate those men thought most qualified to replace Costa e Silva. General Emílio Garrastazu Médici, a supporter of the stricken president and commander of the Third Army located in the state of Rio Grande do Sul, ranked highest. He was followed in popularity by General Orlando Geisel and General Alfonso Albuquerque Lima, the former interior minister. It is reliably reported that Albuquerque Lima had prepared a program of action which he discussed with the officer corps on trips to the various command posts before the final selection was made by the high command of the armed forces. In the end, General Médici received the military nomination for the presidency. Admiral Augusto Hamman Rademaker Grunewald, then serving as navy minister, received the vice presidential nomination.

The sixteenth act stipulated that the elections for president and vice president would be held by the Congress on October 25, 1969; those elected would take office on October 30; their term of office would terminate on March 25, 1974. (The act also clearly reserved the right of legislation to the military ministers even though the Congress had been convened.)

The political parties were given the right to nominate candidates for the offices. ARENA nominated Médici and Rademaker; the MDB did not offer nominations. The candidates of the Revolution were solemnly elected to the vacant positions by the Congress on October 25, 1969.

Institutional Act No. 17 of October 14, 1969, gave the president the power to transfer to the reserves any military officer guilty of violating the cohesion of the armed forces. The preamble of the act stated that "the Armed Forces as institutions that serve to sustain the constituted powers of law and order, are organized on a basis of the principles of hierarchy and discipline. . . ." The act can be interpreted as a warning to those officers in disagreement with the decision of the military high command in passing over Albuquerque Lima in favor of Médici. Also, the act gave to the new president "legal" means of imposing the military's will on the armed forces without having to resort to other forms of coercion or intimidation.

The sixteenth and seventeenth acts were followed by another unilateral decision of the military commanders: Constitutional Amendment No. 1 of October 17, published in the *Diario Oficial* on October 20 and in effect as of October 30. The effect of the amendment led some political observers to refer to the amendment as the 1969 Constitution, even though 95 percent of the 1967 document remained. The amendment, among other changes, reduced still further the powers of the Congress. . . .

The amendment represented the determination of the military to ensure a presidential succession unmarred by dissent or protest. It provided the new chief executive with all the power required for governing and controlling the nation. By moving to promulgate these decisions before the election of General Médici, the military high command assumed collectively the responsibility for the political decision to emasculate the 1967 Constitution. . . .

With the consolidation of internal security and a period of dramatic economic growth following the stabilization period of 1964–67, a new developmental emphasis emerged in the Médici government's domestic program. While the unity of the armed forces was by no means guaranteed, a combination of skillful administration, popular and pragmatic policies, and luck indicated that a majority of the officer corps were willing to support the Médici government's initiatives in the social and economic arenas. . . .

The Post-1964 Economic Performance of Brazil

The Castello Branco government (1964–67) quickly moved to implement a stabilization program to correct the internal and external disequilibria of the postwar period. The expectation was that a draconian program of stabilization would yield high growth rates by the end of the decade. New policy initiatives included restrictive fiscal and monetary measures; a restriction on real wages; the creation of compulsory social security funds which were deposited in the BNDE and in a newly established housing bank (BNH); a "crawling peg" system in 1968 to keep the *cruzeiro* from becoming overvalued; the introduction of a procedure of indexing by which the principal and interest on debt instruments were adjusted to reflect the current rate of inflation, which encouraged savings and noninflationary financing of government deficits; tax and credit incentives for investments in underdeveloped regions and in sectors earmarked for growth, such as exports and capital markets; and the initiation of large government investment projects, principally in infrastructure, with the financial support of the World Bank, the U.S. Agency for International Development, and the Inter-American Development Bank.

The economic reforms, led by Planning Minister Roberto Campos and Finance Minister Octávio Bulhões, worked. While the 1964 to 1967 years resulted in low rates of GDP growth (an average of 3.9 percent per annum) and of industrial expansion (3.6 percent per annum), inflation began to drop—from 87 percent in 1964 to 27 percent in 1967. With the direction of economic affairs in the hands of Antônio Delfim Neto after 1967, and using the Campos-Bulhões stabilization program as a foundation, manufacturing grew impressively from 1967 to 1973 at an average rate of 12.9 percent per annum. The average import ratio of the manufacturing sector increased from an all-time low of 6 percent in 1964 to 7 percent in 1967 and 10.3 percent in 1971. As a result, the share of industry in GDP, which had remained constant at 26 percent between 1960 and 1967, jumped to 30 percent in 1972. Overall, GDP grew at an average annual rate of about 11.5 percent, while the industrial sector and the manufacturing industries expanded at rates of 13.2 and 13.9 percent, respectively.

In addition to the measures taken by the government after 1964, the economic strategy of the Military Republic was aided by a high degree of idle capacity in the manufacturing sector. Also highly relevant was the international environment—a period of rapid economic growth in the industrial world which opened markets for Brazilian exports—and a high level of capital investment in Brazil. Total exports increased from $1.9 billion in 1968 to $6.2 billion in 1973, while manufactured exports grew from $0.4 billion to $2.0 billion, reaching average annual growth rates of about 27 percent and 38 percent, respectively. As a result, the share of manufactured exports in total exports grew from 20.3 percent in 1968 to 32.4 percent in 1973. In the same time period, the share of total exports in GDP rose from 5.2 percent to 7.6 percent.

Brazil's economic expansion was directly related to higher levels of capital investment. Much of that investment came from state company expenditures, but a significant contribution was made by foreign capital. Indeed, the *dependencia* (dependency) school of thought argued that Brazil's—and Latin America's—freedom of action was being severely limited by the role of the multinational corporations in the 1960s and 1970s.

In Brazil, total investment in manufacturing increased nearly four times between 1970 and 1979, growing at an average annual rate of about 15.5 percent in real terms. Significantly, the distribution of investment had been highly concentrated in a reduced number of industries. The share of total investment in metallurgy, transport equipment, and chemical products added up to 47.3 percent in 1969, 62.2 percent in 1975, and 63.5 percent in 1979.

The share of equity in government firms increased from 18.5 percent in 1971 to 22.5 percent in 1979. The share of domestic private firms also increased from 47.1 percent in 1971 to 55.0 percent in 1979, while the share of foreign firms decreased from 34.4 percent to 22.5 percent. These changes in the structure of ownership reflect the significant expansion and diversification of the activities of the public enterprises. . . .

To a remarkable degree between 1964 and 1973, the government achieved many of its economic objectives. Financial markets were reformed; there was a steady decline in the government budget deficit; a new capital market law increased the use of the stock market; and tax incentives were employed to influence the allocation of resources among regions and sectors given priority by the government. Infrastructure projects were begun, and a program to diversify Brazil's exports was successfully undertaken.

The 1973 Oil Shock

As a result of the Arab-Israeli conflict of 1973, world oil prices rose precipitously in 1973–74. Brazil, which imported more than 80 percent of its petroleum needs, was highly vulnerable. The new government of President Ernesto Geisel (1974–79) had a long and complicated agenda it wished to accomplish during its five years in office. Of highest priority was the process of *abertura* (political liberalization). Of importance, also, was an increase in the standard of living of the working class, which had been deliberately suppressed in the preceding decade to finance the rapid diversification of the economy through forced savings and holding down real wages in the industrial sector. The option of introducing measures that would slow the economy was unacceptable to the Geisel administration. The government decided to maintain the ambitious—and expensive—development goals of the Second National Development Plan (1975–79), released in September 1974.

Within a year, it became clear that the financial burden of the import bill was growing rapidly. From 1973 to 1974, Brazil's import bill rose from $6.2 billion to $12.6 billion. The only way to meet Brazil's import expenses, from the government's perspective, was to borrow abroad. Eurodollars were plentiful in this period. Demand for loans was low in the industrial countries because of the oil-induced recession. By the end of 1977, Brazil's net debt had risen to $32 billion. Debt servicing required 51.2 percent of that year's exports. Few observers pointed out that 72 percent of the debt accumulated by the end of 1977 would be repayable by 1982.

The government took a lenient stand with regard to industrial pressure to raise prices in response to rising production costs, linked to energy and labor costs. While price controls were in force throughout the 1970s, the enforcement agencies were lenient in allowing increased costs to be passed along through price adjustments. By the late 1970s the government faced a serious inflationary spiral. . . .

In spite of increasing inflation and the general decline in world economic conditions, the Brazilian economy had performed very well during the 1970s. The World Bank reported that,

> in 1979, manufacturing accounted for 28.0 percent of Brazilian GDP, up from 26 percent in 1960, and the overall industrial sector accounted for 38 percent of GDP. These are very high figures for developing and industrialized countries' standards alike, reflecting a very advanced stage of industrialization of the economy. Brazil's share of manufacturing in GDP is only exceeded by 5 and equaled by 2 of the 76 developing countries for which data are presented in the 1982 World Development Report. Even more noticeable, only 4 of the 18 industrialized countries exceed Brazil's share of manufacturing in GDP.

This was an impressive performance indeed. Equally important, in terms of the overall process of development, the share of industrial sector employment among the economically active population increased from 12.9 percent in 1960 to 23.2 percent in 1976. During this period, manufacturing industry was the main source of employment within the industrial sector; its share among the economically active population increased from 8.6 percent to 15.0 percent. . . .

Direct municipal elections in November 1972 saw ARENA win majorities in mayoral and city council elections in some 4,000 municipalities. In Manaus, Natal, and Pôrto Alegre, the MDB won majorities, but ARENA carried the other nineteen state capitals. There were no elections for mayors in the state capitals or in "zones of national security" such as the Amazon and border municipalities.

In June 1973, President Médici announced the selection of General Ernesto Geisel, the head of the state petroleum company, as his choice in the January 1974 presidential elections. Geisel was a former aide to President Castello Branco. In addition to his reputation as an administrator, he had the good fortune that his brother served as war minister in the Médici cabinet. Because of his identification with the Castello Branco wing of the armed forces, it was hoped that his election would signal the possibility of liberalization of the Military Republic.

In December 1973, President Médici reported to the nation that the economic growth rate that year had surpassed 10 percent. Exports rose, foreign investment continued to flow into the country, and the economy promised to continue to expand and diversify. Shortly thereafter, the head of the National Petroleum Council announced that from September 1973 to February 1974, the price Brazil paid for crude oil had risen 350 percent. The inauguration of General Ernesto Geisel as the fourth president of the Revolution took place on March 15, 1974.

The Fourth Government of the Military Republic: General Ernesto Geisel (1974–79)

Geisel emerged as the key figure in the post-1964 Military Republic. His commitment to authoritarian liberalization—that is, innovation directed and determined at the apex of the political system—profoundly changed Brazil. The five years of the Geisel government witnessed a determined movement away from the grandiose overtones of the Médici team with its emphasis on *grandeza* (greatness), the building of monumental public works projects, and its disdain for civil liberties or human rights. Slowly, but inexorably, Geisel charted a course of liberalization that won increasing support from all sectors of Brazilian society, including the armed forces. When he transferred power to his chosen successor, General João Figueiredo, in

March 1979, Geisel had earned the respect of the Brazilian nation for his honesty and probity.

Geisel demonstrated his desire to separate himself from the Médici government in the organization of his cabinet and palace advisory team. His chief political advisor in the palace was the head of his civilian household, General Golbery do Couto e Silva, a disciple of General Castello Branco and a key architect of the coming liberalization. Golbery had been one of the founders of the National Intelligence Service (SNI) after the Revolution and served as president of Dow Chemical of Brazil as well. General João Figueiredo, chosen to direct the SNI, was a military officer who had worked with both the Castello Branco-Geisel and the Costa e Silva-Médici groups since 1964. His selection was seen as a guarantee that the SNI would be conducted as a professional operation. The key economics positions went to Mário Henrique Simonsen, a well-known economist and banker, who became the Finance Minister, and João Paulo de Reis Velloso, a holdover from the Médici group, who retained the post of Planning Minister. Other appointments appeared to indicate a preference for either competent technocrats or civilian political leaders with prior governmental experience.

In order to better administer the array of complex programs that the Revolution had initiated, decision making under Geisel tended to gather issues around three cabinet-level groups: the Economic Development Council (CDE), chaired by the president, which formulated economic policy; the Social Development Council (CDS), also chaired by the president, which established national policy in the social assistance, health, and welfare areas; and the National Security Council (CSN), previously a principal mechanism for armed forces participation in decision making, but, under Geisel, increasingly an advisory body with little effective veto power over national policy. Reis Velloso and the Planning Secretariat coordinated and reconciled the work of the various councils and attempted to identify priorities within the government's national development plans.

The 1973 oil price shock had a strong impact on the Brazilian economy, although the brunt would not be felt until the end of the decade—at the time of the selection of Geisel's successor, SNI chief General João Figueiredo. The Brazilian economic team, led by Finance Minister Mário Henrique Simonsen, decided to exploit Brazil's comparative advantage and continue to grow. Foreign borrowing escalated—but at relatively low rates of interest. Markets held up, and the trade balance was generally good. Brazilian exports continued to diversify. As Velloso had provided the continuity from the Médici to the Geisel government, so Simonsen would briefly serve as Planning Minister in the Figueiredo administration—and begin to realize the dangers of rising inflation, a growing oil bill, and increasingly rising debt levels. His efforts in 1979 to dampen the economy met with strong resistance, and he was replaced by Antônio Delfim Neto, the miracle worker of the Costa e Silva and Médici periods.

Believing that economic, trade, and investment matters should be left to the technocrats, Geisel, Golbery, and their collaborators concentrated on the political liberalization process. The decision taken in the mid-1960s to allow direct elections for members of Congress and for municipal posts had posed no difficulty through the early 1970s. ARENA, the government party, was returned to office with wide majorities. Some intimidation was involved, of course; many able candidates of the opposition had lost their political rights; many Brazilians actually believed that the government deserved their electoral support; and others became apathetic about voting specifically and about politics in general, and chose not to participate.

By the mid-1970s, with the first economic shock of the increase in petroleum prices, and the emergence of societal pressures for liberalization, elections suddenly took on a different meaning:

> As Brazilian society became more polarized and consciousness levels were raised during the second phase of the post-'64 period, the opposition MDB party was strengthened by being the only available electoral channel for the public expression of disapproval. Thus, the 1974, 1976, and 1978 elections were increasingly viewed as "plebiscites" by the revolutionary government.

In the relatively free elections for Congress on November 15, 1974, the MDB made a strong showing. Of the 22 Senate seats available, the MDB carried 16, for a total of 20 seats in the new Senate (61 percent of the vote in the Senate elections were for MDB candidates and only 39 percent for those of ARENA). The MDB elected 172 deputies to the Chamber, compared with 192 for ARENA (the MDB had only 87 deputies in the previous Congress).

On the state level, the MDB victory was equally impressive. Before the election, the opposition controlled only one state assembly, that of the state of Guanabara (the city of Rio de Janeiro, basically); after the election it had taken six state assemblies, including São Paulo and Rio Grande do Sul. The results of the 1974 election were viewed by many as a plebiscite on the 1964 Revolution—and the regime had either lost or been taught a lesson, or both.

While the election results heartened civilian supporters of liberalization, they created problems for Geisel in dealing with the armed forces. Repeatedly, warnings were issued by both mid-rank officers and members of the high command that electoral politics were precisely what the 1964 Revolution wanted to end. The conservative viewpoint was that elections generally resulted in corruption and subversion. Geisel clearly thought otherwise, but he had to move with care. Using carrot-and-stick methods with both the armed forces and the opposition civilian forces, he tried to give something to both groups—without losing sight of his principal goal. In dismissing the commander of the Second Army in January 1976, for example, he had used a stick against the army and offered the opposition a carrot; he repeated that tactic with the dismissal of Army Minister Frota in October 1977. But the conservative elements of the regime required a "carrot" also, and everyone waited to see how Geisel would react.

Throughout 1975 and 1976, Geisel reacted by publicly cautioning those supporting liberalization to move with care. More concretely, he did not hesitate to use the powers of Institutional Act No. 5 to cancel the political rights of state deputies, federal deputies, and senators charged with corruption, challenging the government, or other vague mistakes. The message was clear—if there was going to be liberalization, Geisel would orchestrate it. To counterbalance his military critics, the president moved military officers frequently, "exiling" those he believed openly hostile to his plans and neutralizing those who appeared uncertain in their support. . . .

In mid-1977, Geisel had an opportunity to offer a carrot to the hardline authoritarians. The Congress had proven recalcitrant in providing a two-thirds majority required to pass a judicial reform bill; Geisel, without warning, recessed the Congress. He then proceeded to promulgate, without political consultation, what became known as the "April Package" of reforms, all of which were seen as regressive. The package canceled the planned direct election of state governors in 1978; they would be selected indirectly by electoral colleges, the majority of which ARENA controlled. The new decree changed the pattern of voting in congressional elections and returned to the old rule whereby the number of deputies was decided not by how many voters a state had, but by how large the population was. This meant that in states with large populations, but small numbers of eligible literate voters, ARENA would do well. The Falcão Law was extended to other elections. The law had been first utilized in the November 1976 elections. It excluded the use of radio and television in electoral campaigns, which again worked against the opposition candidates who were the newer candidates in most cities and states, and less well known to the public. The term of the presidency was extended to six years—beginning with Geisel's successor. And the famous "bionic" senators were created—each state was given a third senator, to be elected by the state assembly, thereby guaranteeing ARENA a solid majority in the federal Senate.

To make it perfectly clear that he was in charge, Geisel proceeded in July 1977 to cancel the political rights of Alencar Furtado, the popular and effective leader of the MDB in the Chamber of Deputies. The party leader, in what was a rare television appearance by an opposition figure, had bitterly attacked the Geisel government. Geisel's decision to act, combined with the April Package of reforms, made it clear by June 1977 that the presidential palace remained very much in charge.

The spring and summer of 1977 were seasons of political turbulence in Brazil. Students, intellectuals, businessmen, church groups, lawyers, and opposition civilian leaders all joined in decrying the regressiveness of the April Package and demanding a stronger commitment to liberalization. An intriguing question is whether or not Geisel and his collaborators deliberately used the April Package to goad the broad forces of the opposition into action. Why? To demonstrate to the hard-line opponents of liberalization that only widespread repression would end the demand for a return to a state of law. Geisel correctly gambled that there were elements in the armed forces opposed to liberalization—but they were not willing to kill their fellow citizens to prevent it from happening. . . .

On December 1, 1977, meeting with members of ARENA, President Geisel made the surprise announcement that he was planning a series of important institutional changes in the 1964 regime. The time had come, he stated, to move ahead with liberalization. The institutional acts were to be replaced with new legislation and new political parties, as well as by other reforms that were to be introduced in 1978. . . .

There were other indications that the process of liberalization was accelerating. In May 1978 the first massive strike since 1964 took place in the São Paulo industrial suburbs. . . . Both the private sector and the government responded hesitantly to this new challenge to the authoritarian regime—particularly given the economic importance of the region for the national economy. But as the strike mentality spread beyond São Bernardo to schools, hospitals, banks, and other public service sectors, the government realized that it no longer controlled workers in Brazil as it had in previous decades. No one emerged satisfied from a messy series of negotiations. The unions prepared for the April 1979 wage negotiations and utilized the time to seek unity in labor ranks and to set out a practical and just agenda of demands.

In June of 1978 the progressive leadership of the São Paulo business community issued a manifesto in which it called for a return to democracy. The government decided to lift prior press censorship which had been in force since 1964. In the same period, at the government's urging, the Congress began to consider a series of government-inspired measures to liberalize the authoritarian regime. Among the most important were the abolition of the institutional acts; the restitution of habeas corpus; the restoration of political liberties, after ten years, to those prosecuted under the provisions of the institutional acts; limitations on the president's power to close Congress; and the creation of new political parties. It was made clear that Geisel, in return, would neither accept any revision of the April 1977 Package nor any change in the application of the Lei Falcão, which regulated political use of radio and television in campaigns. Even with these changes, Congress remained relatively weak. It had no authority over the budget process and could modify neither the National Security Law nor the existing labor legislation, for example. After a series of heated sessions in Congress, the legislation passed in September 1978, but only after the presidential palace implied a return to tighter controls if the president's proposals were not passed as proposed.

In October, the government submitted a new national security law to Congress which incorporated the basic security measures contained in the various institutional acts. The National Security Law was a vital control mechanism for the process of authoritarian liberalization. It was intended to replace the fifth institutional act and to reassure skeptics on the right that the liberalization was indeed controlled from the top. It became law in 1979.

After a spirited presidential campaign, waged throughout Brazil, the ARENA-controlled electoral college convened on October 15, 1978, and, as expected, chose General João Figueiredo as President Geisel's successor. Figueiredo pledged himself to the process of liberalization. . . .

The Fifth Government of the Military Republic:
General João Figueiredo (1979–85)

João Figueiredo assumed the presidency at a difficult moment in Brazilian history. The economic fortunes of the country were poor. The second oil price shock of 1979 and the consequent world recession hurt Brazil badly. The new Planning Minister, Mário Henrique Simonsen, attempted to halt policies of growth and spending, but soon resigned in frustration. His replacement, Agriculture Minister Antônio Delfim Neto, sparked a national commitment to continued growth and expansion that would ultimately end in the debt crisis of 1982–83.

Figueiredo retained not only Simonsen from the Geisel government but also kept General Golbery as his chief political advisor. Senator Petrônio Portella, a wise and experienced member of ARENA, received the post of Minister of Justice with instructions to work out the liberalization process. The cabinet was the usual mix of former military officers and technocrats and evidenced an obvious bias toward those with a commitment to the president's program of authoritarian liberalization. In his first months in office, Figueiredo was confronted with a series of challenges. Of these, two were most significant. One came from organized labor, a second emerged from the growing pressures for accelerated liberalization.

The Labor Unions

The May 1978 strike and its settlement had been the first experiment since 1964 with strikes and collective bargaining. The government had not interfered. The situation was different in 1979:

> The May 1978 stoppages had created a new climate in which rank-and-file mobilizations were rife, and in the city of São Paulo the old union leadership had faced serious opposition during the annual wage-settlement negotiations in November 1978. The new leaders wanted to undermine the power of the pro-government elements in the unions even further. For the government, the annual negotiations would be a test of the degree to which democratization could be kept under control.

At midnight on March 13, two days before Figueiredo's inauguration, a massive strike erupted in the southern industrial belt of São Paulo, centered on the city of São Bernardo and the large auto plants. The metalworkers' union had refused to recognize the agreement negotiated a short time before between the manufacturers and the union leadership. Negotiations continued. Following a threat of government intervention, the union leaders agreed to put forward a proposal for a return to work pending further negotiations over the following forty-five days. Mass meetings of more than 90,000 workers rejected the compromise. The three opposing unions were then taken over by the Minister of Labor, Murillo Macedo.

To advert further polarization, a truce was arranged. The Ministry of Labor promised to withdraw from the unions in which it had intervened and the workers promised to return to work. Negotiations would continue for a new wage and work package. The final determination afforded neither party a clear victory. . . .

Pressures and Counterpressures to Liberalization

By mid-1980 the broad outlines of the regime's authoritarian liberalization were in place, and new parties were formed. Political amnesty had drawn exiled political leaders back to Brazil, and they were now actively involved in the new party structure. Habeas corpus had been restored, strengthening the integrity of the judicial system. Press freedom continued, and government censorship of radio and television diminished. The government had determined to restore direct elections in November 1982 for the country's governorships, an important move to revitalize the federal system. The bionic senators were to disappear when their terms ended in 1986, thereby removing a point of embarrassment for the government. The government also promised to consider revisions in the Falcão Law and to review congressional pressure to restore some of its powers.

In April 1980 the government confronted organized labor in São Paulo once again. After massive strikes, the government intervened and arrested a large group of labor leaders, including Lula. The strike failed, but again the government was warned that labor militancy had become a fact of life in Brazil. In a series of intricate feuds within the Brazilian Communist Party (PCB), longtime leader Luís Carlos Prestes, one of the *tenentes* of the 1920s, was removed in May 1980 and replaced by Giocondo Dias. The feuding on the left pleased the regime and indicated that neither the Communists nor the other Marxist groups actively involved in politics would pose a threat to the liberalization process. Brazil had welcomed Pope John Paul II in July 1980, and his successful visit had pleased the Church, the government, and the people.

The Papal visit had another side, however. A resurgence of right-wing terrorism disturbed the apparent peaceful evolution of liberalization. A prominent member of the Roman Catholic community in São Paulo, and a close collaborator in the Church's human rights effort, Dr. Dalmo Dallari of the University of São Paulo law faculty, was kidnapped, beaten, and stabbed on July 2 by unknown assailants. Dallari had been arrested with others during the metalworkers' strike. Newspaper stands selling opposition material were firebombed.

In September 1980 a secretary of the Brazilian Bar Association was killed by terrorist bombs in Rio de Janeiro; seven others were injured. Rumors circulated that rightist military officers were linked to the violence in an effort to intimidate Figueiredo from proceeding any further with authoritarian liberalization.

In September 1980 more than one million university students and 40,000 professors declared a nationwide strike which closed one-half of the country's universities. Their demand was for increased government spending on education and training. The government confronted a challenge in December 1980 with the publication of a nationalist manifesto in São Paulo, signed by a former government minister and high-ranking army officers.

In retrospect, 1981 was a year of potential crisis for the process of authoritarian liberalization—but the crisis was overcome, thus permitting the holding of the November 1982 national elections. With press freedom guaranteed and habeas corpus in effect, there arose increasing pressure to identify those responsible for the repression of the early 1970s. The armed forces' high command became increasingly nervous about such investigations and communicated its feeling to the presidential palace.

The country was shocked in May 1981 by the explosion outside the Rio Center, a convention hall in Rio de Janeiro, of two bombs on the evening of a May Day concert for working-class Brazilians. An army sergeant died and a security agency captain was badly wounded when the bombs exploded in their car. It was generally understood that the security agencies of the armed forces were involved in the tragic event. Figueiredo confronted a delicate and potentially serious situation. If he pushed for an investigation and prosecution, he would create a direct challenge to the conservative members of the military leadership. If he ignored the incident, his credibility was at stake. Political party leaders rallied around the president and met with him. After a desultory investigation, the case was declared closed although it was made clear in the press, and informally in political circles, that the presidential palace was divided on the government's response. The cautious decision not to confront the military was viewed as a judgment by Figueiredo about his level of support in the armed forces and his desire to continue to proceed with liberalization.

As a result of the differences over the Rio Center incident and about the strategy of the government in pursuing *abertura*, General Golbery suddenly resigned in August 1981. There were rumors of differences with Planning Minister Delfim Neto and also with the SNI chief, General Octávio de Medeiros. The president acted quickly

and called Professor João Leitão de Abreu from the Supreme Court
to take Golbery's place as head of the civilian household and chief
political coordinator for the government. Many commentators noted
that the Médici team was back in place with different jobs—Delfim
in planning, Figueiredo as president, and Leitão as chief advisor to
the president. All three had held high positions in the Médici government in the early 1970s.

The second shock to the political system was the unexpected incapacitation of President Figueiredo in September with a heart attack. After a short period of doubt, it was decided to allow the civilian
vice president, Aureliano Chaves, to become acting president in
Figueiredo's absence. Apparent pressures by the conservatives in the
regime to name an army officer as acting president failed. Supporters
of the *abertura* warmly welcomed the decision. Chaves's conduct in
office was exemplary. The vice president had strengthened the hand
of those who argued that a civilian successor to Figueiredo was both
possible and desirable, and he had enhanced his own chances to become that candidate.

President Figueiredo returned to the palace in late 1981, determined to see through a crucial phase of the process of authoritarian
liberalization—the national elections of November 1982. Taking firm
control of the PDS, he initiated a series of electoral reforms (called
"counterreforms" by many in the opposition). . . .

The Political Implications of the Economic Crisis, 1982–83

With the elections completed in November 1982, the Figueiredo administration turned to the pressing financial problems that Brazil
confronted. The crisis over the Mexican foreign debt, in August-
September 1982, and the uncertainty about Argentina's capacity to
repay, had a negative impact on Brazil's image in the international
banking community. By December 1982, Brazil had agreed to negotiate with the International Monetary Fund as a prerequisite to receiving further loans from the private commercial banks.

As Congress organized in March 1983, the economic crisis and
the deteriorating social conditions of millions of Brazilians who were
without employment, hungry, and sick became a dominant theme in
its debate. In addition, President Figueiredo's desire to postpone discussion of his successor until 1984 was frustrated. As soon as the
elections in November were over, the presidential race opened. With
the social and economic difficulties confronting the government,

1983 became a year of intense national discussion about Brazil's future. . . .

From 1983 to 1985 deteriorating economic conditions—skyrocketing inflation, rising unemployment, exacerbation of the debt crisis, and imposition of austerity measures in response to negotiations with the IMF—intensified the demands by Brazilians for a return to civilian government through the electoral process. Support by middle-class and business groups who had long backed the military regime now eroded and divisions within the armed forces further weakened the military government. As President Figueiredo's term came to an end, Brazil returned to "civilian" government admidst an economic and political crisis more severe (e.g., inflation of over 200 percent per annum) than the circumstances of 1964 which prompted the coup against President Goulart. Nevertheless, the economic and political legacy of two decades of military rule was stamped indelibly on Brazilian society.

CHAPTER 23

Antipolitics in Chile, 1973–94

Background to the Military Coup

In 1970, Dr. Salvador Allende, presidential candidate of the Unidad Popular coalition, won a plurality—but not a majority—of votes from the Chilean electorate. Consequently, and in accord with Chilean electoral laws and the constitution, the Chilean Congress was called upon to vote for the president, and it selected Dr. Allende as the country's new president. Soon thereafter, a wave of opposition to his administration developed among business and middle-class sectors: rightist political movements and parties, entrepreneurial associations, some white-collar unions, as well as groups representing both commercial interests and those of small business. Eventually this opposition determined that "the government of Allende was incompatible with the survival of freedom and private enterprise in Chile, [and] that the only way to avoid their extinction was to overthrow the government."

Gradually this opposition movement spread and consolidated, supported in part by external funding and covert political intervention, to create a conspiratorial Comando Gremialista (the term *gremio* was applied broadly in Chile to include professional and occupational associations) which incorporated truckers, merchants, retailers, industrialists, agricultural landowners, white-collar professionals, and women's groups. These groups eventually took their protests to the streets and highways of Chile, mounted an explosive media campaign against the government, and generally created a climate of instability and tension throughout the country.

For almost three years, Chile became increasingly polarized politically as the Allende government sought to implement a controversial program labeled "the Chilean road to socialism." Polarization was abetted and exacerbated by chaotic economic conditions, which included hyperinflation. Opposition members of Congress accused the government of violating the Chilean constitution and of planning to install a totalitarian regime, and they called upon the military forces to "re-establish the rule of the constitution and the law . . . in order to

guarantee institutional stability, civil peace, security, and development." Under the pressure of these appeals, combined with its own
fervent anti-Marxism and the threat to its integrity posed by leftist
leaders who were urging enlisted personnel to mutiny and engage in
subversion, the military finally acted by instituting a brutal coup d'état
on 11 September 1973.

Political Mission of the Military Regime

Above all else, the new military government blamed Chile's crisis on
"politics" and politicians who had betrayed the nation, engaged in
demagogy, and allowed Soviet-inspired Marxists to gain control of
the Chilean state. According to General Pinochet, speaking at the
University of Chile in 1979, the harsh military action of 1973 was
"intended to repudiate the totalitarian action of the Soviets, enthroned
in a government obedient to their desires, which had practically destroyed the democratic foundations [of Chilean society], through spiritual and material violence." Further, "administrative corruption and
economic chaos had corroded the harmony and democratic
institutionality of the country. . . . we bordered upon fratricidal war."
Only by destroying the old order, by rejecting liberal democracy in
its Chilean variant, by purging the politicians and "extirpating the
Marxist cancer" could Chile be saved from the brink of disaster and
create a new institutionality to guarantee political stability, economic
recovery, and growth.

   Thus, on the one hundredth anniversary of the founding of the
city of Antofagasta, General Pinochet declared, "The Supreme Government has established as its most important objective the creation
and consolidation of a new institutionality, founded on a real democracy, a democracy vigorously defended from its enemies." In 1981
the military government imposed upon Chile the new constitution
approved the previous year in a managed plebiscite. This new constitution codified many of the political practices and emergency decrees through which the military dictatorship sought to construct a
new basis of political legitimacy. Major features of the constitution
included permanent proscription of all parties and movements spreading doctrines undermining the family, advocating violence, or adopting a conception of society, state, or juridical order of a totalitarian
character or based on class conflict (Art. 8); outlawing all groups
"contrary to morality, public order, and national security" (Art. 15);
providing for a number of "states of constitutional exception"—internal and foreign war, internal commotion, emergency, and public

calamity, which, in turn, allow the president of the country to declare "state of assembly," "state of siege," "state of emergency," or "state of catastrophe." These states of constitutional exception authorized suspension, for various periods of time, of civil liberties and constitutional guarantees concerning freedom of association, assembly, press, and other political liberties, including the rights of workers to organize and engage in collective bargaining. In some cases, the constitution authorized the president to expel citizens from the national territory (Arts. 39–41).

Most importantly, the authors of this constitution sought to institutionalize antipolitics or what General Pinochet called "authoritarian democracy." The constitution limited participation of class-based, ideologically motivated, or merely interest-oriented political groups, parties, or movements and founded a military-tutored administrative state. The key concept in the new constitution was national security; every citizen was obligated to "honor the fatherland, defend its sovereignty, and contribute to the preservation of national security and the essential values of Chilean tradition" (Art. 22). Almost all rights of Chilean citizens specified in the constitutional text were limited by the requirements of national security (Art. 19). While national security itself was nowhere precisely defined, the constitution assigned the armed forces the mission to "guarantee the institutional order of the republic" (Art. 90). In this sense, the armed forces became the dominant political force in the new institutionality. This role was further enhanced by creation of a National Security Council dominated by military commanders and responsible for a number of advisory and policymaking tasks (Arts. 95–96).

The constitution also provided *each* of the armed forces with direct representation on regional development councils which appointed mayors, thereby controlling or monitoring municipal administration (Arts. 101–108). Provisions for eventual election of a new congress and participation of newly defined political parties (contingent upon approval of a new law regulating political parties) explicitly included designees of the National Security Council as senators (ex-commanders of each of the four military forces) (Art. 45). Thus, the new constitution clearly provided for a *permanent* militarization of Chilean politics intended to exorcise the evil of "politics" from the political process.

Without hesitancy or chagrin, General Pinochet called this new institutionality "authoritarian democracy." On the second anniversary of the 1980 constitution's implementation (March 1983), General Pinochet declared:

I hereby notify politicians anxious to regain power that we will not tolerate any limits on our exercise of authority beyond that established by the constitutional text. . . . *When government and opposition speak of a "return to democracy," they are not referring to the same thing.* Between one and the other conception are profound differences that no one should ignore. Confronted by the totalitarian threat, and in order to never return to the vices of the past, the government over which I preside is designing, within the context established by the constitution, a political system which delivers the administration and government of the regions and communes to intermediate social entities, decontaminated from the virus of partyism. . . . Without doubt, we Chileans will not at this date allow ourselves to be misled by false visions of apparent redemption, nor by the demagogic deception of politicians from the past.

Regime and Opposition, 1973–80

Not only did the government and the opposition refer to different concepts when they spoke of a return to democracy in the Chile of 1986, but the opposition in Chile remained divided, fragmented, disoriented, frustrated, and subject to episodic regime terror. Most importantly, it was an opposition unable to agree on a viable legitimate alternative, either as a form of government, a socioeconomic strategy, or even a short-term coalition to manage the transition from direct military dictatorship to some form of limited democracy with military participation, as in Brazil or the Philippines.

In short, the opposition in Chile included many oppositions: opposition to specific policies or programs of the military government; opposition to the personal dictatorship of General Pinochet; opposition to military rule; opposition only to *certain aspects* of the authoritarian model (e.g., restrictions upon "democratic" groups versus "Marxist" groups); opposition to the authoritarian model and the constitution of 1980; opposition focused on a restoration, or partial restoration, of Chilean multiparty democracy; opposition to the military regime, liberal democracy, and capitalism which carried some vague "socialism" as its political objective; opposition which still favored the ultimate establishment of a political system based on Marxist-Leninist principles. Both within and among these different types of opposition to the military government existed shifting viewpoints, commitments, and alliances, as well as old-fashioned personal rivalries and factional strife.

In a sense, the ultimate failure of the military programs and policies since 1973 was that not only had *all* pre-coup political movements, groups, parties, and ideologies survived, but that new radical movements and organizations had come into being. This occurred despite state terrorism, recurrent purges, deportation of visible leaders, assassination of exiles, and brutalization of the population. However, the failure of the military government to eliminate its opposition left Chilean society and politics almost as polarized and politicized in 1986 as it had been in 1973. By the early 1980s most Chileans favored a "return to democracy," but with widespread disagreement over the precise definition of "democracy" and, among the forces of the political center and right, over the extent to which leftist political parties and movements should be allowed to participate in any post-Pinochet political process.

A public opinion survey reported by the Chilean weekly *Hoy*, in 1983, found that 21.6 percent of respondents believed that the best government formula for solving national problems was "the current government"; another 15 percent preferred a government without Pinochet but including military participation or directed by a leading rightist politician; 24.2 percent desired a "new government formed by the opposition but without Communists"; and 22.7 percent preferred a "new government formed by opposition elements without exclusions." At the same time, over 75 percent of the respondents favored "reestablishment of full democracy" before 1989 (almost 60 percent favoring this alternative by 1985) in clear opposition to the provisions of the 1980 constitution. Merely recognizing that the Constitution of 1980 enjoyed little domestic support from the majority of Chileans did not, in and of itself, provide any viable political alternative to the present government (as had occurred in quite different ways in Argentina, Uruguay, Peru, and Brazil in the early 1980s). In this sense, the political opposition to the military government in Chile which evolved after 1973 reflected, in all its aspects (focus, organization, tactics, ideological diversity, inability to transcend its pre-1970 historical legacy, etc.), both the concentrated ferocity and power of the dictatorship on the one hand, and the multiple divisions within "the" opposition on the other.

Immediate Responses to the Coup

Initial opposition to the military regime began with a courageous, but disorganized, resistance in factories, workplaces, homes, streets, and centers of detention. This took the form both of physical resistance to military violence and of organizational efforts to survive the immediate repression of leaders of the political parties associated with the Popular Unity coalition, including leaders in the labor move-ment. Because the political left was not organized to offer effective military resistance, it was unable to mount any sustained counterat-tack to the military coup or to the first repressive measures instituted by the junta. The labor movement found itself similarly ill equipped to withstand the harsh measures imposed upon it. These included the outlawing of Chile's major labor confederation, the Central Unica de Trabajadores (CUT), and its affiliates, the military occupation of CUT headquarters, dissolution of two of the largest rural labor federations, as well as attacks upon organizations made up of workers in the pub-lic sector, such as teachers and government employees.

Initially, a segment of the labor movement did support the anti-Marxist and anti-Popular Unity pogrom carried out by the military within the various sectors of organized workers. With the exception of a small minority, most of the Christian Democratic leadership, the political right, the *gremialistas*, and most nonpartisan professional associations also supported military repression of the left. The hier-archy of the Catholic Church, at odds with Popular Unity over pro-posed educational reforms, called on the Chilean population to cooperate with the new regime in restoring order, even though the Permanent Committee of the Episcopal Conference lamented the vio-lence and bloodshed of the coup.

Only slowly, and with painful moderation, did the majority of Chilean political forces begin to challenge the most extreme mea-sures of the military government. Vocal opposition to the coup itself was rare among non-Popular Unity parties, professional associations, Church leaders, and even trade unionists—with the exception of the Movimiento de la Izquierda Revolucionaria (MIR) and smaller revo-lutionary groups. This meant that, at least at first, opposition focused on the junta's national security enforcement practices (later generi-cally labeled "human rights abuses") and on specific policy decisions, for example, reductions in public services and public employment, elimination of price controls on a variety of products, or the ending of subsidies to public enterprises. This latter type of opposition oc-curred among the civilian technicians cooperating with the military government, as well as among certain producer groups, unions, and the political parties in "recess" (the National party, Christian Demo-cratic party, and smaller non-Popular Unity parties).

The outlawing and "dissolution" of parties and movements of the left, along with the murder, "disappearance," detention, or exile of thousands of leaders and cadres, precluded significant public policy debate from these sources. The military government tolerated no serious opposition to its "emergency measures," which overturned the Constitution of 1925, nor to its economic and social policies, even when the government was not always united internally as to specific objectives or methods.

The Church as an Umbrella for
Opposition to Military Government

The hierarchy of the Catholic Church, and a number of other religious groups in Chile, were perceived as opponents of the Popular Unity coalition, or at least as groups hostile to particular policies of the Allende administration. The military government sought, and received, the sanction of the Church in the immediate aftermath of the 1973 coup; Brian Smith reported that twenty-four of the twenty-seven bishops interviewed in his study indicated they believed the coup was necessary. However, the desire of the military to acquire the support of the Church as a source of legitimacy, and the willingness of the Church leadership to collaborate in the "work of reconstruction," also worked to provide Church functionaries and affiliates with a limited degree of insulation from the frontal assaults then being launched against other organizations, such as unions, political parties, and political movements. Over time, although it remained internally divided regarding its role vis-à-vis the new regime, the Church came to provide a fragile umbrella of protection for a variety of human rights, research, social service, and antiregime activities.

Established shortly after the coup, the National Committee to Aid Refugees (CONAR), composed of members of various religious groups, created a nucleus around which an active opposition to the government's severe repression was able to organize. In October 1973 the Committee of Cooperation for Peace (COPACHI) began to provide legal services, food, economic aid, medical assistance, places of refuge, and comfort to victims of the state terror unleashed by the military and the new secret police apparatus, Dirección Nacional de Inteligencia (DINA). Gradually, a national network of safe houses and underground resistance to the regime emerged, frequently in Church buildings or in the homes of people courageous enough to risk their lives to spare others from torture or death. This network won thousands of small victories against the military government, but its willingness to collaborate with Popular Unity and *Mirista* leaders and cadres soon brought down the wrath of the regime. Some religious leaders withdrew from COPACHI after clear evidence of its links to underground and clandestine activities was publicized; in

December 1975, Cardinal Silva, under pressure from both conservative and moderate Catholics, as well as from General Pinochet himself, dissolved the organization while at the same time congratulating it for its humanitarian efforts.

Shortly thereafter, Cardinal Silva established the Vicariate of Solidarity, the single most important umbrella organization, which provided social services to the growing number of Chilean poor and also sought to oppose the human rights abuses of the government. From 1976 to 1986 this Church-supported entity was the foundation of moral and legal resistance to the military dictatorship, just as Church-based community organizations provided at the local level a framework for opposition meetings and planning which the military government attacked on an episodic basis.

While religiously based organizations could mediate certain government policies and challenge human rights abuses openly, neither the hierarchy of the Catholic Church nor its local organizations presented a serious threat to regime policies in other areas or constituted an opposition coalition capable of reforming or overthrowing the military government. Church declarations (such as *Nuestra Convivencia Nacional*, 1977, or *Humanismo Cristiano y Nueva Institucionalidad*, 1978) explicitly praised multiparty democracy and described politics as a noble art consistent with human nature, offering a direct refutation of the regime's derogation of politics and politicians. Even with substantial international support, however, Church work and organization was no substitute for an explicit political opposition which could offer a proposal for transition together with a long-term political program—whether of democratic restoration or some other vision of Chile's political future. The Church functioned primarily as a source of moral opposition to the military dictatorship. It also served as an umbrella which offered partial protection to a gamut of community organizations, research centers, human rights groups, and loosely organized action groups for the opposition. It was unable and unwilling, as was to be expected, to assume the role normally ascribed to other agents in the political process (such as political parties, professional and interest-based associations, or labor) to build coalitions or to elaborate political programs. The Church also suffered from internal division, as some bishops continued to give staunch support to the military government. In addition, significant political cleavages persisted in the wider Catholic community of Chile, with hard-core, conservative, Catholic-inspired organizations such as Opus Dei, the Society for the Defense of Tradition, Family, and Property (TFP), and the Asociación de Católicos Anticomunistas condemning politicization of the Church and defending the military's repression in aggressive fashion.

Nevertheless, some Church leaders, and groups under their auspices, managed to achieve many of the goals which Manuel Antonio Garretón has identified as the measure of "the value and success of opposition forces" under authoritarian regimes (i.e., creation of "breathing spaces" or *espacio político;* maintenance of hope in an alternative; creation of gradual inroads in the regime itself; and organization/support of diverse forms of resistance). Perhaps even more important, the Church's international ties, and the regime's desire to maintain the fiction of its "western and Christian" identification, enabled the Church to play a limited, but crucial, role in opposing the practices, policies, and political objectives of the government.

Universities, Students, and Intellectuals

University students have played a colorful and vital role in Chilean politics since the beginning of the twentieth century. Student movements, aligned with major political parties or groups, have pressured governments for a wide range of social and political reforms as well as for democratization of the university system. Perhaps the most celebrated case occurred in July 1931, when protests by university students helped to precipitate the street demonstrations and general strike that ousted the dictatorial government of General Carlos Ibáñez.

From the 1930s through the 1960s, Chilean universities not only produced new generations of political leaders, but expanded their enrollment in relation to the total population. Politics has always been an essential element of university life, including competition for control of faculty and student organizations by supporters of the country's parties and revolutionary movements. During the Unidad Popular administration, Chilean universities, like most other national institutions, reflected in microcosm the political and ideological conflict extant in the larger society.

In line with its efforts to depoliticize Chilean society, the military dictatorship quickly moved against the universities in 1973 to "purify" (*depurar*) the faculties and eliminate any Marxist influence. Military administrators took over control of the universities and gradually introduced "modernizations" designed to emphasize professional education on the one hand, and to diminish the role and prestige of the humanities and social sciences on the other. Decreased levels of support for both students and universities, together with tightened standards of admission, significantly reduced the opportunities for higher education in Chile.

In the 1980s university enrollment was down by over a third, in absolute numbers, from 1973. Some institutions were affected by the government's programs more drastically than others—most notably the Universidad Técnica del Estado, which had been perceived as perhaps the most politicized, but also the least elitist, of the Santiago institutions of higher learning. Competition for the reduced number of university admissions, combined with the narrower, more technical curriculum and, of course, the systematic purges of politically unacceptable faculty and students, dramatically altered Chilean university life.

In the case of both students and professors, political organization became not only difficult, but dangerous, after 1973. Expulsions from the university for political activity severely dampened overt challenges to the military government from the campus. Penetration of the institutions by secret police and by informants practically destroyed whatever effective intellectual and organizational opposition might have emanated from the university community. While individual faculty members spoke out occasionally, and small groups of students voiced opposition to government policies (especially in the two major Catholic universities) from time to time, Chilean universities, on the whole, failed to generate significant resistance to the military dictatorship until after 1984.

Unlike the purged universities, the expanding number of "independent" research institutes, and loosely connected groups of impoverished scholars and technicians, emerged as a source of intellectual revitalization and, eventually, vocal sources of opposition to the regime. The military's insistence on "decentralization" and "privatization" spawned a surprising number of relatively autonomous research centers. Often associating members or supporters of the same political party (even here sectarianism seemed to survive all efforts of the military to end politics in Chile), these groups produced clandestine films documenting the outrages of the dictatorship, as well as solid investigations of Chile's history and the impact of the military regime. Many individual scholars also contributed to the growing public debate over military policies and the timing of "redemocratization." However, none of these groups had a mass base or influence sufficiently widespread to challenge General Pinochet's hegemony seriously; at will, the general's apparatus censored, imposed self-censorship, shut down, or allowed the reopening of magazines, periodicals, or newspapers critical of the regime. Nevertheless, these groups of intellectuals, students, and professors stubbornly and courageously refused to submit to the military dictatorship, thereby offering technical, political, and moral critiques which undermined General Pinochet's credibility, if not his ability to apply devastating repression when overly annoyed by members of the country's intellectual community.

Political Parties and Opposition to the Military Regime

Prior to the military coup of 1973, the Chilean political party system was highly institutionalized, and penetrated almost all spheres of society. In high schools, universities, unions, peasant cooperatives, local community organizations, and even mothers' clubs, partisan political cleavages mirrored the programs, ideologies, and symbols of national party organizations. In addition, most of the major parties had their own newspapers and theoretical journals; some even controlled radio stations. Parties thus served as the major political instruments in Chilean society, articulating class and interest group positions, representing social movements in Congress, formulating alternative policies and programs, providing government leaders, and competing for the policymaking positions within the state bureaucracy.

Since the 1930s a relatively stable ideological spectrum, from the revolutionary left to the radical right, characterized this party system, with coalition governments, including all but the most "fringe" elements at one time or another. Expansion of the suffrage and post-1958 electoral reforms made for highly competitive elections, accompanied by varying degrees of revolutionary, populist, millenarian, and clientelistic appeals. In the fashion typical of political parties in Western democracies, Chilean party leaders often promised more than they could deliver, engaged in personal and intraparty conflicts, made and unmade coalitions, and hewed, more or less consistently, to certain programmatic and underlying ideological commitments.

Identified as principal targets in the military mission of depoliticizing Chilean society, the initial response of party leaders varied considerably—generally in accord with their role prior to the coup. In almost all cases, however, divisions emerged within the parties that had opposed the Unidad Popular government as well as within the parties of the Popular Unity coalition itself. Even within the National party (formed in the 1960s by a merger of the old Conservative and Liberal parties, who represented the institutionalized right of

Chilean politics), some dissenting voices were heard at the outset. The immediate response of the various parties and movements to the coup set the tone for more than a decade of the political debate, reaction, and antiregime activities.

Movimiento de la Izquierda Revolucionaria (MIR)

MIR, which had predicted a coup all along and criticized the naiveté of a "peaceful road to socialism," declared that neither the left nor socialism nor revolution had been defeated but that a "reformist illusion" had come to its end. MIR advocated armed resistance and confrontation with the "fascist gorillas" (the military). After 1973, notwithstanding penetration by military security, torture, murder, imprisonment of its cadres, and the loss of much of its leadership by 1976, MIR persisted in its revolutionary struggle against the dictatorship—with only limited symbolic victories and without, apparently, gaining the support of much more of the Chilean population than it had in 1973. For MIR, particular policies of the government or the personality of Pinochet mattered much less than the character of the regime, the impossibility of peaceful restoration of "democracy," and the ultimate objective of a socialist revolution in Chile.

Partido Comunista de Chile (PCCH)

Unlike the MIR, the Chilean Communist Party (PCCH) had vocally and repeatedly called for moderation by the more impatient or more revolutionary members of the Popular Unity coalition. The PCCH rejected the *via armada* and sought some reconciliation with the Christian Democrats to defuse the crisis of 1973. Nevertheless, the Communist Party was fiercely attacked by the military government; party, union, peasant, and community leaders were arrested, tortured, and "disappeared."

Facing relentless persecution, the Communist Party went underground and established a directorate in exile. In 1976 almost the entire internal leadership was captured, but by then the party had created a clandestine apparatus. Supported morally and financially by a nucleus of leaders living in Moscow, the Communist Party, against heavy odds, managed to sustain linkages to workers, peasants, students, and community organizations, and to make its presence felt in a growing *public* opposition to the military government (1983–85).

Whereas the Communist Party initially blamed Mirista "ultraleftism" for the isolation of the working classes and the strong middle-class support for the coup, the circumstances of military dictatorship gradually moved the PCCH into a tactical alliance with the MIR and a segment of the Socialist party which favored armed confrontation of the Pinochet government. However, this did not mean giving up traditional political tactics, nor even, at least until 1980, abandoning efforts to forge a new center-left opposition coalition. Meeting in 1977, the party's Central Committee adopted a "program for the reconstruction of Chilean society," which combined nationalistic economic measures with calls to create new democratic institutions. Once again, this program appeared to seek an alliance with the political center, in particular with the Christian Democrats, in order to end the dictatorship. As in the past, however, the Christian Democrats refused to join an alliance with the PCCH.

In 1980 several important Communist leaders publicly acknowledged the need for *all* types of struggle against the military regime. Both internal and external circumstances contributed to the radicalization of Communist opposition tactics. Growing desperation and militancy among the unemployed of Santiago's shantytowns, the evident ineffectiveness of center/left political movements to overcome the dictatorship, and the need to reestablish the party's credibility as an efficacious opponent of the Pinochet government all influenced the decision to incorporate armed struggle into the overall resistance strategy. After approval of the 1980 constitution, which seemed to presage at least nine more years of General Pinochet's authoritarianism, armed struggle seemed to many Communists to be an essential, but not exclusive, revolutionary tactic.

External events only reinforced these tendencies. The victory of the Sandinistas over the Somoza dictatorship in Nicaragua made armed struggle seem more feasible, despite the obvious differences between Chile and Nicaragua. Likewise, the strong support given to Pinochet by the new Reagan administration in the United States discouraged the non-Marxist opposition and reversed whatever pressure for change in regime policies that had been exerted by the Carter administration through its human rights emphasis. Lack of any viable internal alternative to the dictatorship, and loss of hope that U.S. pressure would advance a rapid transition to democracy, made the Communist call for armed struggle all the more understandable—even if unlikely to succeed. Despite its dismal prospects, Communist advocacy of armed struggle only aggravated the difficulty of forging a broad-based opposition coalition against the military government.

The revival of a strategy of armed struggle only served to vindicate General Pinochet's allegation of Soviet imperialism and Marxist terrorism, however, particularly when combined with overt demonstrations of external ties, such as party leaders in Moscow, short-wave broadcasts into Chile from the Soviet Union, and repeated statements of support (both published and broadcast) from the Cuban government of Fidel Castro. On the other hand, the party's ability to maintain a clandestine organization, to recruit new cadres, and to take such a dramatic initiative against the regime may have restored credibility to its historical claim as vanguard of revolutionary struggle in Chile.

In practice, however, the Communist Party was divided, not only with regard to the principal means of struggle to be used against the military government, but also with respect to the relative importance of the external leadership vis-à-vis the internal, clandestine leadership. A group called the Frente Patriótico Manuel Rodríguez (FPMR), representing the armed action element of the party, took responsibility for a number of attacks on military targets, as well as acts of economic sabotage. This raised questions as to the degree of control the party exercised over this group, indeed, questions as to whether a PCCH shift to a more accommodationist line could even be imposed on those favoring armed struggle. Certainly, similar groups in Guatemala, Venezuela, Colombia, and El Salvador eventually rejected party directives and control.

Moreover, permanent repression of the party by the military government meant that an entire generation of cadres had been trained under conditions unique for Chilean Communists, thereby creating a potential source of conflict between Communist youth and those generations of cadres accustomed to a more traditional role for the party in Chilean politics. For the moment, however, refusal of the "democratic" opposition even to consider cooperation with the Communists, plus the military regime's persistent focus on the Communists as Chile's principal enemies, gave the Communist Party no choice but to resist government policies, and to seek destruction of the authoritarian regime, by *all* means available.

Partido Socialista de Chile (PSCH)

Unlike the relative unity of the Chilean Communist Party, the Chilean Socialist Party contained a wide range of social democratic, socialist, Marxist, Leninist, and even Trotskyist groups which periodically coalesced and divided in response to the political moment and the strength of party leadership. After 1973 the always-fragmented Socialist Party splintered into a number of personalist and ideologically hostile factions. Debates over the cause of the coup and the proper goals of the party under the dictatorship from 1973 to 1986 left two major factions—one headed by Clodomiro Almeyda (accepting the thesis of using all means, including armed struggle, against the dictatorship and allied tactically with the Communist Party), and the other identified with Ricardo Lagos, Carlos Briones, and Ricardo Núñez (favoring a moderate line and allied with Social Democrats and the Christian Democrats). Each of these two major factions was subdivided, in turn, into a number of personalist and "ideological" groups, which, when combined with disputes over the power of internal versus exiled leadership, greatly weakened the Socialists as a principal force in the opposition to the military regime.

Some socialists and other small groups (e.g., factions of the Movimiento de Acción Popular Unitaria or MAPU, Izquierda Cristiana, and a segment of the Radical Party) sought to forge a new ideological consensus called the Convergencia. In the early 1980s the Convergencia represented a middle ground between the MIR and PCCH on the one hand, and the Almeyda Socialists and the other major antiregime coalition, the Alianza Democrática (AD) (composed of the major non-Marxist antigovernment parties and some groups which had belonged to the Popular Unity coalition) on the other. Unable to translate minimal ideological consensus into a viable organization, the Convergencia failed to assume a permanent niche in the political landscape. Even with the creation of a "socialist bloc" (*bloque socialista*) consisting of a somewhat more compatible coalition of socialists and leftist Catholics committed to "socialism, democracy, and popular participation," the Socialist Party itself failed to reunite and lost considerable influence in the labor movement, among student groups, and in other traditional organizational spheres penetrated by political activity. Nevertheless, the multiple voices of an always ambiguous socialist political movement were not silenced; key socialist leaders offered plans to reverse policies of the regime and to overthrow the political institutions imposed by the dictatorship. With small numbers of socialists involved in armed struggle and many others collaborating with a variety of "unarmed" opposition groups in a range of tasks, the military regime failed as much in its efforts to eradicate Chilean socialism as it had in its attack on the MIR and the Communist Party. Whether Social Democrats and moderate socialists in partnership with the Alianza Democrática (until the end of 1986), or revolutionary socialists aligned, after 1983, with the PCCH in the Movimiento Democrático Popular (MDP), socialism, however fragmented, remained a significant force in Chilean politics.

Democracia Cristiana (DC)

In contrast to the Popular Unity parties, most of the Christian Democratic leadership initially endorsed the military coup and called upon supporters to "contribute to the new government their technical, professional, or functional cooperation." Expressing their regret for the departure from democratic doctrine, constitutionalist traditions, and also the use of violence, party leaders nevertheless declared that the coup was "primarily the consequence of the economic disaster, the institutional chaos, the armed violence, and the profound moral crisis to which the deposed government led the nation." A minority of Christian Democrats rejected this position from the outset, categorically condemning the overthrow of President Allende even while reaffirming the culpability of the far left and the "sectarian dogmatism" of the Popular Unity coalition.

While the majority of Christian Democrats generally approved of the coup, they also expected a gradual (one- to three-year) restoration of a modified democratic system which would allow ex-President Frei to be reelected to the presidency. As the main source of opposition to the Popular Unity coalition, and with strong links to groups in the labor movement, to peasant organizations, professional and business associations, government employees, and community groups, the Christian Democrats retained the possibility of being able to pose a threat to the military regime. Likewise, their newspapers, radio station, and a variety of newsletters and communications to party-linked social organizations presented the military government with a potentially serious dilemma.

Gradually, the full scope of the military political program pushed the Christian Democrats into more and more public opposition. Christian Democratic union leaders, technicians, government bureaucrats, and even businessmen became a source of visible and vocal opposition—first to government policies and programs, later to the military dictatorship and General Pinochet himself. By 1977 this stance so irritated the military government that *all* political parties were "dissolved." In the meantime, Christian Democratic leaders were harassed, imprisoned, exiled, and even made into targets for assassination. Within the labor movement, among peasant and student groups, and in community organizations, the close ties between Christian Democrats and Popular Unity cadres sometimes caused their fates to be joined in prison camps or "disappearances."

For the Christian Democrats, however, the major thrust of their position was to end the military government and to restore Chilean democracy, or at least a modified version of it which would include a limited role for the Marxist left. In addition, Christian Democrats criticized major policy initiatives of the military regime. Technocratic and programmatic critiques by leading Christian Democrats served to rally public opinion and focus attention on the deleterious effects of government policy for various social sectors; they also served to recruit to the opposition some members of the pro-military coalition who had become inured to various aspects of the radical neoliberal economic program implemented after 1975. This bridge to the political right undermined the unity of those groups most closely associated with the coup: *gremialistas*, professional associations, industrialists, and even some agricultural interests. Since the most important source of legitimacy for the military government, after the initial nationalistic anti-Marxist bombast, was the efficacy of its economic program, Christian Democratic efforts to attack policies and programs on technical and performance grounds began to create chinks in the solid pro-military coalition of 1973, particularly as the economic policies proved to be disastrous in many ways.

The multifaceted opposition of the Christian Democrats—to government policy, to the human rights abuses, to the authoritarian constitution—still failed to overcome the contradictions inherent in seeking to restore democracy without the participation of key groups in Chile's recent political history. Although ex-President Frei's death, in 1982, brought forth a massive demonstration against the military regime, it also emphasized the party's inability to form a coalition capable of both uniting the opposition and *convincing the military* to seek a new political option.

Emergence of Opposition on the Political Right

The traditional political right in Chile, composed of the National Party, the Radical Democrats (a splinter of the Radical Party), and a few members of the Radical Party, provided the principal civilian support for the military coup and also staffed government ministries and policymaking positions under the military government. In addition, right-wing groups (such as Patria y Libertad) and many *gremialista* and professional organizations welcomed the coup and actively supported attacks on the parties of the Unidad Popular, as well as against organized labor, working class, and community organizations.

In some cases, individual party members did oppose the assault on Chilean democracy. Certain of these individuals participated in the "Group of 24," a constitutional study group made up of representatives from many political parties, which sought alternatives to the military constitution of 1980. Similarly, other members of the political right expressed their resistance to the militarization of Chilean politics, opposed specific government policies, and lobbied for a transition to a less authoritarian regime. In general, however, the political right not only supported the military government, but worked actively to secure the long-term political objectives of depoliticizing Chilean society and preventing a return to the "demagoguery" and politics (*politiquería*) of the past.

Even among these groups, however, the abuse of civil liberties combined with the economic disasters resulting from the combination of neoliberal economic policies with the international recession of the early 1980s gradually eroded support for the increasingly personalist administration of General Pinochet. Fragmentation of the political right paralleled fragmentation of the left. An array of "nationalists," *gremialistas*, "liberals," "conservatives," and the old National Party attempted to define their position with respect to the Pinochet government, military rule, the legitimacy of the 1980 constitution, and the type of post-Pinochet government which would be most desirable. The so-called "Group of 8," a loose alliance of diverse elements on the political right who supported the military government, dissolved in 1984; personalist, ideological, and tactical considerations destroyed the fragile coalition.

The severe economic recession (1981–85), which witnessed a concomitant collapse of major financial institutions, numerous business bankruptcies, a burgeoning foreign debt, as well as a decline in living standards for much of the population, significantly undercut support for the Pinochet administration. Groups and individuals who had originally railed vociferously against President Allende, including leading *gremialista* figures and persons with close associations to the early years of the military dictatorship, began to criticize particular aspects of government policy in the 1980s. Many called either for more rapid transition to full implementation of the 1980 constitution than that prescribed in the "Transitory Dispositions" (which included the possibility of Pinochet's "reelection" for a term to last until 1997) or for return to a restricted democracy. Certain rightist individuals and movements sought to distance themselves from the incumbent government sufficiently so as to appear eligible to participate in any transition coalition formed when Pinochet might pass from the scene. While this opposition helped weaken the regime's base of support, it still did not represent a fundamental rejection of the authoritarian model nor did it indicate backing for *full* restoration of the former multiparty system.

A significant number of Chileans on the right managed to deny to themselves the high cost in human rights imposed by the dictatorship. They considered themselves to be both anti-Marxist *and* in favor of democracy. Despite economic difficulties faced by many financial, industrial, commercial, and agricultural groups as a result of the international recession and of government policy, the unwillingness of these groups to risk a "return to chaos" (the Popular Unity years of which General Pinochet constantly reminded them) limited severely both the extent, and pace, of change *within* the regime. Persistent antidemocratic and authoritarian tendencies within these groups, plus fear of the past, continued to undermine efforts to forge a center-right coalition capable of either ousting Pinochet or transforming the government from within.

Labor Movement Opposition

The history of Chile's major labor organizations was tied inextricably to the development of class- and interest-based political movements and parties. All the principal labor unions, federations, and confederations, including the quasi-unions in the public sector among government employees and teachers, were arenas of political competition and played an overt role in national politics. The largest national confederation, the Central Unica de Trabajadores (CUT), had actually been a part of the Popular Unity coalition and had designated ministers in President Allende's cabinet. These realities made labor an obvious target for immediate repression by the military government, not to mention a target for the military's objectives of depoliticizing Chilean society over the long term as well.

In 1973 the military junta lost no time in attacking the major labor organizations of the country, considering them instruments of the political parties and of the Marxist movements which had produced the crisis. In its first months of power, the military dictatorship (1) suspended the processing of all labor petitions; (2) suspended the right to strike and to bargain collectively; (3) first nullified the legal status of the CUT and then dissolved it; (4) allowed layoffs of workers involved in "interruption or paralyzation" of work; and (5) declared a "recess" of all *juntas de conciliación* (mediation boards), and assigned military officers to hear labor disputes. The military government also (6) prohibited union elections; (7) declared that, if any union officer had to be replaced, seniority would determine the identity of the new officer unless that worker belonged to a proscribed organization or movement (i.e., any leftist party); and

(8) outlawed any union meeting held without prior notification to, and approval by, the police as to its time and place. This so-called emergency measure remained in effect until 1979.

Systematic, crushing purges of the old union leadership, combined with infiltration of unions by the new secret police, demoralized workers and allowed imposition of wage and price policies that significantly eroded real wages. Economic policies that removed protective tariffs for most Chilean industry increased unemployment, thus adding to the workers' ills.

Labor's initial responses to policies of the military government were halting but evidenced, nonetheless, a determination to resist to the best of its ability. By January of 1974 the Central Nacional de Trabajadores (CNT), which joined together workers from Christian Democratic and *gremialista* movements, including those of public employees, maritime workers, bank employees, health workers, and even some from the federation of metalworkers, attempted to obtain government recognition of its status as a legitimate voice of labor. Desirous of co-opting the non-Marxist labor organizations, if possible, and thereby obtaining international support for its programs, the military junta gave these groups a public forum by recognizing them as spokesmen for organized labor.

By excluding almost all Marxist and Popular Unity elements, the CNT failed to garner any immediate mass support. Inevitable conflicts arose between the *gremialistas* (most of whom supported the military government) and the Christian Democrats (who saw their role as one of responsible labor opposition) and undermined the possibility of forging any long-term alliance capable of defending the interests of the working class, despite the fact that the *gremialistas*, too, found themselves at odds with government labor policy from time to time. By and large, even the most conservative of white collar and public employee organizations eventually found themselves in the position of seeking to reverse government *policies*, while the rest of the work force recognized much more rapidly the necessity of opposing the dictatorship and working for a return to democracy.

In the meantime, the outlawed CUT established an overseas directorate in Paris, while parties of the deposed Popular Unity coalition undertook sufficient clandestine activity to assure the continued presence of the political left within the labor movement, even though they were temporarily unable to respond to the military repression in a more direct way. During 1974 illegal strikes challenged the dominance of the military but also brought harsh persecution of union leaders.

The government response came from the Minister of Labor, who declared, at the May 1st Labor Day celebration (in 1975), that whereas "September 11 detained Marxism, it did not destroy it; now we must destroy Marxism." However, a month later, in June, a number of labor federations which had previously been affiliated with the CUT (including some Christian Democratic leaders who had rejected cooperation with the government) formed a loosely structured alternative to the CNT: the Coordinadora Nacional Sindical (CNS). This new organization represented an ideologically pluralistic effort by organized labor to resist government policies.

Emulating, in some ways, the labor policies of the Ibáñez dictatorship (1927–31), the military government tried to control organized labor by establishing, in 1976, a National Gremialist Secretariat and also by sponsoring an official National Unity Labor Front. Under the provisions of Decree Law 198, the government removed opposition leaders from their positions within key federations or national unions and replaced them with supporters of the regime. The government also sponsored parallel unions within firms or economic sectors where labor opposition remained strong, for example, among copper workers, port workers, and the National Electricity Industry (ENDESA). In 1977 the government attempted to create official federations of chemical, railroad, and metallurgical workers, rejecting requests to hold meetings on the part of existing labor organizations. The military government tried again, in 1978, to create an official new labor organization called the Unión de Trabajadores de Chile (UNTRACH). While this group sometimes opposed the government's labor and social security policies in an effort to recruit rank-and-file support, it usually avoided questioning the government's legitimacy or overall program. Nevertheless, even under these severe conditions, organized labor refused to succumb. Strikes in the copper mines, among railway and port workers, in factories, and in service industries confirmed the survival of a heterogeneous opposition to government *policies*. Government employees, teachers, shopkeepers, and truckers—in some cases led by the very people who had been the most violent opponents of the Popular Unity government—joined the opposition to government policies even though, at the same time, some of these same leaders still sought "a responsible military officer" to head a transition government.

As in the case of the Church, the external support for labor's demands acted as a constraint on government policy. Threatened by an international boycott, including, significantly, a threat by the AFL-CIO to stop the import of Chilean goods into the United States, the military government moved to institutionalize a new industrial relations system. Beginning with Decree Law 2200 (1978), and followed by a series of decrees purporting to reform the 1931 Labor Code, the military government rewrote the Chilean industrial relations code. Adopted after 1978 as part of the government's so-called "labor plan," the new system made it much easier to dismiss workers without cause and restricted union activity with respect to collective bargaining and strike actions (only plant unions or, in agriculture, only unions in individual farms could present labor petitions and engage in collective bargaining), in contrast to the old system of unions organized by economic sector, by region, or by locality.

In the new 1980 constitution further restrictions were placed on union activity and relationships between labor and political parties, emphasizing the long-term objectives of depoliticizing the labor movement and weakening labor as a national or regional political force. In the same year, the government eliminated the traditional system of labor courts, even dissolving the old *colegios profesionales* (essentially, professional associations of doctors, lawyers, pharmacists, journalists, et al.), and replacing them with *gremialista* associations.

All these measures were resisted, to some degree, by the various labor and professional associations. Militant and public opposition by the CNS leadership led to arrest of the organization's president and secretary-general. Released shortly thereafter, these same leaders were again arrested in June after the CNS presented a "national petition" making a number of economic and political demands on the government—and thus engaging in an illegal act under the terms of the new constitution and labor laws.

In the meantime (April 1981), certain key Christian Democrats, who opposed both the policies of the military government and the resurgence of influence by the left within the labor movement (the CNS), formed the Unión Democrática de Trabajadores (UDT). The UDT challenged the government's "labor plan" and also called for renewed political party activity and a legitimate *political* role for labor. At the same time, however, the UDT rejected unity with the CNS and leftist union organizations—reflecting the continuing ideological and organizational splintering of the Chilean labor movement.

In some ways the labor movement, despite its fragmentation, temporarily replaced the outlawed ("dissolved") political parties as the major visible political opposition to the dictatorship. General Pinochet responded angrily to the national petition (formulated by the CNS and signed by over 400 labor leaders) by labeling the CNS "a front organization for international communism" and threatening the leadership with prosecution under Article 8 of the new constitution, which prohibited the propagation of "totalitarian ideas" or concepts of "class conflict." When a number of ex-politicians, including prominent Christian Democrats, signed declarations of support, they were sent into exile.

Repression of the leadership did not curtail union activity. Strikes occurred among metalworkers, in the shoe and leather industry, and in some large textile firms. Employers retaliated with widespread dismissals of union leaders; and the government retaliated with more violence. In early 1982 the president of the national association of public employees, Agrupación Nacional de Empleados Fiscales (ANEF), and the vice president of the UDT, Tucapel Jiménez, was assassinated.

By mid-1982 the effects of the international recession and Chile's debt crisis pushed unemployment up to 20 percent, thereby producing a desperate situation for millions of Chilean workers and growing impoverishment for even middle sector and professional groups. These unfavorable economic conditions made mobilization of labor for strike actions or political protests quite difficult. Nevertheless, labor protest and activity continued to challenge government policies. In some cases, labor organizations assumed a visible antiregime role in seeking to oust General Pinochet and abrogate the Constitution of 1980.

Late the same year, the military government retaliated by prohibiting unions from receiving outside funds and, during the first half of 1983, by arresting numerous labor leaders. Still seeking the illusive unity which has eluded Chilean labor since the 1930s, labor leaders created a new umbrella organization in 1983: the Comando Nacional de Trabajadores (CNT). The new CNT attempted to organize a "national strike," but was unsuccessful in this effort. Undaunted, the panoply of independent, *gremialista*, Christian Democratic, and traditionally leftist labor organizations continued to oppose government policies and often figured prominently in the overall political opposition to the military regime. Thus, in 1984, in an open letter addressed to General Pinochet and signed by ten leaders of the CNT, the labor coalition called for a return to the 1925 constitution, an abrogation of the military government's "labor plan," and a reversal of government economic policies—in short, it called for a comprehensive change in regime and government policy.

As public protests against the government mounted, in 1984–85, the CNT, CNS, and UDT sought to coordinate opposition to the regime. At the plant level, individual unions returned to represent worker demands for improvement in wages and working conditions. Sectoral federations and confederations also renewed their "bread and butter" demands, along with their participation in the growing opposition to the Pinochet government (1984–87). As was true of political parties, however, dissension and ideological fragmentation continued to plague the labor movement. Despite almost universal opposition to government labor policies, the new labor decrees, and parts of the 1980 constitution, labor proved unable to unify sufficiently either to provide the social base for a transition government or to arrive at a consensus on Chile's political future. Labor's opposition to the Pinochet government and its policies was even more apparent than was that of other professional and occupational groups (*gremialistas*); nevertheless, labor unity, even when confronted by military dictatorship, remained an elusive, perhaps impossible, goal.

Community Organizations, *Pobladores*, Urban and Rural Poor

That segment of the opposition to the military regime's policies/objectives most difficult to identify and to measure, particularly in regard to impact, resides in the multitude of community organizations, shantytowns, rural cooperatives, and seemingly dormant rural labor organizations, women's groups, and local committees. This component of the opposition came into existence shortly after the 1973 coup and continued to function, more or less efficiently, well into the 1980s. Many of these groups maintained tenuous connections to political parties, national labor confederations, and Church-related associations. Others operated practically in isolation for long periods of time, serving either as buffers against government repression or as sanctuaries for those persecuted by the government. A detailed history of this resistance awaits future research.

Of great significance for the military, particularly for the potential they offered for violent resistance to the dictatorship, were the thousands of *pobladores* in the urban shantytowns on the perimeter of Santiago. Repeated confrontations between police and *pobladores*, including recurrent police raids on the *poblaciones*, radicalized many shantytown dwellers and created the possibility, and the fear, that they might erupt at any time into spontaneous rioting, demonstrations, or insurrection. In fact, fear of unleashing this stored-up hatred of the *pobladores* acted as an effective brake on the initiatives of the "democratic" opposition whose (predominantly middle class) constituencies dreaded the possible consequences of popular violence.

While the urban poor of the *poblaciones* had long constituted a dilemma for Chilean political leaders, the misery imposed by the military government's economic policies and political repression hardened political attitudes among these groups of the population. Moreover, the dismantling of the industrial sector of the economy as a result of neoliberal trade and economic policies, and the loss of land and employment opportunities by rural workers as a result of reversing the agrarian reforms of 1964–73, transformed Chile's occupational and social structure. Large numbers of semi-employed, peddlers, dayworkers, and the "self-employed" formed an important new element in Chilean society.

The military government introduced several programs intended to alleviate the impact of massive unemployment, most notably the Minimum Employment Program (PEM)—which expanded from 19,000 participants to over 200,000 in 1982—and the Program for Heads of Household (POJH)—which was instituted in 1982. Thus, almost 8 percent of the labor force was "organized" into government make-work programs. By the 1980s the workers of PEM and POJH had begun to protest against low government wages and limited benefits, while shantytown dwellers organized clandestine resistance committees to oppose the military regime.

Periodic sweeps through the *poblaciones* by military and police forces fostered hostility toward both the military government and its civilian allies. In the countryside, rural workers and dispossessed smallholders, including *campesinos* deprived of the gains only recently acquired through the agrarian reform programs of the two previous governments, patiently awaited the fall of the military government and worked slowly to rebuild the rural labor and cooperative organizations broken up by the regime during the 1970s. Despite efforts of those most marginalized by the regime to combat its gravest injustices, the combination of the exigencies of daily existence plus the systematic coercion of the government rendered most unlikely the success of any mass-based insurrection on the model of Nicaragua, notwithstanding warnings to that effect by conservative academics in the United States.

The Armed Forces as a Source of Opposition

In order to carry out the military coup of 1973, the *golpistas* purged high-ranking officers who appeared most likely to resist the military takeover. Significant numbers of officers were killed, imprisoned, or retired. Enlisted personnel who refused to participate in the coup also suffered execution, incarceration, or other punishment. Later, General Prats, a potential challenger to Pinochet's personalist control, was assassinated in Buenos Aires. Consolidation of General Pinochet's hegemony through creation of the DINA (later, the CNI) further alienated certain sectors within the armed forces. Likewise, the forced departure of Air Force General Leigh from the junta, in 1978, revealed the existence of internal disagreements over policy, nature of the regime, as well as the timetable for restoring democratic government.

Despite some resentment over General Pinochet's increasingly personalized rule and relegation of the Navy and Air Force to secondary roles, most officers and enlisted personnel benefited substantially, both economically and in improved social status, during the 1970s. "Retirement" into the private sector provided military officers with lucrative executive opportunities. Combined with unheard-of modifications in the personnel and retirement systems, these gains by the military and their families made them much more dependent upon the patronage and good graces of Pinochet himself. The national police (*carabineros*) also gained status and benefits when they were transferred out of the Ministry of Interior and "elevated" to co-equal status with the other armed forces.

Perhaps even more importantly, the example of Argentina's treatment (prosecution) of military commanders following restoration of democracy in that country—and the explicit threat by the Chilean opposition also to prosecute military and police torturers when the opportunity presented itself—served to engender a kind of defensive solidarity among many officers within the armed forces. Restoration of civilian government not only threatened prospects for career advancement and present benefits, but it also raised the specter of criminal prosecution for a large number of Chile's military personnel.

These changes within the armed forces represented double-edged swords, inasmuch as the growing personalization of the regime, and of the army hierarchy, also meant a certain *deprofessionalization* of the career system. Resistance to these developments began to interfere with the loyalty to Pinochet of some military officers and even to raise questions as to the desirability of continuing direct participation by the military in the national government. This reluctance did not indicate any rejection of authoritarianism or a change of heart regarding leftist politics and politicians, so much as a sincere concern for the military institutions and future of Chile from the standpoint of a highly nationalistic and patriotic military elite.

By 1985 some officers had become aware that, to minimize damage *to the military institutions*, it might well be to the advantage of the military to extricate itself from government. However, this still left the problem of finding a civilian coalition capable both of (1) providing an alternative to Pinochet; and (2) guaranteeing compliance with any agreement negotiated to transfer power to a democratic civilian government. In this sense, the deep ideological divisions rending the Chilean opposition and the lack of an obvious candidate to succeed Pinochet served to restrain the more concerned military officers from seeking some sort of gradual accommodation with civilian parties and movements.

Prior to 1986, however, these various considerations on the part of the military had failed to present any serious challenge to the Pinochet administration, although they did presage difficulties for the general in the short term and decreased the likelihood of sustaining his personalist administration beyond 1989.

During 1986 selected military officers began to criticize the government openly, influenced on the one hand by Pinochet's seemingly more erratic and arbitrary behavior, and on the other hand by the spreading perception (shared by conservative civilians as well) that Pinochet was losing the support of the U.S. Embassy—a development which placed in jeopardy the massive economic support Chile received from the U.S. and international agencies. This concern within the military took a sharper turn late in 1986, in spite of an attempt to assassinate the general in early September in which a number of his military escort were wounded or killed. Pinochet's response to these signs of disaffection (the assassination attempt, the dissidence within the military, civilian calls for his ouster) was to unleash a new campaign of murder, detention, and terror against his opponents. In the first part of October, he replaced the army representative on the junta with the director of secret police and retired a number of generals. Thereafter, General Pinochet retained control over the army and other armed forces despite the 1988 plebiscite in which Chileans rejected another eight years of his personalist rule.

The Military Junta's Economic Policies

Consolidation of the junta's political power coincided with the gradual development of a new economic program. At first, the economic program had an "emergency" character, focused upon halting hyperinflation and divesting the public sector of the many enterprises acquired from 1970 to 1973. To achieve these objectives, the government devalued the currency, removed price controls from most commodities, postponed scheduled wage increases, freed interest rates for capital market transactions, and modified tax laws in order to encourage domestic and foreign investment. Over 200 firms in the public sector were returned to private owners, and public expenditures and employment were reduced greatly.

The increased oil prices associated with the first "oil shock" of 1973 sharply reduced prices for Chilean exports, while rising interest rates and balance-of-trade problems limited the success of the government program. Unemployment increased dramatically while inflation, though reduced, continued over 300 percent per year. In response, the junta and its civilian advisers decided to introduce an even more profound "shock treatment" to halt inflation and create conditions for economic recovery.

What followed included 15 to 25 percent reductions in government expenditures (but not in the realm of national security) and drastic reductions in the size and role of the public sector; a 10 percent increase in income taxes, tightened monetary policy, loss of perhaps 80,000 government employees, and a decline of some 25 percent in industrial production in 1975. However, inflation did decline significantly—from 300 percent per year in 1974 to 84 percent in 1977—and the government's fiscal deficit practically disappeared by the end of 1975.

In a sense, the government program was tremendously successful. The cost, however, was massive unemployment and underemployment, declines in real wages of 40 percent, and a grim impoverishment of millions of Chileans. The junta claimed this sacrifice was necessary, in the short term, to stabilize the economy and create the conditions that would permit long-term recovery and growth without inflation.

The emergency measures and the "shock treatment" merged eventually into a coherent neoliberal program for restructuring the Chilean economy. This program included privatizing most of the entrepreneurial activities of the government (including banks, insurance companies, exporting firms, major industrial firms); returning much of the agricultural land and assets affected by the previous administrations' land reform programs—and then abolishing the land reform agency (CORA); and opening the economy to private investment and international trade. Taken together, these programs resulted in concentration of financial and productive assets in the hands of a small number of new diversified financial groups which came to dominate the Chilean economy.

The "shock treatment" restructured the Chilean economy. The recovery which followed was based primarily upon improved prices for Chilean products, increasing levels of exports from the agricultural, mining, and industrial sectors, and significant inflows of foreign credit and investment. A wave of financial and real estate speculation fueled a short-lived "boom," with new construction projects in the private and public sector and spectacular nominal increases in the value of urban land, commercial development, and stock prices giving credence to government claims of success. Reduced import duties made possible a frenzy of consumption that seemed to justify the military junta's enthusiasm.

Macroeconomic indicators also seemed to confirm the success of the junta's policies. Inflation went down to only 30 percent in 1979; budget deficits were low and domestic production increased notably. Diversification of markets and product lines for exports contributed to positive balances of payments after 1978. Worldwide economists discussed the "Chilean miracle" and advocates of free market economics held up Chile as vindication of their theories. In an official publication (*Chile: 1980 Economic Profile*), the government declared that Chile had "boldly embarked on a course to revitalize its weakened economy, replacing protectionism with free-market policies" and that "a diversified economy capable of functioning at an internationally competitive level has now been established, thereby assuring economic stability and offering excellent opportunities for domestic and foreign investors."

Opponents of the military government suggested that the "miracle" was only economic recovery from the artificial depression imposed by the "shock treatment." They also noted that unemployment remained over 15 percent, that the gains in consumption were concentrated among the top 20 percent of income earners, and that a growing foreign debt and wild real estate and financial speculating augured disaster.

Between March 1981 and the end of the year, a combination of domestic and international factors confirmed the predictions of the doomsayers. Financial panic and economic collapse followed as international recession, the onset of the debt crisis (short-term foreign debt more than tripled from 1979 to 1982), and the unraveling of the financial pyramids built by the financial conglomerates plunged the country into its worst depression since the 1930s. Rising interest rates and reductions in the inflow of foreign loans and investments which had fueled the "boom" made it impossible to continue the debt service. Declines in copper prices (over 40 percent from 1980 to mid-1982) and prices for other Chilean exports contributed to a growing balance-of-payments deficit. As the economy collapsed, the government was forced to bail out the financial and banking conglomerates (1983). The political opposition sarcastically labeled the process "the Chicago road to socialism," thereby mocking the junta's reliance on University of Chicago-trained economists and economic theory.

The collapse of the "economic miracle" which began in 1981 caused widespread political realignment. Bankruptcies, declining standards of living, and even middle-class unemployment pushed small business operators, professionals, and other supporters of the junta into the camp of the opposition. Leaders of the *gremios*, Chamber of Commerce, professional organizations, and trade associations which had most fiercely attacked the Popular Unity government of Salvador Allende now called the Pinochet administration "the worst government in the country's history." If they had not been outraged by the human rights violations and political repression of the junta, they experienced directly the economic depression in the early 1980s.

Pragmatic and adroit, General Pinochet modified the "free-market" approach enough to ameliorate somewhat the economic collapse. New tariffs, new subsidies, new government programs for employment, construction, and investment all evidenced the general's willingness to depart from economic purity in order to achieve political goals. Holding on in the face of political challenges by a growing opposition, General Pinochet took advantage of the international economic recovery after 1985. The drop in oil prices and interest rates from 1985 to 1987, combined with economic recovery in the United States, Europe, and Japan, provided a breathing space for the Chilean government by bolstering the Chilean economy. A new surge of foreign investment and expansion of exports renewed confidence in the economy; enthusiastic government policymakers reaffirmed the validity of the "free market" and export-driven economic model—though the government had clearly recognized the political necessity of departing significantly from a "pure" market approach.

Social Mobilization, Political Stalemate

The collapse, after 1981, of the "Chilean miracle," an economic boomlet which provided the Pinochet government with a certain amount of social support, was followed by five years of growing opposition activity among all strata of society. A so-called opening (or *apertura*) from 1983 to 1985 produced numerous calls for restoration of democracy, for opposition forces to unite, and for Pinochet to end his personalist rule. Strikes and protest days, even days of "prayers for life," gave the appearance that the dictatorship was losing some of its control. By mid-1984 hopes were high that the military regime was destined for a quick end; daring headlines in opposition media declared, in bold print, "He doesn't want to leave," and in smaller print, "We'll have to throw him out." By August 1985 a significant element of the opposition had hammered out a "National Accord for Transition to Full Democracy" which included agreements on the need for a new constitution (or at least reforms sufficient to destroy the main provisions of the 1980 constitution); a social and economic plan to reactivate the economy, to create jobs, and to redistribute income; and an active state role to reshape the Chilean economy. The Acuerdo also called for an immediate end to states of constitutional exception, for reestablishment of civil liberties and civil rights, for restoration of university autonomy, for an end to political banishment and exile including restoration of citizenship to those deprived of Chilean nationality by decree of the military government.

High hopes for the Acuerdo crumbled before General Pinochet's reaffirmation of the 1980 constitution as the basis of Chilean political life at the same time that the political left was declaring that the Acuerdo was no substitute for armed struggle as the way to achieve a revolutionary transformation of Chilean society. During the next year, new efforts were made to mobilize the civilian opposition which resulted in creation of a "Civic Assembly" (Asamblea de la Civilidad)— still one more attempt to unite opposition groups and movements in an effective way to overcome the dictatorship and achieve "democracy now." Prospects for the Civic Assembly seemed little better than those of previous attempts to forge broad-based civilian opposition coalitions. Chilean society remained severely fragmented, both ideologically and along class lines; the persistent lack of consensus and intense polarization which had preceded the military coup in 1973, combined with the repression by the regime, inhibited successful mobilization against the dictatorship.

This inability of the opposition to resolve the differences (historical, personal, and ideological) which divided them from one another (not to mention the *internal* cleavages in most groups as well) left the military itself as the pivotal arbiter of the government's fate. Lacking viable civilian allies, however, opponents of General Pinochet within the armed forces were understandably hesitant to take steps to end the general's reign.

Transition to Civilian Rule

Paradoxically, General Pinochet's successful consolidation of the 1980 constitutional system ultimately led to his ouster, despite the opposition's inability to overcome the military junta's institutional, political, and economic transformation of the country. The constitution required a plebiscite to determine whether Pinochet should continue in office; the general was caught in his own trap. Fully expecting to win the plebiscite, the regime allowed fair and free elections attended by international observers. With the election results in, Pinochet decided to respect the outcome, to stay on as president for a year (as the constitution stipulated) and as commander of the army to oversee the transition. He remained army commander for the full term of his successor, Patricio Aylwin (1990–94), and was able to ensure that his political and economic legacy endured.

The military junta snatched victory from electoral defeat, institutionalized the premises of antipolitics, and claimed responsibility for restoring democracy to Chile after saving the country from Marxist dictatorship. From 1990 to 1994 they prevented trials for human rights violations and maintained, with civilian allies, the essentials of the 1980 constitution and continuity of the neoliberal economic policies. Into the mid-1990s the armed forces remained proud of their achievements, intent on continuing in their role of "guardians" (*garantes*) of the new political order they had created. Nowhere in Latin America did military antipolitics prove more successful than in Chile.

Stephen M. Gorman

CHAPTER 24

Antipolitics in Peru

Whether the nearly twelve years of military rule in Peru between October 1968 and July 1980 are labeled a "revolution," a "so-called revolution," or a simple "military dictatorship," one fact remains inescapable: the reforms and programs of the armed forces during that period profoundly altered Peruvian society. The military that overthrew President Fernando Belaúnde Terry in 1968 set out to completely restructure social, political, and economic relations in the country. The objective was to promote urban industrial expansion, head off growing political activism among the lower classes, and strengthen the role of the state as an agent of national development and social reconciliation. Peru's military leaders endeavored to create a corporate social order that would be characterized by moral solidarity, social discipline, centralized authority, and hierarchically integrated self-managing socioeconomic units. The fact that the military failed in many of these objectives, and progressively turned away from reformist policies after 1975, does not alter the fact that the military regime nevertheless intentionally changed the nature of Peruvian political life.

The military's intervention into politics in 1968 is somewhat unique within both Latin American politics generally and Peruvian history in particular. In the first instance, although different military factions had been involved in at least eleven coups d'état since the election of Peru's first civilian president in 1872, only once before, in 1962, had the armed forces acted as an *institution* to seize control of the state. On that occasion the military limited its role to convening and supervising "honest" elections, and little more.[1] But in 1968 the armed forces took power with the objective of instituting far-ranging reforms with no intention of returning government to civilian hands in the foreseeable future. Secondly, although the military adopted a political program that had been articulated by progressive sectors of the emerging middle class for more than three decades, the armed forces did not govern as the representative of any specific social class. This is not to suggest that certain groups did not benefit more than others from the military's policies, but this was largely incidental to the broader goals of national development and political stability pursued by the armed forces. Finally, the Peruvian military acted out of extreme nationalism and vigorously attacked the nefarious forms of political, economic, and even cultural neoimperialism that were considered largely responsible for the country's underdevelopment and international dependency. Certainly, other Latin American military regimes have adopted similar antidependency objectives, most notably in Brazil since the early 1970s, but most of these regimes originally came to power in response to perceived internal Communist threats. But for the Peruvian military, the breaking of the linkage between North American imperialism and Peru's ruling oligarchy was an important motivating consideration in the overthrow of the civilian government. . . .

The twelve years of military rule (the *docenio*) are normally divided into the First Phase, corresponding to the presidency of Juan Velasco Alvarado (1968–75), and the Second Phase, corresponding to the presidency of Francisco Morales Bermúdez (1975–80). In point of fact, however, there was a brief period between the overthrow of Velasco in August 1975 and the Lima riots of July 1976 which stands apart from both phases. The First Phase was a period of reformism while the Second Phase is considered rather reactionary, since President Morales Bermúdez presided over the emasculation of many earlier reforms. Morales Bermúdez himself originally characterized the Second Phase as a period of "consolidation" intended to rationalize the reforms that had been effected under Velasco. Throughout the first year of his regime, the emphasis actually appears to have been on consolidating earlier revolutionary gains during a period of economic difficulties. Only after the Lima riots and an attempted right-wing coup within the armed forces in July 1976 were liberal officers purged from the government and a systematic assault initiated against many of the progressive reforms of the earlier period. This shift in governmental policy apparently resulted from the failure of many reforms to produce the results intended by the military. . . .

The military assumed power with an ideology that claimed to understand the past errors of civilian governments that had produced Peru's underdevelopment and international dependency, including the nature of the country's subordinate integration into the global capitalist system. Yet the military rulers proceeded to predicate the success of revolutionary reforms on the expansion of the country's integration into the international market (albeit with some diversification of products, trading partners, and marketing techniques). The result economically was that the generals' approach to development failed in much the same fashion as civilian regimes before them, but on a grander scale.

Ideology and Goals

One of the important characteristics of the Peruvian military is that its officer corps has not been drawn from the upper classes. In fact, officers after the turn of the century were drawn increasingly from the middle and lower-middle classes, especially in the case of the army. Thus, the armed forces, dominated by the army, were not strictly speaking an extension of the ruling classes, although they frequently acted in defense of upper-class interests prior to 1968. The essentially middle-class composition of the army officer corps rendered it especially susceptible to the reformist currents that gained steadily after the early 1930s. Because of early hostilities between the army and the main carrier of progressive middle-class reformism, the Peruvian Aprista Party (or APRA), however, the army was inhibited from embracing the dominant reformist ideology for some time.[2] But with the establishment of the Center of High Military Studies (CAEM), an indirect process of officer indoctrination in middle-class progressivism was initiated under the aegis of military professionalization.

Among the courses offered at CAEM were many dealing with the political history and socioeconomic conditions of Peru. A significant number of the civilian instructors brought in to offer such courses were, at least indirectly, influenced by the writings of Peru's early socialist José Carlos Mariátegui (1895–1930) and the political platform advanced by APRA. New officers became ever more sensitive to the political and economic corruption of the national oligarchy, the domination of the country by foreign economic interests, and the superficiality and decadence of Peru's purely formal democracy and personalistic political parties. All of this promoted a rejection within the army of the sterility of civilian rulers. The final step in the gradual politicization of CAEM officers was the conceptualization of national development as an integral dimension of national defense. If development was indeed essential to a strong national defense, and if civilian politicians were, as the army came steadily to believe, incapable of promoting development, then the army would be compelled to assume the direction of the state in order to fulfill its own mission of national defense.

Without implying that the following goals were universally held within the armed forces, or clearly and consciously understood by the entire circle of military rulers at the outset of the revolution, we can nevertheless identify four major concerns that oriented the military after 1968: (1) Social Justice, (2) Popular Participation, (3) National Independence, and (4) National Development.

Social Justice was a primary and all-inclusive goal of the military revolutionaries, but it was defined in only the vaguest manner. Generally, Social Justice combined a concern for the material well-being of individuals with the teachings of Catholicism. As such, it was analogous to Christian Humanism. But its main emphasis was on the collectivity over the individual, and social responsibility over personal interest. General Velasco Alvarado explained early in the revolution that the military leaders were "humanist revolutionaries" who were intent on moralizing Peruvian society with a set of values completely different from "those that sustain capitalism or communism." The goal of the revolution was to create a society that would "reprieve" man as part of a broader collectivity.

The concept of Social Justice precluded social conflict, which was considered to be a by-product of social stratification based on the special privileges and monopoly over wealth enjoyed by an egotistical minority. Accordingly, Social Justice required that all people share *equitably* (although not necessarily *equally*) in both the wealth and "destiny" of the country. This would be possible only when there arose "free citizens" occupying their "just place in society." It should be stressed that this was not a call for strict egalitarianism since it did not propose a leveling of society, but only a more "just" distribution of social wealth.

Finally, Social Justice imposed certain limitations on formal or legal rights, including property ownership. Stated Velasco, "The Revolution recognizes the legitimacy of all those rights whose observance does not signify perpetuating injustice. . . ." Conversely, the military government refused to respect certain formal rights whose observance "would signify, necessarily, condemning the majority to eternal poverty. . . ." This clearly encompassed property rights. The notion of Social Justice assumed that property might be held in private ownership, but that this would not relieve it of its social obligations. In other words, the right of private property in the productive sectors was conditioned on the use of that property to promote socially beneficial ends.

Participation of the masses in the revolution was another important component of the military's ideology. But participation was redefined and placed within a moral and economic context instead of an essentially political one. That is, participation was not understood in electoral terms. Elections were considered the window dressing of the purely *formal democracy* which had worked only to the advantage of elites in Peru prior to 1968. In a speech to the nation on the 148th Anniversary of Peruvian Independence, Velasco made it clear that the military had no intention of respecting the institutional norms of the civilian political system, including elections, since these had merely permitted the privileged few to deceive and manipulate the vast majority. Not only did participation as defined by the military reject the need for national elections, but it also excluded the need for intermediaries such as political parties. Intermediaries were considered unnecessary, in the first instance, because the national leaders were "interpreters" of popular aspirations, not mere representatives of it. The government and people were *one and the same* (Velasco, in *El Comercio,* July 29, 1969), and thus the functions which political parties purportedly perform to link government and people were superfluous in the case of revolutionary Peru.

What the military meant by participation was the right and duty of all citizens to share in the burdens and benefits of Peruvian development. Also, individuals were to be allowed a wider and more meaningful participation in the operation of social and economic institutions that directly touched upon their own immediate lives, such as neighborhood councils, workers' councils in factories, or other *localized* units. Yet, such grass-roots participation was not intended to serve as a process of reconciliation between opposing interests. The military argued that true participation could only take place within a context of moral solidarity, which meant that it could not occur in the presence of competing interests or values. Consequently, the revolutionary goal of promoting participation had

> as its end the construction in [Peru] of a social democracy of full participation, that is to say, a system based on a moral order of solidarity, not individualism; on an economy fundamentally self-managing, in which the means of production are predominantly social property . . . ; and on a political order where the decision-making power, far from being monopolized by the political and economic oligarchies . . . [is grounded in] social, economic, and political institutions directed, without intermediation or with a minimum of it, by the men and women that form them.

The organic and solitary definition of true participation, thus, entailed a *progressive depoliticization of Peruvian society* [emphasis added, Ed.]. . . .

National Independence was another important objective of the Peruvian revolution, which was dedicated to breaking the country's political, economic, and military dependency on North America. Dependency was defined as the subordination of national will to "imperialist" interests. For the military, subordination occurred whenever national decision makers yielded to foreign pressures or influence. The oligarchy prior to the revolution was considered to have been the active agent of imperialism, and therefore bore primary responsibility for the dependency of Peruvian society. The military promised to resist any and all forms of foreign political influence in the formulation of Peru's domestic and foreign policies.

Nationalism meant, preeminently, national liberation. It required that the government conduct its foreign affairs in strict relation to the national interest, and not in accordance with such outmoded international configurations as the East-West split. Nationalism also meant cultural and intellectual emancipation. A nationalist ideology, for instance, could only be based on, and understood in reference to, the unique heritage of a particular people. Appropriately, Velasco insisted that the Peruvian revolution was neither capitalist nor Communist, but predicated on strictly indigenous values and ideas.

Most significantly, nationalism and the struggle against dependency was taken to mean that Peru should join with the vanguard of underdeveloped nations in pressing for a restructuring of the international political and economic order. To assert the country's new independence, Peru's military leaders broadened diplomatic and commercial ties to include many Communist-bloc nations, and turned away from the United States as the country's chief arms supplier. Lastly, National Independence presupposed national development oriented toward the satisfaction of domestic needs and greater international economic equality with trading partners.

National Development, which was the fourth major revolutionary objective, was intended both as a justification of the revolutionary process (the end that would justify the means), and as a condition that would facilitate the realization of the other revolutionary goals (Social Justice, National Independence, etc.). First and foremost, development required the construction of a modern industrial society, supported by a modern and efficient agrarian sector. Production had to be oriented both toward increasing internal consumption and improving Peru's competitiveness in the international finished goods market. The military realized that foreign capital would be necessary for development, but would have to be closely controlled to ensure that it benefited Peru as much or more than it benefited foreign

investors. It would also require a greater mobilization of Peru's own
domestic resources which would be channeled to the industrial sector. Consistent with these two principal requirements, the revolutionary leaders redefined the rules for investment and altered the
incentives to encourage greater private investment in specific areas
of production, while reserving certain "key" industrial sectors to the
state.

Underlying the military's approach to development was a strong
belief that the state should play a larger role in industrialization and
exercise tighter supervision of foreign capital to direct it into those
economic activities most beneficial to Peru. But even while the state
was to expand its economic role, the military still intended to rely
heavily on private domestic investment, for which reason it was pre-
disposed to permit increasing profits in modern industries to stimulate the accumulation of capital for further investment. Agrarian
reform to stimulate greater production for domestic consumption, and
price controls to hold down the cost of living for urban workers (and
hence the cost of labor for industrialists), were integral elements of
the military's approach to national development. And in a more general context, the military assumed that complete development would
ultimately require national integration in the broadest possible sense.
Only through a simultaneous process of economic, cultural, political, and linguistic integration would it be possible to fully mobilize
human and material resources and build a modern industrial society.

It should be reemphasized that the four principal objectives of
the revolution outlined above evolved gradually over the first year or
so of the military regime. In other words, the military did not take
power with a clear conceptualization of purpose, but rather came
slowly to define its political program through the actual exercise of
power. Toward the end of the Velasco period, one of the president's
close advisors argued that the military had been pursuing a detailed
secret plan of government almost from the outset. But the actual conduct of the military government between 1968 and 1975 strongly suggests that many reforms were ad hoc responses to unanticipated
developments, while others (like the agrarian reform and creation of
so-called Industrial Communities) may actually have been part of a
"grand strategy."

The First Phase of the Revolution

Under Velasco, the military government committed itself to creating
a "pluralistic" economy and a "Social Democracy of Full Participa-

tion." These dual objectives required some far-reaching economic reforms and a comprehensive reordering of the national political environment. On the economic side, a variety of different forms of economic organization were promoted in industry and agriculture, the state assumed a greater role in planning the economy and stimulating industrial expansion, and workers were provided with varying degrees of participation in profits and management. On the political side, the government endeavored to reduce (and eventually eliminate) the role of unions and political parties in the society, depoliticize higher education and increase technological training, and deprive the upper class of its traditional monopoly over political resources (such as control of information). Naturally, economic and political reforms overlapped and were highly interdependent. Nevertheless, it is possible to differentiate between primarily economic and political reform measures in the following discussion for purposes of clarity. While all of the important reforms cannot be reviewed here for reasons of space, we can identify the major programs initiated by the military during the revolution's First Phase.

Economic Reforms
The goal of promoting national development within a context of economic pluralism took the form of recognizing different ownership patterns and organizational forms throughout the economy. The four chief economic sectors that emerged were State Property (involving a government monopoly over certain business, financial, and commercial activities of special importance to Peruvian development), Reformed Private Property (involving worker participation in the profits and management of private industrial firms), Unreformed Private Property (in which companies with less than six employees or $250,000 in annual sales remained essentially unaltered), and Social Property (modeled after Yugoslav worker ownership of industries). Aside from promoting a variety of organizational forms throughout the economy, the military government attempted to restructure the overall economy itself by channeling a greater share of national resources to the modern industrial sector, providing increased opportunities for private capital accumulation, and expanding agricultural production for both export and internal consumption. One of the first and most important moves the Velasco government undertook to stimulate development was agrarian reform.

Agrarian reform. On June 24, 1969, the Velasco regime decreed a comprehensive agrarian reform intended, among other things, to

increase production in order to generate surplus capital for investment in the urban-industrial sector. The reform applied to most coastal
properties above 150 hectares and sierra holdings above 35 to 55 hectares (with regional variations). While expropriated holdings were
compensated for with bonds payable over twenty to thirty years, the
actual value of compensation was "sharply reduced by inflation and
lax law enforcement." Although some observers perceived the reform as an attempt by the military to head off peasant unrest in the
highlands, the pattern of application suggested that increasing productivity was the primary motivation for the law. The large export-
oriented coastal estates were expropriated almost immediately, while
the provisions of the reform were applied only gradually to the highlands on a regional basis.

The reform originally called for transferring roughly 11 million
hectares (out of a national total of perhaps 21 to 23 million hectares
of agricultural land) to some 340,000 rural families (out of perhaps
700,000 rural families). Through subsequent decrees, expropriated
properties were organized along four primary lines, depending on
the size, productivity, and previous organization of the holdings.
Large, profitable coastal estates were constituted as Agricultural Production Cooperatives (CAPs), while the best sierra holdings were
organized as Social Interest Agrarian Societies (SAISs). Fully 76 percent of expropriated properties were eventually organized into CAPs
or SAISs, while the remainder were distributed as individual plots in
either Campesino Cooperatives or Campesino Communities (both of
which suffered from a scarcity of government assistance and credit).
While the peasants in CAPs and SAISs were guaranteed a dominant
voice in the management of their cooperatives, conflicts between
cooperative members and state-appointed technocrats were frequent
over such questions as the allocations of surpluses toward reinvest-
ment or increased pay. Other conflicts concerned the demands of large
numbers of peasants who failed to qualify as beneficiaries of the reform because they had been non-tenant laborers on highland haciendas or only temporary or part-time employees on coastal estates before
the reform. Finally, a considerable amount of land escaped expropriation in the highlands because government delays allowed owners
to carry out their own parcelation of holdings among family members and/or others. . . .

The agrarian reform suffered from a certain ambiguity of purpose from the outset. The "developmentalist" officers viewed the reform as a measure to increase agricultural productivity, while so-called
radical officers favored the reform as a means of income redistribu-

tion (that would mobilize popular support behind the military regime). The revolutionary rhetoric that accompanied the declaration of the reform aroused the expectations of landless sierra peasants, but in practice, the government concentrated on increasing productivity on the already highly efficient coastal estates rather than meeting the demands of highland peasants for the swift and complete expropriation of haciendas. The percentage of Agrarian Bank loans allocated to the agro-export sector increased during the First Phase, and the bulk of public investment in agriculture went toward large-scale irrigation to benefit coastal estates. The fact that most part-time agricultural laborers and non-tenant peasants failed to benefit from the agrarian reform led to serious labor tensions along the coast and land invasion in the highlands.

Partly in response to tensions in the countryside, the military government created the National Agrarian Confederation (CNA) as "the one legitimate organ of expression of farm interests." Established in 1972 by Decree Law 19400, the CNA did not hold its first national convention until late 1974. The CNA was intended to join together all individuals who worked in the agricultural sector to both communicate their interests to government and coordinate regional and national agricultural policies. However, the CNA was "basically a mechanism to enhance the labors of the government" since peasant interests were to be defended by the CNA only to the extent that they were "compatible with the national interest as determined by the Military Government." Although problems continued to disrupt government policies in the countryside even after the formation of the CNA, as the expectations unleashed by the agrarian reform contributed to growing political instability, the situation remained within manageable limits throughout the Velasco period. And although the agrarian reform did not measure up to all of the rhetoric that surrounded its initiation, it nevertheless qualified as one of the most important changes effected by the military.

Reformed private property. The First Phase government attempted to stimulate industrial expansion and harmonize worker-owner relations through the introduction of a series of reforms in 1970. The General Law of Industries (D.L. 18350) required private companies with more than six employees or $250,000 in gross income to reinvest 15 percent of their profits in the name of the workers as a group until workers acquired 50 percent ownership, provide participation in management proportionate to worker ownership in the company, and distribute another 10 percent of net profits directly to individual workers. This was followed by Decree Law 18384, which established the organizational form of the Industrial Communities in each firm through which workers were to share in profits. Finally, Decree Law 18471 in November 1970 significantly tightened the conditions under which industrial workers could be fired or laid off. . . .

Regardless of the intentions of the reform to reconcile the interests of labor and management, worker unrest increased. During the two years preceding the reform of industrial property (1968–69), there had been 735 strikes involving over 200,000 workers (about 10 percent of the labor force), while during the two years following the measure (1971–72), there were 786 strikes involving 292,000 workers (about 15.4 percent of the labor force). More important, the severity of strikes increased. During the period 1968–69, a total of 7.3 million man-hours were lost through strikes. This increased to 17.2 million man-hours during 1971–72. What also changed was the cause of strikes. Whereas in 1968–69, 23.1 percent of all strikes involved layoffs and firings, 17.7 percent involved pay demands, and 15.9 percent involved contract disputes, in 1971 fully 35 percent of all strikes involved pay demands, while the other two issues declined in importance. Certainly not all of these strikes affected the Reformed Private Property Sector, but they do reflect the intensification of labor conflicts in the better organized sectors of the economy which industrial reforms failed to stem.

Even together with a modified form of Industrial Communities (CIS) for State Enterprises (in which workers received bonds instead of stock), industrial reform measures benefited only a minority of Peru's modern work force. In 1972 there were roughly 53,100 workers in mining, 485,200 workers in manufacturing, and 171,700 workers in construction, which together represented 16.2 percent of Peru's labor force. Yet, by the end of the reform period in 1975, only approximately 200,000 workers belonged to CIS, representing less than 4.3 percent of Peru's economically active population. These workers, who were organized into more than 3,500 CIS by the close of the Velasco period, came to pose something of a political challenge to the military government after 1973 when the Ministry of Industry and Tourism sponsored the First National Congress of Industrial Communities. Although the government had not intended to form a permanent national body to aggregate and communicate the interests of CIS (as it had done in the agricultural sector with the formation of the CNA), the workers themselves formed the autonomous National Confederation of Industrial Communities (CONACI) in October 1973 which called upon the government to (1) convert all reformed property to Social Property, (2) increase worker participation in management, and (3) cancel the agrarian debt owed to former landowners. By mid-1974, CONACI had become a serious embarrassment to the regime because of its efforts to push the revolution further left than the generals desired to go. The military responded with an effort to divide CONACI and bring it back within the ideological parameters of the revolution.

The state sector. The expansion of the Peruvian government's direct involvement in the economy under Velasco has been characterized by many observers as a form of "state capitalism." Aside from its other economic reforms, the military created a heterogeneous state sector composed of a collection of industrial, financial, and commercial enterprises. The First Phase government did not intend to either replace or discourage private domestic and foreign investment. Rather, state investment in certain "strategic" areas of the economy was intended to guarantee a rapid development of the industrial infrastructure (e.g., steel production) and promote the expansion of the domestic market. Major export activities were also nationalized to ensure that export earnings were maximized to finance the military's ambitious industrial investment program. Finally, the creation of a state sector was intended to break up certain monopolies held by domestic and foreign capitalists in Peru which acted as obstacles to what the military perceived as the inherent dynamism of the economy. Thus, while foreign investment was still encouraged, it was no longer allowed to freely choose the area and scope of its activities. It was expected to be consistent with, and contribute to, the government's developmental strategies.

Two primary characteristics of the state sector were that it was formed primarily on the basis of existing (mostly foreign) industries, and grew largely out of the pursuit of other objectives, such as the rationalization of a particular area of production or the reduction of external dependency. While the military became intent on centralizing what it perceived as strategic economic activities, it nevertheless remained committed to a notion of "economic pluralism" and had no intention of moving toward a completely state-managed economy. The state sector firms that emerged during the First Phase of the revolution fell into three major categories. In the first group were state enterprises formed from expropriated foreign holdings (including PETROPERU, ENTROMIN, HIERROPERU, ENTELPERU, and ENAFER). These state enterprises gave the government dominant control over the important extractive industries (oil, copper, iron) and public services (electricity and rail transportation). In the second group were formerly domestically owned industries taken over after economic collapses. The fishmeal industry is the chief example, which was converted into the state enterprise PESCAPERU in 1973 at a time when the sector was in severe decline. The third group was made up of already existing and newly created state enterprises, like the steel firm SIDERPERU.

Apart from these primarily extractive and manufacturing firms, the government assumed a dominant position in marketing and credit. Through the purchase of stock, the government came to control most of the banking industry. State monopolies were also created in the foreign marketing of minerals and other products, the domestic wholesale of basic foodstuffs, and industries oriented to processing primary exports to increase the value added.

The military had intended to have the state augment private investment, not replace it. But the rhetoric of the revolution created a climate of uncertainty in the business community that discouraged both domestic and foreign private investments in the economy. Thus, the state's share of fixed investment rose from 29.8 percent in 1968 to 44 percent in 1973. Over the long run the military rulers expected primary exports (especially oil and copper) to finance state investments in heavy industry. But over the short run, the government turned to private international credit which, as it happened, was readily available at reasonable terms during the early 1970s. Indeed, it was the abundance of private credit during this period that allowed the Peruvian government to escape almost completely the effects of the cutoff of official bilateral credits and aid from the United States. The cutoff was in retaliation for the uncompensated expropriation of the International Petroleum Company in 1968, and was not ended until the 1974 Greene Agreement between Peru and the United States resolved all outstanding claims against the revolutionary government.

Even with heavy foreign borrowing, however, the rate of fixed capital formation by the close of the Velasco period remained virtually the same as during the early 1960s. And the growth of industrial output generally, and manufacturing in particular, remained virtually unchanged between the periods 1961–70 and 1971–75. What did change was the economy's dependence on state investment and the country's external public debt (which began to increase almost exponentially). The expansion of the state sector also brought the government into an employer-employee relationship with a sizable proportion of the Peruvian work force. This eventually posed serious political difficulties for the government after 1974 when the military began to react to the first signs of economic crisis by "rationalizing" state-controlled industries (i.e., reducing labor costs).

Social property. As early as July 1971, President Velasco let it be known that the revolutionary government's reorganization of property ownership would not stop with the formation of agrarian cooperatives, Industrial Communities, and the expansion of the state sector. He announced that an entirely new form of property—Social Property—would be created as the foundation for Peruvian socialism. It was not until August 1973, however, that the government finally issued a draft law of Social Property for public comment. After eight months of sometimes intense public debate, resulting in the deportation of certain leading critics, the Law of Social Property (D.L. 20598) was decreed on April 30, 1974. This law provided for the formation of a Social Property Sector composed of Social Property Enterprises (EPSs) which, it was planned, would come to constitute the dominant form of production in the country over the course of twenty or thirty years.

The Social Property Sector was to be presided over by the National Commission of Social Property (CONAPS) which would be responsible for approving the creation of individual EPSs, supervising their early operations, and coordinating policy for the sector as a whole. While EPSs could be formed in any economic field either from scratch or through the conversion of an existing company upon the request of its workers, preference was initially given to the establishment of entirely new firms. To provide state capital for the formation of EPSs, the government set up the National Fund of Social Property (FONAPS) to finance the growth of the new sector. Finally, the law provided for a national Social Property Sector Assembly to consist of EPS representatives elected through regional associations. This national assembly was to meet biannually: in November to plan programs for the sector for the coming year, and in April to evaluate the performance of the sector during the previous year.

The government devoted considerable time and effort to detailing the structure and function of the sector since it was supposed to become the priority area for future public investment. . . . The introduction of Social Property received an enthusiastic response from most workers and leftist intellectuals, but was bitterly opposed by business leaders who feared that it threatened the concept of economic pluralism and was intended to subvert private property. The success of Social Property, however, was jeopardized from the outset by two major difficulties. First, by 1974–75, the military government's investment resources were already severely strained which in turn limited the expansion of the new sector. Second, the high concentration of production in the various branches of modern industry in Peru where EPSs were to be formed threatened the economic viability of the new firms. Their competitiveness within monopolistic conditions could not be guaranteed even with state-imposed restrictions on the expansion of existing private manufacturers. As a result, demands increased toward the end of the First Phase for the conversion of *existing* companies into EPSs, rather than the formation of new enterprises. These and other problems delayed the expansion of the sector, and by the close of the Velasco period, only a handful of EPSs were in operation (with perhaps another one hundred in various stages of planning or formation). The actual growth of the Social Property Sector failed to satisfy the expectations that the reform aroused among workers and intellectuals, and the government's commitment to the Social Property concept waned quickly after 1975.

Political Reforms

While the military's basic approach to development reflected a high degree of confidence in technocratic solutions to economic problems, its approach to the representative duties of government was influenced by a deep distrust of politics and politicians. Labor unions, to the extent that they were traditionally either the creatures of political parties in Peru or, at a minimum, politically oriented, were also highly suspect in the military's eyes. The traditional political system in Peru had operated on the basis of the marginalization of the highland rural population and the segmentary incorporation of different urban and coastal groups by political parties that became their patrons.

The client-patron relationship that developed between the various political parties and their constituencies led to a situation in which the national interest was neglected in favor of particularistic interests. When, as often happened, competing narrow interests could not be reconciled and a consensus for action arrived at, the situation gave rise to the stagnation of the national governmental process. Politics was overwhelmingly a forum for sectarian competition between essentially personalistic political parties. Thus, the military committed itself to the complete depoliticization of Peruvian society. . . . The following measures, although in no way comprehensive, stand out as some of the more important political reforms enacted by the First Phase government to restructure the political environment and foster the growth of a corporatist society in Peru.

Mobilization and participation. The military, or at least a certain faction within the military, was interested in mobilizing support for revolutionary reform and increasing lower-class participation in restructuring Peruvian society. . . . Three options were open to the government: It could create its own revolutionary political party, work through one of the existing political parties (such as the progovernment Communist Party), or attempt to completely redefine the nature and process of mobilization and participation. The military opted for the third alternative and established . . . the National System for Support of Social Mobilization (SINAMOS). The law establishing SINAMOS (D.L. 18896) in June 1971 and the subsequent statute (D.L. 19352) outlining its organization and procedures in April 1972 assigned the agency a number of responsibilities. The most important duties of SINAMOS were to (1) train and organize the popular classes at the local level to promote the implementation of national policies, (2) elaborate a corporatist definition of participation in which individuals would cooperate in localized activities directed from above by the government, (3) coordinate self-help activities among the poor, and (4) undercut the traditional role of political parties as integrative agents for "marginalized" groups.

SINAMOS was given a wide field of operations, including the cooperatives formed by the agrarian reform, the Industrial Communities formed by the Industrial Law, and, most importantly, the squatter settlements (*pueblos jóvenes*) surrounding Lima. To facilitate its manifold responsibilities, SINAMOS was given a dual organizational structure. Alongside a variety of functional departments (dealing with rural organization, labor organization, community development, etc.), the government created a pyramidal national structure with a central office at the top, ten regional offices (presiding over two to five departments), and numerous zonal offices (ideally presiding over about two provinces each). Finally, at the lowest level, were the actual field operatives—or "contact points"—of SINAMOS who initiated or coordinated community activities. . . .

SINAMOS was beset with difficulties almost from the outset. In the first instance, the formation of the agency was a response to the autonomous formation of Committees for the Defense of the Revolution that sprang up around Lima and throughout the country in 1970. . . . Some military hard-liners wanted these committees disbanded, while other officers viewed them as an opportunity to expand the revolution's base of support. Whether this is true or not, SINAMOS was also an attempt to overcome the military's lack of grass-roots structures within the society by which the popular classes could be linked to the government, and give substance to the military's rhetoric of "participation." . . . SINAMOS programs throughout most of the society were visible failures by late 1973; with some notable exceptions, such as in the *pueblos jóvenes* of the Lima/Callao areas. . . .

SINAMOS encountered opposition from virtually every political sector: Government technocrats resented its efforts to interject politics into economic planning, the target communities feared its manipulative potential, and the political parties and unions opposed the efforts of SINAMOS to deprive them of popular leadership. Most significantly, SINAMOS was unable to control many of the mass-based groups it helped bring into existence. Paradoxically, although the military originally created SINAMOS to undercut the appeal of unions, by 1974–75 the government virtually abandoned SINAMOS and in turn attempted to compete with unions directly by forming state-sponsored syndicates in a variety of economic sectors.

Education. The military considered the rationalization and modernization of Peruvian higher education essential to national development, and therefore moved quickly to impose major university reforms. In a highly controversial move, the government issued Decree Law 17437 in February 1969 in a sudden and unexpected manner. The law reduced student participation in university governance from one third to one fourth, reorganized faculties into disciplines, and attempted to depoliticize student politics by setting academic standards for election to student organizations and barring reelections. Most threateningly, the law effectively abolished the traditional autonomy of Peruvian universities by placing them under the supervision of a National Council of the Peruvian University (CONUP) that was placed under the authority of the Ministry of Education. Because of intense reaction from practically all university groups, especially students and professors, the Velasco regime made progressive modifications in the law throughout the remainder of the year. Finally, in November 1969, the government attempted to mollify the university community by appointing an Educational Reform Commission under the supervision of the Ministry of Education to write a new comprehensive educational reform proposal with public input.

It took the Reform Commission until September 1970 to publish its first report for public comment, which sparked considerable public debate. As far as possible, the commission—sometimes under direct pressure from President Velasco himself—endeavored to incorporate the demands of important groups into a new reform proposal. By early 1971 the commission had produced a draft law, but this was not released for public comment until December. After still further modifications in the law in response to pressures and demands from both within and without the universities, the Velasco government finally issued its General Law of Education (D.L. 19326) in March 1972 (more than thirty-four months after the military's first educational reform initiative). . . .

Conflict between the government and the educational community continued at all levels after 1972. In higher education, two major issues of conflict concerned pay for teaching and nonteaching personnel (which failed to keep pace with inflation) and the alleged interference of CONUP in university self-governance. Both the progovernment Revolutionary Students of Peru (formed with the assistance of SINAMOS) and the more radical Student Federation of Peru (FEP) criticized or opposed the reformist measures of CONUP. And the National Federation of Teachers of the Peruvian University (FENDUP) vigorously attacked the government's "rationalization" program in education. Within lower education, popular opposition to the government on a wide range of issues became increasingly radical. In 1970 the strongest teachers' union had been the National Federation of Educators of Peru (FENEP), whose membership was split between followers of the progovernment General Confederation of Peruvian Workers (CGTP) and left-wing Apristas. The Apristas withdrew and formed the Sole Syndicate of Workers of Peruvian Education (SUTEP), which adopted an extremely militant opposition to the military regime.

When the government sponsored elections in the educational establishment in 1973, SUTEP emerged as the dominant teachers' union. The Velasco regime reacted by withdrawing recognition from SUTEP and forming a government-sponsored Syndicate of Educators of the Peruvian Revolution (SERP). The continued dominance of SUTEP among educators, however, led the government to seek a dialogue with the union in July 1974. The "dialogue" came to an end, however, shortly after SUTEP's Secretary General, Horacio Zevallos, labeled the military's education reform as an attempt to promote the interests of the country's "dependent bourgeoisie" at a national congress in November. By early 1975, SUTEP had formulated a political program calling for the overthrow of the existing "bourgeoisie government" and its replacement by a proletarian regime, total opposition to the General Law of Education because of its bias in favor of "power groups," and the formation of a united front to resist the manipulative agencies of the military government (such as SINAMOS and the Ministry of Education).

In reality, the military's approach to education became ever more equivocal after 1973 as opposition mounted to reforms. At times the government adopted a hard-line policy, as with the promulgation of

Decree Law 20201 in October 1973 that authorized the Minister of Education to dismiss any instructor suspected of "subversion" without appeal over the course of a year. At other times, the government (acting through CONUP) struggled to appease student and teacher demands, especially during the first half of 1975. In spite of its obvious disappointment with the response to its reforms, the Velasco government continued to attempt to effect major changes in education right up to the end of the First Phase. For example, in May 1975, Decree Law 21156 established the Indian language of Quechua as one of the official languages of the country, mandated obligatory instruction in the language by the 1976 school year, and gave the judicial system until January 1977 to acquire the capacity to conduct proceedings in the language when requested by defendants.

Information and the press. The Velasco government enjoyed generally good relations with the Peruvian press during its first year in power, but the increasing tempo of reforms invariably caused tension between the military and the wealthy owners of the leading national dailies. The government's first effort to exercise control over the press came in December 1969 with Decree Law 18075. This law imposed stiff penalties for libel against government officials and state entities, and prohibited either foreigners or Peruvian nationals living abroad from owning newspapers. As the government's treatment in the press worsened, more direct measures were taken. In March 1970 two important dailies (*Expreso* and *Extra*) were expropriated and turned over to their workers (who were under the influence of the progovernment Communist Party). The papers, which belonged to Manuel Ulloa (who had served as a minister in the Belaúnde government) were accused of defending the interests of foreign capitalists and the Peruvian oligarchy. In 1971 a third important daily came under indirect military influence when the government purchased the stock of the Banco Popular after the collapse of the financial empire of one of the nation's leading oligarchic families. The bank had served as the holding company for the diverse investments of the Prado family, including the Lima daily *La Crónica*. The paper was renamed *La Nueva Crónica* and placed under the management of an editorial council sympathetic to the revolution. Finally, in January 1972, the government issued Decree Law 19270 that gave the workers in each paper the first option to purchase their dailies, should the owners be forced to sell under the provisions of Decree Law 18075 of 1969.

The crux of the growing conflict between the government and the independent press was that practically all of the leading dailies were owned by extremely wealthy individuals who were deeply involved in the political and economic issues on which their papers editorialized. Indeed, with the exception of *El Comercio* (which was the primary investment of the Miró Quesada family), the leading papers had been purchased by members of the oligarchy precisely in order to protect their investments in other areas of the economy. In other words, left-wing accusations that the national dailies were little more than political organs for the upper class had a great deal of substance. Nevertheless, the rights of the private owners of the press were defended by the more moderate members of the revolutionary government (especially the representatives of the navy), and the efforts by radical officers to take more decisive actions against the press precipitated a political crisis within the Velasco regime between late 1973 and early 1974. Only after these moderates were purged from the inner council of the Velasco regime did the revolutionary government proceed with its plan for guaranteeing "popular control" of information.

In a preliminary move, the government created the National Information System (SINADI) in March 1974 to monitor all mediums of communication to (1) guarantee "truth" in reporting on government programs, (2) "harmonize" reporting with the objectives of the national development plan, and (3) modify the content of news to ensure that it "serve culture." The system was placed under the administration of a Central Office of Information (OCI), whose director was given ministerial rank. The major offensive was contained in Decree Law 20680, issued secretly on July 23, 1974, and put into effect dramatically a few days later. Under its provisions, all national dailies (papers with a circulation of more than 20,000 or distribution in more than half of the departmental capitals) were expropriated. Each of the expropriated papers was assigned to a different sector of the population whose government-recognized participatory organizations were to elect the civil associations that would oversee the editorial policies of each daily. *La Nueva Crónica*, in turn, was placed directly under the authority of the OCI as the official government press. The law brought about the expropriation of the five remaining major dailies (*La Prensa, El Comercio, Correo, Ultima Hora, and Ojo*) which, together with *Extra* and *Expreso*, were designated as the representatives of different socioeconomic groups such as urban labor, campesinos, the service sector, and professional organizations. . . .

While the papers remained generally supportive of the revolutionary government up through mid-1975, they nevertheless exhibited considerable editorial independence. As the government encountered increasing financial difficulties and important reforms failed to meet the growing expectations of the population, this editorial independence became increasingly intolerable to the First Phase regime. Finally, during the last month of the Velasco government, the military reacted to what it perceived as a radicalization of the press with the first of many purges of "subversive" journalists. The Second Phase government subsequently tightened press controls and, finally, completely abandoned the idea of a socialized press in Peru.

The Second Phase and the End of Revolutionary Change

Although many of the reforms of the First Phase were either incomplete or poorly executed, a considerable redistribution of national resources was accomplished benefiting the lower classes. The new or increased responsibilities of the central government in industrialization, public welfare, and other areas, however, placed severe strains on the treasury. With the onset of the international recession induced by increasing energy prices in early 1974, Peru began to encounter serious balance-of-payments problems. Many of the Velasco-era development projects had been financed with private foreign credit, which was to be repaid with the earnings from expanding primary exports. The international recession that set in early in 1974 placed the Velasco regime in a difficult posture: On the one hand, the revolutionary government had become committed to extensive public expenditures, while on the other hand, it needed to come to terms with international creditors who began to press for austerity measures to stabilize the Peruvian economy. The political situation was further complicated by President Velasco's deteriorating health and increasingly personalistic style of rule.

By mid-1975 a coalition of conservative officers within the army had formed around Velasco's Prime Minister, General Francisco Morales Bermúdez. Morales Bermúdez, who was next in line for the presidency on the basis of military seniority, favored conservative fiscal policies to improve the country's national accounts, but otherwise professed support for the objectives of the revolution. In a well-coordinated putsch on August 29, 1975, Velasco was overthrown without bloodshed when the country's five regional army commanders issued an Institutional Manifesto naming Morales Bermúdez president. The action was quickly endorsed by the air force and navy, and encountered virtually no opposition from the popular organizations created by the revolution.

Morales Bermúdez announced that the coup merely signaled a change in personnel, and not a rejection of the goals of the revolution. The government would continue to pursue the objectives of the First Phase, only without *personalismo* or *desviaciones* (personalism or deviations). Nevertheless, the so-called Second Phase reordered government priorities, reduced the influence of reformist officers in decision making, and began to stress the themes of labor discipline and sacrifice. The Second Phase government attempted to "rationalize" First Phase programs, which usually entailed increasing the profitability of public enterprises by adopting wage or employment policies injurious to the working class. Also, a succession of austerity measures (that actually began under Velasco) were imposed that reduced public welfare expenditures and generally raised the cost of living. During its first year, the Morales Bermúdez government kept most of the working-class organizations in line by stressing that Peru's economic difficulties were the result of the collapse of the international capitalist system. The seemingly antipopular policies of the government, it was explained, were only temporary expedients to deal with a transitory crisis. The political space of the Second Phase regime, however, was narrowing as a disproportionate amount of the burdens of the austerity measures fell on the very groups to which the revolution had originally looked for support. By mid-1976 it was clear that the piecemeal austerity measures adopted over the previous year were insufficient to either satisfy Peru's foreign creditors or stabilize the economy. In order to obtain a refinancing of the foreign debt, attract foreign investment, and stimulate exports, drastic action was required. In late June 1976 the ministerial cabinet finally agreed on a set of policies that the ranking reformist officer in the government was forced to announce on national television on June 30. Although numerous reformist officers had been forced into retirement after the Morales Bermúdez coup, enough remained in the Second Phase government to block some of the more onerous policy demands of the most conservative generals, These holdovers from the First Phase were grouped behind General Jorge Fernández Maldonado Solari, who served as Prime Minister and Commander of the Armed Forces by virtue of seniority. The ability of the conservative generals to maneuver Maldonado into announcing the austerity measures, which he certainly had fought against in the cabinet, was probably designed to blunt the public's reaction and direct resentment away from the president.

The austerity package was draconian. It provided for a 12.4 percent cut in government investment in state enterprises, a 12.8 percent reduction in the national budget, a steep increase in consumer prices, and a devaluation of the national currency by 44.4 percent. To help offset the effects of these actions, it was also announced that wages would be increased by 10 to 14 percent. The wage increases, however, did not come close to covering the rise in the cost of living. One immediate effect of the policies was a dramatic increase in the cost of gasoline, which was not compensated for by a corresponding increase in public transportation fares. To protest this fact, the Lima/ Callao transportation cooperatives went on strike the following day. The transportation strike, in turn, sparked three days of rioting that required a full-scale military operation to contain. The violent popular reaction, which was largely directed against government institutions, profoundly altered the military's attitude toward the masses and appeared to confirm the fears of conservative generals that the First Phase had created revolutionary organizations that the government could not be sure of controlling. Many of the organizations created during the First Phase (such as the CNA, CONACI, the Confederation of Workers of the Peruvian Revolution, etc.) joined together in the Front for the Defense of the Revolution that functioned simultaneously as a source of political support for the government and a powerful pressure group designed to push reforms through to completion. As late as June 24, 1976, the Front had remained committed to the military government, but bitterly resisted the conservative orientation of certain officers. In a public communiqué, the Front declared:

> We believe that the world economic crisis and its consequences in Peru, together with the imperialists' and reactionary right's offensive . . . have disrupted the rhythm of the advance of the Revolution in the past ten months. But we are sure that the earlier transforming orientation will be regained shortly, without deviations or foreign influences of any kind. Therefore, we are in the same trench of battle as the Armed Forces, supporting the President of the Republic, General Francisco Morales Bermúdez, and remain confident that he will keep the Revolution on the same road that the People and Armed Forces have been following heretofore. (*El Comercio*, June 24, 1976)

Three days later, reacting to rumors that a major austerity package was under consideration in the cabinet, the coordinating committee of the Front issued another communiqué, stating:

> Whoever has proposed such measures to the government has not considered the suffering of our people, the future of the Revolution and of the country, and therefore we are not in agreement with such policies.

As an alternative, a number of countermeasures were proposed that would attack what the Front termed the capitalist infrastructure of the country, and place the major burdens for contending with the economic crisis on the upper classes. The austerity program unveiled on June 30, therefore, represented a major political defeat for both the remaining reformist officers in the government and the mass-based organizations created under Velasco. Popular support for the military government after the rioting virtually evaporated and the armed forces found themselves politically isolated.

The final blow to the Peruvian revolution came later in the month of July when a power struggle ended in a complete purge of reformist officers from the government. During the rioting in Lima between July 1 and 3, the conservative commander of the Center for Military Instruction (CIMP) ignored standing orders and deployed his troops to protect upper-class suburbs instead of seizing communications centers. General Bobbio Centurión, a strong supporter of austerity measures, incorrectly assumed that mobs were about to attack Lima's upper-class residential districts and took defensive actions without authorization from General Maldonado. Afterward, on July 9, Maldonado used the incident to demand Bobbio Centurión's early retirement. The commander of Lima's second most important military garrison then declared himself in rebellion (expecting support from the archconservative navy). After a brief battle, Bobbio Centurión was placed under arrest and sent into exile after the five regional army commanders and the Joint Chiefs of Staff issued a pronouncement in support of the existing government.

Although the power struggle appeared to have been won by Maldonado, the declaration of the armed forces against Bobbio Centurión was not so much an endorsement of the reformists in the government as an attempt to maintain the outward appearance of military unity and discipline. In reality, Maldonado's actions against Bobbio Centurión solidified the right-wing officers within the armed forces who then forced Maldonado and the other remaining reformist officers into early retirement later the same month. By August 1976 the revolutionary process was over in Peru, and a wide range of First Phase programs were either terminated or, at best, ignored. As Henry Pease García and Alfredo Filomeno observed: "1976 is thus a year of redefinition of the military political project."

At times, the government appeared to be a new regime, distinct from the one that ran the state during the previous eight years. The attack on revolutionary programs was swift. Just five days after

Maldonado's forced retirement on July 16, the government announced that the conditions for transferring the socialized press to complete citizen control did not yet exist, and the papers would therefore have to remain under the administration of government representatives. (Gradually, the military came full circle on the notion of a socialized press and favored the return of the Lima dailies to their former owners.) The following month, in a major address, President Morales Bermúdez declared that the term *socialism* would be dropped from the government's vocabulary because it was a vague and confusing word that merely discouraged private investment in the country. By mid-1977 the government began negotiations with the International Monetary Fund in an effort to appease foreign creditors and investors, which the First Phase government had pledged would never again influence Peruvian decision making. Finally, the government adopted a policy of "labor discipline" to replace the earlier policy of "labor stability," meaning that employers were given a freer hand to dismiss workers for reasons of either profitability or discipline.

The slackening and eventual termination of revolutionary change after the overthrow of Velasco prevented some programs (like Social Property) from ever getting off the ground, and others (like agrarian reform) from expanding their beneficiaries. The case of the agrarian reform is particularly interesting, since it is generally considered to have been the single most important consequence of the revolution. The 1969 agrarian reform had originally aimed at transferring up to eleven million hectares of land (well below the total arable land in Peru) to some 340,000 rural families. Yet, in June 1976, the Morales Bermúdez government declared the agrarian reform at an end (with one year permitted for resolution of all pending cases), with only 6.7 million hectares having been distributed among 269,437 families: 4.9 million of it as CAPs and SAISs. All told, a total of seven million hectares were distributed by the close of the revolution, leaving as much as twelve million hectares unaffected. And even if the original target of 340,000 families had received land (which they did not), those benefited would still have represented only a fraction of an agricultural work force that was calculated in excess of 1.5 million in 1972. In essence, the armed forces simply lacked the resources and resolve to carry through to completion the reforms begun in the First Phase.

In July 1977, President Morales Bermúdez declared that the military would sponsor elections to return government to civilians. The armed forces had exhausted their political capital and seriously damaged their institutional prestige and solidarity. But the military's withdrawal from power proved to be slow and painful. Elections were held for a Constituent Assembly in 1978 that drafted a new constitution which was promulgated the following year. In May 1980 general elections were held for the national legislature and the presidency. During the three years between the announcement of elections and the actual surrender of power by Morales Bermúdez in July 1980, the military found it necessary to rely on openly repressive measures to contend with growing labor militancy. The armed forces ended up devoting their last three years of rule to brutalizing the popular classes in whose name they assumed power in 1968.

Editors' note. Transition to elected civilian government was soon followed by economic recession and a vicious counterinsurgency campaign against the *Sendero Luminoso* and other guerrilla movements. During the next decade of civilian governments, the armed forces greatly expanded both their internal security role and their political influence and authority under new regimes of exception and antiterrorism legislation. For most of the 1980s much of Peru was directly governed by military officers—not as a result of a coup but as the consequence of new laws that established "political-military commands" in "emergency zones." This procedure left much of the country under military jurisdiction. Savagery by *Sendero Luminoso* was matched by military and police brutality. The plague of narco-terrorism and the U.S.-assisted "drug war" further bloodied the country. More Peruvians suffered violent deaths, torture, and endemic fear under the civilian governments than under the 1968–1980 military regimes, while "faceless" (secret and with unknown judges) military courts tried suspected guerrillas and terrorists. Hundreds of innocent people went to prison; thousands more were killed or "disappeared."

Faced with real internal security threats, the armed forces' commitment to developmentalism and antipolitics persisted. In the early 1990s they supported a civilian technocratic president who largely shared their views. President Alberto Fujimori denounced the old political parties and the congress, then effected an *autogolpe* in April 1992 with military support. In language reminiscent of military antipolitical rhetoric, Fujimori denounced the congress for its "irresponsible, sterile, antihistoric, and antipatriotic behavior, which favors the interests of small groups and party leaders over the interests of Peru." He illegally closed the congress and convened a constitutional assembly which adopted a new constitution and gained him reelection; with a clever mix of neoliberal economics and presidential populism he governed Peru in alliance with the armed forces.

Fujimori's antipolitical message and the capture of *Sendero*'s principal leader greatly enhanced his popularity, although he required police and military assistance to quell periodic strikes and demonstrations against the neoliberal reforms. As in Chile, these reforms tamed inflation and promoted economic growth, but at the expense of traditionally protected industries, government employees, the labor movement, and many social programs.

By 1996, Fujimori governed a Peru acclaimed for its reforms by international bankers and transnational enterprises, but the armed forces were still the main bulwark of the government. As in Peru's past, the military was the single most important political force in the nation, and its commitment to antipolitics remained firm.

Notes

1. The following is a list of military coups in Peru since 1872:

1883	General Miguel Iglesias
1886	General Andres A. Cáceres
1914	Colonel Oscar R. Benavides
1930	General María Ponce
1930	Comandante Luis M. Sánchez Cerro
1931	Comandante Gustavo Jiménez
1948	General Manuel A. Odría
1962	General Ricardo Pérez Godoy
1968	General Juan Velasco Alvarado
1975	General Francisco Morales Bermúdez

In addition, there were three notable civilian coups:

1879	Nicolás de Piérola
1895	Nicolás de Piérola (called a revolution)
1919	Augusto B. Leguía

2. The historical rivalry between the military and APRA dates from the 1931 presidential election and an Aprista uprising that followed. Aprista supporters in Trujillo attacked a military garrison and killed a number of soldiers. The military responded with mass executions.

Knut Walter and
Philip J. Williams

CHAPTER 25

Antipolitics in El Salvador, 1948–1994

In December 1948 a number of army officers (led by a group of majors) and civilians overthrew the government of General Salvador Castañeda Castro and installed a junta which sought to legitimize its existence via a new political rhetoric and new ways of ruling. The bywords of the regime of Hernández Martínez and his immediate successors reflected their approach to politics: duty, tranquility, peace, order (social and constitutional), vigilance, protection, property, and guarantees. Although democracy was never mentioned, its dangers were implied in the usual criticism of factions, parties, disorder, and anarchy. Consequently, when the new junta declared that the previous regimes had flouted the popular will, thus provoking political dissent, it also announced that the armed forces would lead the people to a new existence within republican forms of government. In particular, the junta committed itself to observe democratic principles and to respect the popular will, as expressed in free elections.

However, only 11 days following the coup, the junta issued a proclamation which spelled out in more precise terms the exact nature of the democracy under consideration. For one, "liberty" could flourish only within an environment of order, free of extremist views and demagoguery. Thus, while on the one hand the armed forces would become "apolitical," on the other they would be responsible for guaranteeing that "liberty" and for ensuring respect for the law. Not only that: the junta declared that it would be necessary for all Salvadorans to unite to form an "indestructible bloc," made up equally of civilians and the armed forces, in order to achieve national progress and reconstruction.

As a result, the military remained very much a fixture within the new development model that sought to promote industrialization, diversify export agriculture, and increase spending on social services and welfare. It reiterated the armed forces' role as a school for the masses and involved itself directly in support of a national literacy campaign. It decided to improve the preparation of its own officer corps by stiffening entrance requirements and reforming the program of study at the military academy, as well as by creating a general staff college (Escuela de Guerra). It also opened its books to public scrutiny and oversight for a few years (the first and last time) in keeping with its promise to administer funds honestly and efficiently. Nonetheless, military spending as a percentage of the total government budget failed to drop noticeably from the years of the Hernández Martínez dictatorship. Nor was the regime's commitment to political democracy much more than verbal: during the entire decade of the 1950s, opposition parties never gained so much as a single seat in the legislature or control of even one municipality—due to intimidation, fraud, and the government's complete control of elections and campaigning. Though the new rulers disavowed any intention of setting up an "official" party, the rapid creation of the military-dominated Partido Revolucionario de Unificación Democrática (PRUD) might not have seemed, to the average citizen, all that different from the Hernández Martínez Pro Patria party.

Another important element of continuity in the military's role was the maintenance of an extensive paramilitary structure in the rural areas. The local *comandantes* were charged with drawing up the lists of available men for recruitment and then making their selection when the moment arrived. All soldiers who had done their military service continued to register with the local *comandantes* as members of the *escoltas militares*, which were active mostly over weekends, "to guarantee life and property." These reservists were also given talks on topics that included discipline, respect for and obedience to superiors, love of country, flag, and anthem, and the dangers of communism. There were some immediate rewards as well: the headquarters of the *servicio territorial* saw to it that the members of the *escoltas militares* received medical and economic assistance in moments of need, which for a poor peasant family was worth most any sacrifice. Though it is not now possible to make a precise determination of the magnitude of this paramilitary structure, it is possible to arrive at an estimate: if recruits totalled some 3,500 per year (the figure for 1955), by the end of the decade a total of some 35,000 would have been available in addition to all those from the previous years.

Finally, the security forces of the old regime remained pretty much the same in the new order. The National Guard, described by the military hierarchy in ever more glowing terms with each passing year, provided security in all the rural areas. Its services were much in demand, to the point that it continued the practice of the Hernández Martínez years of hiring out retired guardsmen, for a fee, to owners of farms and businesses. As with the conscript army, there are no figures available on the strength of this armed body although, on the basis of uniforms supplied to the force (4,400 in 1955), we can assume that the number was probably close to 2,000. If army conscripts and reservists are then added to the estimated total of guardsmen, it is conceivable that the regime could, by the end of the decade, count on some 40,000 men in the rural areas to provide essential political support and security in a country of two and a half million people, of whom some one and a half million inhabited the rural areas.

Because the military was so preoccupied with maintaining security in the countryside, it was unprepared to deal with the crises that erupted in the urban areas, especially San Salvador, in 1959 and 1960. University students and leaders of the opposition took part in street demonstrations, violently put down by the security forces, which led— ultimately—to another military coup that overthrew the government of Colonel José María Lemus. As in 1948, a coalition of military officers and civilians (mostly linked to the National University) again attempted to establish the groundwork for a new, more open political system, but their government lasted only three months (October 1960– January 1961) when it was replaced by another junta (the Directorio Cívico-Militar) made up of more conservative officers and civilians.

The Governments of "National Conciliation"

The 1960s were years in which the armies of Central America were chiefly involved in a variety of activities designed to counter a perceived Leftist threat emanating from revolutionary Cuba. The United States, through the Alliance for Progress and stepped-up military assistance, sought to promote fundamental social and economic change and guarantee military security. Thus, the civil-military junta (organized in January 1961) found itself caught between the demands of the Kennedy administration that it hold elections and further socioeconomic reform, on the one hand, and the continued resistance of the oligarchy to implementing such changes as land reform, increased direct taxes, and free political expression on the other. To complicate matters, new non-Communist, reform-minded political parties, like the Christian Democrats and Social Democrats, began to emerge, offering the people an alternative. Despite the fact that these parties maintained ties to international political organizations expressly forbidden by the Constitution, those very ties made it impossible to suppress them completely, and they began to attract strong support, especially in the urban areas.

The new military president, Colonel Julio Rivera, proceeded to introduce certain changes, seeking to mollify a number of conflicting interests, within and outside El Salvador. First of all, his administration introduced a system of proportional representation, so that the non-Communist opposition could at least participate in the legislature and in local government. By the end of the decade, the opposition parties controlled nearly half the seats in the legislature as well as a number of municipal governments, including that of San Salvador. Next, a progressive income tax was introduced which increased, to some extent, the taxes paid by the rich, thus providing the government with additional resources for social programs. Nevertheless, there was no attempt to push other important programs, such as land reform, on the Alliance for Progress agenda. Finally, the military introduced a program of civic action (Acción Cívica Militar, or ACM) designed to utilize its resources, both human and material, in assisting projects of local development, in order to fend off any Left-wing attempts to garner support.

Full-scale democracy, however, was out of the question. The military's official definition of democracy was set down early on:

> . . . the system of democratic government is based, fundamentally, on the equilibrium between public powers, in their independence and capacity for *fiscalización recíproca* [mutual oversight].

Furthermore, the new Constitution of 1962 retained one of the provisions of the 1950 document which required the armed forces to uphold public order and guarantee respect for the law and constitutional rights; it also empowered the military to intervene directly if the Constitution's prohibition on presidential reelection was violated.

Of more immediate importance was the open role of the military in furthering economic and social development via the ACM. In 1963 a Dirección General de Acción Cívica was created within the Ministry of Defense to coordinate the military's participation in such programs which, as defined initially, included, among others: construction and repair of schools and roads; transport services for school excursions and food distribution through the Caritas (Catholic Charities) program, medical clinics, donations of cloth for school uniforms, distribution of posters with the symbols of nationhood, blood donations by recruits for hospitals, along with lunch programs and haircutting services for poor schoolchildren. In this way, the resources of the military were pooled with those of the Ministries of Education, Public Works, Health, and the Interior, plus those of a new paramilitary organization, the so-called Organización Democrática Nacional (ORDEN), which was headed by the President of the Republic himself and closely linked to the National Guard.

However, it is difficult to gauge the concrete results of the ACM in terms of coverage and impact. What does seem clear is that the scope and activities of the ACM increased over time, particularly after 1970 when rural unrest spread. For example, in 1966, the ACM gave out food to 16,930 people and Christmas presents to 26,000 children. Five years later, in 1971, this program had expanded to the dispensing of 86,000 Christmas presents, 10,000 pairs of shoes, over 8,000 medical prescriptions, 10,000 pounds of used clothes, 676 tooth extractions and assorted other assistance, in addition to the building of basketball courts, schools, and roads in "hundreds" of communities. Also noticeable is the extension of ACM outreach programs into urban areas (especially San Salvador) after 1975, as the activities of Left-wing trade unions and student groups multiplied and gained momentum.

As opposition increased, the armed forces began to strengthen and expand their military and paramilitary structures. By 1974 they were organizing reserve battalions, which were attached to the various infantry brigades and military posts. Each battalion numbered from 2–3,000 men. In addition, a training school for commandos was set up in the department of Morazán. New equipment and weapons were purchased, not—as the defense minister rather cryptically put it—to make war, but to keep the armed forces in a state of readiness to defend the nation's interests. Finally, the ranks of the *escoltas militares* were expanded due to, in the words of the Minister of Defense, the "increase in population," but, more likely, to the apparent upsurge in peasant "rebellions," as expressed by land seizures, demonstrations, and union-organizing.

What the armed forces, as well as the military presidents—from Fidel Sánchez Hernández (1967–1972) through Arturo Armando Molina (1972–1977) to Carlos Humberto Romero (1977–1979)—were facing was a new enemy: growing numbers of people who (1) were being displaced from their land by the expansion of export agriculture, (2) were being expelled from Honduras (both before and after the disastrous war of 1969), and (3) were being organized by a host of new social actors, ranging from priests to students to peasant leaders. The voices of dissent that came out of these masses, however, had no effective, institutionalized channels of expression because the political opening initiated by President Rivera in the early 1960s was again closed during the early 1970s. The most blatant example of this occurred in 1972, when Colonel Molina was elected via blatant fraud against a coalition of Christian Democrats, Social Democrats, and Communists. Subsequent elections for the legislature and the presidency were either boycotted by the opposition or blatantly rigged by the "official" party, the Partido de Conciliación Nacional (PCN), direct offspring of the PRUD.

Although Colonel Molina's government did try to institute a program of mild land reform (the so-called *transformación agraria*) in 1976, conservative landowning interests scuttled the plan, forcing such a complete reversal that they were even able to impose upon the country the last of the military presidents, General Romero, whose two years in office were characterized by measures of extreme repression. As a result, the solution chosen took the High Command down the path of military confrontation, one for which it was not really prepared. During the 1960s and early 1970s military spending, as a percentage of the total government budget, had declined. Not even the war against Honduras had served to increase the military budget to any significant degree in the years immediately following. And, if they are to be believed, the figures on recruitment and training of new soldiers for the regular army were even lower than in the 1950s: 2,247 for July 1976–June 1977.

One possible explanation for this relatively low level of military recruitment might have to do with declining confidence in the reliability of the regular army as a buffer against popular insurrection. While budget figures give only part of the picture, it is worth noting that the amount spent on all the security forces (which, after 1960, included the Treasury Police) began to increase as a percentage of total military spending. This had resulted in an overall increase in the numbers of National Guard, National Police, and Treasury Police even before fighting broke out in 1981.

During the 1970s the military's control of the rural areas, so carefully managed ever since the peasant insurrection of 1932, began to break down. The explanation is quite simple: the countryside had changed but the military had not. The people who lived and worked in the rural areas (peasants, squatters, migrant workers) were subjected to increased hardship, as land and opportunities for work became ever more scarce. Furthermore, the people in the rural areas were acutely aware of their situation and increasingly willing to take direct action. The military, in its turn, continued to view the rural population as it had in the 1940s and 1950s: a mass of gullible and/or fearful peasants who would provide the raw material from which the military could derive, and mold, a never-ending supply of obedient soldiers and reservists, and through whom they could control the rest. This solution made sense as long as El Salvador was able to "export" its agrarian problem to other areas, that is, as long as the pressure in rural areas could be managed or contained. When the Honduran safety valve, which for decades had siphoned off hundreds of thousands of "excess" rural population, no longer functioned, the military tried its hand at land reform, in 1976. When that failed, due to a combination of limited popular support and strong opposition from within the military itself, the only alternative was to step up repression. The country seemed to have come full circle: in 1979 the country had returned to its same position as in 1932.

The military then attempted, one last time, to undertake the "solution" it had employed in 1944, 1948, and 1960–61: namely, an institutional coup d'état which would bring to the fore a new generation of army officers claiming to represent a clean break with the past. The proclamation that they issued (on 15 October 1979) contained a sweeping indictment of the previous military government and attempted to project a new line of military thinking, one which invoked human rights, political pluralism, electoral freedom, and land reform. There was only one reference to the historic role of the armed forces in the rural areas: ORDEN was to be abolished, but not the *patrullas cantonales*, not the obligatory military service, and not civic action. Furthermore, the proclamation said nothing about democratizing civil-military relations nor reducing the military's well-entrenched position in the state.

Although the military had relied on civilian partners to help it maintain its political dominance throughout the pre-1979 period, it never seriously considered handing formal power over to a civilian president. This reflected not only a basic mistrust of civilian politicians, but also a conviction that the armed forces made up the only institution capable of defending the state and preserving internal order. Thus, while the military was willing to enter into an alliance with different political and social forces, its overriding commitment was to defense of the state and its own core interests.

Even if the civilian-military junta that emerged out of the coup (15 October 1979) had lasted for a period of years with its original members in place, even if the incipient guerrilla forces and the Left in general had made their peace with the new government and supported its fundamental reforms, the issue of the role of the armed forces would still have remained a bone of contention. Not even the most reform-minded of officers were willing to contemplate, much less countenance, the prospect of civil control over the military nor an end to its network of social control in the rural areas. The military could initiate land reform and nationalize the banks (as it did in 1980), it could enter into alliances with its erstwhile political enemies (the Christian Democrats), and it could—later on—support the Right-wing government of the Alianza Republicana Nacional (ARENA), but it could not consider separating itself from its rural power base. A pervasive network of social control in the rural areas was an essential element of the prevailing economic model, since it guaranteed the agro-export oligarchy continued access to land and labor. In the urban areas, generally viewed as less important than rural areas until recently, autonomous political institutions were allowed to evolve, albeit within a restricted political space. However, in the countryside there was no place for labor organizing, permanent political party structures, demonstrations of grievances, or even cooperative ventures. There was only room for the *patrullas cantonales*, the local *comandantes*, the National Guard, ORDEN, and Acción Cívica Militar. All else was off limits, including democracy.

Civil-Military Relations during the 1980s

Paradoxically, during the 1980s, at the very time that a military-dominated junta was transferring formal power to a civilian president, the military was successfully consolidating its presence in the state, expanding its network of control in the countryside, and maintaining its institutional autonomy.

In the wake of the October 1979 coup, very limited progress was made in reducing the military's penetration of the state. Given the intensification of the armed conflict, the military viewed its control over key public institutions as essential to ensuring the state's survival. Civilians did replace military officers at the helm of the national waterworks (Administración Nacional de Acueductos y Agua, or ANDA) and the state industrial development corporation (Instituto Salvadoreño de Fomento Industrial, or INSAFI), and occupied the bulk of cabinet portfolios, including the Ministry of Interior. However, this did not represent a radical departure from the past; traditionally, civilians had held most of the positions in the cabinet. Moreover, the first three civil-military juntas were dominated by military members, and most of the important autonomous institutions remained under the direction of military officers.

During both the Magaña (1982–84) and Duarte (1984–89) governments, there was a more concerted effort to appoint civilians to replace military officers in important public positions, but again results were mixed. Both presidents appointed civilians as Ministers of Interior and replaced those military officers serving as ambassadors. Duarte tried to bring the Instituto Salvadoreño de Transformación Agraria (ISTA) under civilian control, and he created the new Vice-Ministry of Public Security in an attempt to separate the security forces from military control (to be discussed below). What little progress was made, however, was reversed during the subsequent Cristiani government. Military officers once again assumed direction of the Comisión Ejecutiva Portuaria Autónoma (CEPA), as the port authority was known, as well as of ANDA (directed by civilians during the Duarte government); and a retired military officer was appointed Minister of Interior, a post that had been occupied by a civilian since 1979.

Besides administering key state institutions, the military retained an array of prerogatives throughout the 1980s. It maintained control of the security forces and intelligence agencies; the military court system continued to cover large areas of civil society, and the domain where military personnel could be tried in civil courts remained very narrow; the executive exercised little control over military promotions or the military budget; legislative oversight was nonexistent since the military seldom provided the legislature with detailed information regarding the budget or other defense matters; and the military played a leading role in conducting the war, again with little executive oversight.

Many of these prerogatives were enshrined in the 1983 Constitution which, in line with previous ones, accorded the armed forces primary responsibility for (1) ensuring the national defense and internal law and order; (2) guaranteeing compliance with the Constitution and other laws; and (3) defending the "democratic" system of government, including universal suffrage. As one officer put it, civilian politicians "handed over the keys of the nursery to the military." This is not surprising given that the state's very existence had come to depend on the armed forces.

Beyond attending to responsibilities assigned by the Constitution, the military expanded its functions during the 1980s through the nation's counterinsurgency program, which contained political, economic, social, and psychological elements as well as military ones. Among its many aspects was the civic-action project known as "Unidos para Reconstruir," initiated in 1986. Because it was administered directly by the military and implemented in all 14 departments, civilian leadership was seriously eclipsed at both the departmental and local levels. Not only did the military administer and execute the counterinsurgency program, but it also played a decisive role in its formulation.

The goal of the counterinsurgency program, like previous civic-action programs, was to defend, and enhance, social control of the countryside. Besides relying on traditional mechanisms of control, such as the *patrullas cantonales,* the military—under U.S. guidance—set up a system of civil defense units throughout the country. Although the program did not fulfill the expectations of its U.S. sponsors, it did lead to a tightening of control in the rural areas.

Though the military no longer governed directly, one could argue that its political role expanded nonetheless, this time in response to demands of the war. This situation points up the paradoxical nature of El Salvador's transition from military rule. Although one might characterize the post-1979 period as one of transition from authoritarian rule, yet—at least until the peace accords were signed—it in no way constituted a transition toward democracy since, on balance, the military actually consolidated its presence in the state.

Not only did the civil war facilitate an expanded political role for the military, but it also helped to shape the military's perception of itself and of political society generally. Throughout this period, the officer corps continued to regard the armed forces as the only national institution able to defend the state and guarantee public order. This view, combined with a perception that civil society was weak and ineffective, was only reinforced by the habit of civilian politicians to turn to the military for rescue in crisis situations. Such a situation occurred in April 1982 when the Constituent Assembly reached a political stalemate in selecting a civilian president. When it appeared likely that Roberto D'Aubuisson would be named provisional president, the Christian Democrats chose to boycott the proceedings, leading the military High Command to impose (with U.S. encouragement) a more "acceptable" alternative: the independent Alvaro Magaña.

Another such situation arose during the kidnapping of President Duarte's daughter, in September 1985. The president's decision to accede to the FMLN demand that 22 political prisoners, including *Comandante* Nidia Díaz, be released was opposed by several high-ranking officers who believed such concessions only undermined the government's credibility and projected an image of weakness and vulnerability. Both incidents reinforced the notion that civilian politicians put personal and/or partisan interests before the national interest, and that the military was the only institution genuinely concerned with serving the nation.

Besides helping to consolidate the military's position and confirm its distrust of civilians, the civil war enabled the military to maintain its institutional autonomy vis-à-vis the state and society. During the course of the 1980s, the military became much less dependent upon the oligarchy and much more autonomous as an institution with its own set of interests. This distancing of the Salvadoran armed forces from the country's oligarchy began with the decision of the former to support the land reform program initiated in early 1980. However, additional considerations, emerging over time, were also at work. First, military officers increasingly came to view the oligarchy as disloyal and only concerned with its own profit. The military looked on angrily as wealthy oligarchs withdrew their capital from the country and sent their sons and daughters abroad when collapse seemed imminent. Still later, during the peace negotiations, officers again felt betrayed by the oligarchy with a sense that the armed forces had been singled out as a scapegoat after having defended the system from "Communist aggression." On the other hand, certain sectors of the oligarchy came to view the military as a dangerous competitor in the economic realm. They bristled at the military's unfair advantages—such as not having to pay duties on imports—and the involvement of certain officers in the kidnappings of prominent businesspeople. As the negotiations went on, that sector of the oligarchy who had become committed to the need for a negotiated settlement also began to view the military as a bargaining chip which could be used, if not sacrificed, in exchange for concessions on socioeconomic issues. Thus, the convergence of interests between the military and its supporters within the oligarchy was severely tested during the 1980s. As the military progressively developed its own separate set of priorities, it became more concerned with protecting its core interests than with defending the oligarchy at all costs.

Another factor that contributed to the military's developing autonomy during the 1980s was a series of political pacts negotiated between the High Command and political leaders. On the one hand, the pacts helped to establish the ground rules of civil-military relations; on the other, they confirmed the political role of the military and assured its institutional autonomy vis-à-vis the civilian political leadership. Furthermore, the exclusive nature of these pacts contributed little to forging the consensus necessary for a genuine democratic transition.

The first such pact that affected civil-military relations in a significant way was the founding document of the second junta, drawn up in January 1980. Throughout November-December 1979 the growing mobilization of popular organizations had caused the military High Command to adopt, without authorization from the civilian-military junta, increasingly brutal methods of repression. Confronted by escalating violence, the civilian members of the junta and cabinet presented (28 December 1979) the military High Command with an ultimatum: either the military submit to the authority of the junta or the civilian members would resign. The demands included that the Consejo Permanente de la Fuerza Armada (COPEFA) replace the Minister of Defense as the intermediary between the armed forces and the junta; that COPEFA recognize the junta's authority as Commander in Chief of the armed forces; and that restrictions be placed on the ability of the security forces to intervene in labor disputes, subject to specific procedures established by a junta-appointed commission.

On 1 January 1980, COPEFA rejected the demands out of hand. COPEFA stated that, though it recognized the authority of the junta, it could not acquiesce in establishing mechanisms which might "politicize" the military institution. Having seriously overestimated the weight of progressive officers within the military, civilian members of the government had no choice but to resign, leaving the government with only the two military members of the junta, Adolfo Arnoldo Majano and Abdul Gutiérrez, and the Minister of Defense, José Guillermo García.

Upon collapse of the first junta, the military was again forced to look for civilian partners with whom to maintain its political dominance. The logical alternative was the Partido Demócrata Cristiano (PDC) , whose reformist credentials and history of opposition to the military dictatorship lent it some credibility both at home and abroad. In the pact of January 1980 which followed and made public the incorporation of the PDC into the junta, the armed forces agreed to certain PDC demands: (1) to draw up a timetable for carrying out the socioeconomic reforms promised by the first junta, (2) to exclude representatives of the private sector from the cabinet, and (3) to support amendments to the Constitution. Nevertheless, in exchange for progress on the reforms, the PDC accepted the status quo ante regarding civil-military relations. The best it could do was to elicit a vague promise by the military to respect human rights and to support a democratic transition. It is clear that although conservative officers were willing to compromise on the socioeconomic reforms, they were unwilling to accept what they considered a civilian intrusion into the military's internal practices and procedures. By not insisting on new mechanisms to enhance the junta's authority over the armed forces, the PDC had helped ensure the military's continuing domination of the junta.

A second important pact that confirmed the autonomy of the military came in the form of a secret agreement between President-elect Duarte and Minister of Defense Eugenio Vides Casanova, initiated on the eve of Duarte's inauguration in June 1984. The agreement served to reassure both the High Command and the government-elect that their vital interests would be protected. It also helped to formalize a workable relationship between the Duarte government and the High Command, which both considered essential to the war effort.

In general terms, Duarte was concerned that the High Command allow his government to carry out its program. In return, Duarte promised to respect the military's institutional autonomy. For example, regarding Duarte's desire to improve the regime's human rights record, Vides Casanova agreed to the creation of a new Vice-Ministry of Public Security. The idea was to separate the security forces from the military and to bring them under more direct civilian control. The agreement also committed the military to place special emphasis on respecting human rights in all of its training programs. In exchange, Duarte agreed not to prosecute military officials for past human rights abuses, promising, instead, to start with a "clean slate." The agreement also recognized the right of the new government to seek a negotiated settlement to the conflict while, at the same time, affirming the duty of the military to maintain a permanent military offensive aimed at defeating the enemy.

On the issue of institutional autonomy, Duarte promised to defend the unity and institutional integrity of the armed forces, accepting the current composition of the High Command and agreeing to work with Vides Casanova regarding the transfer of other officials. The agreement also accorded the military a leading role in the war effort and confirmed the Defense Minister's role of safeguarding "national interests, institutional interests, and government interests." Finally, Duarte accepted the High Command's insistence that any decisions affecting the military institution be implemented by the institution itself and not imposed by others.

Despite the contributions that pacts can make in furthering a transition from authoritarian rule, their negative consequences are well known. Given the small number of participants involved, pacts are inherently undemocratic. They also tend to freeze into place the existing power structure and limit the possibilities for more far-reaching socioeconomic change. Nevertheless, most observers argue that, in terms of democratic consolidation, the benefits outweigh the costs.

What such observers may fail to see, however, is that pacts can present major impediments to establishment and consolidation of democratic rule. In El Salvador, pacts helped to give a more precise definition to the relationship between the civilian political leadership and the military's High Command. By reassuring both that their vital interests would not be threatened, the agreements minimized the potential for conflict. While this did, indeed, pave the way toward a more harmonious relationship between civilian leaders and the military, at the same time, the pacts worked to preserve and reinforce the dominant position of the military in the state, as well as its institutional autonomy. Consequently, even though the armed forces tolerated a limited political opening, including election of civilian leaders, they retained their right, and ability, to intervene in what they deemed to be undesirable situations. Their continuing control of the state was a formidable obstacle to democratizing civil-military relations.

One last aspect to consider is the impact of military assistance by the United States during this period. U.S. military assistance and training expanded dramatically after 1980 and was a major factor in the massive buildup and expansion of the Salvadoran armed forces, modernization of their arsenal, and dramatic improvement in their warfighting capabilities. Although U.S. aid was adequate to prevent a guerrilla victory, it was not sufficient to assure total military victory. It also meant that, in the wake of the war, efforts to reduce the size of the military and its drain on the national budget would be difficult.

Besides advancing El Salvador's fighting capabilities, United States' assistance was designed to promote democratic professionalism within that country's armed forces. Although it is unclear what degree of importance U.S. officials attached to this mission, it is clear that its progress was negligible. This was reflected in the military's continuing involvement in human rights abuses and in the pervasiveness of corruption within the institution. Moreover, the *tanda* system, about which U.S. officials complained bitterly, remained intact. Under the *tanda* system:

> . . . each graduating class, or *tanda*, from the military academy moves up the ranks together, regardless of ability. Members of the same *tanda* establish deep bonds of loyalty and reciprocity toward

each other—often serving as godfathers to one another's children—
and help shield fellow members from prosecution or punishment
. . . officers are not held accountable for their actions, no matter
how egregious they may be; human rights abuses therefore go un-
punished, military incompetence is tolerated, and corruption runs
rampant.

Loyalty to one's *tanda* often takes priority over one's loyalty to
the institution. Not surprisingly, throughout the 1980s there were
numerous examples of officers protecting fellow *tanda* members im-
plicated in human rights abuses or other crimes despite the potential
damage to the credibility of the institution as a whole.

Decisions regarding promotions and key appointments also continued to be based on *tanda* loyalties and ties of *compadrazgo* rather
than on merit. Minister of Defense Vides Casanova's appointment of
then-Colonel René Emilio Ponce as Chief of Staff is a case in point.
Taking advantage of President Duarte's illness during the latter half
of 1988, Vides Casanova sought to consolidate his power by eliminating his rivals from the High Command. Instead of filling key positions with officials from the *tandas* next in line, Vides drew on the
Tandona (the "big class" of 1966), with whom he had developed a
special relationship since the *Tandona*'s days at the military academy. The upshot was that he skipped over two *tandas* to move up his
unconditional supporters from the *Tandona*.

The lack of progress in professionalizing the armed forces also
was reflected in the absence of a clear chain of command within the
military. Authority continued to be greatly decentralized amongst
brigade commanders, who acted as warlords in the departments under their control. An example of this flawed command structure was
the difficulty in implementing a national basic training program, to
be located at the facilities of CEMFA (Centro de Entrenamiento de la
Fuerza Armada) in La Unión. Despite the fact that the Minister of
Defense issued an *orden general* (general order) to the effect, the
plan was resisted by departmental brigade commanders. By relinquishing their recruits to the national basic training center, brigade
commanders would have lost access to an important source of corruption: funds allocated for recruits' salaries, food, and uniforms.

In short, U.S. military assistance made little headway in
professionalizing the Salvadoran armed forces, let alone fostering
democratic professionalism. This, combined with the legacy of some
60 years of military domination in the political sphere, presented serious obstacles to transforming civil-military relations in the aftermath of the peace accords.

The Military after the Accords

The negotiations, mediated by the United Nations, which began in Spring 1990 between the government of El Salvador and the FMLN, culminating in the peace accords of 16 January 1992, constituted a decisive step toward a genuine process of democratization. The agreement succeeded in forging a minimum consensus between the principal actors in the conflict regarding the basic framework of the new political "game." Our concern here is (1) the way in which the accords affect the armed forces, and (2) the opportunities they create for transforming civil-military relations.

On paper, the peace accords go a long way in reducing the military's institutional prerogatives. Under the terms of the accords and the constitutional reforms agreed to in April 1991, the role and doctrine of the armed forces are completely redefined. The military's primary responsibility is national defense. Its role in public security is limited to situations of national emergency and then only under strict executive control. The armed forces' doctrine is redefined to stress the preeminence of human dignity and democratic values, respect for human rights, and subordination to the constitutional authorities.

Besides ending the military's role in public security, the accords call for the dissolution of the security forces and the creation of a new national civilian police force under executive control. Further, the military-controlled intelligence agency is to be dissolved and a new one set up under direct civilian control. The armed forces' educational system is to be revamped, incorporating into its training programs the new constitutional mission and doctrine. A new academic council for the military school, made up of civilians and military, will be charged with overseeing curriculum, admissions procedures, and faculty appointments.

The accords also call for purging the officer corps, to be carried out under the recommendations of a special Ad Hoc Commission, made up of three prominent Salvadorans. The size of the armed forces is to be reduced to approximately 31,000, and includes dissolution of the specialized combat battalions and civil defense units.

Implementation of the accords affecting the armed forces proved to be a difficult process. Initial problems arose concerning the failure of the military to dismantle the security forces. The government announced the dissolution of the National Guard and Treasury Police on 2 March 1992. However, instead of being dissolved, the two security forces were simply renamed and reincorporated, structurally intact, into the army. Both remained in their original barracks. After repeated protests by the FMLN, United Nations Envoy Marrick Goulding served as mediator of talks in which he negotiated an agreement to dissolve the security forces entirely by 28 June.

Subsequent problems centered on recommendations of the Ad Hoc Commission, which had been set up to evaluate, and purge, the officer corps. Beginning in May 1992, the Commission evaluated the records of 232 officers, or about 10 percent of the total officer corps. On 23 September (1992), the Commission presented its recommendations to the UN Secretary-General and to President Cristiani. The report, whose contents were never made public, called for the dismissal or transfer of 102 officers, including the Minister and Vice-Minister of Defense, and most of the generals and colonels. According to the timetable outlined in the accords, President Cristiani had until 22 November (1992) to implement the Commission's recommendations.

However, fierce resistance by members of the High Command prompted Cristiani to announce (in late October) that he would postpone acting on the Commission's recommendations until after the FMLN had demobilized completely. Mediation efforts by UN Envoys Marrick Goulding and Alvaro de Soto then resulted in a new agreement, whereby the Commission's recommendations would be "incorporated into the year-end 'general orders' of armed forces promotions and retirements to be announced on November 30 and December 31," scheduled to take effect by 6 January 1993. Nevertheless, early in January 1993, UN Secretary-General Boutros-Ghali informed the Security Council that President Cristiani had failed to remove 15 high-ranking officers named in the Commission's report. Cristiani subsequently announced that he would defer taking action against 8 officers until the end of his presidential term.

The impasse was finally broken in March (1993) with the release of the long-awaited report by the United Nations Truth Commission. Unlike the earlier report of the Ad Hoc Commission, which was not published, the Truth Commission findings described, in great detail, the involvement of 40 military officers (including the Minister and Vice-Minister of Defense) in some of the most heinous human rights abuses committed during the civil war. Days before the report was made public, Salvadoran Defense Minister General René Emilio Ponce announced his resignation. Soon after, the Vice-Minister of Defense, General Juan Orlando Zepeda, announced that he was retiring from the armed forces. The fallout from the report, combined with pressure by the United Nations and the Clinton administration, prompted

Cristiani to inform the Secretary-General (in late March 1993) of his decision to remove the remaining officers by the end of June 1993. Although the Minister and Vice-Minister of Defense, along with the rest of the High Command, stepped down on 30 June, the officers remained on availability status and were not slated for retirement until the end of 1993. In this way, the officers were able to retire with honors and with their pensions intact.

Without doubt, significant progress was made in circumscribing the military's institutional prerogatives. Nevertheless, the accords failed to address adequately several important areas in which the military retained political influence. First of all, there was no mention of the military's administration of key state institutions. These included such entities as the Administración Nacional de Telecomunicaciones (ANTEL), the Administración Nacional de Acueductos y Agua (ANDA), the Comisión Ejecutiva Portuaria Autónoma (CEPA), the General Directorate of Land Transport, the General Directorate of Statistics and Census, Customs, Civil Aeronautics, and the Postal Service.

Secondly, the accords did not make sufficient provision for civilian oversight of the military as an institution. For example, the creation of an academic council for the military academy did not apply to subsequent training programs, which apparently were not subject to civilian oversight. Also, the accords did not call for the appointment of a civilian as Minister of Defense, a key element in ensuring civilian supremacy. Finally, while the accords referred to the need to enhance legislative oversight of the military, no specifics were provided regarding how this might be accomplished.

In the wake of the accords, the military showed little willingness to subordinate itself to civilian control. For example, the Ministry of Defense formulated the proposed military service law without any input from civilian politicians. Though the proposed law was debated in the Legislative Assembly, there was no significant modification. Furthermore, General Vargas, considered one of the more enlightened officers in the High Command, told one of the authors that he thought it highly unlikely that the military budget would be debated in any detail in the near future. He argued that El Salvador has no tradition of disclosure and debate of the military budget and that civilian politicians have no experience in military matters. Another officer, Colonel Corado Figueroa, who was even more categorical in his comments, could see no logic in the concept of legislative oversight of the military budget, claiming that civilian politicians (whom he referred to as "subversives") could not be trusted with military secrets.

Neither could Corado envision the possibility of a civilian serving as defense minister, arguing that the public itself would oppose such a move since "a civilian would project an image of lack of solidarity" with the military institution, thereby "weakening the armed forces." General Vargas, on the other hand, viewed the possibility that a civilian might serve as defense minister as "difficult," on the grounds that civilians lack the expertise and "political education" needed for that post, adding that any civilian defense minister "would have to be respectful of the military institution." (Corado was appointed Minister of Defense in June 1993.)

The military's continuing efforts to maintain its institutional autonomy reflect the notion, deeply held, that civilian politicians have no right to intervene in internal military affairs. One high-ranking officer stated in an interview that, of all the conditions stipulated in the peace accords, the most unpalatable was that of creating an academic council to oversee the military academy. He considered civilian representation on the council as constituting "blatant meddling" in the military's affairs. To most civilian politicians, the new academic council does not challenge the institutional autonomy of the military to any significant degree. However, top officers apparently consider continued control of the military academy to be a vital interest.

Finally, the accords did not go far enough in dismantling the paramilitary network in the countryside. With dissolution of the Guardia Nacional and disarming of civil defense units and *patrullas cantonales*, maintaining control over its traditional rural clientele will become more difficult. Nevertheless, in addition to its civic action programs, the military service law guarantees the military an ongoing presence in rural areas, permitting it to establish recruiting centers throughout the country and to maintain a large reserve system as in the past. These recruiting centers, in combination with its civic action programs, will enable the military to continue exercising control over the rural population and to influence the electoral process directly.*

*For example, during the March 1994 elections, troop contingents armed with heavy-caliber machine guns, grenade launchers, and mortars were highly visible along the highways in Chalatenango, San Miguel, and Morazán. While it is impossible to tell what impact the military's presence had on individual voters, it may have served to reinforce the climate of fear in areas most affected by the war. Also, it may have underscored ARENA's dominant campaign theme that a vote for the FMLN was a vote for a return to violence and destruction.

Because of the likelihood that the military will resist direct challenges to what it considers basic, or core, interests, the transformation of civil-military relations will entail more than simply reducing the military's prerogatives. As [Alfred] Stepan points out, achieving more effective civilian control encompasses a multiplicity of tasks in which civil society, political society, and the state all have a role to play.

First, in regard to civil society, universities and research institutes have important contributions to make. Ongoing systematic study of the military is essential in developing new strategies to transform civil-military relations. By dedicating some of their resources to researching the military, universities and research institutes can help legislators to improve, and enhance, their oversight capabilities as well as help to educate the public on their best interests in this area.

In El Salvador, for obvious reasons, academics have been unwilling to study the military in a systematic fashion. Not surprisingly, there are few civilians with expertise in military affairs. Although such research may not have been feasible in the past, today's changed political landscape may offer new opportunities for researching such a delicate topic. Raising public awareness and sharing their expertise with popular organizations and political parties are ways in which academics can contribute to the development of a *política militar*. Public organizations can also educate their membership about the various dimensions of the military problem.

There are some encouraging signs. Throughout the 1970s and 1980s civil society did become more assertive despite the enormous obstacles. Although the "space" available for autonomous social organization and mobilization was extremely limited by state repression, popular organizations aggressively challenged the military's domination of civil society. This was reflected in the significant growth of peasant organizations and trade unions, and in the appearance of new organizations at the grassroots, such as women's movements, the *comunidades eclesiales de base* movement, and neighborhood associations. In the future, popular organizations should be able to find new opportunities to organize and serve their constituencies, thus lending impetus to the efforts of civil society to mount an effective challenge to the military's traditional political dominance.

Second, it is in the interests of the political society to devise a clear strategy to enhance the legislature's oversight capacity. If the military is to be made accountable to elected officials, at the very least legislators will need access to the details of the military budget. Moreover, to be able to debate the military budget in an intelligent manner (when and if budget details are disclosed), legislators need to develop expertise in military affairs. Whether this expertise comes as the result of establishing a permanent legislative committee for military affairs, as recommended by the Truth Commission, or by some other means, is less important than not having to rely solely on military officers for expertise. By developing such expertise independently, political parties will be in a better position to contribute to development of a *política militar*. Currently, none of the parties has made much progress in this regard; rather, most continue to hold a very short-term vision of civil-military relations, with little thought of how these might be transformed over the long run.

Besides reducing some of the military's prerogatives, the executive branch of government can provide essential leadership in formulating an alternative mission for the military and promoting democratic professionalism. One possibility might be to convoke a dialogue, open to all political and social groups, to take up and discuss the proper role of the military. Besides bringing civilian attention to bear on the urgency of formulating a national *política militar*, such a dialogue also might persuade officers of the benefits of fostering democratic professionalism within the armed forces.

Another element in convincing officers of the benefits of democratic professionalism would be to dispel the deep-rooted notion that civilian politicians are self-serving and ineffective. As numerous scholars have noted, government ineffectiveness is likely to provoke the military into assuming a more political role. Given that the peace accords do not address satisfactorily the structural roots of the conflict, further delay in implementing long-awaited socioeconomic change might prove costly. If the country is unable to lay the socioeconomic foundations of a democracy, it could soon find itself faced with a crisis of governability and direct intervention by the armed forces. To avert such a crisis from arising, it is essential to undertake a process of *concertación* (consensus-building) whereby new political mechanisms can be created which allow for the real possibility of achieving structural transformation.

Conclusion

The prospects for democratizing civil-military relations are mixed. If the peace accords are fully implemented, the military's realm of action will be significantly circumscribed. Nevertheless, the military will still remain large by Central American standards and will retain much of its institutional autonomy intact, at least for the near future.

On the positive side, there is a growing antimilitarist sentiment in El Salvador. Even certain sectors of the oligarchy express increasing concern regarding the liability of supporting a large, well-equipped military without a mission. Besides the continuing drain on the budget which this represents, businesspeople also worry about the possible upsurge in kidnappings and other crimes as increasing numbers of former members of the military are demobilized. This antimilitarist sentiment is likely to grow in the wake of the Truth Commission's findings.

It is possible to impose change on the military from the outside. However, unless some of the impetus for change originates from within the military as well, it is unlikely that such change will have a lasting impact. There are few indications that the military's perception of either its role in society or of civilian politicians will change significantly in the short term. On the contrary, in the wake of the accords, high-ranking officers continued to view the military as the only social institution that cherishes the nation's basic interests at heart. Colonel José Humberto Corado Figueroa, Chief of Operations for the High Command (and Minister of Defense in 1995), told one of the authors that the armed forces have always defended the constitutional order and should never allow themselves to be subordinated to the "designs of our enemies." Contrary to the military's new constitutional role, General Mauricio Vargas, Deputy Chief of Staff, stated that the military continues to be "the nation's pillar of support, sustaining [its] institutions."

Top officers also continued to view the military as uniquely qualified to play a leading role in the process of national reconstruction. After the cease-fire went into effect, the military stepped up its civic activities in traditional areas, like repair of the infrastructure, public health, distribution of medicines and medical equipment, and literacy—and entered new areas like conservation and reforestation. On the one hand, the military's frenetic activities were a product of its lack of mission and fear of becoming irrelevant. On the other hand, these activities were both needed and fell well within the military's tradition of civic action and desire to maintain its traditional clientele in the countryside.

Also worrisome was President Cristiani's decision in July 1993 to call out the army to patrol the nation's highways and other high-crime areas where the new National Civilian Police (PNC) had not yet been deployed. Although the FMLN opposed Cristiani's decision to deploy the army, it found itself in a difficult position politically. In a March 1993 poll, crime was considered the number two concern by citizens; and in a September 1993 poll, 66.5 percent expressed support for the army's deployment.* Despite the apparent public support for the measure, it set a dangerous precedent. Instead of assigning sufficient resources to the PNC, the government turned to the army to perform what were in fact public security functions, thereby legitimizing the army's involvement in public security.†

It will not be easy for the armed forces to adapt to the "new era" in their country's history. El Salvador today has no external enemies that threaten its territorial integrity (the border dispute with Honduras has been settled definitively by the World Court); the danger to national security in the form of the Communist menace is gone; internal security will be in the hands of a new civilian police force; the civil war is over and the FMLN is becoming just one of a number of political parties; civil society is more vocal and committed to democratic practices; and the costs of national reconstruction require resources which ought not to be squandered on maintaining a huge military machine. Accepting this new reality will be hard to swallow, even in small doses, since it all points to a future armed force that is small, relatively inexpensive, and politically marginal—which has hardly been the case in the recent past.

*IUDOP, "La Comisión de la Verdad y el proceso electoral en la opinión pública salvadoreña," *Estudios Centroamericanos* (July–August 1993): 714–15; and *La Prensa Gráfica*, 1 October 1993.

†For an excellent analysis of the process of developing the PNC, see William Stanley, *Risking Failure: The Problems and Promise of the New Civilian Police in El Salvador* (Boston: HI/WOLA, 1993).

CHAPTER 26

Military Rule in Guatemala

Three generals ruled Guatemala during the 1970s: Carlos Arana Osorio (1970–74), Kjell Laugerud García (1974–78), and Romeo Lucas García (1978–82). Arana, they say, was the cunning old fox, Laugerud the insipid reformer, Lucas the psychotic tyrant. But these epithets, reducing waves of terror and intervals of reform to a leader's whims, mask the logic and continuity of the military regimes. After twelve years of their rule, a deep political crisis engulfed Guatemala's ruling class.

Capitalist modernization in the 1960s had segmented the bourgeoisie into agrarian, industrial, financial, and commercial fractions, the rhythm of their formation dictated from above by the needs of transnational capital. Conflicts between the MLN and the newer, more dynamic groups were often rancorous. But otherwise, cotton growers and bankers, traders and cattle ranchers, lived in relative harmony until the mid-1970s—as long, that is, as the economic boom lasted.

More important than the internecine disputes of the rich was the changing relationship between the armed forces and the bourgeoisie as a whole. Starting with Arana, the military developed its own economic interests. Brought into government initially as coercive protector of the established order, its senior officers used state power as a launching pad into agroexporting, industry, finance, and real estate. In the process, they became Guatemala's strongest political force. Internal cohesion promoted loyalty to the military caste and squashed any tendency within the ranks toward Peruvian-style reformism.

Military rule neutralized still further the ineffectual parties, and the armed forces filled the vacuum with their own quasi-party structures. A clique of high-ranking officers functioned as a central committee in all but name. The chief of staff held veto power over cabinet appointments.

Though the armed forces encroached on many key areas of the economy and the state through Mafia-like methods, the bourgeoisie was not unhappy with the alliance. The military's extreme laissez-faire approach to economic management, sustained growth rates, and a denial of political reforms provided a large-enough pie for most of the bourgeoisie, even if the military's slice grew dramatically. With blind complacency, the ruling class believed that its economic growth model was eternal. If the political system remained unchanged, the Garden of Eden would continue to bring forth its fruits in abundance.

Like the Garden of Eden, this was ultimately a fantasy world. The fires of class conflict were stoked by suffocating repression and the refusal to open up the political system. Rapid capitalist development brought profound changes in class structure, and agroexporting expansion fueled rural inequalities. Violence, escalating into naked terror during the periods 1966–68, 1970–73, and 1978–82, proved the only means of defending the status quo.

Increasingly, that terror hit the center of the political spectrum. Christian Democrats and social democrats were fair game for the death squads if they threatened to become more than an ineffectual adornment to the military version of pluralism. The fast-growing middle class—never allowed more than crumbs from a rich man's table—stood alienated from the military regime.

Pacification and Growth

Widespread distaste for the brutality of his counterinsurgency campaign of 1966–68 had put Arana in mothballs for a year as ambassador to Nicaragua. But after cementing strong ties to Nicaraguan dictator Anastasio Somoza, he was recalled to be the military's presidential candidate in the 1970 elections. Washington duly signaled its pleasure at Arana's election by dispatching $32.2 million in economic aid during 1972, the second highest annual figure ever to Guatemala.

Defeat of the guerrillas had done nothing to mitigate social tensions, and the bourgeoisie made it clear to Arana that pacification was top on their agenda. So did the U.S. corporations which had invested in Guatemala over the previous decade. With over $200 million in direct investments, the U.S. transnationals far outweighed national industrial capital—most industries employing more than fifty workers were foreign-owned.

By the time of Arana's inauguration, winds of change were blowing through the economy. The limited import-substitution industry of the common market period was grinding to a halt, and after the 1969 Honduras–El Salvador war, regional trade was in disarray. Richard Nixon's arrival at the White House in January 1969, backed by Cuban exiles and Sunbelt investors, paved the way for their invasion of Central America. Their instincts were well suited to rapid-profit speculation in tourism, real estate, and new forms of agribusiness export (fruit, flowers, vegetables, and, later, cardamon).

State power gave Arana—never the most fastidious of operators— a unique platform. Partnership with foreign capital, always attractive, became overtly criminal. Corruption was the norm in government. The 1973 budget granted Arana $12,000 a month in presidential "expenses" and allocated him $1.6 million more a year in confidential discretionary funds.

Though graft was nothing new, Arana raised it to new heights. What *was* qualitatively different was the systematic use of the state apparatus for the enrichment of the bloc in power—senior military officers and their closest civilian and bureaucratic allies.

Arana's abrasive style did not endear him to economic competitors, but Guatemala's first Five-Year Development Plan (1971–75) held out hopes for generating enough wealth to go around. Arana's authoritarian design to modernize the economy argued that not even the solid growth rates of the 1960s were adequate. A booming economy should aim for sustained annual growth rates of 7.8 percent through the 1970s.

The New Infrastructure
To provide energy and communications for the large, foreign-based corporations, and to open up the virgin farmlands of the north, large-scale infrastructure projects got under way by 1974. The second Development Plan (1976–79) gave even greater emphasis to such projects under Laugerud's direction. Three hydroelectric plants alone—Chixoy and Chulac in the highlands and Aguacapa on the south coast—cost well over $1 billion. Add to this a 1.2 billion-barrel-per-day oil pipeline from the Mexican border to the Caribbean, a small oil refinery in Baja Verapaz, a new Pacific port complex at San José, and a $1 billion national highway system, and the concept was awesome.

Chixoy was the pearl of the program. After an initial injection of $7.8 million from the Central American Economic Integration Bank in November 1974, international cash flowed into a project whose 300,000-kw generating capacity was the largest in the region. The World Bank supplied $145 million in 1975 and the Inter-American Development Bank $105 million in 1976—that bank's largest-ever single loan. U.S. representatives eagerly argued the case for both loans. . . .

As well as infrastructure, the transnational corporations gained financial benefits. Legislation put through in 1975 gave them a

100 percent tax exemption on profits for five years, and a one-year exemption from import taxes on machinery, plants, fuel, and spare parts.

By the end of the 1970s, 193 U.S. companies had taken advantage of the "favorable investment climate," 52 of them in agribusiness. Direct investment amounted to $260 million, the largest figure in Central America, and 33 of the world's top 100 firms had established local operations. This was in striking contrast to El Salvador, where only 6 [were] present.

The Army's Political Model

While Arana kept his bargain with foreign capital, he redrew the rules of the political game at home. Bodies began to appear along roadsides in a new wave of terror. In January 1971 alone, 483 people disappeared: not only nameless peasants and workers, to be hastily buried in graves marked XX, but even national figures—intellectuals, trade union officials, moderate party leaders—who had agreed to the military's political rule book. The gunning down in 1971 of Adolfo Mijango López, wheelchair-bound leader of the social democratic Revolutionary Democratic Union (URD), set the tone. Revolutionary opposition was clearly unacceptable, but the political process would now exclude anyone whose views were left of what the armed forces deemed the center.

The military took full control of the electoral machinery, narrowing down the spectrum of "tolerable" opponents. And by opening new agencies like the Army Bank to rationalize its economic holdings, the military showed that its ascent to riches under Arana was no short-term whim. Instead, it served notice that it intended to remain in power, shaping a system under which its economic and political status could never be challenged.

Down the Slippery Slope

No matter how disdainful of public opinion, any ruling group has to find ways of legitimizing its power. The creeping political crisis of the Guatemalan bourgeoisie in the 1970s lies in its failure to build and hold together a viable social base.

Arana, Laugerud, and Lucas each took office at the head of a differing right-wing coalition. Each promised change, Arana offering "Bread and Peace"; Laugerud, "gradual civic reform"; Lucas depicting himself as "the Center-Left Soldier." None could deliver. The ritual of elections, which only the Right could contest and only the

Army could win, degenerated into farce. Each new president burned his bridges to left, right, and center. The military continued to use a list of 72,000 proscribed opponents, drawn up in 1954, adding new names constantly.

General Kjell Laugerud García, a career officer of Norwegian extraction, took office in 1974. Arana had promised that he would use "all the might that goes with holding power" to ensure the election of his hand-picked successor. The previous year had brought an upsurge of working-class mobilization throughout Central America, and strikes in Guatemala by electricity, railroad, and communications workers, teachers, and students. The military high command was united in its belief that "the Army is the only force capable, morally and materially, of governing Guatemala."

By election time the military was sure that the Arana bloodbath had done its job. The economy was booming; the Army not only had ascended to state power, but had become the dominant economic fraction of the ruling class. The military puppet masters could now afford the illusion of electoral pluralism, knowing that they pulled the strings of centrist and reformist participation. However, the rules were clear: A civilian candidate would not be permitted to win.

Two parties dropped their original civilian nominees in favor of military officers. Against Laugerud's civilian-military coalition, the Revolutionary Party fielded Colonel Ernesto Paiz Novales, and a coalition of Christian Democrats and social democrats backed former Chief of Staff General Efraín Ríos Montt.

To Arana's horror, Ríos Montt took 45 percent of the vote, clearly unacceptable. An Army recount showed Laugerud with a healthy 5.5 percent winning margin. General Ríos Montt, though raging at "a regime of absolute illegality," was outmanned and outgunned. As a military man, he understood military realities. After a closed-door meeting with the incoming president—during which money allegedly changed hands—he accepted diplomatic exile in Madrid.

Secure in its fraudulent victory, the Army shored up its political defenses. Since 1970, Mario Sandoval Alarcón's MLN had been its main electoral ally. As president of Congress under Arana, Sandoval had fortified his position, channeling state funds to his paramilitary supporters. But the Army felt increasingly unhappy with the marriage. Economically, the rural oligarchy had been eclipsed by the modernizers; politically, the MLN's warrior-monk image was a liability. By 1974, Arana had broken much of the MLN's free-lance terror machine. Within the military, Laugerud chiseled away at MLN support in the officer corps.

Nonetheless, the fascists' organized power base was an undeniable asset, and Laugerud selected Sandoval as his vice president. In no time, the combative MLN leader was denouncing his boss because of a modest rural cooperative program designed to win peasant support. Anti-Communist bonds notwithstanding, Laugerud judged that new political alliances would be more expedient. The military's Democratic Institutional Party (PID) made overtures to the emasculated Revolutionary Party (PR) and the right wing of the Christian Democrats. The MLN's marginalization from affairs of state finally provoked a split in the party in 1975.

Also crucial to Laugerud's rightist alliance was the Organized Aranista Central (CAO). First conceived as an electoral machine in 1970, the CAO had taken on a life of its own as a personal vehicle for Arana's ambitions of long-term political power. Throughout, Arana remained the power behind Laugerud's throne. His CAO crony, Luis Alfonso López, was corruptly "elected" president of Congress in 1976 amid a bribery scandal, and, according to one Army officer, Arana "was in the *Casa Presidencial* almost every day." During the Laugerud administration, Arana used his influence to further extend his financial tentacles into meat packing, fisheries, timber, construction, vehicle importing, cement works, publishing, broadcasting, and breweries. . . .

Open the Door an Inch

Laugerud's attempt to stabilize military rule embraced a series of tactics. First, consolidate the PID-PR-CAO power axis, squeezing out the MLN. Then separate off the right wings of the Christian Democrats and social democrats, exposing what the generals insisted was a handful of "Communists directed, financed, and incited by the Cuban government." Opening some space for democratic activity, settling strikes by negotiation, and lowering the tenor of repression might win over key leadership of the labor unions and isolate the radical Left. Sustained economic growth, boosted by the post-1976 earthquake construction boom, gave the generals confidence to proceed with their plans.

Their confidence was ill founded, their reforms too little, too late. Inflation, a new phenomenon during 1973, was eroding workers' already meager living standards. The 1974 election fraud told the mass movement that even basic democratic freedoms could not be reclaimed within the framework imposed by the armed forces. Urban tensions erupted.

Evolution of Domestic Consumer Price Index (1961–81)

Year	(avg.) 1961–65	(avg.) 1966–70	1971	1972	1973	1974	1975
Inflation	0.1%	1.5%	-0.5%	0.5%	10.0%	16.0%	13.1%

Year	1976	1977	1978	1979	1980	1981	—
Inflation	10.7%	12.6%	7.9%	11.5%	12.0%	12.4%	—

Sources: United Nations Economic Survey of Latin America (1979); Inter-American Development Bank Annual Report (1981); Boletín Estadístico del Banco de Guatemala; This Week in Central America and Panama.

Union leaders and Army alike were taken aback by the sheer scale of an angry movement which, though moribund, now burst onto the streets. The funeral of a murdered activist could trigger a teeming protest by thousands chanting, "We don't want elections, we want revolution." Striking mine workers from the remote highland town of Ixahuacan found their 300-kilometer march to the capital in 1977 joined by 100,000 united peasant and worker sympathizers. A powerful National Committee of Trade Union Unity (CNUS) crystalized around a 1976 strike at the local Coca-Cola franchise, EGSA, and a devastating earthquake the same year, whose main impact hit urban slum dwellers and highland peasants.

This should not suggest that the entire mass movement became instant revolutionaries. True, the Christian Democrats and fellow reformist parties lost credibility by reaffirming electoral methods after 1974. But they and many of their working-class followers believed that the Laugerud opening, though limited, could be pushed. If not in time for the 1978 elections, a restoration of democracy could surely come by 1982.

Laugerud's reforms were too lukewarm to neutralize the Left, but enough to allow it some space in which to reorganize. As the mass movement swelled in size and confidence, its positions grew more radical. The National Workers' Federation (CNT), largest member of CNUS, severed its ties to the Christian Democratic Latin American Workers' Federation (CLAT). The militant new Committee of Peasant Unity (CUC) registered sweeping successes among south and coast plantation workers. After the earthquake, church groups working in the Indian highlands and foreign aid-financed urban slum projects became an explosive new ingredient in opposition to the regime. Even modest community demands—a new standpipe to the barrio, a drainage system, electric light—took on threatening political dimensions. And a revived guerrilla movement began to inflict stinging blows on the Army.

Slam It Shut Again

Under pressure from his right flank, Laugerud backtracked. Far from stabilizing the regime, his tactics had only succeeded in undermining it further. Real reforms were unacceptable to the agroexporting class, MLN supporters, and Army loyalists alike, and token reforms only opened a Pandora's box. Locked in the classic agrarian mentality of those whose products are shipped straight overseas with little regard for the demands of a local market, the bunker vision of the Right only hardened in response to the U.S. State Department's 1977 designation of Guatemala as a "gross and consistent violator of human rights."

By Lucas García's inauguration in 1978, the armed forces and the rest of the bourgeoisie faced starkly drawn options: thoroughgoing reforms or the full weight of state terrorism against all opponents. Unable to countenance the political repercussions of reform, the regime took the only recourse it knew. . . .

Lucas García: The Descent into Anarchy

Lucas came to power in March 1978 on a record low voter turnout. The MLN—real winners of another flagrantly fraudulent election—protested, but Arana's goon squads and the military high command intervened to uphold Lucas's election. Like Laugerud, Lucas was the protégé of ex-president Arana—reputedly because Arana saw him as the most unintelligent and pliable member of the high command.

Lucas showed some early base of support among the middle class, but in any organizational sense that support was extremely shallow. Since elections were a charade, the Democratic Institutional Party (PID) and the Revolutionary Party (PR), which formed the core of Lucas's electoral alliance, were not effective political instruments, but merely platforms for patronage and enrichment.

The centrist opposition parties were badly split. Opportunistic leaders wanted to gain a stake in the political process; other activists felt their middle-class base might still be brought in from the cold. Lucas shrewdly capitalized on their confusion. The military dangled the carrot of legal registration in front of the FUR [United Front of the Revolution], which obliged by tacitly endorsing Lucas's win and keeping aloof from the new, broad-based Democratic Front against Repression. Christian Democrats, now divided into feuding left and right wings, had spent the 1970s flirting with the idea of building a "centralist alliance" with the PID. Rebuffed in 1974, they nonetheless again fielded a military candidate in 1978, General Ricardo Peralta Méndez.

Lucas's vice presidential running mate was the experienced centrist, Francisco Villagrán Kramer, who had severed his earlier links to the reformist parties. Villagrán Kramer offered Lucas a last veneer of respectability and a last bridge to Washington. By now, Congress had suspended military aid to Guatemala. His own aim, the vice president told a U.S. reporter, was "to avoid a Custer's Last Stand in Guatemala." He was predictably labeled a Marxist by the MLN, and accused by his eventual successor, Colonel Oscar Mendoza Azurdia, of being "an agent of both the United States and the Soviet Union."

The MLN remained the single largest party, with twenty out of sixty-one deputies. But its estrangement from the military power center was complete. MLN decline was exemplified by the enforced choice of retired Colonel Enrique Peralta Azurdia as its presidential candidate. No serving Army officer would accept the albatross of an MLN nomination.

Death Wish?

The October 1978 bus-fare riots had dispelled any remnant hopes of reform under Lucas. His initial hesitation about whether to crush or accommodate the strike exasperated the fiercely right-wing police chief, Colonel Germán Chupina. The colonel, given to hiring out his Mobile Military Police as vigilantes to private businessmen, assigned police provocateurs to inflame the throngs, and thus justify blanket repression. The new Secret Anti-Communist Army, a death squad repeatedly linked to Chupina's office, issued a death list of forty prominent opposition figures, and set about the job of killing them. Terror escalated to unheard-of levels. Ten corpses a day appeared, hideously disfigured by torture, along the roadsides, in storm drains, under viaducts.

Hombres desconocidos (unknown men). Every Guatemalan knows the words; thousands have experienced their meaning. Those who knock on the door at dead of night and speed off in unmarked Cherokee station wagons, dragging away "Communists" whose mutilated bodies will later be left on public display.

The first death squad, the New Anti-Communist Organization, took up operations in 1960. And during the peak years of counter-insurgency (1966–68), the squads bloomed like poisonous flowers. They adopted flamboyant names—An Eye for an Eye, Purple Rose,

The Hawk of Justice. They mutilated their victims' faces and genitals and boasted of their exploits in apocalyptic communiqués. The New Anti-Communist Organization announced publicly that it would cut off the tongue and left hand of its enemies. Open publication of death lists and victims' photographs added to a national psychosis of terror.

In the countryside, security forces, private landowners, and MLN thugs used terror in ways which made one group indistinguishable from the others. Since military commissioners were authorized to bear arms such as machine guns (normally restricted to the Army), many farmers and businessmen simply took out credentials as commissioners to set up their own hit squads. In other cases, officers would use the death squads as enforcers for their private rackets and fiefdoms within the police force.

Fifteen years of this had provided the right climate for private enterprise to reap the harvest of economic growth. The violence was never concealed, especially in the years when the fascist MLN shared power. Even though the first mass disappearances and killings of the 1960s had been quickly tied to Army and national police headquarters and to La Aurora Air Force base, the Army continued to depict the death squads as a spontaneous "civic response" to the Antichrist of communism, a conscious stratagem to offer seemingly independent corroboration of its own harsh rule.

By the late 1970s any distinction between institutional terror—exercised by the state on behalf of the ruling class—and free-lance terror from extralegal groups of the bourgeoisie had blurred into meaninglessness. So had the pretense that death-squad killings were the result of fictitious encounters between "extreme Left" and "extreme Right." The war against communism, Arana argued, prefiguring a line which Argentine generals would later echo, was a dirty business. Innocent people would get hurt. A 1981 Amnesty International report laid to rest any remaining idea that the death squads were independent of the top echelons of the Army and security forces by tracing the chain of command all the way to Lucas's office.

The Psychosis of Terror

The major death squad of the Lucas period, the Secret Anti-Communist Army (ESA), faced a new target—an organized mass movement. The ESA's scale of operations was awesome: 311 peasant leaders killed during 1980, 400 University of San Carlos students and teachers butchered in four months.

Democratic Socialist Party leader Alberto Fuentes Mohr described the death squads' tactics: "Every single murder is of a key person—people in each sector or movement who have the ability to organize the population around a cause." It was his last interview; only days later, he was gunned down in the street. Within weeks, FUR leader Manuel Colom Argueta was also dead, his murder agreed on at a March 1979 meeting between senior Army officers and high-ranking representatives of the private sector.

A decade earlier, Regis Debray had written of the effects of the terror: "Administered in large enough doses over a long enough period, it has an anesthetic effect . . . the obscene becomes commonplace, the abnormal normal." By 1980 the obscenity was still a commonplace, but the anesthetic had worn off. A mass movement revived both in its psychology and its clandestine organization managed to survive the rampant terror. The exhaustion of state terror as an effective means of domination knocked another pin from under the fast-crumbling Lucas regime. . . .

The Garrison State

Since the 1970s the military's role had changed, overstepping its "normal limits" and invading spheres of activity customarily reserved for civil society or the civilian state apparatus. Overlap between the military's coercive role and its ownership of the key means of production severely distorted the function of the state.

The military caste has special privileges. Officers enjoy access to special stores where luxury consumer imports are sold at discount prices. Military entrepreneurs have moved into hotel and real estate speculation on the shores of beautiful Lake Atitlán, Guatemala's prime tourist attraction.

More worrisome than this new wealth is the machinery created for its acquisition and protection—an array of institutions fusing the armed forces with the state. Military men run forty-six semi-autonomous state institutions. Military-controlled agencies include a pension and investment fund—the Institute for Military Social Security (IPM) and the Army Bank. The IPM put up some of the capital for Arana's foundation of the Army Bank in 1972, but even more was siphoned out of public funds. A $5 million appropriation launched the bank, whose charter called for it to open credits for cattle raising, industry, and real estate development. Since then, it has become a financial monster with active capital of $119.2 million in 1981. In

1981, Lucas's Congress approved a further $20 million injection of state funds.

Together with the Bank of America, the Army Bank co-financed the luxury 800-unit Santa Rosita military housing project. IPM funds, in collaboration with the South African Trade and Project Management Service, financed the military-owned Cementos Guastatoya, infringing a long-agreed civilian sector monopoly over the lucrative cement industry. IPM money has also bought the Army a profitable, multistoried parking building in downtown Guatemala City.

This growing domination of the economy by those who wield state power is in no sense state capitalism: The overall trend remains toward the privatization of the economy. Rather, the military has chosen to own what it identifies—through economic self-interest and its particular concept of national security—as key areas of economic life. The profits from these enterprises find their way into the pockets of senior officers and into consolidating the military as an institution.

Fiddling while Guatemala Burns

. . . The Guatemalan military state has proved too voracious to even mediate *intra*-class disputes. The military, now an independent economic power, has used the political-economic levers at its command only for self-enrichment, not to maneuver a stable bourgeois consensus behind its rule. If coffee exporters asked for a tax break, for example, they were likely to be given a tax *increase*, to fatten state revenues for the military's pet projects.

When the effectiveness of terror and the sustained growth of the economy both evaporated under Lucas, previously masked tensions in the ranks of the private sector exploded. With recession sharpening capitalist competition for shrinking profit margins, the individual private sector chambers clamored for special treatment. They found instead that the military only insisted on being cut in on all the most profitable enterprises.

Businessmen excluded from the corridors of power began to mutter that Guatemala was being "Somozanized." The corrupt government bureaucracy—stuffed with self-seeking military officers and technocrats—showed neither inclination nor capacity for pulling the economy out of its nosedive. Plunder replaced planning. By 1981 the military and its immediate right-wing allies were isolated, fast losing control.

A gaping rift even developed between Arana, founding father of the militarized state, and Lucas. . . . Arana, too, now felt the chill winds of economic competition. Through his increasingly vocal party, he proposed the unrestrained machinery of the free market as a path to economic recovery. His harsh Chilean-style monetarism, blaming economic ills on state intervention, sounded like a coherent long-term alternative to many disenchanted businessmen.

Some U.S. policymakers also saw the attraction. Lucas's wild bloodletting, and his willful ruination of the economy, antagonized the Carter administration. Arana, long a favorite son for his counterinsurgency skills, now also offered economic appeal to his backers in the upper echelons of the CIA, Pentagon, and Republican Party.

The Disintegrating Military

Military expansionism affected not only the country's economic base. . . . The military also moved into direct control of culture and education. Army grants pay for young officers to study the "subjects of the future"—electronics, mining, and petroleum engineering. Since 1978 there has been ambitious talk of a military university. In 1979 the armed forces established their own Department of Radio and Television. They also own Channel 5 of Guatemalan television. Control of the press and restrictions on the dissemination of information have tightened.

Ultimately, the military elite have even allowed the legendary cohesion within their own ranks to crumble. Decomposition is rapid. Their monopoly of power has been accompanied by corruption on a massive scale. Even within the officer class, there is potential here for cracks: Generals and colonels control what captains and lieutenants cannot yet aspire to. In the most celebrated case of Mafia-style activity—an arms-buying racket controlled by eight generals—runaway sums were involved. Young officers reported that between 1975 and 1981, the Guatemalan military registered $175 million worth of arms purchases from Israel, Italy, Belgium, and Yugoslavia. The generals reported the value of the sales as $425 million, salting away the difference in private bank accounts in the tax haven of the Cayman Islands. . . .

As the final guarantee of its power, the Guatemalan Army has always been able to resort to its monolithic internal cohesion. The fragmentation of military unity under Lucas was something new, a further Achilles' heel of the military state.

Editors' note. With the election of President Reagan in 1980, the shift of the United States back to a hard-line anti-Communist foreign policy greatly encouraged the Guatemalan military. To meet the resurgent guerrilla challenge and to end the personalism and corruption of General Lucas García's administration, junior officers and their sympathizers carried out a coup in 1982. The new government, headed by General Ríos Montt—a member of a non-Catholic charismatic Christian sect—pledged to end the guerrilla menace and to carry out socioeconomic reforms. Like several of his predecessors in the 1960s, Ríos Montt achieved some early military successes against the EGP guerrillas. The regime declared victory in 1983.

Despite the renewed repression and apparent military victories of the Ríos Montt regime, the Guerrilla Army of the Poor called for an "agrarian, anti-imperialist, and anticapitalist revolution." It was clear, in light of the last quarter century of struggle, that General Ríos Montt's victory could be no more permanent than the "victories" of Peralta Azurdia, Méndez Montenegro, Arana Osorio, and the military governments in the decade 1970–80. Indeed, Ríos Montt himself was overthrown in mid-1983 by more traditional officers who disliked his evangelical religious affiliation and cronyism.

In 1985, following the trends established by Peru, Bolivia, El Salvador, Argentina, Uruguay, and Brazil, the military government headed by General Humberto Mejía Victores held elections and allowed a civilian candidate, Vinicio Cerezo Arévalo, to assume the presidency. However, the Army remained the most important political force in Guatemala into the mid-1990s.

VII

The Persistence of Antipolitics

Cycles of elected, de facto, and military regimes have characterized Latin American politics since the 1840s, leading frequently to mistaken predictions (and wishful thinking) regarding democratization and the end of so-called military intervention in politics. Another cycle of transitions from military to civilian governments began in 1978 in Ecuador; by 1995 no strictly military regimes remained from Mexico to Tierra del Fuego.

Does the round of "democratization" begun in 1978 mean that militarism and antipolitics are over in Latin America? Does it mean that the global trend toward "liberalization" will finally achieve the dream of Latin America's nineteenth-century liberals and twentieth-century social democrats: consolidated democratic systems, subordination of the armed forces to elected governments, respect for civil liberties and rights, and an end to authoritarian practices and institutions?

The two articles that follow, while of necessity overlapping in topics discussed, examine the transitions to civilian government from 1978 to 1995 with these questions in mind. They offer a skeptical, but not deterministic, view of the extent to which transitions to civilian government have achieved real democratization and the degree to which military doctrine and antipolitical attitudes have changed since 1978, especially regarding the relationship between respect for human rights and the military's traditional guardianship mission in Latin American politics. Anitpolitical attitudes and practices die hard. These articles demonstrate their persistence in the 1990s.

365

CHAPTER 27

"Protected Democracies": Antipolitics and Political Transitions in Latin America, 1978–1994

In 1979 over two-thirds of Latin America's people were living under military rule. By 1994, however, not a single military regime remained in Central or South America or the Spanish-speaking Caribbean. Elected presidents (even if former generals, as in the case of Paraguay's first post-Stroessner government) and legislatures replaced military dictators and juntas. Foreign observers certified the "fairness" of elections in Ecuador, Peru, Chile, Honduras, El Salvador, Nicaragua, Guatemala, and Paraguay—even when outgoing military regimes permitted elections only after certain parties or candidates had been excluded from participation. Political parties and opponents of incumbent governments operated openly. Media censorship declined, and fewer cases of politically motivated abuses of human rights were reported.[1] "Democratization" seemed to be under way. Indeed, 1986 was the first time in Central American history that Costa Rica, Nicaragua, Honduras, El Salvador, and Guatemala all had elected civilian governments at the same time.

These positive trends notwithstanding, several events—the kidnapping by military units of Ecuador's President Febrés Cordero (1987), military uprisings in Argentina (from 1985 to 1992), Peruvian President Fujimori's *autogolpe* (1992), and Guatemalan President Serrano's suspension of the constitution and dissolution of Congress (May 1993)—served as harsh reminders that even though democracy may have been on the rise, it had hardly been consolidated. Two unsuccessful military rebellions in Venezuela (in 1992) also served as graphic testimony that, despite more than three decades of routinely holding elections and living under civilian rule, economic crisis and political unrest could still foment unrest and spur military officers to challenge presidents.

The Latin American Transitions

Despite the enthusiasm expressed upon the return of civilian government and the understandable relief that human rights abuses seemed to be on the decline, skeptics doubted the depth and permanence of the transitions. Several invoked past history, noting that previous waves of apparent democratization in Latin America had been followed by a return to authoritarian government. The most pessimistic observers, however, pointed out that there had been no erosion of those underlying impediments to democracy, both social and economic, which had been afflicting Latin America since colonial times: racism, repression of labor, failure to provide the majority of the population with decent living conditions and/or the opportunity for social mobility, and a high concentration of wealth and income in a tiny minority.

However, even the pessimists often failed to remark on the most inglorious aspect of the most recent wave of democratization. The military regimes that came to power in 1964 and the years following exceeded all previous versions of protected democracy. They killed dreams of more egalitarian societies, whether revolutionary, millenarian, or even innocently social democratic. The terrorist states had interred utopia. Decades of repression, the debt crisis of the 1980s, and a grudging conversion to neoliberal economic strategies disarmed and dismantled the Latin American political Left. Reification of "the market" and widespread efforts to reduce the extent of government regulation, privatize public enterprises, and "shrink the size of the State" confirmed the capitalist victory in the Cold War. They also confirmed the ideological and pragmatic surrender of Latin Americans to the international managers of the 1980s debt crisis. As socialism crumbled in Eastern Europe and Cuba found itself undergoing an agonizing economic decline, Marxists were in need of a new star to guide them, as were the progressive political parties, whether Catholic, socialist, or social democratic. The situation was equally unsettling for the military. Faced with the uncertainties inherent in the transition to civilian rule and fearing that civilians wished to weaken (or even eliminate) the armed forces, the military also suffered from the conviction that the end of the Cold War meant the end of U.S. support for their cause. Feeling beleaguered, they fiercely resisted both the efforts to hold them accountable for past actions as well as any prospective loss of institutional prerogatives in the future.[2]

The newly elected governments, for their part, granted a high priority to avoiding any policy initiative that might provoke a new military coup. This was not easy. The neoliberal policies provoked anger, popular protests, riots, and, in several cases—Haiti, Venezuela, and Brazil, for example—attempts at military coups. Moreover, these governments were faced with the daunting tasks of stabilizing the economy, effecting the transition from military to civilian government, and creating a new civil-military relationship simultaneously, any one of which constituted a difficult challenge in itself.

In these circumstances, centrism, pragmatism, and moderation replaced fundamental political and constitutional debate. This usually meant support for private enterprise, a conservative management of the economy, and careful attention to potential flashpoints in civil-military relations. (It also meant walking a tightrope when military-controlled enterprises and military corruption conflicted with the neoliberal program.) Although a less shrill and ideologically polarized polity had its advantages, the apparent lack of alternatives to the neoliberal approach significantly limited the political options and hence the ambitions of the new regimes.

The disarming of the Left in general and of the social democratic opposition to the military regimes in particular had created the conditions that permitted the generals and their civilian allies to contemplate "restoring" democracy. However, most of the changeovers from military to civilian rule took place in the context of international recession, the debt crisis, and economic hardship. The fledgling democracies thus had to face the most severe economic challenges since the Great Depression of the 1930s plus the institutional legacies established by departing military regimes.

This meant that the concept of democracy had been pared to the bone: selecting presidents and legislators through elections. As a consequence, a number of important elements of democracy had to be curtailed, such as political participation (inclusion) and the openness of public contestation. These included (with variations) restrictions on the mass media, on the types and sources of political opposition, on the right to organize or join private associations and labor unions, and on the exercise of civil rights and liberties. The latter extended even to certain modes of personal expression, such as artistic and literary production, and to aspects of private behavior, including religious and family practices. It also meant—in keeping with the spirit of protected democracy—a downplaying of the implied but essential assumption that the election process presumed that those so chosen could exercise their authority to govern without the permanent threat of veto by the secret police, intelligence agencies, or military forces.

Even to achieve this minimalist democracy, the transitions to elected civilian government that took place from 1978 to 1993 required—implicitly in some cases, explicitly in others—the granting (or accepting) of impunity to those civilians and members of the police and military who had tortured, raped, killed, and "disappeared" thousands of those who had expressed opposition to the military regimes, in whole or in part, since 1964. With the partial exception of Argentina during the early years of the Alfonsín regime, the birth of new democracies was made possible only (1) by conceding via "pacts of transfer," formal or informal impunity for crimes committed in the name of national security; (2) by accepting military-imposed limitations on candidates, parties, and procedures in the transition elections; and (3) by observing significant constraints on the authority of the incoming governments.

Nowhere in Latin America did transition to elected civilian government eliminate the principal constitutional, juridical, and political impediments to consolidating civilian-controlled constitutional democracy. This held true even in Argentina and Uruguay, where the most progress occurred. In the words of Uruguayan President Julio María Sanguinetti:

> Trials for the military officers were incompatible with the climate of institutional stability and tranquility . . . if the military challenged the judiciary, we were faced with the [possibility] of a very dangerous institutional weakening [*degradación*] that, in the medium term, was going to result in institutional breakdown.[3]

Despite the armed forces' apparent subordination to civilian government, there were definite limits to this arrangement when, in the view of the military, its institutional interests and prerogatives were threatened. This tension in civil-military relations received clear illustration in Uruguay in 1992, when the Army refused to obey the orders of the president to confront police out on strike, and again in June 1993, when an important former agent of Chile's secret police (Dirección de Inteligencia Nacional, or DINA) was kidnapped, implicating not only Chilean officers but also Uruguay's Army intelligence. The latter event provoked a crisis of sufficient gravity that President Luis Alberto Lacalle was forced to cut short a European trip and return to Montevideo amidst rumors of a coup. The president's only immediate response was to reassign (but not purge or retire) the general then heading the Servicio de Información del Ejército (army intelligence). At the time, General (Ret.) Liber Seregni, leader of the opposition Frente Amplio, observed: "This is a delicate problem, we must proceed carefully." Uruguayans of all political stripes recognized the danger of "pushing the military too far."

The Uruguayan experience illustrated dramatically that despite the different patterns of military "extrication" and transition to civilian government that became the focus of many political theorists, there was an underlying uniformity of outcomes that was frequently ignored. The militaries and their civilian allies imposed major limitations on the transition process itself as well as on important constitutional aspects of the political system that followed. Human rights violations were either not punished at all or were pardoned later. This meant that once in office, civilian governments found themselves in the awkward position of either legitimizing amnesties that the military leaders had already bestowed upon themselves or else granting amnesty to former violators of human rights. Thus, institutions and practices that were either antidemocratic, anticivil libertarian, or both were reaffirmed or strengthened. Though there were significant variations in (a) the extent of the military's veto power, both formal and de facto, over public policy and (b) in the ability of civilians to lessen the asymmetry of civil-military relations, the military everywhere reserved a residual "sovereignty." Civilian politicians looked over their shoulders, consulted with officers, feared offending them, and accepted the "reality" of military guardianship.

These "democracies" were born disabled, unable to enforce the law against those accused of criminal behavior and prevented from exercising fully their constitutional authority. Except for Argentina, they were also forced to accept, both formally and de facto, an overt political role for the armed forces. This meant that many aspects of the "national security doctrine"[4] shared by antipolitical military regimes of the post-1964 period were incorporated into the constitution, into "organic" laws regulating the armed forces, and into laws regarding internal security, terrorism, and public order. It also meant limiting presidential and congressional control and oversight of military institutions—with concomitant increases in the relative autonomy of the armed forces, including intelligence operations responsible for political surveillance—as well as reaffirming a long tradition of governance through regimes of exception.[5] Even in the context of political liberalization, confirmation of the military's expanded political role weakened the legal foundations for civil liberties and rights in much of the hemisphere. For instance, when the Brazilian military violently suppressed a strike at the Volta Redonda steel plant in 1988, leaving three dead and dozens injured, the Minister of Justice sought prosecution of the soldiers involved for excessive use of force. However, not only did the Minister of the Army, a cabinet minister, prevent prosecution, but the Army went on to decorate the soldiers for outstanding performance of duty.

From the 1960s to 1990 the military regimes traumatized millions of Latin Americans. Elected leaders were anxious to avoid returning to the State terrorism that repressed and tortured millions and killed and caused the disappearance of thousands—from the coup in Brazil (1964) to the end of the Pinochet government in Chile (1990). The devastating impact of this experience made the democratizing process a difficult and frustrating one. (It also made transition to civilian government feasible since many of the military's civilian allies realized that the political Left no longer posed a serious threat and were therefore willing to support a return to elected government.) In some cases, the process was tragi-farcical, as in Guatemala. In others, like Peru, the situation became so untenable that it led to President Fujimori's *autogolpe.*

Military officers and their civilian supporters repeatedly warned against government "excesses," indiscretions, or misjudgments in policy regarding the armed forces, the economy, and international relations. Frequent cautions were directed to the media, political parties, labor, and leaders of the opposition not to "insult" or attack military institutions. For example, when alterations to the civil-military relationship were proposed in Honduras (1990), the press spokesperson for the armed forces warned that "the military institution will not permit any group to bring anarchy to this country or any of its institutions. . . . Don't corner the tiger." In May 1993 units of the Peruvian Army, outfitted in combat gear, took to the streets in a move designed to intimidate the Congress, newly reopened, for daring to suggest an investigation into alleged human rights abuses by the Army in the war against the Sendero Luminoso guerrillas. In commenting on this show of force, opposition legislator Henry Pease noted: "Democracy here is like a china shop; [General Nicolás] Hermoza behaved like an elephant in a china shop." In neighboring Chile later the same month, a small number of Chilean soldiers, in combat gear, appeared in downtown Santiago as a reminder to civilian politicians not to go too far in pushing for investigations and criminal prosecutions (even for corruption) or legislation affecting the armed forces. While this so-called *boinazo* apparently involved fewer than a hundred soldiers, its chilling effect on Chilean politics belied earlier claims that the transition from authoritarian government had been completed. Moreover, in October 1993 rumors were circulating in Brazil that elements in the Army would look favorably upon a

Fujimori-like coup in that country, with General Benedito Onofre Leonel reportedly declaring that "the military have always proved to be true leaders in times of turbulence . . . beware the choler of the legions." According to the same report, political scientist Walder Goes added: "For months the military has been saying to authorities, 'Be Careful. Straighten up.' "

From the start, beginning with impunity for violations of human rights to self-conferred amnesties and limits placed on political initiatives of incoming civilian governments, the so-called democratic transitions of the past decade and recent years have been misnamed. Although political authority was indeed transferred, via elections, from military to civilian hands, transition had its price: surrender, in one way or another, to the historical foes of and institutional impediments to full democracy.

General Pinochet's slogan in Chile, *Misión Cumplida* (mission accomplished), could be properly claimed by military leaders throughout the region. The Left had been brought down by violence in the "dirty wars" against subversion. Its defeat had transformed much of the Left ideologically, emasculated the labor movement in most countries, and ended the populism and appeals to mass democracy which had dominated the region for much of the post-World War II period.

However, the greatest triumph of the former military rulers and their civilian allies was their consolidation of protected democracy. This meant, with variation from country to country, the reaffirmation and sometimes strengthening of antidemocratic, anticivil libertarian institutions and practices. These included:

1. regimes of exception as basic elements in Latin American constitutions;[6]

2. prohibition of judicial protection of civil liberties and rights during regimes of exception and/or in applying national security laws;[7]

3. explicit constitutional definition of the internal security and political roles of the armed forces, making the armed forces a virtual fourth branch of government—guardians of the nation;

4. organic laws ("constitutive laws") further embedding the political role and relative autonomy of the armed forces in the legal foundations of the nation;

5. security legislation (laws pertaining to internal security, antiterrorism, and maintenance of public order) that criminalizes

certain types of political opposition (for example, "Marxists," "undemocratic elements," and "totalitarians") and expands military functions and jurisdiction even further (frequently including ample, autonomous internal intelligence roles for the armed forces);

6. restrictions on the mass media justified by "national security" concerns;

7. criminal codes with special provisions for political crimes and "crimes against the State," or against "the constituted government";

8. military jurisdiction (trial by courts-martial or military courts) over civilians for "crimes against internal security," "terrorism," or even "insulting" officers;

9. restriction (or full exclusion) of the jurisdiction of civilian courts over military personnel (as, for example, in the case of allegations of kidnapping, torture, and murder "while in service");[8]

10. formal corporate representation for the armed forces in policymaking (for example, in Congress, the judiciary, executive agencies, public administration, and public enterprises);

11. partial autonomy of the armed forces over its budget (for example, constitutionally fixed minimum budgets in real terms, percentages of export revenues, or revenues from particular public enterprises or taxes, unsupervised [by the legislature] off-the books enterprises used to support intelligence services or special military functions);[9]

12. broad constitutional and statutory autonomy for the military from oversight by the legislature and/or the president over "professional" and "internal" matters, such as military education, promotions, retirements, reassignments, and tenure of service commanders.

Together, these special rights and prerogatives interwoven into the political fabric of protected democracies seriously impair civil authority, constrain liberties and rights, and, to a greater or lesser extent, impede democratization throughout the region, from Guatemala to Chile.

Several legacies from the recent generation of military regimes (1964–1990) are detailed below. First, the various types of regimes of exception that have been incorporated into the new constitutions are outlined, along with examples of their use by the new civilian governments. Second, we look at the role of the armed forces as established by the constitution. Third, national security and antiterrorism legislation is considered and examples are given of how these laws are applied by governments that have only recently made the transition back to civilian authority. Fourth, we examine the extent of military jurisdiction (*jurisdiccíon*), with examples, and assess what this means for democracy. Finally, we sum up the cumulative implications of these legacies for the democratization of those Latin American countries that have effected the changeover from military rule to that of elected civilian governments during this post-1978 period.

Constitutions and Transitions

During the 1970s and 1980s the transition from military to civilian rule in Latin America was usually accompanied by either a new constitution or significant reform of the existing constitution. Only in Argentina was there a return to a nineteenth-century constitution (that of 1853, albeit often amended). When Bolivia returned to civilian rule in 1982, it used the 1967 constitution then extant, which had afforded its previous military governments with broad latitude for their actions through its state-of-siege provisions (Articles 111–114). In Chile, the 1980 Constitution, imposed by the military and amended in 1989, provided a framework for transition. In Uruguay, after voters rejected the military-proposed constitution in a 1980 plebiscite, negotiations between civilian and military elites produced institutional and electoral reforms that made transition possible under the 1967 charter, albeit with some important (temporary) modifications and accompanied by a warning from General Hugo Medina that the armed forces would intervene again should events like those of 1973 recur. Further electoral and constitutional reforms facilitated the transition from 1984 to 1986, but without eliminating constitutional language which dated from Uruguay's 1830 charter, which authorized the president to "take the necessary security measures" (*medidas prontas de seguridad*) to deal with political unrest, and with the temporary addition of a new regime of exception (*estado de insurrección*). In all other cases, new constitutions were adopted before, during, or soon after the switch from military to civilian governments (see Table).

Regimes of Exception

Since independence in the early nineteenth century, Latin American constitutions have routinely included provisions for constitutional regimes of exception in times of "emergency." These provisions ranged from partial or complete suspension of civil liberties and rights, to rule by decree, to temporary suspension of the entire constitution, to martial law. The emergencies justifying such measures varied from country to country, but usually included war, insurrection, natural disaster, "internal commotion," subversion, and threats to the "constituted order." Sometimes economic emergencies could also provoke regimes of exception (for example, Article 190 of Venezuela's 1961 Constitution: sections 6, 7, and 8). These provisions were invoked repeatedly throughout the region from the 1820s to the 1960s, and long before the installation of national security regimes that began, with Brazil, in 1964.[10] In this sense, then, they were not innovations that grew out of national security doctrines or responses to the Cold War. They were accepted, ubiquitous features of Latin American constitutionalism. Whether invoked by presidents or legislatures, such provisions inevitably assigned central political tasks to the military and/or the police.

Transition Constitutions (Military to Civilian Rule), 1978–1993

Country	Year[a]
Bolivia	None. (Military regime used 1967 charter's regime of exception provisions Arts. 111–114, Conservation of Public Order, State of Siege.)
Ecuador	1978
Peru[b]	1979
Chile	1980 (No civilian government until 1990)
Honduras	1982
El Salvador[c]	1983
Panama	1983 (Reforms)
Guatemala[d]	1985
Uruguay	None, but 1967 charter modified by negotiations and amended to include for one year a new regime of exception clause. (Military-proposed constitution rejected in 1980 plebiscite.)
Brazil	1988
Paraguay	1992

[a]Year adopted; implementation later in some cases.
[b]After an *autogolpe* and period of de facto government, President Fujimori orchestrated a constituent assembly and plebiscite on a new constitution in October 1993.
[c]El Salvador adopted important constitutional reforms in 1991 and 1992 leading to peace agreements between the government and the FMLN.
[d]Guatemala adopted extensive constitutional reforms in a referendum in January 1994.

These provisions for legal dictatorship have been subject to intense political debate in every country of Spanish America ever since the earliest days of independence. Military regimes used them after 1964 in order to justify and legitimize their right to take over civilian governments and then expanded their scope. For example, one way of doing this was to broaden the circumstances under which these provisions could be applied, thereby increasing the various types of regimes of exception—state of siege, state of emergency, state of assembly, state of public calamity, state of mobilization, et cetera—as well as the criminal penalties for violations of decrees issued under regimes of exception, including the right of the military to exercise jurisdiction over civilians during emergencies.

Regimes of exception have historically limited democratization and enhanced the political role of the armed forces and secret police in Latin America. They are formal constitutional limits on the full exercise of civil liberties and rights that provide a vague rationale (such as "internal commotion," "threats to the constitutional order," "maintenance of internal order") for restricting the media and repressing political opponents, who are inherently subject to abuse. In Latin America, regimes of exception have frequently "legitimated" tyranny.

Every new Latin American constitution adopted from 1978 to 1993 reaffirmed and/or broadened such regimes of exception. No transition to civilian government eliminated or seriously restricted them, with the possible exception of a somewhat delimited *estado de excepción* in the 1993 Paraguayan Constitution. In most cases, indeed, relatively long, complex sections of the new constitutions elaborated provisions for drastic regimes of exception.[11] Beginning with Ecuador in 1978 and Peru in 1979, broad, frequently vague provisions for draconian regimes of exception appeared in the constitutions of most of the "new democracies."

After their respective transitions to civilian government, regimes of exception were invoked repeatedly in both Peru[12] and El Salvador, where ongoing guerrilla wars justified an almost permanent application. Other countries—Honduras, Bolivia, Ecuador, Guatemala, and Argentina—have also employed the regime of exception upon occasion. Suspension of civil liberties and rights has permitted governments to repress students, crush labor strikes, halt peasant land occupations, and stifle protests against government economic policy. In practice, neither courts nor legislatures have been effective in enforcing limits on such "emergency powers." Regimes of exception became and remain routine instruments of constitutional dictatorship. The possibility that such regimes can be applied at any time keeps the region's democracies permanently on edge in a situation that is tentative, insecure, and conditional, while continuing to ensure a political role for the national police and armed forces.

The Constitutional Mission of the Armed Forces

The fact that national constitutions both define and enshrine a political mission for the armed forces acts as a further constraint on civilian governments, subjecting them to military guardianship. Constitutions and supplementary quasi-constitutional legislation (so-called "constitutive laws" or "organic laws") in Spanish America and Brazil have frequently given the armed forces explicit responsibility for functions that go well beyond national defense, including maintaining internal order and security, defending the constitution and the republican form of government, preventing usurpation of authority by presidents or other government officials, and even supervising elections. Over 80 percent of nineteenth-century Spanish-American constitutions assigned a constitutional mission to the armed forces, thus making them, in some sense, almost into a fourth branch of government. This pattern still continues in the present. Latin American constitutions rarely fail to spell out the mission of the armed forces and detail their duties.

In the 1950s and 1960s the leading military elites expanded this constitutional mission even further by defining national security in broader, more all-inclusive terms which were subsequently disseminated throughout the hemisphere. In Peru, for example, General Edgardo Mercado Jarrín, an influential military intellectual and policymaker, defined national security as "the guarantee that the State affords the nation through social, economic and military policies to obtain and maintain national objectives," adding that without development, there could be no security and without security, no development. In broadening the meaning of national security, it logically followed that the armed forces would be required (1) to operate intelligence networks that were increasingly more comprehensive; and (2) to collect and manage data of a socioeconomic and political nature. This inevitably led to the development of ever larger, more autonomous agencies whose missions extended to political espionage and counterintelligence activities, including infiltration of civilian political movements and parties, labor and religious organizations, and, indeed, of any group considered a potential threat to domestic security. The armed forces saw themselves as founders of their nations, reservoirs of patriotism, and guardians of their nations' permanent interests against internal subversion and external threats. This hyperbolic view was best expressed in an article entitled "El ser militar" (published in *El Soldado* magazine of January-February 1984):

> The carnal, concrete, living expression of the *patria* in sovereignty is the armed forces, whose mission is the defense of unity, of integrity, and of honor, as well as of everything else essential and permanent in the country: the Supreme interests of the Nation.[13]

In many cases, the transition constitutions of the 1970s and 1980s not only recognized a legitimate political role for the military but also served to expand it, justifying military participation at all levels of policymaking and administration. Indeed, in much of the region, it could hardly be suggested that the armed forces ever "intervene" in politics; they are, like the congress, the president, and the judiciary, assigned their own mission by the constitution. At times, this mission approaches the impeachment power of the U.S. Senate or that of "judicial review with bayonets" as, for example, in Guatemala and El Salvador, where constitutions charge the armed forces with preventing presidents from seeking reelection or "staying in power." Frequently, the armed forces are assigned the mission of protecting the "constitutional order" and serving as "guarantors" of the constitution (see the 1980 Chilean constitution and the 1988 Brazilian Charter). Again, this is not a new development but a reaffirmation of a central feature of Latin American politics that has served to inhibit full democratization since the early years of the nineteenth century. The rationale for this military mission after 1959 as well as justification for its support by the U.S. government rested on defending the nation from communism and the prevention of "more Cubas." In the past, other enemies and heretics had served the same purpose.

In effect, these arrangements make the military a semiautonomous branch of government with the responsibility for judging the behavior of legislators, judges, and the president and the power to veto policies or institutional reforms it deems inappropriate. More than ever before, the armed forces have become the unelected but constitutionally designated political arbiters of the new democracies. This role is legitimized in the constitutions governing the transitions and is supplemented by organic (or constitutive) laws that define the role and regulations of the armed forces in considerable detail. In some cases, such laws have quasi-constitutional status, thus requiring the virtual equivalent of a constitutional reform to deprive the armed forces of exclusive jurisdiction over (a) the organization and curriculum of military schools and colleges, (b) procedures for promotion and retirement, and (c) appointments to high military posts. In Chile the Armed Forces Organic Law even obligates the congress to finance the costs of implementing regimes of exception, and it also guarantees the armed forces a budget for nonpersonnel expenses and secret operations (*gastos reservados*) at least equal to that of 1989 and adjusted for inflation in accord with the consumer price index (Articles 94–99).

The constitutional mission of the armed forces, as defined in the post-1978 constitutions and further enlarged in regimes of exception (as indicated earlier), ratified most of the tenets of the dominant national security doctrine (even when the language was subtly changed, such as from "national security," with its stigma of State terrorism, to the more neutral "national defense" or "national stability"), including the need to protect democracy from itself.[14] The accompanying constitutional charge to be "apolitical" was translated to mean "above party and ideological disputes" but also meant to defend

> what is permanent, . . . the *patria*, against threats to its existence, to the principles that provide foundations to society. . . . at that moment national security is in danger, and the Army must act.[15]

Reminding Latin Americans of Simón Bolívar's unfortunate words that "in times of danger a Congress has never saved a Republic," proponents of a tutelary role for the military decry a "principle of apoliticism that turns military officers into automatons"; instead,

> in this age of profound social changes, especially in developing countries, the armed forces frequently acquire the role of arbiters, in others a more important role, . . . finding themselves in some instances as the only factor that guarantees the permanence of the State.[16]

This concept of the armed forces, reinforced by a national security doctrine and embedded in so-called democratic constitutions, encourages the military's exercise of power by portraying it as a legitimate constitutional mission. Though not all military officers share this view of their role, it is pervasive enough that no Latin American nation has seen fit to delete this tutelary guardianship role for the military from its constitution during the recent democratic transitions.[17] As long as this concept remains as the foundation of protected democracy, voters may select presidents and legislators, but the armed forces reserve the right, guaranteed by the constitution, to protect the country against the errors of elected officials.

National Security Laws

Like the regimes of exception and the constitutionally designated
missions for the armed forces, Latin American laws that seek to preserve the "internal security of the state" hark back to the criminal
codes of the nineteenth century and to legislation and decrees of the
early twentieth century. Each country has its own archive of legislation that permits political repression, censorship of the press, and
the selective persecution of those deemed undesirable at the time:
anarchists, socialists, communists, fascists, *apristas* (Peru), *peronistas*
(Argentina), *adecos* (Venezuela), or just ambiguously defined
subversives, terrorists, and bandits (opponents of the incumbent
regime).

The concept of "security" is always vague. The Cold War produced definitions that grew ever broader, borrowing from older geopolitical ideas and partly from French and U.S. elaborations of earlier
doctrines. When the Organization of American States (OAS) adopted
the Caracas Declaration in 1954 (conceived to justify U.S. intervention in Guatemala), the concept of collective security in Latin America
was expanded to encompass the perceived threat from international
communism. The Cuban Revolution (1959) expanded this sense of
collective defense yet again by adding the threat from internal insurgencies to that emanating from outside the hemisphere. This linking
of two kinds of security threats, internal and external, which was
prompted in part by the Cold War doctrines of the United States and
buttressed by its military assistance programs, meant "a shift in military emphasis from hemispheric defense to internal security." However, the two concerns were never entirely separated; post-1960s
insurgencies became a de facto part of the superpower conflict. They
were considered an instrument of international communism, applied
in this hemisphere as part of the Communists' global war on "the
Western Christian tradition."

Thus, in the 1960s, while U.S. policymakers and military officers were viewing this as a shift in focus for the Latin American military establishments, the latter, on the other hand, were just reinforcing
and expanding their dual historical and constitutional missions: e.g.,
protecting internal and external security. However, at this time the
two missions were more closely connected since the guerrilla insurgents and their Leftist civilian allies espoused exotic (i.e., antinational)
ideologies and were supported by an international adversary that rejected both God and *patria*. At the same time, the concept of "security" was greatly enhanced as the doctrine that developed within the

United States, Brazil, Peru, and Argentina made security virtually synonymous with public policy. In the Brazilian version elaborated by the Escola Superior de Guerra (ESG), security became:

> The guarantee by the State in particular, to the degree feasible, for the benefit of the Nation, by means of political, economic, psychological and military actions, of securing and maintaining Permanent National Objectives, in spite of existing or potential antagonisms and pressures.[18]

In Peru, a similar security doctrine was defined at the Centro de Altos Estudios Militares (CAEM), typified by such comments as those of General Mercado Jarrín, cited earlier. This doctrine soon spread to most of Latin America. In this context, the new national security legislation that was adopted in much of Latin America still reflected Hispanic traditions of long standing but with a new focus on the Cold War and an amplified definition of security.

National security laws—sometimes called public order laws, organic laws regulating regimes of exception, or national security laws (Ecuador, 1979; Chile, 1958)—are a particular type of repressive instrument. They outlaw political opponents and certain types of political activity in the name of defending national security, the nation, constitutional order, the legal government, patriotic values, and national interests. Such laws often outlaw propagation of ideas considered subversive, limit the freedom of association, and otherwise restrict civil rights and liberties that are respected elsewhere. They serve to criminalize behavior normally considered legal—for example, suggesting that a monarchy be replaced by a republican government or accusing a military officer of corruption. This type of legislation acts as a permanent limit on civil liberties and rights even when no regime of exception is in force. It is inherently antidemocratic, anticivil libertarian, and prone to abuse. It conflicts with even minimalist procedural definitions of democracy, which focus on free, fair elections and open public contestation, by permanently inhibiting public debate, stifling opposition, restricting the press, and criminalizing the exercise of civil liberties—all in the name of national security. Epitomizing this sort of legislation was El Salvador's Law for the Defense and Guarantee of Public Order (1977), which instituted press censorship, banned public meetings and strikes, and made it a crime "to disseminate information that tends to destroy the social order." At the same time, it eliminated normal constitutional protection for infractions and subjected the accused to military justice.

Typically, the post-1964 military governments modified existing laws, introduced new "institutional acts," and/or decreed new national security legislation. Much of this legislation remained operative after transition to elected civilian governments in the 1980s. In some cases, changes have been made in national security legislation after the transition. However, on the whole, such changes failed to alter the essentially antidemocratic features of this type of legislation.

National security laws, even when comprehensive, are often supplemented with "antiterrorism" laws, gun control laws, provisions for media censorship, and proscription of particular politicians, "dangerous" political movements, and parties. Violators of these laws are sometimes subject to military rather than civil jurisdiction, thus losing their right to protection under due process and other constitutional limits on arbitrary detention, interrogation, and routine criminal procedure.

Elected governments that took office after years of military rule, often confronting socioeconomic and fiscal crises, insurgencies, and the threat of new coups if they failed to meet these challenges, found themselves burdened with draconian national security laws that had been bequeathed to them by the former military regimes. In no case have such laws been eliminated. Nevertheless, in some instances— Chile and Argentina, for example—they have been modified to reduce criminal penalties and diminish the extent of military jurisdiction. Elsewhere, however, new and harsher security laws have been passed in order "to defend democracy." For example, Peru's Decreto Legislativo 46 (1981) made any "incitement to terrorist acts," whether on radio, television, or in print media, into a criminal act punishable by four to six years in prison. In addition, "any public defense (*apología*) of a terrorist act or of a person sentenced as a terrorist or an accomplice" was punishable by three to five years in prison (Peru, 1981). Maintaining the essential features of national security legislation such as this has significantly altered the meaning of democracy in Latin America by imposing severe constraints, both psychological and legal, on the extent to which public life can be carried out, whether in the areas of public contestation, electoral competition, and/or opposition to the incumbent government.

This trend further weakens the democratic character of the transition governments even when these governments claim that they are only seeking to "protect" democracy through the exercise of their authority under this kind of legislation. Implementing the law against "enemies of democracy" must, of necessity, rely heavily upon the police and the military. This serves only to confirm previous claims of those institutions that order and progress are possible only through repression of political opposition, dissidents, and those dubbed "terrorists." Notwithstanding the terrible dilemma of a government faced with massive terrorism (the Sendero Luminoso in Peru), right-wing death squads and persistent guerrilla war (in Guatemala and El Salvador), or small groups of violent political extremists (Chile, after 1990), acceptance of these national security laws continues to legitimize authoritarian legal attitudes and practices of the past and extend them into the future.

Perhaps the most dramatic use of such laws by the "new democracies" took place in Peru after 1981, as the government battled the emergent Sendero Luminoso and other armed movements. The application of a number of these legal measures in combination—repeated decrees of regimes of exception, the military's assumption of control over newly designated "emergency zones," implementation of antiterrorism laws, plus certain provisions of the 1979 constitution—virtually abolished civil rights and liberties in Peru. Even President Alán García (1985–1990) conceded that the government was "fighting barbarism with barbarism." Thousands were tortured, mutilated, and murdered as military communiqués announced the deaths of "subversive delinquents," and the Sendero guerrillas killed peasants, police officers, and village leaders. In 1986, responding to three prison uprisings, the armed forces and police liquidated 250 accused terrorists. Two years later, the Andean Jurists Commission reported that Peruvian security legislation allowed the military "virtually to supplant civilian officials, with broad authority (*poder amplísimo*) and no defined limits."

Similar occurrences were common in El Salvador and Guatemala from 1984 to 1992. National security legislation placed whole civilian populations under military jurisdiction, erasing their civil liberties and rights. In the process, it also eroded the legitimacy and perceived relevance of civilian government. Elsewhere, the enduring legacy of such national security legislation led not only to military surveillance of civilian politicians (Brazil, Chile) but also to its intervention in the formulation and implementation of policy in a number of areas: labor policy, foreign policy, and policies regarding agrarian reform (in Honduras, the constitution cites this as a mission of the armed forces).

The broadened concept of security associated with Latin American national security doctrine was transferred implicitly, if not explicitly, into most national legal systems, thus legitimizing even more the idea that the armed forces were the logical custodians of civilian institutions. Any matter that affects security, either internal or external, is ipso facto a military concern. Indeed, all civilian associations—political parties, labor movements, religious organizations—may represent threats to the future security of the nation; monitoring their activities becomes, therefore, a "natural" function for the armed forces and security agencies. This means that any public protests, disturbances, or activity by political parties, social movements, and labor are legitimate security concerns, requiring efficient, ongoing surveillance by military intelligence. In more obvious situations, when disorder occurs or an insurgency appears, the demands of national security oblige the military to respond.

Even in Uruguay, where the post-1984 civilian government and the political party system have made significant gains, negotiating a reduction in the military budget and reasserting civil authority over the armed forces via the Defense Ministry, the national security mission still remains as a sword of Damocles. Thus, Minister of Defense General (Ret.) Hugo Medina, who played a key role in negotiating the transition to civilian government, was able to declare:

> If terrorists are inactive here it only means the timing is not right for them, or that their international leaders do not think terrorist action would be to their benefit or lucrative enough at this particular moment. When they decide that the time is ripe, here or anywhere else, they will strike, and we need to be ready. It would be inexcusable not to be prepared. The *raison d'être* of any army is to be ready to defend the country from internal or external threats.[19]

The permanent vigilance and protection of internal security by the armed forces of the sort imagined by General Medina and less moderate officers elsewhere make Latin American democracy permanently insecure. According to Chilean Major Luis B. Olivares Dylsi, it is precisely during the transition to civilian government that "subversion may gain force, more sometimes, less others, depending on the extent of infiltration and adhesion of local Marxists." This threat requires the special attention of the armed forces to prevent subversive forces from infiltrating both the State and civil society —leading to the military's unavoidable exercise of its mission of salvation.

If the use of national security laws was most dramatic in Peru, the application of similar laws in other countries—Guatemala, El Salvador, and Ecuador—justified and resulted in significant human rights abuses throughout the 1980s. Political repression, torture, and disappearances also increased in Honduras following its transition to elected civilian government as the Fuerza de Seguridad Pública (FUSEP) and Dirección Nacional de Investigaciones (DNI) sought to quell small guerrilla insurgencies and combat "terrorism."

In Ecuador, national security legislation as implemented by civilian government is among the most revealing in many ways. In that country, the Ley de Seguridad Nacional (1979, with amendments) assigns a long list of policy areas to the heads of the armed forces (*comando conjunto*), who serve as permanent advisers to the president in matters of national security. Their responsibilities run the gamut from planning and organizing internal security and the use of the national police (Article 48) to advising on treaties, trade integration, boundary issues, construction of ports, roads, airports, and communications systems, and contracts and concessions for the exploration and exploitation of petroleum and other minerals or strategic materials. Thus, under this law, commanders of the armed services are responsible for, and oversee, a very broad range of policy concerns.

In addition, should the president invoke his constitutional power to declare a state of emergency, the security law permits him to grant *facultades extraordinarias* (extraordinary powers) to civil or military authorities. This delegation of authority enables the government to operate by means of promulgating *bandos* (decrees), a system that is tantamount to the institution of martial law since violators of the *bandos* are automatically subject to the military's penal code (Articles 145–147). The law further nullifies all other laws, decrees, and dispositions in conflict with its provisions, thus prevailing over all contrary dispositions.

During the 1979–84 period, the national security law was invoked to control and/or suppress strikes, protests, peasant demands for land and better working conditions, and opposition political movements. When the newly instituted neoliberal economic program sparked large-scale protests, the government used the law to suppress the demonstrations. In October 1982, for example, the Frente Unitario de Trabajadores (FUT, or United Workers Front) called for a "national peoples' strike" to protest the government's policies. In response, President Osvaldo Hurtado used the Law of National Security to decree a security zone across the entire national territory, which enabled his government to suspend civil liberties and rights, intimidate the press, and close certain radio stations. Again, in 1984, he issued Executive Decree 2511 to declare a security zone in Napo and Esmeraldas provinces in order to put down strikes and counter protests.

The regulations covering how and when the national security law was to be applied were published the day before the outgoing military regime turned over the presidency to Jaime Roldós (who died in 1981, to be succeeded by Vice President Hurtado). These regulations gave the military wide latitude in carrying out the surveillance of, and exercising jurisdiction over, civilians. The 21-point platform on which the Roldós-Hurtado ticket had campaigned acknowledged this fact by calling for

> the participation of the armed forces in the creation of the new democracy and in the achievement of the permanent national objectives, as well as the concrete tasks of socioeconomic development. . . . [For the military], national security is to the permanent national objectives what these are to the very survival of the nation.[20]

In effect, the national security law gave the military carte blanche to take part in policymaking whenever the officers were so inclined and anticipated that the country's "permanent national objectives" might be affected.

Ecuador's new president, León Febrés Cordero, took office in 1984 and promptly implemented an orthodox neoliberal economic plan which weighed heavily on the population and was met by an increase in public protests, strikes, and open opposition. The government dealt with these harshly, provoking both international human rights groups and administration opponents to denounce secret detention centers, the use of torture, and political repression. However, concern for national security cut both ways. The president found himself "detained" at Taura Air Force Base by a rebel officer, Air Force General Frank Vargas, who was competing with the Minister of Defense and Commander of the Air Force for control of the armed forces and who opposed a number of the chief executive's initiatives. The situation was resolved by negotiation, thus saving the president and the country from the nightmare of assassination, but also serving as a vivid reminder to the country at large that civilian government was not beyond challenge from the military.

More important than the tragicomic confrontation between the general and the president, the national security legislation remained an ever-present instrument to defend the nation's permanent interests. As Patricio Ycaza succinctly stated:

> The Law of National Security is the most complete negation of the real democracy to which the workers and the people aspire. . . . Its derogation is an urgent necessity.[21]

Much the same could be said for the national security laws and related repressive decrees and regulations throughout the hemisphere. The doctrine of national security (DSN) and the laws derived from its premises are incompatible with the exercise of those civil liberties and rights associated with authentic democracy. So long as these assumptions prevail and national security doctrine and implementing legislation exist to reinforce the internal security mission of the military, the process of democratization will be held hostage to the demands for internal order and protection of the "permanent interests of the nation." No clearer statement of this dilemma can be found than in the conclusions of Chilean officers Lt. Col. Juan M. Gallardo Miranda and Lt. Col. Edmundo O'Kuingttons Ocampo, which were published in *Military Review* in 1992:

> [The armed forces' mission] is not only defense against external threats, but also internal threats that affect society and the nation as a whole . . . their function transcends governments, groups, and persons, responding only to the permanent interests of the nation, where the principle of National Security predominates over all others.[22]

Without sweeping revision or repeal of national security, antiterrorist, and public order laws, Latin American democracy will remain hostage to its military guardians. A vivid reminder of the extent to which such national security doctrine pervades Latin American politics, not just military institutions, was reflected in the reason given by El Salvador's Supreme Court for rejecting the report of the International Truth Commission on the violations of human rights in that country: "[The report] passes over the legitimate and the permanent interests of the country. . . ." This is to say that considerations of national security were sufficient to justify thousands of deaths, of *desaparecidos* (persons "disappeared"), and acts of torture. In El Salvador, as in Guatemala, Ecuador, and Chile, the "permanent interests of the nation" took precedence over all other legal and constitutional norms and requirements. Combined with the regimes of exception and the expansion of military missions enshrined in national constitutions, these national security laws work to impede the full working of democracy on the one hand while retaining the judicial supports of an authoritarian past on the other. Even in nations where the old national security doctrine has been formally rejected (or modified, as in the Guatemalan military's "thesis of national stability"), the armed forces typically seek to restrict the initiatives of elected government and to "co-govern" their nations. As Alfred Stepan found in his interviews with Brazilian officers in the 1980s, the armed forces in Latin America continued to believe that

> the National Security Law [Brazil, 1978] was precisely the type of instrument needed for a "strong democracy" instead of a "liberal democracy." The key to a "strong democracy" was that it somehow institutionalized the principle of self-defense.[23]

Military Jurisdiction over Civilians

Spanish and Spanish-American legal traditions include special privileges and legal jurisdictions (*fueros*) for military personnel. The *fueros* provide specified immunities from ordinary civil and/or criminal jurisdiction and give military tribunals jurisdictional priority in certain cases. For example, military courts may have jurisdiction in cases involving criminal charges against military personnel, such as murder, torture, or abuse of civilians. Such military jurisdiction may effectively bar trials of accused military personnel in ordinary criminal or civil courts.

Historically, the particulars of these immunities and priorities have varied in both Spain and Spanish America. Though important differences continue to exist in Latin America in the 1990s, there are also certain basic commonalities. In Latin America, military jurisdiction implies the application of military penal codes, typically without the protection of civil liberties and rights (*garantías*). This includes the absence of certain elements of due process which the constitution affords to civilians. This voiding of basic constitutional protection for those subject to military *fueros* is justified on the overriding need for discipline in military forces in peace as well as in war.

The routine application of military law and the extension of military jurisdiction to civilians for certain crimes and/or during periods of emergency, whether formalized by imposition of regimes of exception or de facto, significantly erodes civil liberties and rights and discourages open political opposition or competition. Depending on the extent of such jurisdiction, it may well (a) have a chilling effect on the mass media and/or constitute effective censorship; (b) prevent public opposition to government policies; and (c) subject civilians to lengthy imprisonment, interrogation, and even execution without recourse to habeas corpus, *amparo* (protection), or other constitutional remedies. This was common under most of the military governments from 1964 to the 1990s—both under regimes of exception (such as state of siege) and in accord with decree laws and institutional acts promulgated by the juntas. (It was also true for some civilian governments; for example, the Venezuelan Organic Law of Security and Defense [1976] subjected civilians to military jurisdiction and application of the Code of Military Justice for infractions committed under states of emergency when "mobilization" had been decreed [Article 39].) In particular, the laws already mentioned—national security, antiterrorism, and gun control—provided expanded military jurisdiction over civilians. When applied under regimes of exception, they also often prevented recourse to judicial review of military decisions.

The scope of military *fueros* and jurisdiction over civilians has been an important issue in Latin America ever since the early nineteenth century, when the first constitutions were drafted. Over 80 percent of Spanish-American constitutions of the period reaffirmed the military *fuero* as a prerogative of the officer corps; only 23 (out of 103) national constitutions precluded the military's right to exercise jurisdiction over civilians in all circumstances. In Brazil, in particular, the military enjoyed a special legal status. In some cases—Mexico, for instance—military tribunals were eventually prohibited from exercising jurisdiction over civilians (Article 13: *los tribunales militares en ningún caso y por ningún motivo podrán extender su jurisdicción sobre personas que no pertenezcan al Ejército*). In most cases, however, Latin America—like Spain, France, and Portugal—provided for military jurisdiction over civilians in the case of particular crimes such as banditry and "crimes against the internal security of the State." A legacy of Spain's Bourbon reforms in the last quarter of the eighteenth century, this stipulation not only survived into the nineteenth century but into the twentieth as well, when it was expanded to apply to anarchists, socialists, Nazis, Communists, and assorted "subversives and terrorists" who "threatened the constitutional order."

In the twentieth century, in fact, as regimes of exception and the application of specialized antiterrorist/national security legislation became more frequent, military jurisdiction over civilian populations actually expanded, particularly from the 1960s to the 1980s. For example, the military junta in Peru (1962–63) instituted a new legal code that gave the military jurisdiction over those

> who by spoken or written word, whatever the medium might be, or by deed, publicly slander or offend the Armed Forces or Auxiliary Forces, with the goal of undermining their prestige, impairing their discipline, or provoking their disintegration.[24]

The code also stipulated imprisonment for "outrages against the nation, its representative symbols, and the armed institutions." In addition to the chilling effect this was to have on both the media and political opponents, this expansion of the military's jurisdiction allowed governments engaged in waging "internal wars" against putative subversion to subject members of their civilian populations to court-martials and special *consejos de guerra*.

This jurisdiction of the military over civilians was authorized through a variety of legal mechanisms: in constitutions, criminal codes, special legislation and decrees, military codes of justice, and via pseudoconstitutional statutes adopted by military governments to modify existing constitutions. For many decades, it was an important weapon in the arsenal employed against so-called terrorists, guerrillas, leftists, and opponents of the regimes in power. In El Salvador, for example, the 1962 Constitution (Articles 175–177) stipulated that in the event of war, invasion, rebellion, sedition, catastrophe, epidemic, or "other grave perturbations of public order," certain civil liberties and rights could be suspended. Upon government suspension of the *garantías*, in accord with Article 175 of the Constitution, the jurisdiction of the military was immediately extended to cover crimes of treason, espionage, rebellion, sedition, and "other crimes against peace, independence of the State, or human rights" (*derecho de gentes*). Even after *garantías* were restored at the conclusion of the regime of exception, military tribunals were to retain their right to jurisdiction over any cases that had originated while the regime of exception was in force (Article 177).

After 1973, Chile, Argentina, Peru, and Uruguay expanded the reach of military jurisdiction through extensive use of constitutional "reforms,"[25] legislation, and decree powers, while Ecuador and Brazil were not far behind. Infractions of the law committed under regimes of exception and violations of antiterrorist, gun control, and security laws could all subject a civilian, after periods of incarceration and interrogation in military installations, to trial by a military court. The usual protections afforded such citizens by the constitution were held in abeyance and did not prevail. This placed citizens at the mercy of, and unprotected from, abuse by government authority, which was free to abrogate basic constitutional rights and liberties and permit military officers to administer draconian "justice"—sometimes "on the spot."

With some exceptions, most of these provisions for military jurisdiction over civilians are still in place [1995] and have not been eliminated since transition to civilian government. Most elected governments have been unable to overcome the legacy of military *fueros* and the expansion, in recent times, of jurisdiction by the military.

Since 1990, for example, journalists and politicians in Chile have been called before military courts for "offenses against the honor of military officers" (*desacato*). Even after President Eduardo Frei took office (in 1994), a military judge (*fiscal*) was able to order the arrest of a human rights lawyer for "seditious" comments in violation of the Military Code of Justice, Article 176: to wit, *sedición impropia, inducción al desorden y a tibieza en el servicio de las tropas*. In Peru, Ecuador, and El Salvador (until 1992), the military routinely exercised jurisdiction over the civil population during the war against revolutionary guerrilla movements and terrorism. While further, more detailed analysis of the complexity of military jurisdiction is required for each of the countries considered in this study, it is clear that the Mexican model (absolute prohibition of military jurisdiction over civilians) has not been instituted in most of the region as part of the political transitions that have recently taken place. No absolute prohibition on applying military law and criminal penalties to civilians has been mandated in constitutions regulating the transition to civilian government in Ecuador, Peru, Bolivia, Argentina, Uruguay, Brazil, Chile, or Paraguay. (The Peruvian Constitution, approved in 1993, provides that civilians can be tried in military tribunals for treason and "terrorism," as determined by Article 173.)

In contrast, the constitutions of both Honduras (1982: Article 90) and Guatemala (1985: Article 219) clearly prohibit military jurisdiction over civilians. El Salvador, in its reform of the constitution in 1992, agreed to curtail, though not prohibit entirely, the right of the military to exercise jurisdiction over civilians (DL 368, 1992). Similar prohibitions have been written into the new 1991 Colombian Constitution (Article 213) and adopted in Spain during transition from the Franco dictatorship as part of the reform of the Military Code of Justice (Law 9/80, 6 November 1980). In Paraguay, military jurisdiction over civilians has been limited to situations that involve international conflict (Article 174). These reforms represent significant achievements by those struggling to reassert the prerogatives of civilian government since they involve the erosion, if not always elimination, of long-standing bulwarks of protected democracy. If these reforms endure, they will markedly enhance the possibilities of further democratization.

The Legacy

More complete democratization in Latin America is hindered by constitutional guarantees of regimes of exception and expanded missions for the armed forces, buttressed by statutes and national security laws enacted both during and since military rule, by military jurisdiction over civilians as well as by lingering fears of a military response should civilian governments be deemed to have acted "imprudently" in matters of concern to the armed forces. These represent significant (though not the only) barriers to broad public contestation, to truly free and fair elections, to the normal exercise of civil authority and right to initiate policy by elected governments, and to the effective usufruct of civil rights and liberties. One of the most enduring victories of the authoritarian regimes that installed themselves in the post-1964 era has been their ability to legitimize these antidemocratic practices by embedding them in constitutions and so-called organic laws.

The military rulers and their civilian supporters have emerged as victors in more ways than one from their self-proclaimed "internal war" of the last three decades. Not only do they claim congratulations for having saved their countries from what they viewed as the mortal threat of subversion, but they have also won (with rare exceptions) impunity from being held accountable for the harsh measures and abuses of human rights employed in waging that fight. In addition, they have also won important, if incomplete, political victories. In so doing, they have been able to condition, control, and limit the extent of democratization in Latin America, while installing themselves as arbiters of national politics. In this role, they retain the support of those civilian parties and movements that remember populist and Leftist threats from the 1950s to the 1970s and thus favor protected democracy. Other features of protected democracies also work to reinforce the political victories of antidemocratic military regimes even in the context of transition to elected government.

These victories may be mitigated by elections, by a less restricted press, and by the ongoing process of civilian government. They may even be tempered by an indisposition to reassume management of the socioeconomic morass which military rulers bequeathed to their successors and an unwillingness to confront external pressures for "democratization" imposed by the apparent victors in the Cold War. The lack of a substantial threat to internal order or stability (again, with such exceptions as Peru, Guatemala, Colombia, and Nicaragua) also undercuts any legitimate justification for the military to exert overt pressure on an elected civilian government. Even where internal insurgencies continue, their lack of any credible assistance from, or linkage to, hostile external allies will further invalidate any military attempts at interference. Some or all of these factors have com-

bined to enable civilian governments to whittle away at military prerogatives even to the point of instituting significant reductions in
military budgets and/or privatizing industries formerly under military aegis.

Some liberalization of political regimes has taken place almost
everywhere in the region. Nevertheless, despite a conjunction of favorable developments (like civilian successes, the winding down of
the Cold War, and a redefinition of the role and mission for Latin
American armed forces), the philosophical, constitutional, legal, and
institutional foundations of protected democracy and military guardianship have frequently—though not uniformly—been legitimized and
strengthened since 1978. What the camouflaged revetments of this
protected democracy conceal may be violently revealed in the event
that civilian leadership flounders or fails, civil strife erupts, military
prerogatives and institutional interests come under heavy challenge,
or a threat to "the permanent interests of the nation" is perceived.
This may be particularly true in those situations where the legal foundations of military guardianship were substantially weakened after
transition to civilian government, as in Argentina and Uruguay, or
even more so in such cases as Guatemala, Honduras, Peru, and Ecuador, where civilian constitutional government remains fragile, if not
fictional. . . .

Beneath the veneer of elected civilian government, both authoritarian legal institutions and a political mission for the armed forces
have been consolidated. The memories and lingering fears of renewed
repression, reinforced by occasional military saber rattling, discourage attempts to dismantle the edifice of protected democracy.
Antipolitics, as institutionalized from 1964 to 1990, remains the cor-
nerstone of Latin American politics as we approach the twenty-first
century.

Constitutional and legal reforms will neither end militarism nor
guarantee consolidation of democracy in Latin America. That development will depend, among many international and domestic factors, upon the long-term strengthening of civilian political institutions
combined with changes in the socialization of the professional military. However, until and unless these impediments are removed, Latin
American democracy will remain in its present tentative and tenuous
state.

Notes

[The original version of this article contained extensive notes and tables, deleted
here.]

1. This was not, however, universally the case. In Honduras, Peru, El Salvador, and Guatemala, the human rights records of civilian governments were far from enviable (see Americas Watch Committee, *El Salvador's Decade of Terror: Human Rights Since the Assassination of Archbishop Romero* [New Haven: Yale University Press, 1991]; Americas Watch Committee, *Peru under Fire: Human Rights Since the Return to Democracy* [New Haven: Yale University Press, 1992]; Amnesty International, *Honduras: Autoridad civil, poder militar, violaciones de los derechos en la decada de 1980* [London, 1988]; and L. Funes de Torres, *Honduras: Derechos humanos* [Tegucigalpa: Centro de Documentación de Honduras, 1984]).

2. In the wake of the new liberal economic policies adopted in the region and the apparent focus of the United States on democracy and human rights, military nationalists and populists bitterly attacked the new regional and international agenda. Attempted coups in Venezuela and Argentina were illustrative. Coup leaders, who saw the new agenda as hostile to their institutions, viewed the following as responsible: ideas of the Italian Marxist Antonio Gramsci, the model of the Spanish Defense Ministry (particularly the military reforms instituted after the death of General Francisco Franco), and the new U.S. security agenda for the region (see, for example, R. Jassen, *Seineldin: El ejército traicionado, La patria vencida* [Buenos Aires: Editorial Verum et Militia, 1989]; and Hernán Grüber Odremán, *Antecedentes históricos de la insurrección militar del 27–N–1992* [Caracas: Centauro, 1993]). In his prologue Admiral Grüber remarks:

> *Debe quedar claro que nos rebelamos contra un gobierno comprobadamente inmerso en el fango de la corrupción, en procura de una democracia decente; que si los políticos indiferentes y los jefes militares que conocieran de mis alertas y constantes llamados a la correción de errores, huberian sido receptivos y obrado con sensatez, ni mis compañeros del "Movimiento 5 de Julio" ni yo, hubiésemos tomado el camino de la rebelión contra el gobierno y su entorno, en protesta de un ordén constitucional sistemáticamente violado y en procura de la democracia que respeta el estado de derecho, que garantiza la justicia igual para todos y que no depreda el tesoro nacional; la democracia que ha sido siempre esperanza de un pueblo mil veces engañados que clama por su redención.*

The admiral provides a good example of the military's role in protected democracy: the obligation to defend national values and to uphold the constitution as the ultimate reservoir of sovereignty and defense against corrupt and incompetent politicians, and even their military collaborators.

3. Cited in Gabriel Ramírez, *La cuestión militar, Democracia tutelada o democracia asociativa, El caso uruguayo*, II (Montevideo: Arca, 1989), 97. See also Julio María Sanguinetti, *El temor y la impaciencia, Ensayo sobre la transición democrática en América Latina* (Buenos Aires: Fondo de Cultura Economica, 1991).

4. A greatly expanded definition of "national security" from the 1950s to the 1970s, which covered everything from economic development to ideological censorship, provided the rationale for expanding the role of the armed services. A very large literature on this topic—in English, Portuguese, and Spanish—linked the doctrine to the 1960s–1980s military regimes, though usually neglecting to discuss the nineteenth-century origins of military participation in regimes of exception and the liberal foundations of the "national security state."

5. Regimes of exception, such as the state of siege, suspension of habeas corpus and civil liberties, the granting of broad decree powers to presidents, and the subjection of civilians to military jurisdiction in times of "emergency," are not unique

to Latin America. However, they are used much more routinely in Latin America than in Europe, where they originated—first in ancient Rome, and then in the republican constitutions adopted after the French Revolution and in Spain's Constitution of 1812.

6. Regimes of exception are constitutional and statutory provisions that allow for the temporary reorganization or redefinition of governmental authority and procedures for the explicit purpose of dealing with an emergency condition. These conditions may range from war, natural disasters, epidemics, economic "emergencies," rebellions, and strikes, to civil war. The most typical regimes of exception involve the partial or complete suspension of civil liberties and rights, an expansion of the president's decree power, delegation by the Congress of its legislative authority to the executive, a total suspension of the constitution for the duration of the emergency, the expansion of military jurisdiction over civilian populations, imposition of full or partial martial law (which assigns legislative, executive, and judicial authority to military officers for the duration of the emergency), or specially named regimes of exception that may entail some or all of the above, like the state of siege, state of emergency, state of internal war, state of public calamity, and so forth. Declaring a regime of exception has often proved a handy way to implement policies in a State-declared "emergency," as illustrated by the case of the Menem government in Argentina, which "issued as many decrees during 1989–92 as were issued by all his civilian predecessors since 1922 put together. Meanwhile, Paz Estenssoro in Bolivia put through the whole stabilization plan of 1985 [the neoliberal policies] in the form of a decree."

7. For example, the 1980 Chilean Constitution stipulated that habeas corpus and *amparo* were not applicable (*procedentes*) in "states of assembly" and states of siege (Article 41: 3); Peru's Ley de Habeas Corpus y Amparo (7 December 1982) established the inapplicability (*improcedencia*) of habeas corpus and *amparo* in regard to suspended *garantías*. In contrast, Argentina's Ley Nacional de Habeas Corpus (24 October 1984) strengthened the authority of the judiciary to review the reasons for detaining persons during states of siege, and even to decide whether the executive had properly exercised its authority to declare a state of siege. In 1985 the Supreme Court used this new authority in a request for habeas corpus by Jorge H. Granada, who had been arrested by the Alfonsín government during a state of siege (see Hector Fix-Zamudio, "La justicia constitucional en América Latina," in *El constitucionalismo en las postrimerías del siglo XX, Constitucionalismo* IV [México: UNAM, 1988–89], 451–532).

8. Thus, in early 1993, the Peruvian military assumed jurisdiction over cases that involved the violation of human rights, murder, and the disappearances of students and a professor in the now infamous La Cantuta University case (July 1992), alleging that no civilian court could proceed so long as the case corresponded to the *fuero militar*. In new legislation, President Fujimori and the Congress expanded the jurisdictional priority of the military courts in the La Cantuta case even further in February 1994.

9. In Ecuador, for example, the armed forces obtained a fixed share of petroleum revenue, estimated at 23 percent of the total; in Chile, they assured themselves of a minimum budget that was guaranteed never to fall below that of 1989, in real terms; and in Honduras, the armed forces secured for themselves direct participation in numerous public and "private" enterprises, including their own bank. Also in Honduras, where the national police are a dependent of the Ministry of Defense and represent a fourth branch of the armed services, they have an official "special services" branch that competes with private security companies, using police personnel to guard banks, factories, mines, and other enterprises. Income from this

enterprise goes into police coffers. In Guatemala, as well, the Policía Militar Ambulante (PMA) has a special services unit that charges fees for security services offered to private enterprises. The Nicaraguan "transition" from Sandinista rule to the government of Violeta Chamorro has allowed considerable autonomy to the Ejército Popular Sandinista, including the right to establish and operate their own enterprises, ranging from the manufacture of furniture to operation of air transport, health services, and construction activities. In addition, a number of enterprises operate "off-the-books," providing resources to the armed forces (or its individual members) that go unscrutinized by the Congress.

10. According to a preliminary study on the state of siege and protection of human rights in the Americas (1963) done by the Inter-American Commission on Human Rights of the Organization of American States (OAS), there were over 100 occasions in which the state of siege was either declared or extended in the Americas during the 1950–60 decade, a period that was without either external war or armed invasion. However, the state of siege is one of the many kinds of regimes of exception used in Latin America.

11. It should be noted that this also applied in the situation of nations that were not under military rule in the 1970s and 1980s. For example, Colombia's 1991 constitution contains broad provisions for regimes of exception (Articles 213–215). In addition, both Peru (through its new 1993 constitution) and Guatemala (via an extensive reform of the constitution, approved in a plebiscite on 30 January 1994 that drew only a 15 percent turnout of the voters) further expanded the power of the president on the one hand, while greatly weakening legislative initiatives and ability to oversee executive action on the other.

12. Under provisions of Article 188 of the Constitution, the Peruvian Congress delegated decree power to President Fujimori to deal with economic, defense, antidrug, and terrorist policies. In November 1991, Fujimori issued several decree laws that virtually militarized the entire political system, restricted civil liberties and rights, created a new Sistema de Inteligencia Nacional (SINA), limited press coverage of terrorism and "defense issues," and greatly enhanced the role of the military and national police through new organic laws. For a summary of these decrees, see Coletta Youngers, "Peru under Scrutiny: Human Rights and U.S. Drug Policy," Issue Brief No. 5, Washington Office on Latin America, Washington, DC (July 13, 1992): 24–29.

13. "El ser militar," in *El Soldado*, no. 94 (January-February 1984), cited in Carina Perelli, "The Military's Perception of Threat in the Southern Cone of South America," in L. Goodman, J. Mendelson, J. Rial, eds., *The Military and Democracy* (Lexington, MA: Lexington Books, 1990), 97.

14. In a personal interview, General Gramajo (now retired) indicated that it was also necessary to "win the semantic war," thus the change in emphasis from "national security" to "national stability."

15. Hermann Oehling, *La función política del ejército*, Memorial del Ejército de Chile, Edición especial y restringida (Santiago: Biblioteca del Oficial, Estado Mayor General del Ejército, 1977), 142–43. The author here cites approvingly the comments of J. A. Primo de Rivera: "El ejército es la salvaguardia de lo permanente; por eso no se debe mezclar en luchas accidentales. Pero cuando es lo permanente mismo lo que peligra; cuando está en riesgo la misma permanencia de la Patria— que sucede si las cosas van de cierto modo, incluso perder la unidad—el ejército no tiene más remedio que deliberar y elegir." *Obras completas* (Madrid, 1964), 321.

16. Oehling (1977), 380.

17. While the focus here is on the transition constitutions, similar provisions for regimes of exception and constitutional missions for the armed forces exist in Ven-

ezuela and Colombia, countries that have avoided formal government by the military even though they were frequently subordinated to regimes of exception from the 1960s to the 1990s. The Nicaraguan constitution adopted by the Sandinistas also contained such provisions. In contrast, Argentina's Constitution of 1853, much amended and re-adopted after repeal of Juan Perón's 1949 charter, did not assign such a mission to the armed forces. Although the Argentine military refers to its "historical mission," this is based upon a corporate mystique and authority derived from statutes rather than from a constitutional mandate.

18. This concept evolved from the 1950s, when Juárez do N. Távora formulated the original definition for the Escola Superior de Guerra (ESG): "the pursuit and safeguarding of its [the State's] national objectives against adverse internal or external factors."

19. Cited in Paul W. Zagorski, *Democracy vs. National Security: Civil-Military Relations in Latin America* (Boulder, CO: Lynne Rienner, 1992), 136–37.

20. Colonel Alfonso Littuma Arizaga, *La nación y su seguridad* (Editorial Publitécnica, n.d.), 187, cited in Patricio Ycaza, "Seguridad nacional y derechos humanos," in *Los derechos humanos: El caso ecuadoriano* (Quito: Editorial El Conejo, 1985), 273.

21. Ycaza (1985), 278.

22. "El rol de las fuerzas armadas en la sociedad, Doctrina militar en el acontecer político de Sudamérica," *Military Review*, Edición Hispanoamericana (November-December 1992): 14.

23. Alfred Stepan, *Rethinking Military Politics: Brazil and the Southern Cone* (Princeton: Princeton University Press, 1988), 53.

24. *Código de Justicia Militar* (Peru), articles 100–103.

25. The military governments typically sought to legitimate their actions with quasi-constitutional reforms called "institutional acts," "constitutional acts," or decree-laws. In some countries, such as Uruguay and Argentina, previous legislation by civilian governments had already extended military jurisdiction to cover cases involving subversion and/or terrorism.

Brian Loveman

CHAPTER 28

Human Rights, Antipolitics, and Protecting the *Patria*: An (Almost) Military Perspective

Para la patria, porque es ella a quien debemos todo;
porque todos nuestros esfuerzos deben sumarse para
hacer de ella lo que un buen hijo anhela para su madre
amada; porque es la Patria la suprema madre. (1974)[1]

La fuerza armada a diferencia de cualquier otro de
los organismos que crea y sostiene el Estado para
servir los intereses de los asociados, tiene una
misión muy clara y definida, esta misión es vencer. (1977)[2]

Los que de palabra, por escrito, por medio de la imprenta.
grabado, estampas, alegorías, caricaturas, signos, gritos ó
alusiones, ultrajaren á la Nación, á su bandera, himno
nacional ú otro emblema de su representación, serán castigados
con la pena de prisión correccional. . . .

Los que de palabra ó por escrito, por medio de la imprenta,
grabado ú otro medio mecánico de publicación, en estampas,
alegorías, caricaturas, emblemas ó alusiones injurien ú ofendan
clara ó encubiertamente al Ejército ó á la Armada . . . serán
castigados con la pena de prisión correccional. (1890, 1906)[3]

The gradual transition from military to civilian governments in Latin America from 1978 to 1994 brought demands for trials and punishment of armed forces personnel accused of human rights violations during the recent periods of military rule. Demands for "justice" also arose in nations ostensibly ruled by civilians, such as Colombia and Venezuela, where the armed forces engaged in prolonged counterinsurgency and antiterrorist operations to protect national institutions and security. Under attack, military officers from Central America and the Caribbean to the Southern Cone sought to defend the dignity and honor of their institutions, reaffirm the salvational mission they had victoriously effected in the battle against international communism and internal subversion, and avoid personal criminal responsibility in particular cases of alleged human rights violations.

In some countries so-called Truth Commissions were created to investigate and report on the alleged violations.[4] In others, civilian governments indicted individual officers and prosecuted notorious offenders in the spotlight of the recently uncensored mass media.[5] Despite these efforts, political and legal bulwarks, immunities and amnesty decrees established during transition, lack of appropriate evidence, and threats—both implicit and explicit—against the new civilian governments generally impeded successful prosecution.[6]

Political constraints on prosecution for alleged human rights violations did not prevent widespread dissemination of detailed descriptions of abuse, torture, murder, "disappearances," and mass graves. International human rights organizations had routinely denounced these crimes for years; domestic human rights activists, political parties, Church groups, and other regime opponents had done likewise.[7] Calls for punishment not only threatened individual officers but also besmirched the institutional integrity of the armed forces, threatened their role and relative autonomy in the new political systems, and questioned the legitimacy of the patriotic mission recently completed.

The armed forces rejected revisionist histories, such as those contained in the Truth Commissions' reports, that ignored the circumstances that had required their intervention (for example, Brazil, Bolivia, 1964; Chile, Uruguay, 1973; Argentina, 1976). They reminded their compatriots of the international "war" of communism that threatened their nations' sovereign existence and of the internal subversion, terrorism, and impending civil wars that they successfully overcame. They also reminded their critics and accusers of the calls made by civilian legislators, party leaders, judges, and the business community for the military to save their nations from chaos and destruction. With national variations, the armed forces elaborated a coherent historical, constitutional, legal, doctrinal, and political defense. This defense is important because it not only sought to legitimize "dirty wars" but also served as a more extensive moral, philosophical, ideological, and institutional rationale for *protected democracy*, the "new" political model that emerged in Latin America in the 1980s and 1990s.[8]

The moral, legal, and political foundations of the armed forces' defense against allegations of human rights abuses are described schematically in this chapter, using material from Argentina, Chile, and El Salvador to illustrate the main premises. The defense includes their version of nationality, sovereignty, nation-building, and their own historical and political missions and obligations. The schema presented necessarily neglects differences among countries and within their armed forces. National idiosyncrasies, characteristic internal social and political variation, and distinctive political histories shaped the Latin American armed forces and are still extant. This variation, however, does not prevent describing the armed forces' shared historical conceptions, doctrines, and constitutional missions as well as their claims of "residual sovereignty" (*las ultimas reservas morales*) in their respective nations when "permanent national interests" are threatened.[9] These common premises buttress their defense against accusations of human rights violations and legitimate their current insistence on a continued role in national politics. Although these premises are under serious challenge in the 1980s and 1990s, they remain embedded in the structure of military doctrine and self-perception.[10]

The Historical Vision

The Latin American armed forces routinely trace their origins to Spain's colonial armies and militia. Institutional myths and official histories trace their martial glories to imperial Spain's Western Hemispheric conquests, settlements, and the defense of *las indias* against other European powers and Indian resistance. In some cases, the very creation of nationality and the "new race" is attributed to the Army— an army that *precedes* the nation, eventually creates the nation, and defends the new nation against Spanish reconquest and other external and internal threats.[11]

The armed forces were tasked with defending the new nations against external threats and maintaining internal security. These are the primordial purposes of the State, recognized as such by Thomas Aquinas, Machiavelli, Thomas Hobbes, Adam Smith, and almost every Latin American military officer since 1810. These officers base their mission on a presumed natural law: despite efforts to achieve peace, there will always be war. This "law of war" imposes "the obligation to maintain a permanent army," charged with "the guardianship (*salvaguardia*) and defense of our liberty and independence."[12] The formal source for this mission statement is taken from Article 274 of the French Constitution (5 Fructidor, Year III): "The armed forces are instituted to defend the State against external enemies and to assure maintenance of internal order and compliance with the laws."

This concept was included in Spain's 1812 Constitution and in later Latin American charters. But even without (and before) national constitutions, the armed forces regard themselves as the "carnal, concrete, living expression of the *patria*."[13]

Members of the armed forces are religiously dedicated to patriotism and the *patria* and a reverence for national symbols such as the flag, national anthem, and coat of arms (*escudo*). They are professional soldiers, but also a holy brotherhood, with barracks like monasteries. They have inherited the warrior-priest tradition of the Spanish *reconquista*, the Inquisition, and the conquest of a new world for God and king. In a Guatemalan version:

> The visible representation of the *patria* is the **national flag**: these are the blessed colors that wherever they are displayed . . . with the coat of arms (*escudo*) of the Nation, an immaculate white at its center, represent our beloved *patria*. Their acoustic representation, to put it that way, is the **National Anthem**, whose beautiful notes bring joy and make our hearts flood with inexplicable emotion and happiness.[14]

The armed forces have a historical mission: the defense and salvation of the nation's traditions and its permanent values.[15] They are the "last bulwark of nationality."[16] In this mission the armed forces find a fixed moral rationale for drastic defensive measures against the *patria*'s enemies. The "Army has a paternal mission: think always of the *patria* to defend it against whatever could cause pain to its children."[17]

This historical mission is iterated and reiterated in military publications, speeches, and rituals. A typical example is Colombia's General Fernando Landazábal Reyes's 1993 reminder to his beloved (and politically besieged) comrades: "Our armed forces are the undeclinable supports (*sostenedores indeclinables*) of national integrity, and [they] must not forget that beyond the political interests of transitory governments (*gobiernos pasajeros*), in their hands is the historical responsibility for preserving it, without tarnishing its honor, in the plenitude of its sovereign splendor."[18] This location of "historical responsibility" for the *patria*'s defense and security in the hands of the military is a basic premise shared by the Latin American armed forces.

Similar citations abound in military pronouncements, texts, and academy curricula from the nineteenth century to the present. This premise constitutes a sacred duty that cannot be subordinated to any transitory government—meaning, of course, to *any* government, since any government will be "transitory" relative to the life of the *patria*. A corollary to this premise is that civilians generally lack the moral, spiritual, physical, and patriotic qualities of the true soldier, making them ultimately unreliable guardians of the Holy Grail, unable to protect the *patria*. Thus, "the barracks is the school of character and civic virtue, the forge that molds the ideals of the *patria* . . . the crucible where men's purest and dearest thoughts are melded. . . . The army is a model of the *patria* itself, in its hierarchical and ordered constitution."[19]

Civilians and political elites have accepted this historical vision often enough to give it credence and legitimacy. Colombian president Julio César Turbay, for example, addressing in 1979 the Thirteenth Conference of Commanders of Latin American Armies in Bogotá, declared: "Naturally, in extreme cases, confronted with an ostensible political vacuum that leads toward generalized anarchy, the armed forces must (*se ven precisadas*) exercise power to reestablish the rule of authority."[20] Chilean ex-president Eduardo Frei Montalva, commenting on the 1973 military coup in that country, stated: "The military has saved Chile. . . . [The armed forces] were called on by the nation and they fulfilled their legal duty. . . . If a people has been so weakened and harassed (*acosado*) that it cannot rebel, . . . then the Army substitutes its arms and does its work."[21] Most of Latin America, even those nations governed by popularly elected presidents with democratic values, expects the armed forces, "in crises," to exercise their "historical mission" to "save the *patria*."

The Constitutional Mission

The armed forces' historical mission is legally confirmed in a secular sacrament—the constitution. Latin American constitutions almost always define a broad obligation and authority for the military: external defense, internal security, upholding the laws, and protecting the constitution and national institutions. Variations in wording and mission evolved in the nineteenth century and changes occurred in the twentieth. Typically, however, the armed forces have constitutional status, much like the congress, the presidency, and the judicial branch, and are often defined as "permanent institutions." This constitutional mission reinforces the armed forces' perceived historical role and legitimizes actions taken to protect, defend, and conserve the *patria*.[22]

Whatever the precise language, the military's constitutional mission requires exercising discretion in deciding when and how to protect the *patria* and its institutions. Evidently, this task is assigned to the military (and sometimes to the police) because it theoretically possesses the resources and power to achieve it. This custodial, guardianship, protectorship role *is* the armed forces' specialized constitutional and political mission. "If the mission of the Army . . . is sustaining the *patria*'s independence, the integrity of its territory, and maintaining [internal] peace and respect for order and the legitimate institutions of the State, this imperative constitutes for those commanding troops an undeclinable obligation that must be achieved at all cost."[23] If politics and elections degenerate into *politiquería* and "promote disorder and endanger national honor and integrity," then "fulfilling its patriotic duty, the armed forces must reimpose order and legality (*los fueros de la legalidad*)." The soldier must dedicate himself exclusively to the "defense of the *patria* and the institutions that give it life."[24]

This tutelary role of the armed forces has a long history in Latin America. Through constitutional reforms and modification of military ordinances, efforts to erode this constitutional rationale for military review of civilian decisions have mounted in the late 1980s and 1990s. Combined with the military's "historical mission," however, this institutional foundation for intervention remains viable, if dormant. It played a significant role in justifying the military *pronunciamientos* and the policies of the military regimes from 1964 to 1994 that stand accused of human rights violations.

Constitutional Regimes of Exception

Latin American constitutions typically allow suspension of civil liberties and rights to meet all manner of emergencies: natural disasters, "internal commotion," threats to the constitutional order, insurgency, rebellion, and internal war. To the extent that human rights (including the right to life, liberty, due process, and the "rule of law") are interpreted as constitutional rights and liberties, these may disappear by presidential decree, legislative action, or, in certain circumstances, through decisions made by specialized governmental agencies such as the ministerial cabinet, permanent congressional commissions, or even the military high command. Frequently, the implementation of a regime of exception extends special authority to the armed forces and police, subjects civilians to military jurisdiction (laws, courts, and courts-martial), and even permits summary execution of "terrorists," "subversives," and "traitors."

One type of regime of exception is "internal war," formalized in a variety of juridical modes such as "state of siege," "internal commotion," "state of assembly," and others. At war, the rules of war apply. The basic rule is that the enemy may be killed. Indeed, one important objective of armies is to meet and destroy the enemy. If political opponents become "enemies" in a war, undeclared or declared, their extirpation is no longer a violation of human rights or even a common crime but rather a legitimate function of armies engaged in combat. Military intelligence agencies seek the whereabouts of the enemy; interrogating prisoners is one way to locate its resources and forces and destroy its combatants.

What in peace would be murder, in war becomes righteous, particularly if in doing so the *patria* and the "national way of life" are conserved. Declared regimes of exception that suspend civil rights and liberties, even without a declaration of "war," enhance the military's (and police's) authority vis-à-vis citizens to carry out their mission. They also legitimize violence and withdraw the "normal" constitutional restraints on coercion.

Regimes of exception are the result, in constitution-making, of a priori philosophical, moral, and political decisions that, at times, "human rights" must be subordinated to "protecting the *patria*."[25] In the words of Argentina's General Adcel Vilas, "The offensive against subversion presupposes in the first place freedom of action in all areas . . . *a series of special procedures*, an instantaneous response, *a persecution to the death*."[26] Even before the 1976 coup, Argentina's elected government had declared a "state of war" against terrorism. The 1853 Constitution's state-of-siege provisions and related security legislation imposed a drastic regime of exception. (And eventually the government went far beyond pre-1976 legality and constitutionality in the antiterrorist war.) In Chile, in 1973, the military junta decreed a "state of siege in all the national territory . . . and in Decree Law No. 5 declared that the state of siege imposed implied a 'state or time of war' for legal judicial purposes, as established in the Military Code of Justice."[27]

Internal wars and regimes of exception change the rules; civil liberties and rights are "suspended." Protection of "human rights," as defined in international treaties or natural law, succumbs to the "law of war" and the fundamental rights of all states to preserve their own existence. The military's historical and constitutional missions are ratified in regimes of exception that recognize the existence of crisis, the need for special rules and drastic action, and the duty of the armed forces and police to protect the *patria* and its institutions.

National Security and Military Law

No Latin American nation is without an internal security law, provisions for media censorship, military ordinances, and a military justice code that potentially expands the armed forces' authority in times of "crisis" or even provides routine military jurisdiction over civilians. There is great variation in the extent of the jurisdiction of military courts over civilians within Latin America; since the 1980s more nations have sought to reduce or eliminate this jurisdiction. However, the historical influence of this legislative and judicial "patriotic security blanket" reached its peak in the post-1964 regimes now under criticism for human rights violations. In many instances, however, the security legislation and military jurisdiction over civilians provided clear legal bases for actions deemed, retrospectively, as regrettable or, more forcefully, as human rights violations.

No detailed discussion of these laws and practices is possible in the present chapter. Excellent comparative and monographic summaries exist for some countries and less detailed versions for others.[28] Among the best studies of the evolution of the patriotic security blanket is Francisco Leal Buitrago's *El oficio de la guerra: La seguridad nacional en Colombia* (1994). After discussing the historical background, Leal describes Colombia's 1978 *estatuto de seguridad*, adopted under a "state of siege" and "leading to outrageous, indiscriminate detentions and torture of [various persons] considered to be leftists." All these episodes "were framed by application of military justice . . . and continuing military operations against the guerrillas."[29]

This description of the impact of security legislation and application of military codes and jurisdiction to civilians under an elected government reflects the general consequences of such legislation in most of Latin America. It also clearly identifies the apparent *legal* foundations for much of the action later condemned as human rights violations. In military regimes such legislation, admittedly, was often expanded, but the basic provisions had long existed.[30] They were accreted over more than 150 years by numerous governments to protect the State, the institutional order, internal security, and the *patria*. The military and police were to carry out their duty—indeed, were ordered by civilian and military superiors to carry out their missions.

How could fulfilling this historical, constitutional, legal, and organizational mission be called "human rights violations"?

Obediencia Debida and Individual "Excesses"

Military personnel not only have historical missions and constitutional and legal duties, but they also have specific military obligations defined by ordinances, military law, and orders. In almost all of Latin America, military personnel are trained to obey superior orders unhesitatingly. With few exceptions,[31] this obligation is not contingent on the legality of the orders issued, as it is in the United States, Britain, and much of continental Europe.[32] Superiors may violate the law and exceed their authority; they are legally responsible, not the personnel who dutifully comply with the orders. This principle of *obediencia debida* was reaffirmed in Argentina and elsewhere in response to the dilemmas of human rights trials and liabilities. When individual soldiers and officers exceed their authority and commit crimes against other individuals, they commit individual "excesses," which are properly punishable, unlike actions taken in accord with *obediencia debida*. Those who exceed their authority or order others to act illegally should be brought to justice; those who obey illegal orders may claim this principle as a valid defense. *Los órdenes se cumplen, no se discuten.*[33]

The Cold War and the New National Security Doctrine

Traditional military missions, constitutional obligations, defense and security legislation, and military law and ordinances provided firm moral, historical, and legal foundations for the armed forces' protection of the *patria*. The Cold War after World War II, the global struggle between communism and "freedom," and the incorporation of Latin American nations into the 1947 Rio Treaty for regional security introduced new threats to the *patria*. International communism—godless, morally abominable, nefarious, resolute, and imperialistic—denied the historical and sovereign "essence" of Latin American nations. It recruited internal adherents from political parties, labor unions, university and community organizations, and the mass media. It sought to subvert patriotic values, even to penetrate and poison the armed forces.

The Cuban Revolution and its subsequent support for revolutionary political and guerrilla movements brought this threat directly and convincingly to the Western Hemisphere. Military leaders did not invent guerrilla *focos,* Communist parties, a shrill Leftist media, and calls for revolution. They witnessed executions of Cuban officers after Fidel Castro's victory, attacks on the Catholic Church, Havana's alignment with the Soviet Union, and radical transformation of the island's society. They heard clearly the Cubans' call for continental revolution, for overthrowing the old order and establishing revolutionary socialism. They saw Cuban support and training of local insurgents. They suffered losses in combat and through terrorist attacks. There was a real enemy—an enemy that had declared war on the *patria*, its institutions, and the military itself.

Borrowing from classic geopolitical formulations, from French counterinsurgency doctrines developed in Algeria, from U.S. Cold War doctrine, and with the original contributions of Peruvian and Brazilian military theorists, the Latin American armed forces adopted a new national security doctrine (NSD), which permeated the hemisphere's military institutions. Informed by national political and economic conditions, shaped by individual experiences with revolutionary movements and insurgency, and influenced by U.S. military assistance missions, training, and the inter-American defense establishment (the Inter-American Defense Board, Inter-American Defense College, School of the Americas, and many other "faces" of the regional security network), the new NSD became, in its national variations, the dominant view of the Latin American military. Despite objections and reservations within all the military establishments, the basic premises of the NSD buttressed the military's historical, constitutional, and legal mission.[34]

Many studies of the NSD and its influence have appeared since the 1960s.[35] In the present context a bare outline suffices. The NSD expanded greatly the concept of security, making it virtually synonymous with political, social, and economic development. It located the source of Latin American unrest and insurgency in (1) internal socioeconomic and political conditions that made the poor and others vulnerable to subversive proposals; (2) the efforts of international (and Cuban) communism to take advantage of these conditions, importing "exotic" (Marxist, socialist, revolutionary) ideology and "converting" disciples and followers in Latin America; and (3) domestic revolutionaries, subversives, fellow travelers, and naive idealists, who furthered the Communist plan by deed and omission.

The NSD required a multifaceted national effort to overcome the internal conditions that favored subversion and revolutionary movements, to defeat international communism's ideological and organizational thrusts into individual countries, and to direct military action against political movements, university, labor, and other organizations, the media, and, of course, politico-military groups that operated underground and overtly. This effort was essentially a call for a permanent and total war by the State against the enemy threatening the *patria*.

This enemy was perceived as evil—evil incarnate. It was also unscrupulous, devious, perverse, even satanic. Communism "seeks to implant the reign of materialism over the spiritual, rancor and fear instead of love, lies against truth, arbitrariness in place of justice . . . the return of slavery, the end of freedom."[36] And "communism is an intrinsically perverse doctrine, meaning that whatever springs forth from it, however salutary it appears, is rotted by the venom that corrodes its roots."[37] In Brazil a military officer asked rhetorically who were the Communists, the "internal enemy." The response: "Fanatics, patient in obtaining their final objectives [world conquest] . . . persistent in their subversion, vassals of the party, . . . radical, . . . cynical, . . . antireligious."[38] The Communists would use the uninformed, the well intentioned, the naive, indeed anyone, to achieve their objectives. Their tactical flexibility allowed temporary alliances, pacts, collaboration, and even professed adherence to "democratic" rules of the game. They would infiltrate the Catholic Church and invent "Christians for socialism." Their cynicism also allowed using terrorism while denouncing terrorists, and calling for free press and respect for civil liberties while ultimately intending to abolish these. The enemy was flexible, but single-minded and untrustworthy. Those who lent themselves, however inadvertently, to the enemy's cause were also a danger to the *patria*. Such an enemy could only be defeated in a total war—a war without mercy, a war that addressed the underlying socioeconomic conditions that nurtured discontent, but also a war that extirpated the enemy and collaborators.

Communism threatened the "Western Christian way of life" and its Latin American versions; the entire "civilization" was at stake along with the survival of the *patria*. Even when not operating overtly, communism was actively plotting, conspiring, and planning its next move. Time was on its side; the enemy had a strategy without time limits for its victory. Communism sought "to weaken those societies that the Red sect does not control, to grasp them in its claws at the opportune moment, to convert them into new satellites of Soviet imperialism."[39] In Uruguay the military junta told the Inter-American Human Rights Commission that "the declaration of war by Marxism-Leninism against the Western world is a state of 'permanent aggression,' as Karl Marx affirmed in 1848."[40]

And were these ideas incorrect? Did not the Soviet Union and the Cubans openly proclaim their ultimate goals? Did not "peaceful coexistence" bring bloodshed, insurgency, and revolutionary war to Latin America? Was not the *patria* in grave danger? Should not the armed forces be prepared to carry out their moral, historical, constitutional, and legal missions?

Conjunctures

The moral, historical, constitutional, legal, and strictly military rationales for saving the *patria* always exist. They become operational only if a "crisis" occurs. Only the crisis (or in some cases, imminent threat of one) justifies military action. The post-1964 military regimes all claimed to save their nations from a combined external and internal threat posed by international communism and its internal allies. As elements of the Cold War anti-Communist alliance and the Inter-American Security System designed after 1947, the Latin American military combined French, U.S., and their own new "national security doctrine" to legitimize expanded military political participation and, eventually, military government. The NSD provided new twists on old themes, identified "the enemy," and gave immediacy to the military mission.

Conjunctural political and socioeconomic crises in individual Latin American nations provoked military responses, installation of military or civil-military regimes, and fierce repression of "the enemy." Military regimes dominated South America and Central America from the 1960s to the 1980s; most civilian governments that engaged in counterinsurgency operations also used NSD-type strategies and methods. Colombia, for example, endured more years of regimes of exception—the application of harsh national security laws and military jurisdiction over civilians—and experienced many more dead and tortured from the 1960s into the 1990s than some countries with military governments.[41]

In some cases (Colombia, El Salvador, Guatemala, Peru) these conflicts persisted into the late 1980s and 1990s; in others (Chile, Uruguay, Argentina) "the enemy" was defeated, transformed, or pacified. In most cases a legacy of this struggle was the demand for "justice," for trials of "human rights violators," for punishment of "criminals." (And in some cases a legacy of the struggle is continuing internal conflict, narcoterrorism, and organized crime.) The armed forces respond that they are heroes who saved the *patria*, in accord with their moral, historical, constitutional, legal, and conjunctural obligations. Are they wrong? Consider Argentina, Chile, and El Salvador, where individual "excesses" certainly occurred. And consider the official legal and political responses of the armed forces to their accusers.

Review, first, in Argentina, General Osiris G. Villegas's defense of General Ramón Camps, accused of homicide, illegal deprivation of liberty, and torture of prisoners:[42]

1. Colonel Camps participated in a war against subversion, a war in every sense. In war the enemy is attacked with whatever violence is necessary to destroy it. This war was the result of subversive attacks on the political institutions of Argentina, virtually in collapse by the time of the 1976 military *pronunciamiento*.

2. In accord with the law, the armed forces participated in the war against subversion until its annihilation, as ordered by the constitutional government. This included the declaration of a state of siege in 1975, the outlawing of the ERP and Montoneros,[43] the prorogation of the state of siege, the laws adopted against subversion and sabotage, and the arms control law.

3. The police and security personnel supported the armed forces in this war.

4. Colonel (General) Camps, acting as police chief of Buenos Aires Province, acted in accord with existing laws and regulations, followed superiors' orders, and conformed to the concept of *obediencia debida*.

5. In war, the laws of war apply, including the Geneva Conventions, if accepted by the belligerents—something the subversives were unwilling to do, as evidenced by their terrorist tactics. In this war the armed forces reacted to the subversive enemies' terrorist methods in accord with international law, which allows "response in kind" when the parties do not abide by international conventions on warfare.

6. The Marxist subversives sought power by destroying the principles and values that constitute our national essence (*el ser nacional*) to impose their atheist, materialist model. They intended to destroy the moral and legal foundations of the State. These objectives were clearly at odds with our "fundamental law."

7. The aggressor was international communism, directed by the Soviet Union through Cuba and their agents in Latin America, covert authors of the war suffered by Argentina then, and now [1986] by El Salvador, Nicaragua, and Peru.

8. The [new] constitutional government [of President Raul Alfonsín] has acknowledged that the fight against subversion was a war (Decree No. 157/83) declared by the previous de facto government. The conflict between the armed forces and the subversives was a "casus belli." The decrees of the [Isabel] Perón government declared that "to combat the enemies of the people is converted into an imperative of the moment."

9. The participation of the defendant in this war was the result of operations that implied making decisions under extreme situations (*situación limite*), in full combat, on the front line, with the accompanying passion that combat generates in its inevitable atmosphere of destruction and death.

10. Colonel Camps operated openly, lawfully, and with the presumption of a "state of war." He conformed to the natural chain of command and "obedience," ending with the Commander in Chief of the Army.

11. The real "accused" in this trial is the Army, as an institution, in a "political trial." Acts of war are not brought to trial; they are not justiciable. Camps and other officers who defended their *patria* and its institutions are being tried under the terms of ex-post laws and in the glare of the media. This allows the subversives who lost the war to determine their [the officers'] fate in collaboration with a government seeking revenge and political advantage rather than justice. All this with no effort by the same government to bring to justice the terrorists and subversives or to subject them to public exposure and repudiation, as has been done with military officers.

Why attack the Army that had defended the *patria*? Why hold Camps accountable for fulfilling his duty, obeying "orders," and winning the war against terrorism and subversion? What if the terrorists had been victorious? Who would have defended human rights against godless, materialistic, satanic Marxist-Leninist Soviet imperialism and its Cuban satellite?[44]

Consider next the victory of the Chilean armed forces against the Popular Unity coalition, the Soviet menace, international communism, and Cuban intervention. Seventeen years after saving the *patria* from destruction and orchestrating economic recovery and institutional reform, including a new (1980) constitution that permitted a "transition to democracy," the Rettig Commission accused the armed forces and police of human rights violations. The Chilean Army answered as follows:[45]

1.   The [Salvador] Allende government (1970–1973) acted illegitimately, destroyed national unity, fomented class struggle, drove the country toward fratricidal strife, broke the law, operated outside of constitutional norms . . . [such that] anarchy prevailed, that the internal and external security of the country were in peril, that the very existence of Chile as an independent state was in jeopardy, and . . . in accord with our historic conceptions (*pensamiento*) we deposed the illegitimate and immoral government, assuming the moral duty that the *patria* has imposed on us.[46]

2.   The congressional majority and the Supreme Court previously called upon the military to restore order, the rule of law, and constitutional government.[47]

3.   The Rettig Commission's report ignores the circumstances that provoked the 1973 *pronunciamiento* and the fact that only due to the energetic and drastic action taken by the armed forces was a bloody civil war avoided.

4.   The report also ignores the existence of subversive war before and after the military government assumed control, and that once engaged in war a military institution can only seek total victory.

5.   The report also fails to evaluate the magnitude and danger of the terrorist action and armed subversion, actual and imminent, from 1973 to 1990.

6.   These were part of a planned strategy by international and domestic Marxists to regain the power they lost in 1973, make the country ungovernable, and, ultimately, attempt the assassination of the president [General Augusto Pinochet] in 1986.

7.   The armed forces and police acted legally to repress these threats and adopted constitutional and legal reforms as required. A new constitution was approved in the plebiscite of 1980, with a transition to civilian government occurring as programmed in that constitution [in 1990].

8. The institution [the Army] insists that a state of war existed from the publication of Decree Law No. 5, 1973, and that the courts, which remained operative, did not challenge this decree.

9. The courts-martial that tried civilians operated under ordinances, dating from 1839, that regulated the operations of *tribunales de tiempo de guerra*. These were not inventions of the military junta and acted in accord with Chilean law, including the Military Code of Justice.

10. The Army with the other branches of the armed forces and police intervened in 1973 to overcome the moral, institutional, economic, and social crisis afflicting our country, in response to the clamor of the citizenry, that resulted precisely from the great trust that the people of Chile have had throughout history for these institutions.

11. For this reason, it is unacceptable to link, even indirectly, supposed criminal activity committed by individuals with the historic role of the Army in national life and, moreover, when these supposed crimes (*delitos*) are founded in the declarations of persons who claim to be affected [by the action of members of the armed forces].

12. The Army and the other armed forces and police were called upon to intervene in the worst institutional crisis in this century, as the ultimate recourse against a serious threat to national sovereignty and social peace (*las bases mismas de la convivencia*). They completed their mission, defeating the totalitarian threat; and they reconstructed and modernized the economy, restored social peace and democracy, and returned political authority to civilians in a free country. . . .

13. The Chilean Army certainly sees no reason to ask pardon from anyone for having taken part in this patriotic effort.

14. In particular, the Army rejects the Rettig Commission's conclusion that there was not a state of war in the country. This is an offense against those [soldiers] who died in this war.

15. The Army also repudiates the campaign to besmirch its members in the press with accusations of torture and other crimes, instead of the appropriate procedures required in a state of law. It will not accept being put on trial in this fashion for having saved the liberty and sovereignty of the *patria*, at the

insistence of civil society. Still less is this acceptable when among the principal accusers are those responsible for the tragedy, as leaders of the Popular Unity [coalition].

16. The Chilean Army reaffirms its decision to continue fulfilling its mission, guarding the institutional order of the Republic and respect for its external sovereignty.

According to Army leaders, the armed forces fulfilled their mission. Individual "excesses" may have occurred, but these should be treated according to the rule of law, gathering evidence and bringing offenders to trial as appropriate (with the exception of most crimes committed before the self-amnesty decreed in Chile in 1978). This did not give the press, the ex-Allendistas, the subversives' families, or anyone else license to excoriate the armed forces publicly, offend their honor, or deny the success of their patriotic mission. They had saved and reclaimed the *patria*—at civilian request. In the 1970s ex-president Frei and then President [Patricio] Aylwin (1990–1994) had recognized the armed forces' victory over Marxism and the need for their intervention. Now that they had returned the *patria* intact to the civilians and to the politicians—even to politicians who had participated in the 1970s debacle—what right did these same civilians have to denigrate their accomplishments and to forget their sacrifice? Under such conditions they would be forced to maintain vigilance over the *patria*, preventing the return of subversion: "The survival of the incipient Latin American democracies depends, and will depend, with more emphasis in the future, on the action of Marxist subversion within each State. . . . If the democratic regimes are capable of defending themselves against subversion and totalitarian ideas they will be strengthened, and a new and more promising political era will begin in this continent."[48]

Published just before the transition to civilian government in Chile and full implementation of *perestroika* in the Soviet Union, these words may seem archaic in 1995. Not so to Chilean and other Latin American officers still standing watch over their *patrias'* destinies. War, threat of conflict, and internal disorder are in the nature of human beings. The armed forces are the last bulwark, for each nation, against the inevitable consequences of human nature itself. How can the armed forces be faulted for carrying out their mission—a mission that F. A. Hayek, the champion of human freedom and idol of the neoliberal hegemony sweeping Latin America and the globe, compared to organic survival:

When an external enemy threatens, when rebellion or lawless violence has broken out, or a natural catastrophe requires quick action
by whatever means can be secured, powers of compulsory organization, which nobody normally possesses, must be granted to some-
body. Like an animal in flight from mortal danger, society may in
such situations have to suspend temporarily even vital functions
on which in the long run its existence depends if it is to escape
destruction.[49]

To save the *patria* from destruction, the suspension of civil liberties and rights and the defeat of its enemies are essential. In war there
are no "human rights" so long as the enemy attacks, resists, and remains an enemy that puts the *patria* in mortal danger. There can be
no "rights" without survival, no survival without defense, defeat of
the enemy, and eternal vigilance. The armed forces made survival
possible; and not just survival, but renewal, growth, modernization,
and hope for the future. For the *misión cumplida*, there should only
be profound gratitude. With their victory over the mortal threat, discussion of human rights now has meaning.

Consider, finally, El Salvador. The Salvadoran armed forces were
unable to obtain "total victory," but with massive U.S. military assistance prevented a repetition of the Sandinista defeat of the Somoza
government in Nicaragua. In 1992 the Salvadoran military was forced
to settle for peace accords, a political settlement after a prolonged
civil war. As in Argentina and Chile after the transition to civilian
government, charges of human rights violations threatened the armed
forces with trials, public criticism, and institutional reforms. No one
could seriously contend that the Salvadoran military had not been at
war. Casualties on both sides were numerous, though most dead,
wounded, and "disappeared" were civilians. The *Informe de la
Comisión de la Verdad* also identified human rights abuses perpe-
trated by the Salvadoran armed forces and the guerrilla armies.

Much like their Chilean and Argentine comrades, the armed forces
in El Salvador rejected the contextual and moral assertions of the
Truth Commission. They responded publicly and vehemently.[50]

1. The Commission's conclusions falsify historical reality and
   formulate accusations totally lacking in foundation and objectivity, affecting thereby the process of pacification that is
   supported by all Salvadorans (*todos los sectores ciudadanos*).

2. Once again the armed forces reaffirm their faith and essential
   principles and values, those that have guided them in fulfilling their duties to society throughout their history.

3. Therefore, we remind the citizenry that we soldiers did not provoke the war, nor did we incite any of the civilian population to rise up in arms against their brothers and against the laws of the Republic, nor did we assign ourselves the ignoble mission of destroying the infrastructure that sustains work and progress.

4. The armed forces act, and have always acted, complying with the orders of the highest State authorities and supporting the public administration. These actions were legitimated by the populace as demonstrated in multiple free and democratic elections.

5. The armed forces reaffirm their will to continue fulfilling their constitutional mission of defending the sovereignty of the State, even when this implies the greatest of sacrifices.

6. As a permanent institution at the nation's service, the armed forces will use the necessary legal recourses that they consider adequate to the legitimate right of defense against those who promote their destruction and that of the Republic.

7. The armed forces feel pride in having fulfilled their mission of defending society and the juridical-political system of the State. . . .

8. As the guarantee (*garante*) of the State's sovereignty, the armed forces cannot accept that the Truth Commission's report fails to recognize its constitutional authority to defend the *patria* against aggression in any of its forms.

9. In preparing its report, the Commission used sources and methods that ensured its reaching preconceived conclusions, with no other objective than staining (*mancillar*) the honor and dignity of the [military] institutions, causing the public to believe that the armed forces and its members systematically violated human rights.

10. The report does not mention the horror and suffering that communism's so-called "prolonged popular war" caused all strata of the population.

11. The FMLN [terrorist group] used violence, destruction, kidnappings, assassinations, and systematic attacks on the citizenry in its effort to attain total power, obligating the country's legitimate government to use arms to repel the aggression that attacked it.

12. The armed forces are proud to have fulfilled the mission of defending the people (*pueblo*), . . . and to have contributed to the pacification and preservation of our republican, democratic system at the cost of blood and sacrifice, supported by our faith in God and our unending spirit of service to the nation.

The *patria* was threatened; extreme measures had to be taken. The armed forces fulfilled their duties, saved the nation from the Communist onslaught, and even received the approval of the citizenry in elections. The political party that had most consistently supported a hard line against the subversives won the presidency again after the peace accords. And now the Truth Commission and even some government politicians attacked the honor of the armed forces, purged officers who had defended the *patria*, and pushed for trials of so-called human rights violators.

In their view, the armed forces were again betrayed by civilians unable to deliver the promised pensions, jobs, and land for retired veterans. Now they were accused of "crimes" for actions that had made possible the nation's survival. What recourse was left to the armed forces but to retrench and remind the citizenry of the military's historical, constitutional, legal, and moral missions to protect the *patria*'s permanent interests? And also to remind them that, like their Chilean comrades, should the civilians fail to protect these permanent interests, the armed forces might be forced to do so. This antipolitical perspective continues to frame Salvadoran and Latin American politics in the 1990s.

Epilogue

Perestroika and the end of the Cold War brought new threats to the armed forces and the *patria*. The United States lost interest in anticommunism and was discomfited by authoritarian allies and repressive policies. Past human rights abuses were viewed in a new light; support for "democratization" and reduction in military expenditures replaced counterinsurgency and low-intensity conflict as buzzwords in official proclamations by the United States.

Military nationalists saw U.S. support for human rights investigations, and even for introducing human rights courses in military curricula, as a deliberate effort to weaken or destroy the Latin American armed forces. Feigned concern for human rights by the world's strongest power barely masked its intention to subordinate Latin

American *national* security and development to the United States'
regional and international agenda. Arms control, limitations on technology transfer, pressures for reductions in military budgets, and a
new emphasis on environmental problems and drug trafficking were
all part of the strategic plan to impose U.S. hegemony in a unipolar
"new world order."

A plot existed, a great "plot to annihilate the Latin American armed
forces and the nations of Ibero-America." This plot was denounced
in a best-selling book, widely read by Latin American officers, edited by Argentina's Colonel Mohamed Alí Seineldín and U.S. "political prisoner" Lyndon H. La Rouche: "Ibero-American military history
is, in every case, the vertebral column in the life of each of our peoples.
For that reason the current masters of the world (new world order)
have resolved to eliminate the armed and security forces of Ibero-
America, the last barrier to these nations' total submission."[51] In two
inflammatory volumes, officers from Brazil to Guatemala denounced
the conspiracy to cripple the Latin American armed forces through
budget cuts and the introduction of exotic doctrines into the military
academies, and thereby to subvert Ibero-American sovereignty. As
part of this conspiracy, the bugaboo of human rights abuses and the
demand for trials is used to denigrate the armed forces and subordinate national law and security to international human rights agreements. Perhaps the most blatant case of this strategy occurred in El
Salvador, where the Lying Truth Commission (*la Mentirosa
"Comisión de la Verdad"*) imposed international demands for constitutional change and purges of the armed forces:

> The most devastating, perhaps definitive, blow to El Salvador's
> sovereignty was the appearance of the United Nations' Truth Com-
> mission, 15 March 1993. The report not only treats the FMLN as a
> legitimate belligerent force, instead of considering it the
> narcoterrorist group that it is, but based on this redefines the war,
> initiated by the FMLN, as "State terrorism" and characterizes the
> casualties that occurred as "violations of human rights.". . . The
> report not only demands the immediate purge of the armed forces'
> command structure, but also the dismissal of all of El Salvador's
> Supreme Court. . . . Far from being impartial investigators of the
> truth, the "legal experts" integrating the Commission are old sup-
> porters of the Communist insurgents whom their report absolves of
> all important culpability.[52]

The Salvadoran Defense Ministry published a pamphlet in March
1993, *La amenaza a la soberanía nacional y la destrucción del estado*.
This pamphlet asked the (rhetorical?) question: Who could benefit

by diffusing such lies and by maligning the armed forces? It answered: "Communism has not disappeared. Its immediate objective in El Salvador is the destruction of the armed forces to complete its assault on [the nation's governmental power]."[53] The Salvadorans, like Seineldín and his coauthors—Panama's General Noriega, Venezuela's General Visconti and Admiral Grüber, Brazil's General Frota and Admiral Tasso, among others—believe that international concerns for human rights and attacks on the armed forces are part of a continuing global conspiracy to erode Latin American sovereignty:

> In the last years the [Brazilian] armed forces have been victims of permanent attacks, professionally elaborated and orchestrated by certain national and international mass media against their moral character. The strategic objective of this campaign is the systematic demoralization and maximum debilitation or the total destruction of the national military institutions. . . . Any pretext may be used for this purpose: drug trafficking, ecology, protection of Indian rights, etc.[54]

General Frota's colleague, Admiral Tasso, added: "I believe firmly that just as the forces of the devil cannot overcome the Church of our God, while the armed forces exist, no one and nothing will limit Brazil's sovereignty or impede her struggle for peace, liberty, and justice."[55]

The armed forces' victory over subversion and defense of the *patria* must not be undone by the creation of a new international order that destroys sovereignty. The armed forces are, in General Frota's words, "the last bastion"; they must defend themselves and their nations from the international human rights conspiracy whose victory would signify the demise of their nations. In the 1990s the armed forces sought to prevent the ploy of human rights and the return of "politics" from destroying their institutions and their *patria*.

Notes

1. Jaime Aníbal Maldonado, *Con la espada y la luz* (Guatemala: Editorial del Ejército, 1974), 61.

2. Gen. Carlos Dellepiane, *Historia militar del Perú*, 6th ed. (Lima: Ministerio de Guerra, 1977), 2:448.

3. *Código de Justicia Militar, 27 Septiembre 1890*, as amended March 23, 1906 (Madrid: Talleres del Depósito de la Guerra, 1906), 250.

4. For an overview and discussion of the dilemmas of dealing with human rights violations see José Zalaquett, "Confronting Human Rights Violations Committed by Former Governments: Principles Applicable and Political Constraints," *Persona y Sociedad* 6, no. 2–3 (Santiago, n.d.): 51–80. See *Nunca más: Informe de la*

420   *The Politics of Antipolitics*

Comisión Nacional sobre Desaparición de Personas (Buenos Aires: Editorial Universitaria de Buenos Aires, 1985); Servicio Paz y Justicia, *Uruguay, Nunca más, Human Rights Violations, 1972–1985*, trans. Elizabeth Hampsten (Philadelphia: Temple University Press, 1989); *Informe de la Comisión Nacional de Verdad y Reconciliación* (Santiago: Ministerio Secretaría General de Gobierno, 1991); and *Informe de la Comisión de la Verdad para El Salvador, De la locura a la esperanza* (New York: United Nations, 1992–93).

5. For example, in Paraguay, the former chief of the secret police was tried and sentenced to prison; in Argentina military leaders were tried and imprisoned (then pardoned); in Chile police were tried in the case of the *degollados*, and the ex-chief of the DINA [Dirección de Inteligencia Nacional, or secret police] tried for the murder of Orlando Letelier in Washington, DC; in El Salvador military personnel accused of killing nuns and Jesuit priests were also incarcerated. However, the hundreds of thousands of tortured, murdered, "disappeared," and abused in nonnotorious circumstances rarely saw their victimizers brought to trial.

6. Patrice McSherry, "Military Power, Impunity, and State-Society Change in Latin America," *Canadian Journal of Political Science* 25, no. 3 (September 1992): 463–88.

7. For a list of such publications see *Human Rights Watch* current publications catalog and that of *Amnesty International*.

8. For a more detailed discussion of *protected democracy* see Chapter 27 in this volume.

9. See Col. José D. Ramos A., *Nunca será tarde (seguridad democrática)* (Santiago: Gráfica Andes, 1988), 14.

10. A frontal assault on these premises is being made in El Salvador in the 1990s as a result of the "peace accords" ending the long civil war. See Ministerio de la Defensa Nacional, *Doctrina militar y relaciones ejército/sociedad* (El Salvador: ONUSAL, 1994). After 1985 in Argentina some efforts were made to redefine the internal role of the armed forces but in a fashion less comprehensive than in El Salvador.

11. For a fascinating study of the "poetic system" (underlying myth and metaphor) in the Chilean Estado Mayor General's *Historia del ejército de Chile* see Hernán Vidal, *Mitología militar chilena: Surrealismo desde el superego* (Minneapolis, MN: Institute for the Study of Ideologies and Literature, 1989).

12. Col. Manuel Rodríguez Solís, *Deontología militar, tratado de los deberes militares*, comp. Col. Juan José Solis Morales (Guatemala: Ministerio de la Defensa Nacional, 1964), 35.

13. "El ser militar," in *El Soldado*, no. 94 (January-February 1984), cited in Carina Perelli, "The Military's Perception of Threat in the Southern Cone of South America," in L. Goodman, J. Mendelson, and J. Rial, eds., *The Military and Democracy* (Lexington, MA: Lexington Books, 1990), 97.

14. Rodríguez Solís (1964), 28 (emphasis in the original).

15. Lt. Col. Carlos Molina Johnson, 1973, in *Algunas de las razones del quiebre de la institucionalidad política* (Santiago: Instituto Geográfico Militar, 1987).

16. Benjamín Rattenbach, *El sistema social-militar en la sociedad moderna* (Buenos Aires: Editorial Pleamar, 1972).

17. Rodríguez Solís (1964), 40–41.

18. Fernando Landazábal Reyes, *El equilibrio del poder* (Bogotá: Plaza & Janes, 1993), 146.

19. Rodríguez Solís (1964), 45. Similar language can be found in military texts and *memorias* from Chile to Mexico. This Guatemalan example simply illustrates the "priest-warrior" self-image in relation to profession, morality, and *patria*. See

also Frederick M. Nunn, *The Time of the Generals* (Lincoln: University of Nebraska Press, 1992), for a global comparison of "military lore."

20. *El Tiempo* (Bogotá), November 6, 1979, 1–A, 8–A. Cited in Francisco Leal Buitrago, *El oficio de la guerra: La seguridad nacional en Colombia* (Bogotá: Tercer Mundo Editores, 1994), 55.

21. Molina Johnson (1987), 91–92.

22. Costa Rica is an obvious exception, with abolition of the Army after 1948. In some other cases the armed forces are not created in the constitution—for example, the Argentine 1853 Constitution. For a more detailed description of this constitutional mission see the previous chapter in this volume.

23. Rodríguez Solís (1964), 121.

24. Rodríguez Solís (1964), 142.

25. See Brian Loveman, *The Constitution of Tyranny: Regimes of Exception in Spanish America* (Pittsburgh: University of Pittsburgh Press, 1993).

26. Cited in Donald C. Hodges, *Argentina's "Dirty War": An Intellectual Biography* (Austin: University of Texas Press, 1991), 125.

27. "Informe presentado ante el Consejo de Seguridad Nacional por el Comandante en Jefe de la Armada de Chile, Almirante Jorge Martínez Busch," March 27, 1991, published in *La Nación*, March 28, 1991. This was the Navy's response to the Rettig Commission's report on human rights violations by the military government. Reprinted in "Respuestas de las fuerzas armadas y de orden al informe de la Comisión Nacional de Verdad y Reconciliación," *Estudios Públicos* 41 (Summer 1991).

28. See, for example, Alvaro del Barrio Reyna and José Julio León Reyes, *Terrorismo: Ley antiterrorista y derechos humanos* (Santiago: Programa de Derechos Humanos, Universidad Academia de Humanismo Cristiano, 1990); Leal Buitrago (1994); Felipe González Morales, "Modelos legislativos de seguridad interior: 1925–1989," *Revista Chilena de Derechos Humanos* 11 (November 1989): 18–24; Americas Watch, *Peru under Fire: Human Rights since the Return to Democracy* (New Haven: Yale University Press, 1992); Human Rights Watch, Americas, *State of War: Political Violence and Counterinsurgency in Colombia* (New York, 1993); and Americas Watch, *El Salvador's Decade of Terror: Human Rights since the Assassination of Archbishop Romero* (New Haven: Yale University Press, 1991).

29. Leal Buitrago (1994), 54–55.

30. See, for example, Ministerio del Interior, *Orden público y seguridad del estado* (Santiago: Editorial Jurídica de Chile, 1993), for an updated compendium of such legislation.

31. El Salvador's 1934 military code had an ambiguous provision that has been interpreted, retrospectively, as an obligation, or at least authorization, to disobey illegal orders. Article 9 of the 1934 Ordenanza del Ejército read: "Las órdenes *legales* del superior deben cumplirse por los subordinados sin hacer observación ni reclamación alguna, sin vacilación y sin murmurar" [emphasis added]. However, the text continued: "pero podrán reclamar si hubiera lugar a ello, después de haberlas cumplido." Cited in *Doctrina militar* (1994), 58–59.

32. See *Doctrina Militar* (1994), 53–57, for relevant language from military codes in the United States, England, Germany, France, Spain, and Italy. The section concludes with the observation that "the current doctrine in armies in Western democratic nations imposes the obligation of legitimate disobedience to those orders that imply illegal or criminal action" (p. 56).

33. In a major departure from this concept, Argentine Army commander Lt. Gen. Martín Balza declared in April 1995 that "those who give or comply with immoral orders are criminals." If Balza's opinion were to become doctrine in Argentina's military schools and courts, the long-standing tradition of *obediencia debida* would

be seriously undermined. At this time, it is not certain that resistance to Balza's ideas in the Army and other armed services will be overcome.

34. The most important early versions of the NSD were Peruvian and Brazilian. Adaptations and revisions occurred throughout the hemisphere, were discussed among officers, and published in military journals. See, for example, Gen. Golbery de Couto e Silva, *Planejamento estrategico* (Rio de Janeiro: Biblioteca do Exército, Vol. 213, 1955); Gen. Fernando Landazábal Reyes, *Estrategia de la subversión y su desarrollo en América Latina* (Bogotá: Editorial Pax, 1969); Col. Osiris G. Villegas, *La guerra comunista* (Bogotá: Librería del Ejército, 1964); Gen. Edgardo Mercado Jarrín, "El ejército de hoy en su proyección en nuestra sociedad en período de transición," *Revista militar del Perú* 685 (November-December 1964): 1–20; "La política y la estrategia militar en la guerra contrasubversiva en la América Latina," *Revista Militar del Perú* 701 (November-December 1967): 4–33.

35. A useful overview is found in Genaro Arriagada Herrera, *El pensamiento político de los militares* (Santiago: CISEC, Edición Privada, n.d.), 109–207; Joseph Comblin, *The Church and the National Security State* (Maryknoll: Orbis Books, 1979); Margaret E. Crahan, "National Security Ideology and Human Rights," in M. E. Crahan, ed., *Human Rights and Basic Needs in the Americas* (Washington, DC: Georgetown University Press, 1982), 100–127; David Pion-Berlin, "Latin American National Security Doctrines: Hard- and Soft-line Themes," *Armed Forces and Society* 15 (Spring 1989): 411–29.

36. Col. Osiris G. Villegas, *Guerra revolucionaria comunista* (Buenos Aires: Biblioteca del Oficial, 1962), 46.

37. Gen. Augusto Pinochet, "Discurso en el tercer aniversario del gobierno," Santiago, September 11, 1976.

38. A. De Lannes, "Conhecendo o inimigo interno. A ação revolucionaria," *Revista a Defesa Nacional* 675 (January-February 1978): 180.

39. Pinochet (1976).

40. Ministerio de Relaciones Exteriores, *Los derechos humanos en Uruguay: Respuesta del gobierno al informe de la Comisión Interamericana de Derechos Humanos, de fecha 24 de Mayo 1977* (Montevideo: Ministerio de Relaciones Exteriores, 1977).

41. For details see Leal Buitrago (1994).

42. A brief synopsis and paraphrase follow of parts of Villegas's *Testimonio de un alegato* (Buenos Aires, 1990). The synopsis cannot do justice to the complex substantive and procedural arguments whereby Villegas requests the acquittal of Camps. Villegas's brief, his appendixes, and his mastery of the security legislation, military codes, and procedures are impressive. This schematic overview merely attempts to illustrate the overall "argument" and defense, not to replicate it in its nuances and technical ferocity. The defense was never presented because the case was transferred from military to civilian jurisdiction. For that reason, Villegas published the entire *alegato* that he intended to present to the Consejo Supremo de las Fuerzas Armadas.

43. The ERP, or Ejército Revolucionario del Pueblo, and the Montoneros were two of the most important revolutionary organizations committed to armed struggle in Argentina. See Hodges (1991) for details.

44. The Argentine version of this view suffered a severe blow with the publication of ex-Lt. Comdr. Adolfo Scilingo's "confessions" of Navy flights from which live prisoners were thrown into the ocean (Horacio Verbitsky, *El vuelo* [Buenos Aires: Planeta, 1995]). Each of the armed forces' chiefs issued statements lamenting human rights abuses during the "dirty war." Thus, Lt. Gen. Martín Balza admitted that the Army had used "illegitimate methods, including the suppression of life,"

and Navy commander Adm. Enrique Molina Pico acknowledged that "we used mistaken methods which caused unacceptable horrors even in the context of a cruel war."

45. A synopsis and paraphrase follow of parts of the "Informe presentado ante el Consejo de Seguridad Nacional por el Comandante en Jefe del Ejército de Chile, General Augusto Pinochet Ugarte," March 27, 1991, reprinted from *La Nación*, March 28, 1991, and in *Estudios Públicos* 41 (Summer 1991). As in the case of the Villegas defense of General Camps treated above, this paraphrase of the Army's official response to the Rettig Commission's report does not do full justice to the document, but rather seeks to capture its main thrusts and "spirit."

46. "Bando No. 5 emitido por la Junta de Comandantes en Jefe de las FF. AA. y Director General de Carabineros de Chile el 11 de Septiembre de 1973."

47. The armed forces make reference here to the "Acuerdo de la Cámara de Diputados sobre el grave quebrantamiento del orden constitucional y legal de la República," August 23, 1973, and the "Pronunciamiento de la Corte Suprema sobre la quiebra de la juridicidad en Chile," May 7, 1973.

48. Maj. Luis B. Olivares, *Subversión política y transición* (Santiago: Estado Mayor General del Ejército, Biblioteca Militar, 1988).

49. F. A. Hayek, *Law, Legislation, and Liberty* (Chicago: University of Chicago Press, 1979), 124.

50. A synopsis and paraphrase follow, taken from "La fuerza armada de El Salvador, Posición ante el informe de la Comisión de la Verdad," in *El informe de la Comisión de la Verdad: Análisis, reflexiones y comentarios* (San Salvador: Estudios CentroAmericanos, 534–35 (April-May 1993), 47:484–86.

51. *El complot para aniquilar a las fuerzas armadas y a las naciones de Iberoamérica*, 2 vols. (México: Edición exclusiva para el Ejército Mexicano, Secretaria de la Defensa Nacional, 1994), xiv.

52. *El Complot* (1994), 1:169–72.

53. *El Complot* (1994), 1:188.

54. Brig. Gen. Ivan Moacyr da Frota, commander of the Brazilian Air Force, "Las fuerzas armadas, El último baluarte," *O Estado* (São Paulo), May 12, 1993, reprinted in *El Complot* (1994), 2:390–96.

55. Admiral Sérgio Tasso Vasquez de Aquino, "Las fuerzas armadas de Brasil y la conyuntura nacional," in *El Complot* (1994), 2:402.

Acknowledgments

Grateful acknowledgment is made to the publishers and authors of the following selections for their permission to reprint in whole or in part. Sources for the documents in Chapters 15–20 are cited at the end of each selection.

"An Overview of the European Military Missions in Latin America," by Frederick M. Nunn. *Military Affairs* 39 (February 1975): 1–7.

"Origins of the 'New Professionalism' of the Brazilian Military," by Frank D. McCann, Jr. *Journal of Interamerican Studies and World Affairs* 21, no. 4 (November 1979): 505–22.

"The Military and Argentine Politics," by Robert A. Potash. Adapted from Chapters 1, 2, 3, 4, and 8 of *The Army and Politics in Argentina, 1928–1945: Yrigoyen to Perón* (Stanford, CA: Stanford University Press, 1969), with the permission of the publishers. © 1969 by the Board of Trustees of the Leland Stanford Junior University. Footnotes omitted.

"The Military and Brazilian Politics to World War II," by Ronald M. Schneider. From *The Political System of Brazil: Emergence of a Modernizing Authoritarian Regime, 1964–1970* (New York: Columbia University Press, 1971), pp. 37–48. Reprinted by permission of the publisher and the author.

"The Military in Chilean Politics, 1924–32," by Frederick M. Nunn. First published as "A Latin American State within the State: The Politics of the Chilean Army, 1924–1927," *The Americas* 27, no. 1 (July 1970): 40–55.

"The Military in Peruvian Politics, 1919–45," by Víctor Villanueva. Translation of Chapters 3–5 of *El militarismo en el Perú* (Lima: T. Scheuch, 1962), pp. 52–107.

"The Guatemalan Military and the Revolution of 1944," by Kenneth J. Grieb. *The Americas* 32, no. 4 (April 1976): 524–43.

"Guerrilla Warfare in Underdeveloped Areas," by W. W. Rostow. *Marine Corps Gazette* 46, no. 1 (January 1962): 46–49.

"Post-Vietnam Counterinsurgency Doctrine," by Col. John D. Waghelstein. *Military Review* 65, no. 5 (May 1985): 42–49.

"The U.S. Southern Command: A Strategy for the Future," by Col. Antonio J. Ramos, USAF; Col. Ronald C. Oates, USMC; and Lt. Col. Timothy L. McMahon, USA. From *Military Review* (November 1992): 32–39.

"Military Government and State Terrorism in Argentina," by Juan E. Corradi. First published as "The Mode of Destruction: Terrorism in Argentina," in *Telos* 54 (Winter 1982–83): 61–76.

"The Post-1964 Military Republic in Brazil," by Riordan Roett. From *Brazil: Politics in a Patrimonial Society*, 3d ed. (New York: Praeger Publishers, 1984), pp. 125–78. Abridged and reprinted with permission of the author and the publisher.

"Antipolitics in Chile, 1973–87," by Brian Loveman. Reprinted and revised from *Journal of Interamerican Studies and World Affairs* 28, no. 4 (Winter 1986–87): 1–38.

Revised and edited from "Antipolitics in Peru, 1968–80," by Stephen M. Gorman. From *Post-Revolutionary Peru: The Politics of Transformation* (Boulder: Westview Press, 1982), pp. 1–32.

Revised and updated from "The Military and Democratization in El Salvador," by Knut Walter and Philip J. Williams. *Journal of Interamerican Studies and World Affairs* 35, no. 1 (Spring 1993): 45–73.

Reprinted and edited from "Military Rule in Guatemala," by George Black. From "Garrison Guatemala," *NACLA Report on the Americas* 17, no. 1 (January–February 1983): 19–25. © 1983 by the North American Congress on Latin America, 475 Riverside Drive, #454, New York, NY 10115-0122.

Revised and updated from " 'Protected Democracies' and Military Guardianship: Political Transitions in Latin America, 1978–1993," by Brian Loveman. *Journal of Interamerican Studies and World Affairs* 36, no. 2 (Summer 1994): 105–89.

Latin American Silhouettes
Studies in History and Culture

William H. Beezley and
Judith Ewell
Editors

Volumes Published

William H. Beezley and Judith Ewell, eds., *The Human Tradition in Latin America: The Twentieth Century* (1987). Cloth ISBN 0-8420-2283-X Paper ISBN 0-8420-2284-8

Judith Ewell and William H. Beezley, eds., *The Human Tradition in Latin America: The Nineteenth Century* (1989). Cloth ISBN 0-8420-2331-3 Paper ISBN 0-8420-2332-1

David G. LaFrance, *The Mexican Revolution in Puebla, 1908–1913: The Maderista Movement and the Failure of Liberal Reform* (1989). ISBN 0-8420-2293-7

Mark A. Burkholder, *Politics of a Colonial Career: José Baquíjano and the Audiencia of Lima*, 2d ed. (1990). Cloth ISBN 0-8420-2353-4 Paper ISBN 0-8420-2352-6

Kenneth M. Coleman and George C. Herring, eds. (with Foreword by Daniel Oduber), *Understanding the Central American Crisis: Sources of Conflict, U.S. Policy, and Options for Peace* (1991). Cloth ISBN 0-8420-2382-8 Paper ISBN 0-8420-2383-6

Carlos B. Gil, ed., *Hope and Frustration: Interviews with Leaders of Mexico's Political Opposition* (1992). Cloth ISBN 0-8420-2395-X Paper ISBN 0-8420-2396-8

Charles Bergquist, Ricardo Peñaranda, and Gonzalo Sánchez, eds., *Violence in Colombia: The Contemporary Crisis in Historical Perspective* (1992). Cloth ISBN 0-8420-2369-0   Paper ISBN 0-8420-2376-3

Heidi Zogbaum, *B. Traven: A Vision of Mexico* (1992). ISBN 0-8420-2392-5

Jaime E. Rodríguez O., ed., *Patterns of Contention in Mexican History* (1992). ISBN 0-8420-2399-2

Louis A. Pérez, Jr., ed., *Slaves, Sugar, and Colonial Society: Travel Accounts of Cuba, 1801–1899* (1992). Cloth ISBN 0-8420-2354-2   Paper ISBN 0-8420-2415-8

Peter Blanchard, *Slavery and Abolition in Early Republican Peru* (1992). Cloth ISBN 0-8420-2400-X   Paper ISBN 0-8420-2429-8

Paul J. Vanderwood, *Disorder and Progress: Bandits, Police, and Mexican Development*. Revised and Enlarged Edition (1992). Cloth ISBN 0-8420-2438-7 Paper ISBN 0-8420-2439-5

Sandra McGee Deutsch and Ronald H. Dolkart, eds., *The Argentine Right: Its History and Intellectual Origins, 1910 to the Present* (1993). Cloth ISBN 0-8420-2418-2   Paper ISBN 0-8420-2419-0

Jaime E. Rodríguez O., ed., *The Evolution of the Mexican Political System* (1993). ISBN 0-8420-2448-4

Steve Ellner, *Organized Labor in Venezuela, 1958–1991: Behavior and Concerns in a Democratic Setting* (1993). ISBN 0-8420-2443-3

Paul J. Dosal, *Doing Business with the Dictators: A Political History of United Fruit in Guatemala, 1899–1944* (1993). Cloth ISBN 0-8420-2475-1 Paper ISBN 0-8420-2590-1

Marquis James, *Merchant Adventurer: The Story of W. R. Grace* (1993). ISBN 0-8420-2444-1

John Charles Chasteen and Joseph S. Tulchin, eds., *Problems in Modern Latin American History: A Reader* (1994). Cloth ISBN 0-8420-2327-5 Paper ISBN 0-8420-2328-3

Marguerite Guzmán Bouvard, *Revolutionizing Motherhood: The Mothers of the Plaza de Mayo* (1994). Cloth ISBN 0-8420-2486-7   Paper ISBN 0-8420-2487-5

William H. Beezley, Cheryl English Martin, and William E. French, eds., *Rituals of Rule, Rituals of Resistance: Public Celebrations and Popular Culture in Mexico* (1994). Cloth ISBN 0-8420-2416-6   Paper ISBN 0-8420-2417-4

Stephen R. Niblo, *War, Diplomacy, and Development: The United States and Mexico, 1938–1954* (1995). ISBN 0-8420-2550-2

G. Harvey Summ, ed., *Brazilian Mosaic: Portraits of a Diverse People and Culture* (1995). Cloth ISBN 0-8420-2491-3   Paper ISBN 0-8420-2492-1

N. Patrick Peritore and Ana Karina Galve-Peritore, eds., *Biotechnology in Latin America: Politics, Impacts, and Risks* (1995). Cloth ISBN 0-8420-2556-1 Paper ISBN 0-8420-2557-X

Silvia Marina Arrom and Servando Ortoll, eds., *Riots in the Cities: Popular Politics and the Urban Poor in Latin America, 1765–1910* (1996). Cloth ISBN 0-8420-2580-4   Paper ISBN 0-8420-2581-2

Roderic Ai Camp, ed., *Polling for Democracy: Public Opinion and Political Liberalization in Mexico* (1996). ISBN 0-8420-2583-9

Brian Loveman and Thomas M. Davies, Jr., eds., *The Politics of Antipolitics: The Military in Latin America*, 3d ed., revised and updated (1996). Cloth ISBN 0-8420-2609-6   Paper ISBN 0-8420-2611-8

Joseph S. Tulchin, Andrés Serbín, and Rafael Hernández, eds., *Cuba and the Caribbean: Regional Issues and Trends in the Post-Cold War Era* (1997). ISBN 0-8420-2652-5